About the Author

HOWARD SOUNES was born in 1965. He is the author of five works of nonfiction, published in thirteen languages, addressing diverse subjects. Each book is based on a huge amount of research and exclusive interviews conducted over a number of years, revealing a great deal of new information. Sounes's recent books include a celebrated biography of the American poet Charles Bukowski and *Down the Highway: The Life of Bob Dylan*. Sounes lives in London.

ARNOLD PALMER,
JACK NICKLAUS,
TIGER WOODS,

. . .

and the Business
of Modern Golf

THE
WICKED
GAME

. . .

HOWARD SOUNES

Perennial Currents
An Imprint of HarperCollins*Publishers*

First Perennial Currents edition published 2005.

DESIGNED BY DEBORAH KERNER / DANCING BEARS DESIGN

The Library of Congress has catalogued the hardcover edition as follows:

Sounes, Howard.
    The wicked game: Arnold Palmer, Jack Nicklaus, Tiger Woods, and the story of modern golf / Howard Sounes.—1st ed.
      p. cm.
    ISBN 0-06-051386-1
    1. Palmer, Arnold. 2. Nicklaus, Jack. 3. Woods, Tiger. 4. Golfers—United States—Biography. 5. Golf—United States—History—20th century.
I. Title.

GV964.A1S68 2004
796.352'092'2—dc22

[B]   2004042565

ISBN 0-06-051387-X (pbk.)

05 06 07 08 09 ❖/RRD 10 9 8 7 6 5 4 3 2 1

"Golf!" he said. "After all, what is golf?

Just pushing a small ball into a hole.

A child could do it. . . ."

—P. G. WODEHOUSE,
The Salvation of George Mackintosh

CONTENTS

PREFACE

So familiar a sight is Tiger Woods in his golfing attire that it seemed strange to see him in evening wear—a black suit, highly polished shoes, and a gray shirt buttoned to the neck—all dressed up for the PGA Tour Awards. Tiger looked good as he slipped into the ballroom of the Hilton Hotel, but perhaps not as striking as he does in his natural habitat.

On the golf course, Tiger cuts a fine and distinctive figure that easily differentiates him from his fellow PGA Tour players, those members of the professional association that sanctions and administers a tour of prize-money events in the United States. His difference is not necessarily because of the color of his skin. In fact, in this respect he is a chameleon, not readily defined as black, white, or Asian, though the racial backgrounds of his parents mean he has all those genes and more. One of Tiger's sponsorship deals is with Disney, and he puts one in mind of the hero of an animated film, a figure of universal appeal created by artists who blend together characteristics of the people of the world. He could be a cartoon character, with his flawless skin, brown button eyes, jet black hair cut so close it appears sprayed on, and candy red lips that part to reveal teeth so white and large that one wonders if he has more than the usual number. Still, what sets Tiger apart from his peers are not his beguiling, multiracial features, but his youthfulness, his sense of style, and his athletic physique. In a game where athleticism is not mandatory, Tiger, at six feet two inches and 180 pounds, is an athlete of classical proportions. His upper body forms the ideal V shape. A lifetime of swinging golf clubs has swollen his arms like Popeye's, and there isn't an ounce of fat on the man. If you asked Woods to "pinch an inch," he'd have to find his hapless rival Phil Mickelson and pinch his belly. If the ancient Greeks had played golf and the great museums of the world featured marble statues of men not only wrestling and throwing the discus but also driving and putting golf balls, then those statues would resemble Tiger Woods.

On the course, he dresses in customized Nike clothes. Unlike most young people who dress in Nike—making one think of refuse bags filled with tires—he looks truly elegant. On his feet, he wears black Nike golf shoes with a tick logo—what the company likes to call a swoosh—neatly inscribed on the outside of each heel. His trousers have knife-edge creases, and another swoosh is woven above the back right pocket, from which droops a snow white golf glove. On final days, Tiger offsets his black pants with a red top, red being a lucky color in his mother's Thai culture. Years ago Lee Trevino used the same gimmick when he was playing in finals on tour (red and black were his "payday colors"). The last piece of apparel, the ubiquitous Nike cap, completes Tiger's outfit like the lid on a pot and enhances his appearance, because without it he has the high forehead of incipient baldness. Tiger looks every inch a winner in his golf uniform, and of course he plays the game sublimely. Little wonder thousands flock to see him at tournaments, clustering around the tee box excitedly as he prepares to drive. Addressing the ball, Tiger is picture-perfect. When he swings through the ball, the ground seems to tremble. Onlookers exhale a collective "Oooh!" as they watch the ball streak away from the tee, a hiss in its slipstream, soar against an azure sky, and drop down beyond the point, in the far green distance, where anybody can see clearly. Then Tiger hands his club to his caddie and sets off down the fairway, head erect, chest out—an almost soldierly deportment—and maybe ten thousand people stumble along in his wake to see him play again, wishing *they* were Tiger, so cool and talented, with more money than he can ever spend. And he seems to be a nice fellow, too, though he ignores his fans for the most part.

Tiger out of uniform, stepping onto the stage at the Hilton at Torrey Pines—the golf course north of San Diego, California—was not as impressive or exciting a spectacle, but interesting nonetheless. As he took his seat next to the lectern, I reflected upon the fact that he is the most famous sportsman in the world today, the first time for a golfer. Woods is also the highest-paid sports figure in the world. Having earned $69 million from prize money and endorsements in 2002, he could probably have bought and sold everybody in the room: a gathering of PGA Tour officials, media, fellow players, and members of the Century Club of San Diego, host to that week's tour stop, the Buick Invitational. Indeed, the money he had made in 2002 was partly why he was making this appearance on Wednesday evening, February 12, 2003.

To some extent, success in professional golf is judged by how much money players make. The PGA Tour has a Money List, and for coming out on top in 2002, for the fourth year in a row, Tiger was to receive the Arnold Palmer Award, named for the player who popularized golf in the 1950s and '60s and in the process made himself and many of his fellow golfers very rich. Palmer was not at the Hilton in person but was represented by a bronze figurine of his youthful self posed like the Academy Award, with a golf club where Oscar clutches his sword. The other giant of the modern game is Jack Nicklaus, the hefty, plainspoken Midwesterner who usurped Palmer as world number one and went on to become the greatest golfer ever, winning eighteen professional "majors"—the four annual events that are the summits of the game: the Masters, the United States Open Championship, the (British) Open Championship, and the PGA (Professional Golfers' Association of

America) Championship. With two U.S. Amateur titles as well—which many golfers, including Nicklaus, consider majors—he had twenty major titles in all. That is why Nicklaus is regarded as the best, and that was why another award Tiger was receiving, the Player of the Year Award, was in the form of the Jack Nicklaus Trophy. Nicklaus, long past his prime, overweight and walking with the aid of a synthetic hip, was represented by an effigy of himself leaping triumphantly at the 1975 Masters.

After some words from the PGA Tour commissioner, Tiger's best friend on tour, Mark O'Meara, got up to introduce the star of the evening to the audience. A stout man in his midforties, O'Meara became mentor and neighbor to Tiger when he turned professional in 1996, at the age of twenty, and moved from his native California to live in the gated community of Isleworth, Florida, that O'Meara also calls home. Tiger valued O'Meara's counsel, and it was comforting to know he could always have dinner with the O'Meara family if he felt lonesome at Isleworth, and he did find it a lonely life at first, separated from his family and the people he had grown up with. As they practiced together and traveled on tour, O'Meara reaped a benefit from the relationship, finding that Tiger inspired him to play better than he had ever done. Proof came in 1998, when he won two majors—his first ever—in a year when Tiger was off form and, as O'Meara reminded the audience at the Hilton, that was the year *he* had picked up the Jack Nicklaus Trophy. Of course, Tiger had all the others handed out since he began playing the tour full-time.* "What can you say about Tiger Woods?" O'Meara asked, rhetorically. "Fourth consecutive Player of the Year for the Jack Nicklaus award. That's an incredible accomplishment. He's won five of the last six. Probably would have won six of the last six, except some old guy here—gray and balding—had to clip him in 1998." Tiger, sitting beside O'Meara on stage, along with the recipients of other, lesser

---

*Tiger had little opportunity to win the award in his first year on tour, since he did not start competing as a professional until the late summer of 1996.

tour awards, grinned broadly at that remark. O'Meara added that he was most proud of his buddy not for what he had accomplished on the golf course but for the person he was away from the course: a humble man, apparently, and a role model. "So, Tiger, congratulations."

As the audience applauded, Tiger stood and took his friend's place at the lectern. "I paid him well, didn't I?" he began, a small joke that went a long way with this partisan crowd. Tiger is likable, undoubtedly. He looks good, as noted, and that is important in terms of how sports stars are marketed and how the public relates to them. Intelligence shines from his eyes, which is not the case with all professional golfers. Tiger is not brilliant, but he is smart, certainly shrewd enough to know that he should make a good impression when he has to say a few words in public, which he does invariably. "Last year was very special," he continued, his voice lowered in sincerity, his eyes dipped modestly. He speaks well, though either out of laziness or because of the innate shyness that is part of his complex character, he does not open his mouth quite wide enough and therefore does not enunciate as clearly as he might. His voice can sound muffled, as if he has cotton wool in his cheeks. "To have a chance to win five tournaments, to win a major championship, that is special. To be lucky enough to win two, that makes it so much more special." He thanked everybody for what they had done to make the tour what it was, saying how grateful he was to be part of it, and he did not forget to mention the men sitting alongside him, including Gene Sauers, who was receiving the dubious honor of Comeback Player of the Year. "Congratulations to all you guys," said Tiger. "Have an absolutely fantastic year. . . . It's quite an honor to get this. Thank you." Then Tiger posed for photographs and, while most people were turning to the bar, he slipped out the door. As he did so, I walked up and introduced myself, and the subject of this book, to him.

Sometimes referred to as "the wicked game," because it is so fiendishly difficult to play, golf, in the parlance of Woods's generation, is a wickedly good game—more fashionable now perhaps than it has ever been. At the same time, the game has a history of discrimination—against minorities, the less well-off, and women—that is wicked in the true sense. The golf establishment is hidebound and elitist, and few games are so entwined with money, politics, and big business. This is the rich story of golf explored in this book—not just the process of knocking balls into holes—and it is told through the lives and careers of the three most famous, successful, and influential players of modern times: Palmer, Nicklaus, and Woods. Having met and interviewed the two older men, I worked hard to get an interview with Woods for this book. But whenever I asked, he was not available *at that time*, whatever time that was, and not knowing for sure whether his underlings were relaying my requests to him and his reply to me, or whether they were thinking *for* him, finally I had to ask him myself, explaining the premise of my book, and what I was trying to achieve.

Tiger listened as we walked, saying little enough in reply. With the polite business of accepting awards over and done with, he had reverted to a character I had observed before as I traveled from tournament to tournament: a closemouthed young man who is suspicious of strangers and somewhat aloof. As we proceeded down the corridor, surprised passersby, who had not been expecting to see Woods, yelped gleefully, "Tiger! Tiger!" He ignored them, for the most part, walking on as if wrapped in his own dreamworld. Most people in his position—certainly Palmer and Nicklaus—would pause to say hi and sign autographs and go through the duties of celebrity. Not Tiger, who has an almost imperial manner.

As we climbed an escalator toward the ground-floor lobby, I told him about some of the other notable people who had given me interviews, telling him this because celebrities will often talk only when they know their peers have already done so—that it's an okay thing to be a part of. One of the major characters in this book is Mark McCormack, an attorney who became Arnold Palmer's agent in the early 1960s and, on the back of his client's success, built the largest sports agency in the world, International Management Group (IMG), creating the model by which all sports stars are marketed. Nicklaus was one of McCormack's clients. So was Woods. His agent, Mark Steinberg, who was riding the escalator behind us, was an IMG employee. Meanwhile, McCormack was in a coma in New York, having suffered a heart attack. Shortly before he was stricken, he had been gracious enough to meet me. Tiger did not seem much interested in hearing about that, though; he seemed more concerned with trying to make a call on Steinberg's cell phone. He couldn't get a signal, however, and was obliged to listen as I added that I wanted to speak to him in part to ensure that what I wrote about him would be as accurate as possible. "Well, thank you. I appreciate that," he replied sarcastically, sarcasm being his preferred form of humor.

Nevertheless, I pushed on, reminding him that I had also recently met his father, Earl, a remarkable man and another central character in this book. For as Mark McCormack made Arnold Palmer (and vice versa), Earl Woods created Tiger. In fact, I had mentioned his father to him earlier that day at a press conference, inviting Tiger to talk about his parents. "My father's a beauty, as you probably have come to realize," he'd told me, speaking through a microphone, even though we were sitting less than six feet apart (I was in the front row of the press tent at the Buick Invitational; he was sitting in an easy chair on a low dais). His demeanor then was similar to how he was onstage later at the Hilton: composed and agreeable, apparently wanting to give a good account of himself. Yet he did not speak with the natural warmth that is characteristic of Palmer, nor with Nicklaus's bluntness. Rather, there was a slippery quality to Woods's speech making, as if he was concerned primarily about not saying the wrong thing. In fact, it was his father—a former information officer in the U.S. Army—who taught Tiger to be this way: when he had to speak in public to reporters, and when he was accepting trophies and awards (which he had been doing regularly for a long time), Tiger should talk directly and be polite. But there was no perceived value in giving away more of himself than he had to. This was military training in a sense: name, rank, and serial number. It also had to do with Earl's being an African American, a man whose life had been shaped by experiences of racism, both real and possibly sometimes imagined. Earl is suspicious of the white-dominated world. And Tiger seems suspicious, too. "He is a person I truly love. Same with my mother," Tiger continued in answer to my question. "And they've meant everything to me. Without their guidance and their support, throughout the years, I wouldn't be where I'm at right now. There's no way. I have the greatest time talking with them, the greatest time being around them, and it's not like we're mother-son, or father-son. We don't have those type of relationships. It seems like we're like best friends." Although he made eye contact and smiled as he answered (only those who ask the stupidest questions don't get a smile), I got the impression that Tiger was not overjoyed to hear his "pop" had spoken with me for this book. My experience of Woods—again quite different from my dealings with Palmer and Nicklaus—is that he is uncomfortable with the people in his life talking about him. Indeed, he tries to stop it.

It was raining by the time we emerged into the parking lot of the Hilton. In the morning, Tiger would play in his first tournament round after a two-month layoff due to corrective surgery on his left knee, and no doubt he had his mind on the challenge ahead (he would win the Buick Invitational easily). Before that he was going out for dinner with some friends. As he made his way to an anonymous Buick sedan, I asked finally whether there was anything he wanted to say in a one-on-one interview. "No. I'm sorry. Not on unauthorized about me," he said. "I have my own books." I tried to persuade him, giving good reasons why he might make an exception to his rule, but Woods was steely. "I have my own books," he repeated. Still he remembered to be polite, as his parents had taught him. "Thank you, though." And I thanked him. Then he left.

No blame is attached to Tiger for not doing an interview. That is his right, and considering the many demands on his time one cannot be altogether surprised, much less angry, when he declines a request. Some may even consider his decision to be wise, a way of protecting himself.

However, his attitude is contrary to the tradition of the game whereby most players talk freely to fans and the media when asked. Many of the biggest names in golf enjoyed talking about the game, and their place in it, for this book. Tiger—despite his engaging Disney-like look and apparently affable persona—is not like the other great stars of golf, past and present. For the most part, Tiger does not chat with strangers. He is warier than that, and when it comes to giving his time, he does so usually only in controlled situations and in exchange for money. As we shall see, Tiger is very business-minded. He is, after all, a brand name. Everything Tiger Woods does and says is under contract (which is why an IMG agent trails behind him). The Nike clothes he wears, the Buick he drives, the TAG Heuer watch on his wrist, the American Express card in his wallet—everything is a deal. As he says, he has his own books. At the moment, his publishing career extends to an instruction book, *How I Play Golf*, put together for him by the staff at *Golf Digest* magazine, to which he contributes ghosted instruction articles.

Despite Tiger's lack of cooperation, I hope this book is a revealing and worthwhile look at the wicked game. It is a critical book, because I believe there is much in golf to be critical of. Yet little or no criticism appears in the main publications of golf; the golf press, working as it does hand in golf glove with players and their agents, constitutes little more than a publicity department for the game. As someone who comes to the game as an outsider, a writer of diverse books of nonfiction and biography—about a murder case, a poet, and Bob Dylan—I don't have a vested interest in the golf establishment. I'm someone like you, perhaps, who enjoys watching events such as the Masters on TV, hits a few golf balls now and again to very little effect, and finds Palmer, Nicklaus, and Woods interesting because they are unusual people of outstanding achievement who, above and beyond golf, stand tall in popular culture. Although Tiger himself said little more to me than the few words you have already read, many important people in his life did speak to me at length, and this book reveals aspects of Woods's life, and what might be called the Woods family mythology, that may be surprising, casting his story in a new light. However, this book is bigger than Tiger and his family, starting as it does with a player of a different stripe: Arnie Palmer, the sunburned hero of 1950s America, a steel-town boy who went on to play golf with presidents and became the first great sports star of the nascent television age. Then came Jack Nicklaus, a golden-haired gladiator for the Technicolor years. Others competed in the 1980s to replace Palmer and Nicklaus in terms of fame and success—such as Severiano Ballesteros, Greg Norman, and Tom Watson—but the only golfer to have galvanized the interest of the general public since has been Tiger Woods. That is why Palmer, Nicklaus, and Woods are the focus of this book and, being American men, that is why this is largely the story of men's golf in America.

Over a period of two years, from St. Andrews in Scotland to Augusta, Georgia, more than 150 people were interviewed. I would like to thank the following: Arnold Palmer; his brother, Jerry; the staff at Bay Hill Club and Lodge in Florida, particularly Mr. Palmer's secretary, Pat Boeckenstedt; the staff at Latrobe Country Club in Pennsylvania, including Mr. Palmer's assistants Donald "Doc" Giffin, Cori J. Britt, and Gina Varrone. Thanks also to Ed Seay at Palmer Course Design Company; Dick Tiddy of the Arnold Palmer Golf Academy; caddie James "Tip" Anderson; Palmer's flying instructor, Eli "Babe" Krinock; Palmer's physician, Dr. Bob Mazero, and his dentist, Dr. Howard "Howdy" Giles (two of his close friends); Ed Bignon (formerly of Arnold Palmer Golf Management); and journalist Larry Guest.

I am grateful to Jack and Barbara Nicklaus; to Mr. Nicklaus's sister, Marilyn Hutchinson; and the staff at Muirfield Village Golf Club in Ohio. Thank you to Nicklaus's three best friends at Muirfield: Bob Hoag, Pandel Savic, and Ivor Young; Scott Tolley at Nicklaus in Florida; former business associate Putnam S. Pierman; journalist Kaye Kessler; Robin Obetz, the best man at Nicklaus's wedding; Dom Lepore at Scioto Country Club in Ohio, where Nicklaus learned the game; and Gerald Goodson at the Jack Nicklaus Museum.

I am also indebted to Tiger Woods's father, Earl; to his aunt Mabel Lee "Mae" Moore; and Earl Woods's first wife, Barbara Ann Gary. I also spoke with two of Tiger's siblings, Kevin and Royce Woods, though they declined full interviews. Thank you to Tiger's former girlfriends Dina Gravell and Joanna Jagoda (who helped with fact checking).

The late Mark H. McCormack talked about the founding of International Management Group and his work with Palmer, Nicklaus, and Woods. Thanks also to IMG agent Mark Steinberg and Vice President Publishing/Golf Bev Norwood. At Nike, Inc., thanks to Director of Golf Marketing Kel Devlin and Carolyn Wu (Global Issues Management). Thank you also to Ineke Zeldenrust at the Clean Clothes Campaign in Holland, and Tim Connor at NikeWatch in Australia. I am grateful to John Franklin Merchant, Tiger's former lawyer, and Greg McLaughlin, executive director of the Tiger Woods Foundation.

Thanks to Tiger's caddies, Mike "Fluff" Cowan and Steve Williams, and his former sports psychologist, Dr. J. Jay Brunza. Thank you to his coaches (in chronological order): Rudy Duran, John Anselmo, Claude "Butch" Harmon Jr., and Wally Goodwin (formerly of Stanford University in California). Thanks also to Tiger's Stanford teammates—Notah Begay III, Eri Crum, Joel Kribel, Casey Martin, Jake Poe, and Conrad Ray—and to amateur player and friend Trip Kuehne.

In Earl Woods's hometown of Manhattan, Kansas, friends and former neighbors helped unravel the Woods family history: Bill Baker, Dr. Charles Bascom, Rosa Hickman, Gene Holiwell, Denzil Kastner, Jerry Keck, Harold Robinson, Patty Schrader (née Keck), Don Slater, and Marion Socolofsky. Thank you also to Earl's former schoolteacher Elbert Fly, and his former Kansas State University baseball coach Ray Wauthier. Special thanks to Cindy Harris, Pat Patton, and Cindy Von Elling of the Department of Special Collections at KSU. I am also grateful to Linda Glasgow at the Riley County Historical Museum.

Thank you to Tiger Woods's childhood/school friends and acquaintances: Lesley Aldrich-Linnert, Mickey Conahan, Mike Kruse, and Kelly Manos. And staff past and present at Cerritos Elementary School in Anaheim, California: Diane Baer Linda Behrens, Maureen Decker, Jerry Friedman, Donald Hill, Jane Orbison, and Joy Rice. Thank you to the staff at Western High School in Anaheim: Ron Butterfield, Don Crosby, Corrina Durrego, Cia Fermelia, Doug Munsey, Bill Murvin, Jim Tozzie, and Ed Woodson. Heather Gruenthal helped with photographs. Thanks to Bill Orr, who customized Tiger's clubs during his amateur career, and Jimmy Burns, Paul Moreno, Ron Nichols, Walter Olsen, and Bob Rogers at the Navy Golf Course in Cypress, California.

Since turning professional, Tiger Woods has lived within the guarded confines of Isleworth Golf and Country Club in Windermere, Florida. Isleworth owner Joseph Lewis, and his daughter Vivienne Silverton, invited me in to meet them and tour Isleworth. Thanks also to Lisa H. Richards, Isleworth golf pro Marty De Angelo, and Tiger's Isleworth neighbor Mark O'Meara.

Thanks to notable golfers not previously mentioned: Tommy Bolt, Mark Calcavecchia, Jim Dent, Bruce Devlin, Ernie Els, Dow Finsterwald, Doug Ford, Tony Jacklin, Byron Nelson, Charlie Owens, Gary Player, Nick Price, Chi Chi Rodriguez, Doug Sanders, Adrian Stills, Tom Watson, Tom Weiskopf, Ward Wettlaufer, Kermit Zarley, Stanley Ziobrowski, and Frank Urban "Fuzzy" Zoeller. Also, thanks to William Spiller Jr., son of the late Bill Spiller.

Thank you to senior administrators in the game: Peter Dawson, secretary of the Royal & Ancient Golf Club of St. Andrews (and to John Uzielli, former captain of the R&A); David B. Fay, executive director of the United States Golf Association; Jim L. Awtrey, chief executive officer at the PGA of America (and Julius Mason, director of Public and Media Relations); former PGA Tour Commissioner Deane Beman; and Henry Hughes, senior vice president of the PGA Tour.

I am grateful to James Bell, tournament director of the Bay Hill Invitational, and Bob Berry, formerly of the Buick Challenge. Hall W. Thompson, founder of the Shoal Creek Country Club in Birmingham, Alabama, also spoke to me. At the Augusta National Golf Club in Georgia, thanks to Dr. Stephen W. Brown and Frank Carpenter. I am grateful also to Linda Poitevint Beck at the Augusta Public Library and the Rihl family of Augusta.

Those not previously mentioned include golf coach David Leadbetter; former head of CBS Golf Frank Chirkinian; founder of the Golf Channel, Joseph E. Gibbs; director general of Rolex, Patrick Heiniger; and player-broadcasters Bill Kratzert (ESPN), Bob Rosburg (ABC), and Ken Venturi (CBS). Thank you to veteran caddies Alfred "Rabbit" Dyer, Sam "Killer" Foy, and Irving McLean; to golf course builders and designers Dave Harman, Michael Hurdzan, and Jay Morrish; to Bill Osborne, an attorney in the Isleworth/Lake Bessie court case (and litigants Don Greer and Bob Londeree); civil rights/golf activists Dr. Martha Burk, Maggie Hathaway, and Porter Pernell, the former president of the United Golfers Association; M. Grant Batey, cofounder of the Meadowbrook Country Club in North Carolina, one of the oldest black-owned country clubs in the United States; Joe Louis Barrow Jr. at the First Tee; and Barbara Douglas at the National Minority Golf Foundation. Thanks also to Professor Herma Hill Kay at the University of California at Berkeley (Boalt Hall School of Law).

Finally, thank you to Russell Galen of Scovil Chichak Galen, Inc., in New York; Jonathan Lloyd at Curtis Brown Ltd. in London; Henry Ferris at William Morrow/HarperCollins Publishers Inc. in New York; and Ingrid Connell at Pan Macmillan in London.

1

MISTER PALMER'S
NEIGHBORHOOD

The hands are large and unusually strong, with the leathery feel of a workingman's hands. With hands like that a fellow could be a smith in a steel mill, which might have been the fate of Arnold Daniel Palmer had he not trained his fingers into the Vardon grip at an early age and swung himself into the history of golf. The hands were resting on the controls of the golfer's jet as he descended through the rain clouds to the Arnold Palmer Regional Airport in his hometown of Latrobe, Pennsylvania. There was a time, thirty or so years ago, when Palmer was the only professional golfer successful enough to afford a private airplane, dispensing with those wearisome road trips between tour events. Now there is so much money in the game that practically every tour player flies to work. Still, few own their planes. Even Tiger Woods leases. Palmer owned this $16 million Cessna Citation X and, at the age of seventy-two, he was the pilot.

When he made contact with the control tower, it was the slow, sonorous voice of a thousand television commercials—for Pennzoil and myriad other products—an instantly recognizable and engaging, though slightly too loud voice, for Palmer is a little deaf. The tower welcomed him home and gave N1AP permission to land; he lifted the flaps and the jet came roaring in over the rooftops of this gray steel town southeast of Pittsburgh. It is not the prettiest town in America. In truth, Latrobe has a tired look. Its vitality has been seeping away since the 1970s, when the steel industry went into recession, and the population has dwindled to less than nine thousand. But Latrobe still has its pride. Rolling Rock beer is brewed here. And, of course, Latrobe has Arnold Palmer, or one might say that Arnold Palmer has Latrobe, for he owns great swaths of the place and much of the rest is named in his honor.

Each spring, when he returns after wintering in Florida and California, where he also has homes, Palmer collects a new Cadillac from the parking lot of the Arnold Palmer Regional Airport. It is left there for him by Arnold Palmer Motors, the local General Motors dealership. In late April 2002, he picked up a Cadillac Escalade and drove down Arnold Palmer Drive into Youngstown, the neighborhood he grew up in, and where he is very much a king of all he surveys. Many of the houses along the road are owned by Palmer or members of his family, and much of the surrounding land is his, including the wooded hillside in the distance, land that Arnold and his late wife, Winnie, acquired so developers could not spoil the countryside. Since Winnie's death from cancer in 1999, Palmer has also established the Winnie Palmer Nature Reserve at the edge of town, a fond tribute to a beloved spouse. They were a famously close and happy couple, though some friends were taken aback when he started dating again soon after her death, keeping company now with a well-preserved woman in her early sixties by the name of Kathleen Gawthorp, who looks more than a little like Winnie did: petite and pretty and brunette. Arnie always had been popular with women.

Soon the fairways of Latrobe Country Club came into view, the golf course where Arnold's father worked as greenskeeper and club professional. Arnie owned the club now, and his kid brother, Jerry, managed it. Turning left opposite the entrance, Palmer powered the Escalade up a steep, tree-lined road to a parking area in front of a low, white-painted building. These were the stables where his daughters, Amy and

Peggy, used to keep ponies. Now that the girls are grown, with children of their own, Palmer has had the stables converted into offices. The welcome mat is embossed with his corporate logo of a multicolored golf umbrella. Inside are bright, interconnecting rooms, offices to five assistants led by Donald "Doc" Giffin, an owlish former *Pittsburgh Press* writer who has been Palmer's man Friday since 1966. Adjacent is the ranch-style house Arnold and Winnie built shortly after they married. This compound and the club across the road are Palmer's summer base, and it is a homely place without any of the obtrusive security young Tiger Woods needs to surround himself with in Florida. Palmer is protected by the fact that he is part of the community here in western Pennsylvania, where he was born and raised, and local people like him. They remember that when he became famous and reporters asked him where he was from, he didn't say he came from a place near Pittsburgh, as others would have, because almost nobody had heard of Latrobe. "Near Pittsburgh was not a phrase Arnie used," says Bob Mazero, his school friend and now doctor. He was Arnold Palmer of Latrobe. He was proud of the place, and that made people proud of him.

Virtually every day of Palmer's life is filled with business, with the golfer speaking frequently by telephone with his assistants and associates across the country, including Ed Seay, who runs the Palmer Course Design Company in Florida. Of the plethora of celebrity golfers in the lucrative industry of golf course design and construction, the most successful are Jack Nicklaus and Arnold Palmer, with Palmer's company building more courses, though Nicklaus's are considered superior* and are usually more expensive. Still, a Palmer course is hardly cheap, costing up to $500,000 *per hole,* and, with 250 courses in thirteen countries, this is one of the reasons he is so rich.

Another major source of income is endorsement work. The day after Palmer returned home, there was a photo shoot for the International

---

*In 2001 the Golf Research Group ranked "Nicklaus Signature" courses number one in terms of "architect's value" and other indices. Palmer came in sixth.

GLUV Corporation, one of many companies he is contracted to. The cameras for the shoot were set up in the office foyer, the centerpiece of which is an array of trophies representing his ninety-two wins, including seven professional major wins. Other mementos of a full life include framed photographs of Palmer with Queen Elizabeth II, the emperor of Japan, Muhammad Ali, and almost every incumbent of the White House since Dwight Eisenhower, who was a close friend. There is also a portrait of the quintessential American golfer by Norman Rockwell, mounted in a gold frame and hung at the end of a corridor adjacent to Palmer's private office, the colors of the picture bright in the morning sunlight.

When Rockwell painted his picture, Palmer was in his prime—slim-faced with thick brown hair. As the golfer stepped back into his office in 2002, he was an old man, portly around the middle and shorter than one imagined. The face was fuller than when Rockwell captured him, Florida-tanned and folded into creases, and the hair had become thin and white. Palmer was still a handsome and distinguished figure, however, sharply dressed in the style of another era: a black shirt with a yellow cashmere sweater draped over broad shoulders, a gold Rolex studded with diamonds. He has presence, and his inner sanctum has the corresponding ambience of a presidential office crossed with the den of a member of Sinatra's Rat Pack or even a Mafia don. One enters via double doors to find windows on three sides overlooking woodland. The walls are hung with framed photographs, the tables ornamented with memorabilia, including models of airplanes he has owned, golf medals, and hole-in-one balls. Palmer sat at a large solid wood desk, sunlight on his back, as he received delegations of staff. Two cheerful secretaries, Deborah and Gina, entered bearing piles of items sent in by fans wanting autographs: there were regular requests by letter, photographs people wanted signed, golf balls, even golf clubs. Using a black marker pen, he signed everything without complaint, taking his time to do it properly, grunting the occasional question in a pleasant way and receiving the prompt, positive replies due to a man of his age and importance.

Then the secretaries departed and Palmer turned his mind to reminiscence—first about his long association with the Augusta National Golf Club of Georgia and its Masters tournament, which occupies center stage in his life and in our story. The Masters was fresh in his mind because, two weeks earlier, Palmer had made his forty-eighth appearance in the championship, and he had told the world that it was his last.

With the exception of the Royal & Ancient Golf Club of St. Andrews in Scotland, which is the historic home of golf* there is probably no golf club in the world so famous as the Augusta National, and no golf championship—Britain's Open notwithstanding—is as celebrated as Augusta's invitational. To Palmer, Nicklaus, and Woods, the Masters is everything.

Although it is the youngest of the major tournaments, founded seventy-four years after Britain's Open, the Masters feels like golf's quintessential event. The fact that it is the only major played at the same venue each year lends a particular sense of tradition, which is a quality valued highly in golf. The venue is, of course, an exclusive private club closed to the public for all but one week of the year, in early April. One of the charms of golf is that it is a pastoral game played in beautiful places, and the Augusta National is a golfer's wonderland, an unusually spacious course maintained in pristine condition. Its seemingly endless fairways narrow to jewel-like greens framed with pine trees, guarded by bunkers filled with sand of an unusual brightness, and beautified with colorful flowers. It is partly because of the attractiveness of the setting that the Masters is enjoyed not just by golf enthusiasts but by the general public as a television show. When the

---

*The earliest written reference to golf in the British Isles can be dated to 1457, and the earliest reference to golf being played on the links at St. Andrews, which is land linked to the sea, was in 1552, when the townspeople were granted by charter the right to pursue "golff, futball, schuteing and all gamis" on land adjacent to the beach. Although the Dutch played a similar stick–and–ball game, they didn't hit the ball into a hole. Therefore, golf as we know it is generally agreed to be a Scottish invention. The R&A was founded in 1754.

weather is still cold in much of North America and in northern Europe, viewers switch on the Masters and the screen is suffused with spring, for spring comes early in the South. The cameras of CBS, which has had the exclusive rights to the Masters since 1956, linger on the magnolia trees that line the approach to the plantation clubhouse, and pan through the flowering white dogwood, golden bells, and azalea planted at the 11th, 12th, and 13th holes, those holes at the bottom of the hill, around Rae's Creek, known as Amen Corner. With the broadcast comes soothing music and an oleaginous voice-over from Jim Nantz, CBS golf anchor. "Well, it's the annual celebration of spring," Nantz croons, "an awakening of new life at this national treasure down in Augusta, Georgia . . ." And syrupy though his words are, the effect is charming.

Great golfers have been defined by their performances in the Masters since the tournament was first held in 1934. The young Arnold Palmer won four times between 1958 and 1964, which was then a record, thrilling the crowds and the new television audience with his bold play. So many people came to follow him around the course at Augusta that the local newspaper dubbed his thousands of fans "Arnie's Army," supposedly the largest private army in the world. An exceptionally personable young man, he also won over the club's founders, the legendary amateur Bobby Jones and his associate Clifford Roberts, and Palmer became close to the club's most distinguished member, President Dwight Eisenhower—all now long dead, of course. But Palmer remains a fixture at the Masters.

Back when the Masters was young, Jones and Roberts decreed that champions would be eligible to compete for as long as they lived—exempt from the usual rules of qualifying for a place in the tournament—and several had taken them at their word. Before the 2002 tournament, however, club chairman William "Hootie" Johnson wrote to three old-timers—Gay Brewer (seventy), Billy Casper (seventy), and Doug Ford (seventy-nine)—asking them respectfully not to play again. At the end of their biblical allotment of years, some had trouble walking the course, which is long and hilly, let alone making the cut.* If Brewer and the others had to go, Palmer should, too, by rights. He was already older than Brewer and Casper. But owing to his great fame, because the fans still loved to see him, and taking into account that Palmer is one of only two professional golfers to have been made a member of this club (the other being Jack Nicklaus), it seemed unlikely that anybody would have the temerity to ask *him* to stop. Still, when the others got the letter, Palmer got the message. On Thursday, April 11, 2002, after ending round one of the Masters at the bottom of the leader board with a 17-over-par score of 89, he made an announcement.

"Tomorrow will be it," he growled at the sportswriters. "That's it. I don't want to get a letter." There was some indulgent laughter at the reference to Chairman Johnson's by now notorious missive, but Palmer was serious, and privately disgruntled that the lifetime exemption apparently no longer pertained. "Augusta has meant an awful lot to me over the years, and it may be the one tournament that really kicked me off and got me started on my career," he added sadly. Saying goodbye was like admitting his life was over, which was a melancholy thought indeed. Palmer had always been a sentimental sort, and now, in old age, lachrymose thoughts came even more easily. "I recognize the fact that, you know, someday I'm going to die. I don't want to die, but I'm going to," he said a tad melodramatically. Despite a bout of prostate cancer in 1997, his health is excellent.

So, in April 2002 Palmer played what everybody thought was his final round at the Masters, over two days because he was interrupted by a storm on Friday. And fans from across the country hastened to Augusta to catch golf's original TV star in his farewell show. Of course, most couldn't get tickets. Due to an eccentric ticketing policy, only those on the club's list of patrons are offered tournament-round badges each year. Because of oversubscription, the list has been closed to new

---

*The midway point at which players who have not done so well are eliminated from the tournament.

applicants since 1972. Inevitably this system has fueled a thriving black market with many of the patrons on the list selling their tickets to scalpers who congregate, like fleas on a dog, outside the club, along Washington Road. Last-chance badges for Arnold Palmer were changing hands for $1,300 and more. Palmer's final round made the evening news and the morning front pages. Fellow players such as the Australian star Greg Norman paused to pay tribute. "Everybody who plays the game of golf should thank Arnold Palmer for what he's given the game of golf and every professional golfer should thank Arnold Palmer for putting every dollar they have in their pocket," said Norman, an exaggerated statement that held a kernel of truth. "Because Arnold was the guy who turned the game of golf around. Arnold was the guy who brought corporate America to the game, brought charisma to the game, brought a different atmosphere and ambience to it. Everybody should take their hats off to him and salute him and say, thanks for everything." And so Palmer received a standing ovation at every green, and there were some tears and a good deal of nostalgia for what had been and would never be again. Only it wasn't quite as simple as that.

"[It's] kinda sad, because I'm not going to be playing anymore. I'm not very happy about that," said Palmer, reflecting back home in Latrobe on the 2002 tournament shortly after saying good-bye to Augusta. As he spoke, he became quickly and surprisingly emotional all over again. His voice thickened. His eyes became misty. "Augusta is very special, and always has been," he said. "It's a tournament that I looked forward to long before I ever got there, and then to get there and have the experiences that I've had, and to [have had that] opportunity for forty-eight years, is even more special."

In fact, it was more than he could bear to say good-bye. Shortly before the 2003 Masters, Arnie would sit down and write a letter to Hootie Johnson expressing his displeasure at this silly age restriction and making it clear he wanted to come back and wave some more for the folks. Arnie didn't want to play *forever*. He didn't want to become so doddering that he drove a ball into a spectator's face, like poor Sam Snead did at the

2002 Masters (shortly before Snead himself died at age eighty-nine). But having competed forty-eight times, Arnold thought fifty would be a nice round number. Then Jack Nicklaus wrote to Johnson backing Palmer up, asking the club to rescind the age restriction (which had become official after the 2002 tournament—players had to be under sixty-five and to have competed in a certain number of events the preceding year). It would have been more dignified, perhaps, if Palmer had stuck by his original decision. But one of the failings of old golf stars is that, having defined themselves by aiming at and achieving records, they are loath to give up the habit. In his heyday, a record of Masters wins was Palmer's target. In his seventies, a record number of Masters *starts* had to suffice. And one of his weaknesses, perhaps, is that he loves to be loved. Tiger Woods might be cold and aloof, but Palmer goes almost too far the other way. Without the adulation of fans, he was lost, and nobody, including Hootie Johnson, was going to refuse his sad, old face, because golf is all about tradition, even when tradition becomes a deadweight.

Still, you couldn't blame the man for being attached to Augusta. As Palmer says, "That was my life, and my living." The living proved an exceedingly good one, as is evident when one visits him in Latrobe. His fortune is estimated to be a high eight-figure number, maybe as large as $100 million. Palmer was the progenitor of the career that every subsequent professional golfer has aspired to and, though only a handful have come near his financial success, even journeyman players on tour are millionaires in the twenty-first century. As Norman said, the wealth exists to some extent because of the attention Palmer brought to golf, and the way in which he attracted corporate investors to tournaments, where weekly purses are now $5 million and rising. "I suppose, in some ways, I worked to try to have that happen, to a degree, and I certainly have no problem with the fact that they can win the kind of money they win," says Palmer. "You can only hope that they appreciate it, and will return it to the game so that the people following them will have the same opportunity." He does not like to talk too much about money, considering such conversation impolite and, anyway, he didn't set out to be rich. Money was a by-product of success in the game he loved. "My goals were to become the greatest player in the world, [and] at some point in my career I think I did that. Then, of course, Nicklaus came along," he added, and you couldn't help but think that he still wished that Nicklaus had not ended his reign quite as soon as he did.

Golf has always been a game enjoyed by the privileged, excluding more people than it has embraced, and Nicklaus was typical of the country club–type who have long dominated the game. "Golf has been labeled a snob sport, and was," Palmer concedes. But Palmer's story runs contrary to the norm, because his background is humble. "One of the reasons that I [think] the people accepted me, and took me into their hearts and minds, was the fact that I was a steel-mill-town boy," he says. "I was born in a depression. We had nothing."

Arnold's father, Milfred Jerome Palmer, known for obscure reasons as Deacon or Deke, was born and raised in Youngstown, the son of a house painter. Preferring the outdoor life to work in the Stygian steel mills, Deacon was one of the laborers who built Latrobe Country Club in the 1920s, a project commissioned by Latrobe Electric Steel in an affluent decade. Later he became greenskeeper and then golf professional— selling equipment and giving lessons at the club. Deke married Doris Morrison and they had four children, starting with Arnold, who was born on September 10, 1929. Two years later there was a sister, Lois Jean, known as Cheech. After a thirteen-year gap there were two more children: Jerry in 1944 and Sandy in 1948.

Arnie came into the world six weeks before the Wall Street Crash. There have been few more challenging times in which to grow up than the Great Depression. Yet he was also born into a golden age of golf. It was shortly after his first birthday that Robert Tyre Jones Jr.—better known as Bobby Jones—thrilled America by winning the U.S. Amateur in Philadelphia. By doing so, he achieved his historic Grand Slam, which comprised winning in one season what were then considered the four major championships—the Amateur and Open championships of both Britain and the United States. It is difficult now to appreciate how famous and glamorous a figure Jones was. An indication of his celebrity is that he was honored with a ticker-tape parade in New York during his Grand Slam year, a parade to rival that of aviator Charles Lindbergh, who had made history three years earlier by flying the Atlantic solo. Jones would be a golfing hero and benchmark for generations of players, including Palmer and then Nicklaus, who would in turn become the role model for Woods. As Nicklaus says, tracing the history, "It seems as though every record I shot at was Jones's and every record [Tiger] shot at has been mine."

One of Jones's friends was the dour Clifford Roberts, whose severe personality had been formed by a difficult and frightening childhood. At sixteen he burned down his family home in a frightful accident. When he was nineteen, his mother killed herself with a shotgun. His father apparently chose to take his own life, too, when he was crushed by a train.* Despite his upbringing, with little money behind him and scant education, Roberts made a fortune on Wall Street, where he proved an astute investor and collector of friends. He adored Bobby Jones and together they decided to build a golf club that would be part tribute to Jones's achievements in the game and a place for themselves and their wealthy cronies to get together and relax and talk business. They decided upon an old indigo plantation in Augusta, Georgia, near Jones's hometown of Atlanta. "Perfect!" exclaimed Jones when he saw the land. "And to think this ground has been lying here all these years waiting for someone to come along and lay a golf course on it."

Built during the Depression, the Augusta National was not an immediate success when it opened in 1933, struggling with financial problems and finding it hard to attract enough members in the first few years. But it evolved into one of the most exclusive and extraordinary private clubs in the United States. There are not many members, about three hundred in total, and when one sees them about the place, they are mostly old men,

---

*Clifford Roberts continued the family tradition: he shot himself dead in 1977, when depressed during an illness.

shriveled up like tortoises in their green club blazers, seemingly too frail
to do much at all. But appearances are deceptive. These men are among
the richest and most powerful in America. The current chairman may go
by the comical nickname of Hootie, but he also happens to be the former chairman of the executive committee of the mighty Bank of America. There is in fact a tradition of bankers leading the club. Johnson's
predecessor, Jackson T. Stephens, is chairman of one of the largest investment banks in the country, Stephens Group, Inc., and is personally
worth $1.5 billion. Some members are even richer, including the rela-
tively youthful Bill Gates and Warren Buffett, the two richest men in the
world. And with big money comes great power. Back in 1952, the membership demonstrated this power by boosting one of its number, General
Dwight D. Eisenhower, into the White House as president of the United
States. The financial and moral support of the members, together with
widespread connections at the highest level in American society, were a
great asset to the campaign. Eisenhower was a Republican president, of
course, and the Augusta National is a deeply conservative, even reactionary, institution with a history of discrimination that is part of the tradition of its invitational, and the history of golf. For most of its existence,
the Augusta National shunned African Americans as it now shuns
women. It has been said that Jones and Roberts wanted no blacks inside
the club or in their tournament—only caddies and kitchen staff. Though
this statement is apocryphal, the fact remains that no black golfer played
in the Masters until 1975, decades after other American sports had been
integrated. There were no black members until as recently as 1990 and
there are still no women. Sexism is the last barrier of discrimination in
golf and, though the club is under increasing pressure to admit women,
it still chooses to discriminate in this way as it has in other ways. This is
part of the unpleasant background of Jim Nantz's "national treasure."

Just as the Augusta National was an all-white preserve, so was
the more modest club where Arnold Palmer's father worked in Pennsylvania. Indeed, until recent times most golf and country clubs across the

country have been bastions of a type and class of people. Latrobe Country Club did not admit blacks, Jews, or Catholics when Arnold was a boy. The members were a homogeneous group of white professionals: doctors from the local hospital, steel mill bosses, and other citizens of substance. That isn't to say the members were bad people. Quite the contrary. Among the original membership were the Rogers, for instance, an upstanding family who owned a die-casting business in Latrobe. They had a son, Fred, who was a year older than Arnie; in adult life he epitomized wholesome, small-town American values as the creator and host of the iconic children's TV show *Mister Rogers' Neighborhood*. That imaginary neighborhood had much in common with Latrobe in the years of Arnie's childhood and youth. Latrobe was an unpretentious, tight-knit community where people respected each other and took an interest in one another's well-being, without overstepping polite inquiry. Your place in the community was part of who you were, as Deacon Palmer told Arnie repeatedly, and this philosophy formed Arnie's character. Perhaps his most marked characteristic is his solicitude. When he talks to you, he seems genuinely interested in what you say and to want to help you. And although Palmer's speaking voice is gruffer than that of the late Fred Rogers, his manner is not altogether dissimilar to the slow and thoughtful way in which Mister Rogers spoke to his young audience.

When he was six, Arnold's family moved into a small wood-frame house backing onto the 6th fairway at Latrobe Country Club. Although Arnold would grow up with the country club as his backyard, Deacon Palmer laid down strict rules about how his children treated the course and other facilities (he had rules about everything). They were certainly not encouraged to use the course as a playground. Instead, they played on the little-used highway in front. "Few if any automobiles came out this way, except to maybe come to the club, so [we] had a great road in front of our house with no traffic that we could play on and ride our bikes," recalls Jerry Palmer. The clubhouse was off-limits, as was the swimming pool. The Palmer kids swam in the stream. And there were few luxuries at home, because money was so tight. "We were very poor," adds Jerry. "During the Depression my parents had to raise farm animals—pigs, chickens—to get along." To ease his worries, Deacon sometimes drank too much, and he had a temper that he directed at Arnie, the oldest child. But still the boy loved his father, and it was his father who introduced him at the age of three to the game that became his life.

"Hit it hard!" Deacon ordered. Then: "Go find it and hit it hard again." This simple golfing advice was not quite as early an introduction to the game as Earl Woods later gave Tiger (who was ten months old at the time). But one of the commonalities among Palmer, Nicklaus, and Woods is that all three were introduced to golf by dominant, sports-crazy fathers whom they adored. For his part, Arnold developed a distinctive style of play on the fairways of Latrobe Country Club that involved hitting the ball low and hard, with a slight curve or "draw." His wasn't an elegant or sophisticated swing. Deacon believed that what felt good was probably right. And Arnold's weak point was his short game, partly because he didn't get enough practice around the greens. (Deacon didn't want Arnie digging lumps out of the precious turf.) But what he lacked in style, Arnie made up for in enthusiasm.

As his interest in golf grew, the boy naturally wanted to play as often as possible, so he would accompany his mother and her friends when they played the course on ladies' day. There was a ditch one hundred yards from the 6th tee that some female players could not clear easily. Helen Fritz had particular difficulty, and so Arnie offered his assistance. "I'll knock your ball over the ditch for a nickel," he suggested, and he did, earning his first money from the game. Mindful of her son's appearance in company, his mother would chide him: "Arnold, pull up your pants and tuck your shirt in." He got into the habit of hitching up his trousers, which became one of his trademark gestures in later life. As he grew older, he worked on the course with his father: tending the fairways, minding the pro shop, and working as a caddie, which meant he could play the course on Mondays, too.

For a short time in high school, Arnold was distracted from golf by football, which was the glamour sport in Latrobe, with most of the male population going to the local stadium on Saturday during the season. He was big and strong enough to be good, and Bob Mazero recalls that he and the other boys at Latrobe High badly wanted Arnie on the football team. But Deacon warned his son that a football injury could derail his golfing, so he gave up on the idea. From the age of twelve, Arnold had been playing in junior tournaments and, increasingly, he was thinking of becoming a professional: a tournament golfer playing for prize money, not a club pro, like his father, at the beck and call of members. Perhaps surprisingly, part of his inspiration was Mildred Didrikson "Babe" Zaharias, who became a great celebrity in women's golf in the 1940s after an early career as a gold medal–winning Olympic athlete. The Babe, as she was known, beat Annika Sorenstam—the leading female player of modern times, who made headlines in 2003 by competing as the only woman in a PGA Tour invitational—by decades when she made the cut in several men's tour events, proving that women could compete against men in golf and that the public enjoyed seeing them play against men. When Arnie was a boy, the Babe gave an exhibition of her golfing skills at Latrobe Country Club, and he was deeply impressed by the excitement she caused. Wouldn't it be wonderful to bask in that kind of attention himself? In 1946 he competed in the state high school championship and had a little gallery of local people following him around the course. At one stage in the latter part of the tournament (which he won), Arnie found himself in the rough with a choice between a conservative recovery shot to the fairway and a risky shot through the trees to the green. He took the latter option, and the excitement he caused when he successfully shot the ball through to the green showed him that he could get the kind of attention the Babe had received. It was just a matter of having a distinctive persona, something slightly different, and in his case recovery shots would become one of his trademarks. By getting into the same kind of trouble as weekend golfers but having the ability to blast his way out, often daringly, Arnie connected with everyday players. His willingness to acknowledge and exploit this bond showed Arnie's natural desire to be a star. It is important to understand that he always wanted to be popular.

While competing in a junior tournament at Oakland Hills Country Club in Detroit, Arnie met Buddy Worsham, another golf-crazy teenager, who became the most significant friend of his young life. Buddy was from a distinguished golfing family. His elder brother, Lew, won the 1947 U.S. Open and, almost as significantly, in 1953 he won the World Championship of Golf at the Tam O'Shanter Country Club outside Chicago, the first golf tournament televised live across the United States. (Worsham helped get televised golf off to a flying start by holing an improbable eagle for the title.) Buddy told Arnie that after high school he was going to Wake Forest College, a Baptist college near Durham, North Carolina. The climate was so warm down there you could play golf year-round, which sounded like heaven. But Arnie would have been hard-pressed to get a scholarship on the strength of his academic work. He was not the most impressive student at Latrobe High, where he was in a class for the less academically inclined. Neither could his family afford to pay his way. It was fortunate therefore that the athletic director at Wake Forest was persuaded to offer him a sports scholarship.

Palmer's college life was formative in several ways. Aside from the close friendship with Worsham, who became his roommate, an education in the conservative South crystallized his political views as a staunch Republican. Inevitably his character also developed. At first he was shy, as longtime friend Dick Tiddy recalls. "Today he is very outgoing and quite different," observes Tiddy, who met Arnie in his second year. "I think it was fame and fortune made him different." Golf took up most of his time at college, as well as his recreation time, and Arnie was increasingly successful in amateur events, including winning the West Penn Junior and Amateur tournaments. When he was home, he worked with his dad at the golf course and, one Christmas, as a bricklayer in the steel mills. Holiday jobs gave him pocket money for going to dances and taking girls out. Arnie was swinging carelessly through life—having a wonderful time, in fact—when a tragedy occurred. One Saturday night in the fall of 1950, Buddy asked Arnie if he would like to go on one of their jaunts into Durham, where there was a homecoming dance. Arnie declined, pointing out that they didn't have dates and, anyway, he wanted to stay behind to see a movie. So Buddy went without him. On Sunday morning Arnie woke to the news that Buddy and another boy had died in a car wreck during the night. When he went into town to find out what had happened, Arnie was given the ghastly task of identifying the bodies, which he recalls as probably the worst shock of his life. In part he blamed himself for what had happened. Had he gone to the dance, as Buddy had asked, Arnie probably would have been the one who drove home and maybe he would have driven more safely. More than half a century later, a photograph of Buddy hangs on the wall of Palmer's Latrobe office.

It was because of his friend's death that Arnie quit Wake Forest in January 1951 and joined the U.S. Coast Guard, serving for three years, initially at Cape May, New Jersey. He did not have much opportunity to practice during his years in the service and won relatively few tournaments, though he got to the fourth round of the 1953 U.S. Amateur. In January 1954 he returned to Wake Forest, where he had been offered a chance to complete his education. Golf took up most of his time, though. That year he won several tournaments, including the Ohio Amateur. (Among the competitors was a fourteen-year-old Ohio schoolboy named Jack Nicklaus, who watched Palmer admiringly.) Palmer had never taken his education particularly seriously, and when summer came, and he had to choose between studying and playing golf, it was no contest. The dean at Wake Forest warned him about missing classes and, ultimately, Palmer had to leave college without a degree. He went to work for a friend, Bill Wehnes, who sold paint. Palmer became a paint salesman, too, though a good deal of his time was spent playing golf, and his future was decided by one very significant tournament during that summer of 1954.

In August the U.S. Amateur Championship was held at the Country

Club of Detroit in Grosse Point Farms, Michigan. Palmer was twenty-four, and it was his fifth attempt at the title, which was the crowning achievement of any amateur career and at that time still considered one of the majors. The format was match play,* and a fellow had to win eight matches before he could claim the golden trophy. After some easy matches and some hard fights, Arnie met Bob Sweeny in the 36-hole final. In the 1950s the players who dominated the U.S. Amateur were mature men, many of whom were of independent means. A distinguished gentleman who dressed immaculately for the tournament in white linen, like a character out of one of F. Scott Fitzgerald's novels, Robert Sweeny Jr. was a forty-three-year-old investment banker from New York with a home in Palm Beach, Florida, and another on the French Riviera. Palmer was a simple young man in chinos and a sweaty, short-sleeved shirt who, having flunked out of college, was making a meager living. Yet his lack of sophistication was part of his appeal, together with his audacious style of play and his open, expressive manner. When Arnie hit a poor shot, his disappointment was written on his face. When he struck a good one, he sparked up a cigarette, dragged on it deeply, and stalked down the fairway to go again, and his enthusiasm was infectious. Still, the older man was a fine player, too, the winner of Britain's Amateur Championship in 1937, and he ended the morning round 2-up.

There were 18 more holes in the afternoon, and as the hours of a long, warm day passed, the two men traded birdies. Three times Palmer drew even, before moving ahead at the 32nd and then going 2-up at the 33rd. Sweeny was not done, though. He proved his mettle by halving the 34th and won the penultimate hole. With just one shot in it the tie was still very much alive down to the last, but Sweeny drove into the rough and, having put himself out of contention, conceded. Arnie was

---

*A game decided by the number of holes won, as opposed to medal or stroke play, where the number of shots are totaled and the lowest score wins. To win 2 and 1, for example, means to be two holes up with only one left to play.

the champion, 1-up, winner of the beautiful trophy that had been held by Jones and would in years to come pass into the hands of Nicklaus and eventually Woods. Doris Palmer hugged Arnie proudly and even Deacon broke into a smile as a brass band struck up. "I've never had a better moment than winning the U.S. Amateur Championship in 1954," says Palmer. "That was the turning point which made everything else possible." The press was delighted with a personable and approachable winner. Arnie was not the most cultured player in the world; he swung like a truck driver. He looked like a greenskeeper. But he made golf exciting, and he was empathetic in a way a high-society figure such as Bob Sweeny was not. Crowds loved Palmer because he was someone like themselves, and that was why the young man from Latrobe would almost single-handedly transform golf from a "snob sport," as Palmer puts it, into a game for everyone—apart from black people, that is.

2

AN INVISIBLE MAN

If Arnold Palmer had been born an African American—an apparently strange notion, but a pertinent one—the story of golf would have been very different. "He would have had no chance. None at all," says Tiger Woods's father, Earl. "He would have been excluded from golf." In 1950s America, black golfers were invisible men, to paraphrase Ralph Ellison,* shut out of the game as if they did not exist, and it is worth taking a moment to see how deep and widespread discrimination was.

Even though the United States was reforming in regard to race in the 1950s, the golf establishment lagged behind mainstream society for years. For example, in May of 1954, the year Arnold Palmer won the U.S. Amateur, the Supreme Court ruled against the divisive "separate but equal" principle that had hitherto been a halfway house between segregation and integration in the southern states. According to this principle, African Americans could be denied access to schools,

---

*Ellison begins *Invisible Man,* his 1952 novel about the experience of being black in America: "I am an invisible man . . . simply because people refuse to see me."

restaurants, and other facilities used by white people as long as equivalent facilities were provided for blacks. This was far from an equal share in society for African Americans, of course, and it was this injustice that the Supreme Court corrected. Henceforth, blacks and whites would have to integrate (though there would be violent conflicts before this was achieved). Despite this legislation, the golf establishment did not even begin to reform, however; golf was played and run for the most part within private clubs—grand establishments, like the Augusta National, and family clubs, like the Latrobe Country Club—and the members of these clubs could employ any kind of discriminatory practices they wished. What members wanted was to associate with people like themselves: well-heeled white people. Out of this clubbish environment came the men who ran golf, as well as its early champions, and for the most part these men shared and perpetuated what are essentially reactionary values. To be blunt, the institution of golf was racist. It was also sexist, and certainly elitist, and in many ways it has not changed.

Blacks were accepted in other sports at the highest level. Moreover, they were among the luminaries of sport, and had been for years: Jesse Owens was the star of the 1936 Munich Olympic Games; Joe Louis became heavyweight champion of the world in 1937. Althea Gibson would soon become champion of Wimbledon and the U.S. Open; in 1947, Jackie Robinson became the first black man to play Major League Baseball in the United States, giving hope to a generation of black boys (and their baseball-crazy fathers, as we shall see). Robinson went on to be one of the biggest names in baseball. In the late 1940s, black football players were signed to National Football League teams. But despite that historic Supreme Court ruling of 1954, black Americans made virtually no headway integrating into golf, neither as professionals nor as amateurs in white-owned private clubs, where they were not welcome for the most part. (There have been only a handful of black-owned golf clubs in the United States.) They were not even welcome to play on publicly owned municipal golf courses. On

December 7, 1955, in Greensboro, North Carolina, Dr. George C. Simkins, a black dentist, and five of his friends played nine holes at Gillespie Park, which was a public facility. However, local white golfers had circumvented the Supreme Court ruling by leasing the course for a nominal sum and establishing a bogus, whites-only membership. Because Dr. Simkins and his friends were not "members," the club pro took the view that they were trespassing and called the police. The black golfers were arrested and ultimately sentenced to thirty days in jail.

An outrageous incident such as the Simkins case can be blamed partly on racism in society, at a time when blacks suffered many injustices. But golf had a particular problem with color that went far beyond garden-variety prejudice. Golf was institutionally racist. Race discrimination was ingrained in the very executive of the game, actually written into the rules of the Professional Golfers' Association (PGA) of America, the organization that represented all golf professionals in the country, including club pros and—at that time—tour players. The PGA had restricted membership since 1934 with these words:

ARTICLE III
Members
SECTION 1. Professional golfers of the Caucasian Race, over the age of eighteen (18) years residing in North or South America, who can qualify under the terms and conditions hereinafter specified, shall be eligible . . .

The so-called Caucasian clause of the PGA of America is one of the most disgraceful facts in the history of American golf, a thing so brazen that it is still shocking. And it is very significant. If nonwhites could not belong to the PGA, they could not get jobs as club professionals, which cut them out of the game at an important stage, and even if they found a way to play and develop their skills to tournament level, they could not gain invitations to compete in official PGA Tour events.* Shameful though this is, the injustice was apparently of little concern to the distinguished tournament players of the day. In 1935 the future champion golfer Byron Nelson was hired by George Jacobus to work as his assistant at Ridgewood Country Club in New Jersey. As Jacobus was also president of the PGA, Nelson had a better-than-average overview of the game and its iniquities. Although he has a sharp memory for most things in his grand old age, Nelson says he has little or no recollection of the Caucasian rule and does not seem much troubled by what it represented. "I don't remember anything about that. I know [minorities] had some problems, but nothing serious that I knew anything about," he says.

Black Americans were the minority group most obviously shut out of golf. Yet, inevitably, some learned to play, typically as caddies at white clubs, though they usually had to sneak games, often playing at night by the light of the moon or using a system of lookouts to warn them when the club pro was coming. Many of these caddies had considerable skill, such as Sam "Killer" Foy, who began caddying at the Houston Country Club as a twelve-year-old in 1941, later becoming one of the best-known caddies on tour. Men like Foy dreamed of playing in tournaments for money. "Every caddie wanted to play," he says. But then reality dawned on him, as it did on others: "I got that off my mind." The professional game was closed to blacks. Partly it was a financial problem. By and large, blacks had less money than whites and golf is expensive. Young African Americans taking up the game would improvise the most ingenious equipment, using clubs made of tree limbs and balls fashioned from bottle caps. Porter Pernell, who grew up in Selma, Alabama, in the 1940s, and later became president of the African-American United Golfers Association (UGA), recalls that the only chance most blacks had to acquire real clubs was when a white

---

*The professional tour in the United States was part of the PGA of America until 1968, when it split from the association and became known as the PGA Tour.

player broke his—often in anger—and they salvaged the remains. But it is wrong to assume that blacks have been shut out of American golf only because they did not have the financial wherewithal to buy equipment and pay green fees. Even if a black man became a professional member of the well-paid middle class, like Dr. Simkins of North Carolina, he might still be jailed for playing golf on a public facility as the result of sheer racist spite.

Some black golfers pursued the game despite all the obstacles, but they found it brought them more than the usual amount of frustration. When Porter Pernell left the South to live and work in Hartford, Connecticut, he was allowed to play on the municipal course in town, Keney Park, though he and his black friends were hardly made to feel welcome there. But when Pernell and his friends wanted to obtain handicaps, they discovered they could only apply to the governing body of American golf, the United States Golf Association (USGA), via the Keney Park Club, and even though Pernell and his friends were playing on the Keney Park course, the club would not admit them as members because they were black. Pernell wrote to the USGA asking if he and his friends could obtain handicaps directly from the association. "They responded that they couldn't do that. Why? Because they wanted to recognize only one club." It was because of similar infuriating incidents happening across the country over many years that black golfers got together as early as 1925 and formed their own association, the United States Colored Golfers Association, later the UGA, of which Pernell later became president. At its height, the association claimed an impressive fifteen thousand members (by comparison, the PGA of America currently has twenty-seven thousand), and it organized its own professional tournaments, with modest cash prizes often put up by breweries. A number of black players rose to prominence through these events—especially the annual UGA National Open—notably men such as Bill Spiller and Teddy Rhodes, who was personal pro to the boxer Joe Louis, himself a keen golfer. The likes of Rhodes and Spiller were clearly good enough to graduate to mainstream tour events—and wanted to do so—but they could not play "the tour" simply because they were black and the PGA did not allow blacks to be members of its association. And white PGA professionals paid little heed to the plight of black players trying to break into the tour. "I don't think any of them were good enough players to have been on the tour," says Byron Nelson, expressing a typical opinion. This was a view that neither his black contemporaries Rhodes and Spiller nor the fans who came to watch them compete in the National Open would have shared. Against such a background, it is easy to see why it is so significant that a man of color, Tiger Woods, eventually came to dominate golf.

The year Arnold Palmer won the U.S. Amateur, Tiger Woods's father married for the first time and joined the army. The experiences of Earl Woods's early life shaped his character and explain much about the life and achievements of his son. For these reasons, it is important to find out where Earl came from and how he became the man he is.

He was born Earl Dennison Woods on March 5, 1932 (of the same generation as Arnold Palmer) and raised in Manhattan, Kansas, a small town 125 miles west of Kansas City. Manhattan was segregated when Earl was growing up; the blacks lived in a distinct neighborhood—or ghetto, if you will—south of Poyntz Avenue and north of the Kansas River, which flooded when Earl was three, causing mayhem. The black neighborhood was the least desirable part of town, where most of the roads were unpaved and railroad tracks ran between the blocks. From the alley behind the Woodses' home, you could hit the Rock Island Line freight trains with a stone as they went rumbling by. Even if blacks had the money to live in the more salubrious parts of Manhattan, they could not integrate into white society. They were not allowed to eat in restaurants such as Scheu's Cafe (though they worked in the kitchen). At the Wareham movie theater they were obliged to sit upstairs (though they paid the same price for their tickets). Naturally they were not welcome at either of the local golf courses, Stagg Hill or the Manhattan Country Club. Blacks were not even allowed in the City Park, except on August 4, the celebration of the Emancipation Proclamation. Earl's sister Freda, who worked for a time as an elevator operator at Coles department store, was moved to packing in the basement because white customers did not want to share an elevator with a black person.

The injustices seem scandalous in retrospect. At the time, most of the black residents of Manhattan took segregation as the norm. Indeed, many of Earl's contemporaries talk fondly about the old days in the neighborhood, nostalgic for the strong sense of community and common values that bound people together: respect for elders, hard work, and honesty. The influence of the church was strong in the community, maybe because God didn't seem to care what color you were. "God loves everybody. He made us all, and made us all colors," says Rosa Hickman, a former neighbor of the Woods family.

Earl's father, Miles Woods, was a Baptist who was born in Louisiana in 1873 and came to Manhattan as part of the mass northern migration of blacks following emancipation. He first married Etta Viola Mitchell, who gave him five children before dying in childbirth in 1905. His second wife, Earl's mother and Tiger's grandmother, was Maude Carter, born in 1893. Unlike most black women from rural Kansas in this era, Maude had a college education. She met Miles while she was a student at Kansas University in Lawrence and, though he was twenty years her senior, they married in July 1919. She then finished her education at Kansas State College (now known as Kansas State University) in Manhattan, earning a bachelor of science degree in home economics. Maude's pride in her education and her sense of the importance of education as a means of getting on in a white world would be transmitted to her six children who survived to adulthood:* Miles, Hattie Belle, Freda, Lillian, Mabel Lee (known as Mae), and Earl, the youngest.

The family lived in a simple wood-frame house at 1015 Yuma Street, one block from downtown. Miles worked in a lumberyard, as a janitor,

---

*A son, James, died within two days of birth.

and finally as a street cleaner. By the time Earl was born, his father was fifty-eight and in poor health. He was an epileptic and would have "spells" in the night. When this happened, Maude called upon her second-born and most capable child, Hattie Belle, and they would restrain Miles, sometimes putting a spoon in his mouth so he wouldn't bite his tongue. Miles was a sickly, distant figure to most of the children, including Mae, who could not understand why her well-educated and relatively youthful mother had married this "old, fussy, cussy man" who wore tattered overalls and, though he didn't drink or smoke, swore like a soldier. Earl recalls his father could swear for thirty minutes without repetition, "and I picked up on it."

Of all the children, Earl was perhaps closest to the old man because of their shared love of baseball. The Woodses lived near Griffith Park, where baseball games were played, and Miles was scorekeeper. Earl became bat boy, running from the dugout to pick up bats dropped by players and retrieving home-run balls, for which there was a nickel reward. ("Go get it, Tiger," Miles would urge his son, as the boy pelted out beyond the fence.)* Miles coached his son in baseball and became convinced his boy had exceptional ability as a catcher. "He had one single obsession and that was for me to be a professional baseball player," recalls Earl. But on August 28, 1943, a few hours after keeping score at an evening baseball game, Miles died. Earl was eleven. "My mother put her arm around me after the funeral and said, 'You're the man of the house now.' I became the father that young, looking out for everyone else," said Earl. The family had struggled in recent years, what with Miles's failing health and the aftermath of the Depression. With Miles dead, life became even more difficult. Although Maude had a degree and wanted to teach, the only work she could get was cleaning for white folks, including at the Phi Delta Theta fraternity house. This humiliation had a shattering effect on Maude, who would sing the Kansas State alma mater plaintively when

---

*Though Miles Woods did call Earl "Tiger" on occasion, Earl's inspiration for naming his son Tiger was different, as will become apparent.

she was depressed. "I hate Manhattan, Kansas, because they didn't give Mom a chance to do anything," says Mae, Earl's only surviving sibling. "Mom had to work as a maid and that broke her heart." Then, at fifty-four, Maude Woods suffered a stroke and died.

Hereby springs a curious tale. As Tiger Woods has risen to fame, Earl has given reporters a well-polished account of his life and times— the background to who Tiger is. It is an engaging story, particular aspects of which make one sympathize with Earl and what he has had to overcome as a black American, and, by association, make one sympathetic to Tiger. Certainly, African Americans of Earl's generation have suffered considerable injustice. But Earl has consistently made statements that are untrue.

In chronological order, the first of these is that he was thirteen when his mother died, leaving him an orphan. Earl has told this story repeatedly. It appears in numerous newspaper and magazine stories and in books, including Earl's memoir, *Training a Tiger*. Tiger himself has taken up the story. "He has overcome so many obstacles in his own life," Tiger wrote in the introduction to another of Earl's books, *Start Something*. "By the time he was thirteen his parents had died."

When I met Earl at his home in California in 2003, I was careful to check that this was the claim:

HS: [May] I ask how old you were when your mother died?
EW: I was thirteen.

Earl was born in March 1932. His mother died in November 1947. He was therefore fifteen years and eight months when she died. Young, but not as tender an age as thirteen. Not such a good story. When I put this to Earl, he conceded immediately that I was correct (curious, as he had been saying something quite different for years). "OK. That may be a clarification that I, as a young person, wasn't aware of. That is what you call corrections of history. . . . My perception was that she died when I was thirteen." One wants to give Earl, and his perception of when he was orphaned, the benefit of the doubt. But this is not the only example of the facts not matching his story.

When their mother died, Hattie Belle took over the role of mother and provider. "If we had to circle anybody six times, we'd have to circle Hattie, because it was Hattie who made Earl and I possible," says his sister Mae. "It was Hattie who kept the family [together]." After graduating from Kansas State in 1944, with a degree in home economics, this serious, bespectacled young woman became a teacher at the black school in town, the Douglas School, where African American children were educated through the sixth grade. Although Hattie Belle was courting, she stayed home with the younger children, having decided it was her duty to keep the family together and see her younger siblings through college. (When she married medical student Jesse Spearman in Earl's senior year, he moved in, too, becoming the "man of the house.")

Hattie Belle raised her younger siblings with a firm hand. "Hattie was a little dictator," says Mae. "You followed Hattie's rules. There was no playing around." At the same time, the older sisters fussed over Earl, with Hattie in particular telling him that he was special and that he would do better in life than neighborhood boys so long as he attended to his studies and didn't waste his time. As a result, Earl came to have a high opinion of himself; he was a somewhat stuck-up child with few friends. "See, the whole family was kind of clannish," recalls former neighbor Don Slater, who was seven years younger than Earl and admired his baseball skills. "Earl's always been sort of selfish [because] Hattie Belle made him that way," he adds. "He's always had this one thought from Hattie Belle: you are going to be better than others. . . . She put him on a pedestal. That's what his problem was."

Earl could certainly be a charmless boy. One time when Slater was watching him hit balls, he complimented Earl on a particularly fine stroke. "Earl, that was a nice home run," he said, as the ball whizzed over the fence.

Earl retorted: "Get away from me, Don Slater, you little brat."

Earl was known to the kids in the neighborhood as Frog, a nickname derived from the appearance of his eyes, which were oval-shaped and set wide apart. His eyes were in fact a clue to the complicated racial background of Earl and his siblings, who weren't just African American. As Mae says, "We were all mixed. . . . [Kids] used to tease me and Earl [because] we had these slanted eyes, [and] none of us are the same color." Their mother had been light skinned, as were many members of her side of the family. According to Mae, Grandmother Carter was "the prettiest blonde you ever saw." And one of their maternal aunts was Native American. As a result, several of the Woods children had light skin. Their father, Miles Woods, who had come north as part of the migration of blacks after the Civil War, was probably of African American slave stock. He was darker, or "just brown," as Mae puts it, and some of the Woods siblings took after him in coloring. However, the shape of Mae's and Earl's eyes indicated Asian blood in the family. In the nineteenth century Chinese immigrants worked in the construction of U.S. railroads and, as Mae recalls, it was a family joke that somewhere in their background was a Chinaman who "didn't stay on his railroad job." There was probably some truth in this. Earl and his siblings were part African American, part Native American, part Asian, and, apparently, part European. This racial palette became significant in Tiger's career when he was marketed as a racial everyman, and when he was forced into addressing the thorny issue of whether he considered himself "black."

Earl graduated from Manhattan High in 1949 and was featured prominently in that year's *Blue M* yearbook for his part in school sports. He played football and basketball for the school and also American Legion baseball. It was taken for granted at home that now that Earl had graduated he would go on to Kansas State College, as Mae already had. And this is where we come to another discrepancy in the story of Earl's life.

Just as he has claimed he was thirteen when his mother died, Earl has repeatedly said he was such a good baseball player that he was given a baseball scholarship to Kansas State, and thus became the first black athlete in what was then the Big Seven Conference* league of Midwestern colleges. "My American Legion coach happened to be the baseball coach at Kansas State University, and he got me a scholarship to play there," Earl told *Golf Digest* in 2001. "I was the first—and only—non-white in the whole conference." He added: "I was good enough in baseball that it never dawned on me that I couldn't get a scholarship." He made much the same claim in his book *Training a Tiger,* and Tiger himself has repeated this story. It is a good story, because it makes Earl seem special, and once again Earl confirmed it in his 2003 interview with me:

> HS: Do you mean you were the first black in the conference, or the first black baseball player in the conference?
> EW: First black in the entire conference in all sports.

This is a big claim, and again it is untrue. The first black player in the conference was Earl's childhood friend and neighbor Harold Robinson, who, by the by, had a tougher childhood than Earl's. Robinson really was orphaned at thirteen, and he had to take a job washing dishes at Scheu's to put himself through school and help support his two younger brothers. In September 1949 it was Robinson who broke the color bar in the Big Seven by playing football for Kansas State, after the coach got permission from the university's president, Milton Eisenhower (the brother of the future U.S. president, who hailed from nearby Abilene). Earl was the first black *baseball* player in the conference.

The fact that Earl has repeatedly claimed to be the one who broke the color bar—in all sports in the conference, a much bigger claim—is frustrating to Harold Robinson, who is proud of his place in history. "I was the Jackie Robinson, you might say, of the conference," he states. "Earl came after me." This is a well-known fact in Manhattan. Yet when Earl

---

*The "conference" was a league of regional college sports teams, including baseball, basketball, and football.

told me in 2003 that he was the "first black in the entire conference in all sports," he did not speak carelessly. He spoke slowly and definitely so I would understand. I challenged his recollection:

> HS: [But] Harold says he was.
> EW: Who?
> HS: Harold Robinson, your friend.
> EW: That's right! That's right! Harold was. Harold Robinson in
>   football was the first black and then Veryl Switzer [a foot-
>   ball player from Kansas], myself, and Gene Wilson [a bas-
>   ketball player from Indiana] followed. I was the first
>   baseball player.

Again, it is peculiar that Earl has persisted so long in saying something that is not quite true—an improvement on the truth, let's say—and that, when presented with the facts, he recants so readily.

There is more:

> HS: The scholarship. You had a baseball scholarship?
> EW: Uh-huh.

Earl maintained that he went to Kansas State on a baseball scholarship and, as we have seen, he told *Golf Digest* that his American Legion coach got the scholarship for him, for the same coach was in charge at Kansas State. However, the coach, Ray Wauthier, denies this is what happened. "He didn't get a scholarship from me. . . . I think he put that in the story to make it sound a little better."

When I put this to Earl, he changed his story slightly. "Well, he is correct technically," he said. "Coaches don't give scholarships. Schools give scholarships. . . . I got a scholarship with my tuition paid." Wauthier insists a "baseball scholarship" would have had to come through him, and he didn't give one to Earl. Another former student, Gene Holiwell, recalls how he and Earl approached Wauthier shortly after enrolling in college in the fall of 1949, asking if they could simply try out for the team. "Weren't any scholarships," says Holiwell. "I never heard the word [scholarship] mentioned." Both practiced with the team through their freshman year (freshmen weren't allowed to play varsity ball), and then Earl was picked to play on the team in competition in his sophomore year of 1951, breaking the color bar *in baseball* in the Big Seven.

Whether he got a baseball scholarship or not, by being the first and only black baseball player in the league Earl came into contact with some of the harsh realities of racism in America. During away games, he sometimes had to eat and sleep apart from his fellow players. Coach Wauthier had warned him that this would be the case. "I explained all that to him before he ever came out for baseball," he says. "I told him that the way the social situation was in the country, at that time, he would have to be kind of segregated at night and at mealtimes. But where I could keep him with us, and have him eat and sleep with us, I would do it. And if he was willing to play under those conditions, that would satisfy me. . . . He knew what he was getting into." Still, it was a humiliating experience to be taken aside from the others when they got into town, to have to find a hotel in the black neighborhood and stay there alone until morning. Coaches of rival teams complained about bringing a black baseball player into the league, and Earl was subjected to hurtful and unwarranted comments simply because of his color.

Scouts from the white professional teams would come to watch games, and Earl became excited about his chances of being picked for stardom with a major league team, but the coaches never asked for him. Earl believes this was racism. "Because of my race, I wasn't eligible to play in the major leagues," he told *Golf Digest*. This is questionable. By 1951–53, when Earl was on the team at Kansas State, blacks were being signed by teams across the country. "We had black players getting in the American League, with the Cleveland Indians [and so on]. It was becoming more acceptable," recalls Wauthier, who does not believe Earl's ethnicity alone was a reason for his not getting picked. Maybe he just wasn't good enough. Earl says he received one offer, from the local black pro team, the Kansas City Monarchs, which played in a less prestigious league than Earl aspired to. When he and Hattie Belle talked it over, they agreed their mother would have wanted Earl to continue his education. So he turned down the Monarchs and never became a professional ballplayer. Is this the thwarted ambition that propelled his son Tiger into the spotlight? Did Earl seek success in professional sports vicariously through his youngest son, as his father did through him? "Hell, no," he says indignantly. But it looks that way from the outside.

The experience of discrimination, whether real or partly imagined, helped form Earl's singular character, though he is in some ways remarkably forgiving. By contrast, his sister Mae is very bitter toward Manhattan, Kansas, which she calls a "nasty little prejudiced town." She describes racism as "like a thousand little poison darts" and says it was probably even worse for her brother because men had to go out and work in the racist world. Indeed, Mae feels her brother's character was *distorted* by his early experiences as a black man. As we sat together in her home near Palm Springs, California, Mae reminded me that as a white man I could not have the remotest idea of how cruel white people are to blacks, and maybe it is true that white people can have no real comprehension of what the journalist Alistair Cooke calls "the privations and public humiliations" of African Americans. From Mae's point of view, black people are remarkable in that they have not vented their anger more often and more violently, because the ugliness of racism is there from childhood, a constant antagonism. "The fact that Tiger and Earl had to penetrate this . . . I don't know how they survived. I swear to God . . . distortions have to take place. The black male who is successful has to be distorted as he matures."

Earl matured into what his first wife describes as a "kinda complex individual." Barbara Ann Hart, who prefers to be known as Ann, dated Earl when he was in college, and recalls an intelligent and attractive but antisocial young man. "I remember him making the remark that he didn't need friends as long as he had a good book. . . . He tried to be an island unto himself." Although highly opinionated, and therefore not particularly suited to taking orders, Earl had joined the Reserve Officers' Training Corps (ROTC) when he was at Kansas State and was commissioned as a second lieutenant on May 24, 1953, the day he graduated with a bachelor of science degree in sociology. Earl then worked as a civilian at Fort Riley, the local army base, and began to think seriously of a career in the military. Options were limited for a black man in Manhattan. Because of his ROTC training, he could enter the service as a regular officer and, by doing so, he would at least be able to get away from Manhattan and start a new life with Ann. On March 18, 1954, Ann and Earl married in Abilene and then drove to Fort Benning, Georgia, where Earl was to begin active army basic training. At the end of August, he would be posted overseas, initially to West Germany, where he and Ann started their family—the family Earl later dismissed as a "trial run" for the main work of his life: raising Tiger Woods.

3

BLACK AND WHITE

As platoon leader Earl Woods traveled to Europe, back home in the United States sports reporters were clamoring to know when Arnold Palmer, the exciting new champion of the U.S. Amateur, would turn professional. In retrospect, it seems surprising that he hesitated for a moment. But Arnie had no inkling of the great wealth that awaited him in professional golf and, from his perspective, the obstacles to being a tour player appeared considerable, including the fact that in 1954 the PGA did not allow players to collect prize money for the first six months they were on tour and did not make them full members of the PGA for five years—enough to test anybody's patience, and one of the subtle ways in which the PGA shut the working classes out of the game. "Most people have no idea how, when I came into the game, how even I was treated as a young player coming along," says Palmer, who railed under the restrictions at the time and recalls them with some indignation now. "[Even though] I had won the U.S. Amateur Championship, and numerous amateur events around the United States, [I] couldn't even take the money that I was winning playing golf. There was no such thing. And I also had to serve a five-year apprenticeship to become a PGA member, which no one ever knows or thinks about today."

It was while he was debating with himself whether, or when, he should take the plunge and turn professional—and how on earth he could afford to do so—that Arnie met his future wife. It is a classically romantic story. On Labor Day in 1954 Arnie arrived at the Shawnee Inn resort, near Shawnee-on-the-Delaware in Pennsylvania, to compete as an amateur in the Bill Waite Memorial tournament. Walking back to the inn after a practice round, he stopped to talk with a pretty girl by the name of Winifred Walzer. Nineteen years old, she lived in Bethlehem, Pennsylvania, and was at college studying to be an interior designer. That week Winnie and a girlfriend were working as hostesses at the tournament. Winnie and Arnie met on a Tuesday. Saturday afternoon, he won the tournament. Saturday evening at the award ceremony, five days after they met, Arnie asked Winnie to marry him and she said yes, having been quite bowled over.

Winnie suspected her father would not give his consent, however, and she was too young to marry legally without it. Why would any father want Arnie Palmer for a son-in-law? The young man had no college degree, he earned nothing from his golf, and he was supporting himself halfheartedly selling paint. Indeed, he was so broke he had to borrow money to buy a small engagement ring. Despite the obstacles, the couple talked about marrying in the spring and using the forthcoming Walker Cup (a prestigious biannual tournament between amateur teams from Britain and the United States) as their honeymoon. In 1955 the Walker Cup was being held at St. Andrews in Scotland, and Arnold was invited as U.S. Amateur champion. But then Arnie decided he wanted to turn professional without delay. By hustling games (playing less talented golfers for money), he paid off some of the money he'd borrowed and in November he signed what was then a standard sponsorship deal with Wilson Sporting Goods ($2,000 on signature, plus $5,000 a year) whereby he would carry a Wilson golf bag. Though $5,000 was a sizable lump sum in 1954, due to the fact that rookie professionals could not accept prize money during their first half-year on tour in official PGA events, this represented Palmer's only guaranteed income for the six months ahead, out of which he had to find his traveling expenses, so money would be tight. Then he went to Florida for his first professional event, the Miami Open. He missed the cut in Miami, and because Winnie's father was implacably opposed to their union, Arnie and Winnie eloped to Virginia, where they married a few days before Christmas 1954.

Winnie discovered straightaway that her husband had conservative views about marriage, as he did about most things. He would earn the money; her job would be wife and mother. "He's old-fashioned about that," she said. "It was made perfectly clear from the outset that my job was to mind the home. Well, we didn't have a home in those days, so it meant driving coast-to-coast across America supporting him at every tournament." In the new year they drove out to California to join the tour, counting the nickels and dimes as they went and, after a while, hooking a trailer to the back of their secondhand Ford to save on motels. It was not an ideal honeymoon, and far from what Winnie had dreamed of. As she said: "I was not pleased with the idea that, instead of going to Europe for our honeymoon, I was now driving around in a trailer with this guy that had no money!"

There was some romance to the life, however. Country club golf was often a listless affair, but making a living on the professional tour, in the days before television and rich endorsement deals brought big money to the game, was a risky, vagabond existence that attracted, and created, larger-than-life characters of a type rare in professional golf now. Even their jaunty nicknames were evocative of high jinks: Ed "Porky" Oliver, E. J. "Dutch" Harrison, "Slammin'" Sammy Snead. "Everybody was different," remembers Chi Chi Rodriguez, a wisecracking Puerto Rican who became another mainstay of the tour. "Now everybody looks like clones." The culture was one of engaging with galleries and promoting oneself shamelessly, often with a gimmick. Any kind of angle would do—like Snead or Rodriguez, a fellow might wear a certain type of hat, or adopt the image of a boozer like, for instance, the prewar golfing great Walter Hagen—and there was a great emphasis on showmanship during the rounds. All so different from today, when most PGA Tour players are as sober as a judge, with the mind of an accountant and the self-regarding manner of a movie star. Tiger Woods does not even look at his galleries and signs autographs without making eye contact. "In my day, [Ben] Hogan and Snead and Nelson and Arnold, [we] never went to psychologists to tell us not to make eye contact with the people because, if we do, they will want something. I *want* people to want something from me," adds Rodriguez. "You know, if a man is making five or ten million a year he shouldn't mind if somebody says, 'Hey, give me your autograph.' "

One of the first friends the Palmers made on tour was one of its biggest personalities: Tommy Bolt, known affectionately as Terrible Tommy or Thunder Bolt, because of his explosive temper. Bolt was a bull of a man ten years Arnie's senior. He had a lantern jaw and a powerful chest, which he stuck out like a soldier on parade. A natural showman, Bolt would march up to galleries before a round and invite them to walk the course with him and, in the days before fairways were roped off, they could do precisely that. By winning people's interest and building a gallery, Bolt made himself well known, which got him invited to more events and therefore he made more money. In return, fans were entertained by his powerful driving of the ball and displays of ferocious temper that were sometimes spontaneous and possibly calculated to amuse at other times. A wonderful ball striker, Bolt had a less impressive short game and would sometimes fly into a rage when his ball failed to get near enough to the hole. The stories are legion, mostly involving clubs being tossed about without apparent regard for where they landed or whom they might hit. One time in the second round of the Canadian Open, on the back 9, Bolt hit a 4-iron to the green to see his ball travel only twenty-five feet, falling pathetically short of the target. He was so perturbed by this that he rammed his iron into the damp fairway, which took about nine inches. "And of course he walked off and here was his caddie struggling to pull the golf club out of the earth," recalls his partner in the match, Ward Wettlaufer.

Looking back, Bolt remembers how much fun he and his colleagues had before TV and sponsorship money changed the nature of the professional game, but he notes how difficult it was to make a living. "We had monetary pressures," he says. "Those kids nowadays don't have monetary pressures. They have their pockets stuffed full of money before they get on the tour, so they don't have any real pressure. I think we had the best of it, though. You get big money involved, big business, you have a lot of pressure there. [You] have to win enough money to support all your managers and your psychiatrist and your trainers and [so forth]." Tournament purses were typically about $10,000 in total and there were great players—some of *the* greatest, such as Ben Hogan—competing for the little money out there. Palmer struggled at first in such company, borrowing from Winnie's family to stay on the road. It was a hard life. By the time the Palmers reached Florida, seven weeks into the tour, their Ford was almost worn out and living in a trailer had become insufferable. Still, there were compensations: the friendship of characters such as Tommy and his wife, Shirley (until the night the Bolts had a violent fight and threw kitchen knives at each other, which made Arnie and Winnie think they might be safer traveling alone), the freedom of the open road, and the opportunity to visit some of the golf courses Arnie had dreamed about since childhood. In April 1955, he was thrilled to drive down Magnolia Lane to the Augusta National clubhouse, for instance, meeting Bobby Jones and Clifford Roberts, both of whom took a liking to the young man from Latrobe, such an agreeable fellow with such a pretty wife. Palmer, who had a Masters invitation by virtue of being U.S. Amateur champion, finished tenth.

After the Masters, the Palmers and the Bolts traveled through the Midwest together and over the border to Toronto, where in August Arnie enjoyed his first professional win, at the Canadian Open. It was a turning point for the fledgling pro and the $2,400 prize money set the Palmers straight. When he and Winnie returned to Pennsylvania at the end of the season, they had the wherewithal to buy a three-acre plot of land across from Latrobe Country Club, and on this land they built the six-room, ranch-style house that remains Palmer's primary residence. Their first child, Peggy, was born on February 26, 1956, and when the season resumed, mother and baby went back on the road with Arnie. (When their second daughter, Amy, was born in 1958, they all traveled together.) Over the next couple of years, Palmer established himself as one of the most successful players on tour, winning two PGA events in 1956 and four the following year. A major title eluded him for the time being. His best finish in the majors in his first three years was seventh. Still, he was making a living, learning the game, and making friends.

One friend and contemporary of Palmer's was Charlie Sifford, the first African American to win on tour and therefore a significant minor character in our story. Born in North Carolina in 1922, Sifford began work as a caddie at thirteen and later became the personal golf coach to the bandleader Billy Eckstine. A talented player, Sifford won a string of UGA National Open titles and, naturally, aspired to compete in regular tour events, wanting to pit himself against the best players in the country, people like Bolt and Hogan and Snead. Yet, as we have seen, PGA rules specifically excluded nonwhites from membership in the association and thus from officially sanctioned tournaments. Most events would not even let a black player attempt to qualify for an exemption, and on those rare occasions when African Americans did find a way into a tournament, it was made abundantly clear that they were not welcome.

In early 1952 the boxer and amateur golfer Joe Louis used his celebrity to obtain exemptions for himself and a number of his friends, including Sifford, to try to qualify for the Phoenix Open. But when they got to Phoenix, no hotels would put them up; they were not allowed in the locker room at the country club where the tournament was being held, and they were obliged to play their qualifying round all together early in the morning before the white players went out. When their group got to the first hole, Charlie Sifford found that someone had taken a shit in the cup. Not surprisingly, he failed to qualify.

Worse happened at other events that Sifford competed in, up to and including death threats. As Sifford has said, it was an incongruous feeling to walk onto a golf course afraid for one's life. This was a game meant to be enjoyed, after all. Some players believe that if Sifford hadn't had to deal with so many obstacles and so much harassment, he would have developed into a truly great champion, disproving the assertion some white players make that there weren't any first-class black golfers in this era. "He was one of the greatest players that ever lived," says Chi Chi Rodriguez. "But he would have been even greater [had] he been given a chance when he was young."

In 1957 at the relatively late age of thirty-four, having left Eckstine's employ, Sifford made a determined effort to earn a living as a touring professional, despite the fact that most events were still closed to him. One of the few tournaments he did get into was the Long Beach Open in California, a short, 54-hole tournament that was not an official PGA event, but it was cosponsored by the PGA and there were well-known players such as Bolt in the field. On Sunday, November 10, 1957, Sifford won the Long Beach Open. A psychological barrier was thereby broken; a black golfer *could* compete against the best white golfers and beat them. But this did not open up the tour. Black golfers were still excluded from membership in the PGA and therefore most tournaments. The injustice made Sifford an outspoken critic of the way golf was run. "Underneath the façade of gentility of which golf is so proud, I found an ugly streak of racism that starts in the country clubs and runs all the way up through the PGA itself," he wrote in his autobiography, *Just Let Me Play,* a devastating critique. As Sifford says in his book, he became ashamed of the game he loved. To his credit, he did not give up. Eventually the Caucasian clause would be dropped. Eventually he

would be given a so-called tour card, allowing him into PGA tournaments, and in time he would become the first black player to win a full-
fledged PGA Tour event, the 1967 Greater Hartford Open. His fellow
players did not help him in this struggle, however.

"Charlie Sifford and I played together from the day I started playing," recalls Arnold Palmer. "The first tournament that I won, Charlie
Sifford and I were tied after the first round, [and] we became good
friends." Yet Palmer did not lobby the PGA to give his friend a tour
card. Palmer and other white players did not see that as their role. They
were sportsmen, not politicians, and Palmer would argue that he didn't
have that much influence anyway at this stage in his career. If one looks
beyond golf for a moment, though, one is reminded that in the late
1950s all America was politicized by civil rights. It was a time for ordinary people to take a stand, no matter what their walk of life, to help
the process of integration. When Sifford won the Long Beach Open in
the fall of 1957, down in Little Rock, Arkansas, black schoolchildren
were risking their lives to attend Little Rock Central High, which had
previously been the preserve of white students. The country watched
aghast as racists mobbed the school, shouting obscenities and threats at
the nine black children who had the courage to exercise their civil
rights. When the Arkansas National Guard failed to maintain order,
President Eisenhower sent in the 101st Airborne Division so that the
children could go to classes. If children could so bravely confront
racism, surely a few tour golfers might have gone to the men who ran
the PGA and said, "It's about time we did away with this stinking Caucasian clause and let black golfers like our friend Charlie Sifford into
the game," or words to that effect. They did not. Tour golfers and the
golf establishment remained part of the race problem in America, not
part of the solution.

Most people would say that President Eisenhower had done no more
than he should have by sending the troops into Little Rock. It was,
however, a deeply unpopular decision among his friends at the Augusta
National. Since the deep pockets of the chairman, Clifford Roberts,

and the members had helped Eisenhower into office in 1952, the president and his wife, Mamie, had used the club as a frequent retreat from Washington, D.C. They visited so often that Roberts had a holiday home built for them adjacent to the 10th tee, the Eisenhower Cabin. Roberts and the members were very proud of their association with the presidency; Ike was very much their man, after all. But by taking the side of the black students at Little Rock Central High, many members thought Eisenhower had made a serious mistake. Roberts himself worried that the intervention might spark a second civil war. In short, the Augusta National—and golf itself—remained a bastion of reactionary values in a time of social change.

Some might say the men who ran the Augusta National, and the membership, were racists, plain and simple. The story told by Charlie Sifford and others is that Roberts decreed there would be only white golfers and black caddies at the Masters as long as he lived.* Though the story is apocryphal, despite his success on tour Sifford certainly never received an invitation. As far as he was concerned, the Augusta National was "the most racist and hateful spot on the golf globe" and its invitational "the worst redneck tournament in the country, run by people who openly discriminated against blacks."

Much of the ill feeling Sifford and others bear toward the Augusta National is directed toward Roberts, the gloomy financier who did so much to shape the club and its tournament, and whose influence is felt still at Augusta. Roberts's supporters believe he has been unfairly characterized as a bigot, pointing out, for instance, that he was fond of several long-serving black employees.† That is true, though only in the sense that one can have affection for a pet. One such favored employee was Claude Tillman, a "little black fellow [who] couldn't read or

---

*In fact, Roberts would welcome a black player into the championship before the end of his life, but as we will see, the invitation was a long time coming.

†The case for Roberts was put forth most recently in *The Making of the Masters: Clifford Roberts, Augusta National, and Golf's Most Prestigious Tournament* (Simon & Schuster, 1999), written by David Owen with the cooperation of the club.

write," as Roberts wrote in his memoir, *The Story of the Augusta National Golf Club*. Tillman worked originally for a member of the club and, when the member died, his widow sent Tillman to Roberts with a Christmas wreath around his neck and a card attached to it addressed to the chairman. After discussing the matter with his steward, Roberts placed what he called his "gift" in the club kitchen, where Tillman would work from then on. Roberts related this story in his 1976 book as if it were an amusing anecdote. Yet the notion of a black servant being passed from the employ of one wealthy white man to another, *with a wreath around his neck,* is reminiscent of slave ownership.

Aside from his memoir, Roberts's racial views are on record in an oral history he dictated for Columbia University. He made it clear in this testimony that he considered whites to be superior to people of color. Blacks were second best in his racial hierarchy. And he had total disdain for people of mixed race. The children that resulted from mixed marriages were, he asserted, "worthless . . . in every respect." One wonders what he would have made of Tiger Woods.

Flawed though the Augusta National is, its championship has for long been one of the greatest events of the golfing year, the defining tournament in so many careers. And it was here that Arnold Palmer was elevated to stardom.

Having been on tour for a couple of years, Arnie had built up a following among the general public. But when he arrived at Augusta in April 1958 for the Masters, he found he had an unusually vociferous and numerous new band of supporters. Servicemen from nearby Fort Gordon, enrolled by the club to operate the scoreboards at that year's tournament, had decided Arnie was their man. Whenever he came into view, they cheered loudly and waved placards, bringing the rambunctious flavor of a football game to the hitherto prissy business of Masters golf. This was such a phenomenon that a headline writer at the *Augusta Chronicle* coined a name for Palmer's new supporters. They were "Arnie's Army," and the pun stuck, coming to mean all those fans who would follow Palmer during his long career. Not until the advent of Tiger Woods, almost forty years later, would golf see such fans—thousands of people whooping and yelling and getting so involved in their hero that, when he ducked into a portable toilet to relieve himself during a round, they would stand and stare until he emerged. Not all Arnie's colleagues were pleased by this. "They're not real golf fans," sniped fellow player Frank Beard. Others realized the army was evidence of what Palmer was doing to rouse golf.

Palmer shot 70-73-68 in the first three rounds of the 1958 Masters, then lay in bed Saturday night listening to heavy rain drenching Augusta. The course was so soggy on Sunday morning that there was a suggestion that the final might be postponed. Still, twenty thousand fans came through the gates to watch, and the tournament got under way as scheduled, with Palmer paired with Ken Venturi, a tall, thin Californian who tended to stutter and mangle his syntax when he was under stress. And stress there would be.

At the start of the day, Palmer and Venturi, together with Doug Ford and Fred Hawkins, all seemed to have a shot at the title. Palmer edged a stroke ahead of the pack at Amen Corner, with Venturi in second place. Now was when the Masters was decided—the back 9 holes on Sunday afternoon—and Palmer set about his work with a rare sense of purpose. Always a powerful driver of the ball, he hit such a muscular tee shot at the par-3 12th that his ball embedded itself in the ground between the green and the rear bunker, plugged deep into the wet turf. The crowds, sitting in bleachers on the other side of Rae's Creek, a couple of hundred yards away, then watched what the *New York Times* correspondent described as a pantomime. They could only guess at what was going on by the animated gestures of the men on the green and the strange actions that followed. When Palmer got to the green, he made it clear he was not happy about the lie of his ball, which was stuck in the wet ground, and told the rules official Arthur Lacey that he did not want to play it as it was. Lacey said he had to. Palmer argued that under wet weather rules he was entitled to remove, clean, and drop his ball before he hit it again. Lacey said that wasn't done at Augusta. Palmer consulted with Venturi, who took the view that he should play the ball, as Lacey said. Arnie told them that he would play *two* balls and appeal to the rules committee for a final decision. So he dug the plugged ball out of the ground and moved it eighteen inches, then chipped and two-putted for a double-bogey (which would have lost him the lead). To the bemusement of the crowd, who still had no clear idea what was going on, Palmer then dropped a fresh ball where the first had been and, with a chip and a putt, he holed this for par. Venturi was outraged, but the matter had not yet been ruled upon. As the men continued on their round the officials conferred among themselves as to whether what had happened was legal or not and, such was the importance of the decision, no less a personage than Bobby Jones came down from the clubhouse to join them.

At the age of fifty-six, Jones presented a sad sight. The former Grand Slammer was suffering from a crippling illness, syringomyelia, that twisted a once-handsome man into a gnarled stump of a human being. To cope with the pain of the illness and the indignity of his situation, Jones drank heavily and smoked like a demon, and the booze and cigarettes further debilitated him. By 1958 he could barely walk. So when he came down from the clubhouse, he did so in a customized golf buggy that looked like a carnival bumper car. Wearing a sun hat, with his eyes masked behind dark glasses and a cigarette smoldering in one clawed hand, the erstwhile golden boy of golf parked under a tree where a gaggle of tournament officials gathered around him to debate the matter of Palmer and the plugged ball. Meanwhile, Arnie played on, half-thinking he might be ruled against or even disqualified. The pressure seemed to spur him. He powered his way to the green at 13 for an eagle that seemed to rattle Venturi into three-putting at 14. The pair were on 15 when they were called over to Jones's cart. To Palmer's relief, he was not disqualified. Moreover, the lower score would be recorded for the 12th hole. Venturi was so discombobulated by the decision that he promptly three-putted again. Palmer finished his round with a birdie at

18 and then waited inside one of the club buildings while Doug Ford and Fred Hawkins completed their rounds. When both ended on 285, Arnie was declared the winner by a stroke. In the process, he made an enemy of Venturi, who tied for fourth and has never forgiven Palmer for the incident at 12. "Why [should I]? He was wrong," he snorts. "I wasn't arguing for myself. I was arguing for the game of golf [and] the other players. I was arguing for Fred Hawkins and Doug Ford."

Palmer could learn to live with Venturi's resentment, however. With his win at the Masters, and the donning of the green club blazer that went with the silver trophy, life opened up like a magnolia flower. Among other things, Palmer was introduced to President Eisenhower, who became a close and important friend, and whose contribution to the growth of the game, and to the fame of Arnold Palmer, was considerable.

Eisenhower was a very popular president—a hero of World War II, whose homely charm often won over even some of those who disagreed with his politics. Although an inept golfer, he loved the game, and the image of the president hacking away each weekend like a regular guy was endearing. For some, certainly, the image was inappropriate in a time of civil unrest and cold war fears, and it gave his opponents material to use against him. At the 1956 Democratic convention, Tennessee governor Frank Clement accused Eisenhower of "looking down the long green fairways of indifference." But for the most part, golf didn't do Eisenhower any harm in terms of public relations and, in return, the president's patronage lifted the profile of the game. When the president was seen playing with the young champ Arnie Palmer, everybody benefited. "Eisenhower was interested in golf and he was seen a lot on television playing golf, and the fact that I played with him a lot was something that helped contribute to the whole scenario," explains Palmer. The friendship was one of several felicitous elements that came together at the right time to promote the young man from Latrobe as the preeminent star of the game—perhaps beyond his ability and achievement.

Arnie was a gutsy player, a performer on the golf course, but he would never rival the number of wins Sam Snead achieved. Contemporaries such as Billy Casper, whose name has largely faded from the public consciousness, won almost as many tournaments. Jack Nicklaus would win more, and many more of the all-important majors. Most aficionados would say Bobby Jones had an infinitely better swing, and some are disdainful of Palmer's technique. "He's got a terrible swing," reckons Ken Venturi, though he adds that this helped Palmer's popularity, because weekend hackers saw themselves in him. "Everybody said, 'Hey, that looks like me!'" notes Venturi. "If he had a very aesthetic swing, he wouldn't have been Arnold Palmer." Aside from the way he struck the ball, Palmer was blessed with an uncommonly likable personality. Almost everybody warmed to him. Men and women. Young and old. From the president to a crusty old character like Clifford Roberts, people were won over by this friendly fellow who genuinely seemed interested in others first. Arnie also reached his prime just as the television age was dawning and, moreover, his personal charm came across on television, which is not always the case with the medium. "Palmer became famous because of television," opines Tommy Bolt. "Snead and Hogan were greater players, actually, than Palmer, [but they] weren't as lucky, because television didn't come [in until later]."

Today, television is taken for granted. When Arnie was growing up in Latrobe, there was no TV. In 1949, when he was a student at Wake Forest, a mere 2.3 percent of American homes had a television, and most of them were in the metropolitan Northeast. Then came the deluge. By 1962, 90 percent of American homes had the box. Television was everywhere and almost anybody on TV became a celebrity—comic, anchorman, game show host, golfer. Though golf was not the networks' first choice when it came to choosing sports events to broadcast—tournaments were long and were played over huge areas of land at the mercy of the elements—some golf was shown on TV, and the player America saw winning was Arnold Palmer.

The Masters had been at the forefront of televised golf since it was first broadcast by CBS in 1956, and by the time Palmer came to defend his title in 1959 it was favorite viewing with those fans who had access to television. Palmer was tied for the lead after the first three rounds of the 1959 championship and seemed set for a satisfying back-to-back win when, on Sunday, again at the 12th, he ran into trouble. This time he sent his ball into Rae's Creek, leading to a calamitous triple-bogey. Maybe the gods were avenging Venturi for what had happened the previous year at this hole. A fellow Pennsylvanian, the quiet, nondrinking, nonsmoking Art Wall Jr., put together a series of birdies that resulted in victory. Still, Palmer had been a wonderful player to watch, for the thirty thousand who crowded into the club and the millions following on television. And the men in the CBS truck knew they were getting good pictures. "The camera fell in love with Arnold hitching up his trousers and flipping his cigarette away and expanding his nostrils," recalls Frank Chirkinian, who took over the CBS producer's chair in 1959. "The camera fell in love with Arnold, and it's still in love with Arnold to this day, [because] he exudes so much charm and charisma. It's infectious."

Frank Chirkinian is another significant minor figure in the story of modern golf. A man of strong personality and innovative ideas, he ran the Masters broadcast for thirty-eight years and in that time introduced many features that are now standard to golf coverage. These included having the inside of the cups painted white so they showed up on TV and using the plus-and-minus scoring system, which made it easier for viewers to see how players were doing in relation to one another (as opposed to giving only cumulative totals). He introduced famous and distinguished commentators to the viewing public, including the English writer Henry Longhurst. It was Chirkinian who brought the Goodyear blimp to golf, with a camera to film the action from above. ("The bloody thing's been going around up there ever since.") The Masters telecast was unsophisticated in its first few years, however. Only the last four holes were shown initially, partly because the limited number of cameras available were all fixed in position, and furthermore they could be no more than a thousand feet from the control truck. The broadcasts were also in black and white, of course, which did not do justice to the setting. So much of the glory of Augusta is in the verdancy of its fairways, the colors of the flowers, the pine trees against a blue sky. Chirkinian was also acutely aware of the inherent problems of golf as television, noting that if one added up the time it took actually to strike the ball in a round of golf—those few seconds of swinging the club—the essential action, if you will, would boil down to about five minutes per player. "So we watch an awful lot of people wandering about or standing still and tossing grass in the air."

Paradoxically, golf was also suited to television. It is usually an uncomfortable and unrewarding experience to attend a major championship in person, because the numbers of people who crush around the greens make it difficult to see the action and, with matches being played all over the course simultaneously, it is difficult to get an idea of the overall picture. Ben Hogan once observed, "I don't know why anyone would go to a golf tournament." Aside from its ridiculous ticketing system, the Masters is better run than most big tournaments. Although as many as two hundred thousand people attend each year (the numbers have grown dramatically since the 1950s), the course is so large and well designed that one can walk about comfortably and, for the most part, get a reasonable view. There is an atmosphere of easiness. People regard each other with an air of mutual appreciation, as if all are attending a smart garden party. The club adds to this atmosphere in subtle ways. It does not charge exorbitant prices for souvenirs and refreshments. The spectator guide, a model of what such guides should be, is distributed for free by cheerful helpers. Lunch is a bargain, though sugary pink lemonade and pappy sandwiches—Pimento Cheese is the classic—are hardly good food. Still, for all this, it is easier to watch the Masters, or any tournament, by staying at home. As John Updike wrote astutely: "No sport is as much improved for the spectator by television as golf."

Bobby Jones had very particular ideas about how he wanted his tournament broadcast, and what should and should not be said by CBS commentators on air. He asked Frank Chirkinian's men not to talk about the prize money for one thing. "Because the money is really not the primary reason that the players are here," explains Chirkinian. "Players are here to win a championship. The championship is symbolized by a trophy and a jacket. These things will be there for the player forever. When the money is all gone, they still have the trophies." To this day, CBS never announces how much the winner receives. When Palmer won his first green jacket in 1958, this was a small matter because his prize was only $11,250. But when the first prize came to exceed $1 million, as it does now, it seems like a conspicuous omission. Jones also frowned on certain phraseology common to sports reporters. In most sports, fans are simply that. Or they are crowds. In golf, they are referred to genteelly as galleries. Even this was too vulgar a term for Jones, who insisted that the people who paid to watch his Masters should be referred to on air as the club's "patrons." Silly. Yet over the years these eccentric details have helped give the tournament a unique flavor, one that has proved enduringly popular. With all the problems and restrictions, TV had a wonderful show in the Masters, and a TV star in Arnold Palmer.

With his burgeoning fame, it was evident that Arnie was going to make a lot of money. Already he was being paid to carry a Wilson golf bag and to wear Munsingwear and Haggar clothing. There was an Arnold Palmer golf column and talk of an eponymous golf academy. But all this was relatively small-time, little deals put together by Palmer himself, with the help of Winnie, who was handling most of his paperwork, as well as raising their daughters. The first person to realize Palmer's full earning potential, and to set about managing and exploiting it, was a shrewd and ambitious Cleveland attorney who was also a good enough golfer to have competed in the 1958 U.S. Open (though he missed the cut). Mark H. McCormack was his name, and he is one of the most important figures in the history of modern golf.

Almost everybody who knows Arnold Palmer speaks of him with great affection, but Mark McCormack was a man who commanded wary respect. Most acquaintances would agree that he was exceedingly clever, but few seemed to warm to a man who was, as former client Doug Ford puts it, a "hard nut." Born in 1930, Mark Hume McCormack was the only child of a Chicago publisher, Ned McCormack, a man of British descent, and a half-Irish mother, Grace, whose methodical disposition Mark inherited. He grew into a sharp-faced, sandy-haired youth. Tall and strong, he had an above-average ability for golf, which he played with distinction at the College of William and Mary in Virginia. Still, he was wise enough to know that he did not have the talent to make a good living as a tour professional. Instead, he decided on a career in business. He graduated from Yale Law School with an LL.B. and joined the Cleveland law firm of Arter, Hadden, Wykoff & Van Duzer in 1957. On weekends, professional players who were friends would ask him advice about legal matters, and it occurred to McCormack that there was money to be made in the business of golf. Perspicaciously, McCormack also recognized that golf could be exploited in ways other games could not. Unlike football or basketball fans, for example, most of the people who follow golf also play the game. In order to do so they purchase expensive equipment and change it regularly. Golf balls, clubs, bags, and clothing could all be endorsed by their favorite tour players (as was already happening in a small way). Golf fans would also pay to get advice from their favorite stars or to watch a demonstration of their skills. With all this in mind, McCormack went into partnership with Dick Taylor, who ran the Carling Open in Cleveland. "I had this idea for exhibitions," McCormack explained in one of his last interviews conducted shortly before his death in 2003. "I felt that country clubs around the Northeastern parts of the United States, at least, didn't want to turn their course over to a tournament, because it would keep the members—during a fairly short season—away from the course for a couple of weeks. But I figured that no matter how exclusive the course they would always want to see a leading player play the course. So when you had your guests out there you could [say], 'Arnold Palmer got on here with a 7-iron.' So we set up an exhibition company, Taylor and I. And we knew the players—me through the golf I played, and he through sponsoring the tournament—and we mailed clubs about exhibitions, and we got a pretty good response. We started mailing clubs on golf accessories and stuff for endorsements. That was pretty good [too]." The company McCormack and Taylor formed was National Sports Management. Early clients included Billy Casper, Dow Finsterwald (a close pal of Palmer's), and Doug Ford, all of whom were asked to help with start-up funds. "We had all put up, I think, two hundred apiece to put him in business," recalls Ford. It was a reasonable investment, considering that personal appearances were worth about $200 each. Ford soon became disenchanted with the brisk way McCormack conducted business, however, as would other clients in subsequent years. "He'd call us in the morning and say, 'You gotta be at Macy's tonight.' And things like that, and we got a little upset with this . . . you never knew where the hell you were." So Ford quit, and he claims McCormack never forgave him.

But McCormack already had a bigger and better client. At the 1959 Carling Open, the attorney struck up a friendship with Arnie Palmer. Aside from a mutual passion for golf, the men were the same age with similar values. Both had very close relationships with their parents, for example. Arnie had even considered a career as a lawyer at one time, though he decided, tellingly, that he was too nice to be good at the work. All this helped form a bond. Also, McCormack entered Palmer's life at exactly the right time. The golfer urgently needed a professional manager to cope with the paperwork that was becoming too much for Winnie to deal with. "Arnold said, 'Look, I'm looking for somebody to take over all [the] money stuff, you know, insurance and estate planning and taxes and fan mail and all that stuff. But I don't really want to be part of a group, so would you think about doing that?' And I said, 'Yes,' and told Dick [Taylor] I would either buy him out of our company, or he could buy me out, and basically he bought me out, [and] I went on with Arnold." The deal was settled on a handshake. Thus Arnie became the founding client of International Management Incorporated, which grew into International Management Group.*

To some extent, McCormack made Palmer. "He was the first player that was really marketed on tour," says Tommy Bolt. "Mark McCormack [is] partially responsible for his being as much noticed as he is." At the same time, Palmer, with his charisma and established success, was the foundation upon which McCormack built IMG. Today the company is an impressive international corporation, representing a multitude of sports and entertainment personalities, including the biggest names in golf over successive generations, as well as major sporting events such as the Open Championship and Wimbledon, and exerting an influence on television programming. For all these reasons, McCormack became known as the Most Powerful Man in Sports. ("I'm flattered that people say that," he said, though it was not always meant as a compliment.)

It started with one client who, as McCormack saw it, possessed five distinct qualities that made him especially salable. "One: his appearance." Palmer was handsome, and this is important in advertising. "Two: the fact that he was the son of a golf pro and a caddie and had grown up the American way, sort of, not from a wealthy family." An underdog image, in other words. "Three: the way he played golf, and the way he wore his emotions on his sleeve on the golf course, in a nice way, as opposed to screaming and yelling and slamming clubs. And he took chances, and people liked that. Four: the fact that he had some very spectacular finishes right when television was hitting—Cherry Hills, the Open, at the Masters—doing these dramatic things and beginning the Palmer charge and all that stuff." The fifth and final point was that Palmer was good with people. "He could relate to people whether they were President Eisenhower or a truck driver, in the same way. And [he] was a very genuine, very patient person."

---

*McCormack didn't begin using the name International Management Group (IMG) until the mid-1960s.

That isn't to say Arnie was an easy touch. If he wanted so much as a pair of new golf shoes sent to him, he would get McCormack on the telephone and ask him to attend to it personally. And Palmer was just as ambitious for his career as McCormack was. Together they created and sold a product that has proved one of the most valuable and enduring brand names in sport: Arnold Palmer, the template by which all sports stars are marketed today. The strategy for selling Palmer was a clever one. McCormack associated the golfer with upmarket products as much as possible, knowing Palmer could later move downmarket, but it would be hard to go the other way. Realizing that even the greatest sportsmen don't win forever, he refrained from marketing Arnie on the back of a specific victory. Instead, he sold the Arnold Palmer persona. One of the virtues of golf as a business is that it is a truly international pursuit, unlike baseball, for instance. Therefore, the best golfer in the world was as marketable in Canberra as he was in Cleveland, and McCormack lost no time in selling Palmer all over the world. He also realized that they had a lot of time to exploit the Palmer name, because golfers have long careers. In an essentially gentle game, tour players keep going well into middle age and beyond and are rarely troubled by serious injury, let alone any greater calamity arising from playing the game. (Though he later branched out into motor sports, McCormack noted that race car drivers had an inherent disadvantage as clients: in their sport, they sometimes got killed.) Palmer was going to be playing golf for a long time. So they tried to build relationships with companies such as Pennzoil that would last for many years.

At the time of their handshake deal, the golfer was earning approximately $60,000 per year. Within two years he would be making half a million annually, and the figures kept getting bigger as America moved out of the Eisenhower era—what is sometimes called the black-and-white era—into the exuberant 1960s. The turn of the decade would see the election of John F. Kennedy, a continuing boom in consumerism and leisure, and one of the greatest seasons Palmer ever enjoyed. The future would be broadcast nonstop on television, in color, with the blue-collar kid from Latrobe, where they forged steel and brewed Rolling Rock, as the first superstar of golf and seemingly its invincible champion. However, a prodigiously talented young man from Ohio named Jack Nicklaus had other ideas.

4

· · ·

GOLDEN DAWN

There is a particular beauty to the American Midwest, especially in summer when the expanse of land between the Rocky Mountains and eastern Ohio is streaked with sunshine and all outdoors is as
warm as an oven. It seems like such a healthy place, the beating heart of
the country. Jack Nicklaus is in many ways the archetypal Midwesterner, born and raised in Columbus, Ohio, a man of Midwestern values, personality, and appearance. In contrast, his great rival Arnold
Palmer is perceived to be the product of the industrial Northeast. In
fact, Latrobe and Columbus are only about three hours apart by car,
with the demarcation line of the Midwest—the eastern border of Ohio—
between them, and both men could be said to have the characteristics of
Middle Americans. Another popular perception of the differences between these golfers is that Palmer was a regular, blue-collar guy and
Jack was raised a spoiled, rich kid. "The American Dream was Arnold,
and Jack was, you know, born with a silver spoon in his mouth," as
Mark McCormack expressed it.

Jack and his little sister, Marilyn, were the only children of Charlie
Nicklaus and his wife, Nellie, known by her middle name of Helen,

though Charlie called her Sissy. Both were of German stock—Helen's maiden name was Schoener—but probably because their forebears didn't want to appear foreign, the Nicklauses pronounced the surname Nick-lus, rather than Nick-louse, which would have been logical. The men had a distinctly Germanic look: stocky physiques and blond hair (a look common to the Midwest, of course, where so many families are of North European descent). Moreover, as Jack grew up, he showed himself to have what are often taken to be German characteristics. "Hardworking . . . hard-driven. Very focused," suggests his sister. He was born on January 21, 1940, three years before Marilyn. Their father was a stout man with a cheerful demeanor and a strong resemblance to the comedian Lou Costello. A pharmacist by trade, he built up a string of local stores called Nicklaus Drugs, the first of which was on the campus of Ohio State University, northwest of downtown Columbus. As business prospered, the family moved several times, but the house that Jack and his sister considered their real home, where they came to live when Jack was about seven, was a five-bedroom, mock-Tudor house on Collingswood Road in Upper Arlington, an affluent suburb. Charlie established a new pharmacy on nearby Lane Avenue and life was good. "We had everything we needed," says Marilyn. "Probably everything we needed and more. I would not say my dad was a wealthy man, but we were certainly comfortable." Upper Arlington was not a rich neighborhood, in the true sense. The rich of Columbus—the families who owned the newspapers, the radio stations, and the bank—congregated for the most part in the much grander suburb of Bexley. Upper Arlington would correctly be described as upper-middle-class, as were the Nicklauses.

Life for the Nicklaus family in the late 1940s and into the 1950s was analogous to that of the Cunninghams in the TV show *Happy Days*. Like Howard Cunningham, the patriarch of the TV family, Charlie Nicklaus was a successful store owner, known to virtually everybody in town—a thoroughly decent and likeable fellow, fat and jolly and popular. The Nicklaus house was filled with friends, and friends of the children, playing games, listening to music, watching television. "The first TV set I ever saw was at Jack's house," recalls Robin Obetz, son of a local doctor and future golfing partner. The music Jack and his sister enjoyed was the uncomplicated, cheerful songs of the Four Freshmen and the Dells, music Jack still loves. The family walked to the First Community Church together on Sundays. In times of stress, a Nicklaus might exclaim "Oh Lordy!" or "Gracious!" as Jack and Marilyn still do. As the kids grew older there would be school dances, the innocently named "sock hops." In short, Jack's upbringing was a 1950s middle-class, suburban idyll.

Part of this wholesome life was sports. Charlie and Jack were *nutty* for sports, as Jack would put it, and enjoyed almost any game. As the seasons turned, through the snow of winter into the blaze of summer, father and son worked their way through almost every outdoor activity, and Jack grew into a strongly built boy who excelled at every game he played. Part of the reason the family home was always so full of kids was that Jack was forever putting together a team for some game or other. Like Arnold Palmer, young Jack loved football in particular. In fact, the Nicklauses lost a maid one time when Jack burst in from a football game and decided to practice a tackle on the poor woman. Having almost been knocked down the stairs into the cellar, the maid quit. Then golf came into Jack's life, as it had into Palmer's. It happened for Jack by chance when, around the time he was nine, his father broke a bone in his left ankle playing volleyball. Charlie's doctor advised moderate exercise, two hours of walking a day would be good, and so he took up golf, a game he had played in his youth. Close by was Scioto Country Club, named for the Scioto River, and Charlie started to play there. Naturally, Jack had a club put in his hand and began swinging along with his father. Around the same time, a new golf professional joined Scioto: Jack Grout, an amiable thirty-nine-year-old who had been playing the tour without much success. Happening to see Charlie and his son on the course one day, he hailed them with a proposition. "Mr. Charlie, I noticed you and your boy out walking the golf course," he said. "We have a nice junior program starting. Maybe he'd like to play in that?"

Jack Nicklaus joined the program and entered a junior tournament in 1950. When Jack Grout saw the kid in competition, he was so excited he called sportswriter Kaye Kessler at the local newspaper, the *Citizen-Journal*. "You know, Kaye," he began. "We had our first tournament and one of the boys, Jack Nicklaus, shot a 53 for 9 holes."

"That makes me sick!" exclaimed Kessler enviously. He then went out to see Jack, and thus became the first journalist to document his golfing career.

Soon Grout was giving Jack private lessons, which Charlie paid for happily, and the boy was golfing with the passion he brought to every game, and more. "He played about 27 holes every day and hit about 200 balls," recalls Dom Lepore, who worked for Grout and is still to be found behind the counter in the Scioto pro shop. "His mother used to call here late at night and say, 'Tell Jackie he's got to come home for supper.'" Jack was not only lucky to have found a fine coach in Grout but also fortunate to be learning the game on one of the best courses in the United States. Arnold Palmer's testing ground, Latrobe Country Club, was a rinky-dink 9-hole affair when he started to play.* Scioto's 18 holes had been laid out by Donald Ross, one of the most famous names in golf course design, and was of such a high quality that the PGA Championship was held there in 1950, when Jack was ten, giving him a first glimpse of a major tournament and its stars.

At ten, and again at eleven, Jack won the Scioto Club Juvenile Trophy and then went on to win a series of state junior championships in his early teens, establishing himself as the best junior golfer in the region and impressing almost everybody he met in golf with his maturity. "He [was] remarkably poised, remarkably focused for a kid going through those early teens," recalls Kaye Kessler, who became a family friend. "I always had the impression that he was a kid who never was a kid. . . . He was

---

*It was later extended to 18 holes.

always so bent on becoming the wonderful golfer that he became." There are parallels here with Tiger Woods. Putting aside for a moment the racial and economic differences, both had an exceptional ability to concentrate on the game at a young age, and their focus was such that they appeared old before their time. Furthermore, Tiger and Jack had strong fathers behind them (and doting mothers). Charlie was less of a "stage parent" than Earl, however. "Charlie was not at all pushy, like Earl Woods," says Kessler. "He was very good about escorting [Jack] around all the junior tournaments. But Charlie was never in the forefront. It was always Jack." Charlie was content to finance his son's junior career and follow it as a spectator, in the company of a group of friends who became known as "Charlie's Gang." They were golf cronies from Scioto, such as local Buick dealer Bob Daniels, who had the time and money to travel to tournaments.

Here lies another similarity between Jack and Tiger, who are closely linked in the modern history of golf, as the greatest player ever and his challenger, and have much in common as far as personality is concerned as well as in respect to how they were brought up (granted that the Nicklauses had more money). From an early age, both kept company with people much older than themselves, such as their fathers' golfing cronies. Because of their precocious ability in the game, they also tended not to compete with boys their own age but with older youths and young men. At Scioto Jack played with Bob Hoag, Pandel Savic, and Ivor Young, who were between seven and fifteen years his senior (and these men became his closest friends in adult life). In tournaments he played against, and beat, older boys on a regular basis. For example, in 1953, at the age of thirteen, Jack competed in the U.S. Junior Amateur Championship in Oklahoma. In the first round, he came up against sixteen-year-old Stanley Ziobrowski of New York, whom he beat easily. Ziobrowski's friends teased him about it. "They said, 'How could you get beat by a thirteen-year-old kid?' And I said, 'You want to know something? You'll be reading about this thirteen-year-old.'"

For the time being, Jack continued to pursue other sports, too, playing basketball with particular distinction at Upper Arlington High, where the school team was known as the Golden Bears (though this is not the derivation of Jack's most-often-used nickname, the Golden Bear, which was bestowed later by sportswriter Don Lawrence based on Jack's physical appearance). Despite his talent for basketball, and indeed most sports, Nicklaus gradually gave up everything in favor of golf, simply because golf appealed to him more, and he seemed to have a special facility for it. As each year passed, he became a better player. When he won the Ohio Open at sixteen, he knew with the wonderful clarity only the truly talented enjoy what he would do with the rest of his life. "I was just interested in being a golfer. And when I started playing golf, I just wanted to be the best I could at playing golf." This clarity and confidence had a negative side in that as Nicklaus matured he could seem a little dull. Arnold Palmer had a passion for golf and life. Nicklaus was more like Tiger—a golfing machine.

Despite his great talent for and ambition in golf, Jack did not think at first that he wanted to be a professional player. After graduating from high school in 1957, he enrolled at nearby Ohio State to study for a degree in pharmacy so he could work with his dad in the family business. That way he could support himself while he played as an amateur, as Bobby Jones, who was an idol to both Jack and his father, had done. It was in his first week at Ohio State that Jack met Barbara Bash, a strong-willed young woman who was studying to be a teacher. They became engaged to be married, and Barbara would be a vital part of Jack's success: a stable, intelligent life partner who supported him loyally, but was also one of the few people who could make a bullheaded man see when he was wrong. Aside from meeting Barbara, the other significant development during Nicklaus's college years was that he put on a lot of weight. He had always been a hefty boy, but a tendency to overindulge himself meant that a strong, muscular frame was covered with layers of blubber so that he became very big, like a wrestler. At college, Jack was nicknamed "Blob-O" and "Whaleman." But he didn't much care what people said about him—he never would, or at least he never allowed people to know if he did, which would be a strength in competitive golf—and the weight didn't hinder his golf. In his youth, he was strong enough to carry all those extra pounds. In 1958 he competed in his first tour event, the Rubber City Open in Akron, and he played against Arnold Palmer for the first time in an exhibition match, finding himself charmed by Arnie as most people were. For his part, Arnie noticed the boy's power and talent and filed away the fact that this might be someone who would worry him in the future. In the spring of 1959 Jack was enormously excited to be invited to compete in the Walker Cup at Muirfield in Scotland, winning his foursome and singles matches. Selection for the Walker Cup team also meant an invitation to the Masters, where he met Bobby Jones for the first time, which was as thrilling for Nicklaus as it had been for Palmer.

In September 1959, when Jack was nineteen, all these valuable golfing experiences came together at Broadmoor Golf Club in Colorado, the venue of the U.S. Amateur. Nicklaus had a good feeling for his chances going into the tournament, though the high elevation meant he had to rethink his usual club selection (balls travel farther in thin mountain air and he was liable to overshoot). He began his campaign by beating Bob Jones III, son of Bobby Jones, 7 and 6—that is, he won by being up seven holes with six holes left to play—and also won his next two games easily. Playing Dave Smith in fog was a tougher challenge, but Nicklaus scraped a victory. The semifinal was a hard match against a middle-aged amateur, Gene Andrews, the golfer credited with being the first to use a system of yardages. Though every tournament player and his caddie now keep careful note of distances to each tee at every course, as well as a diagram of the green, in the late 1950s Andrews was virtually the only one doing so. Despite the advantage his yardage book gave him, Andrews lost to Nicklaus, which led to a final match against Charlie Coe, another gentleman amateur several years Nicklaus's senior. The players contested the title keenly over 36 holes, but in the afternoon round Coe made mistakes allowing Nicklaus to win, 1-up. Victory in the U.S. Amateur was momentous for Jack, as it had been for Palmer in 1954 and

would be for Woods in the 1990s. It was also a defining moment for the
Nicklaus family. An emotional Charlie told Jack's mother: "Sissy, I
think our son's been born to greatness."

Meanwhile, the new superstar of professional golf was entering
the golden phase of his career. Arnie Palmer won four tournaments
in the lead-up to the 1960 Masters, including three in succession, the
first time that had happened since 1952, and arrived at Augusta exuding confidence. He led through the first three rounds, giving a magnificent display of power and determination. But on Sunday Ken Venturi put
together a terrific round of 70 for a total score of 283. Finishing ahead of
Palmer, Venturi looked to be the likely winner. Friends congratulated
him as he went inside to watch Palmer's final few holes on television. "I
haven't won it yet," Venturi cautioned his supporters, which were wise
words as it turned out. Palmer soon began to close the gap. The turning
point was a birdie at the 17th. A par at the last would have tied him
with Venturi, forcing a play-off. He did better than that and birdied for a
1-stroke victory. Without displaying any emotion, Venturi stepped outside to congratulate the man who had vanquished him again.

The next major was the U.S. Open at Cherry Hills Country Club,
high in the Rocky Mountains, where the air was so thin the USGA provided oxygen for the players. In the 36-hole final, Jack Nicklaus, competing as an amateur, found himself leading the field at one point, while
paired with no less a person than Ben Hogan, a remarkable man who
achieved his greatest success on tour after returning to professional golf
in his mid-thirties, following a near-fatal car accident, becoming only
the second player (after Gene Sarazen) to win all four modern majors.
Hogan's personality was as severe as the Depression. He said little and
had a curious, hard-bitten way of expressing himself when he did speak.
(After winning the 1951 U.S. Open at Oakland Hills, he commented:
"I'm glad [I] brought this course, this monster, to its knees.") In many
ways, Hogan was the antithesis of the genial Arnold Palmer. But
Palmer's smile wasn't doing him much good at Cherry Hills. He finished

the third round on Saturday morning in 15th place, with Hogan and Nicklaus among those ahead of him.

During the lunch break, Palmer was eating a hamburger in the locker room when he overheard his friend the sports reporter Bob Drum talking with some of the other players about the championship. Palmer joined the discussion, turning it to his own prospects in the afternoon round. As things stood, he was seven shots behind the leader, Mike Souchak. "Bob, what do you think?" he asked Drum. "I think I can shoot 65 out there this afternoon. What do you think that'll do?"

"It wouldn't do you any good!" retorted the reporter.

"Sixty-five makes me 280 and 280 wins Open championships," the golfer returned hotly. "And besides that I'm going to drive the 1st green. I'll see you later." With that, Palmer put down his unfinished burger and hastened to the course.

Standing at the 1st tee, Palmer had something to prove—to himself and Bob Drum. He had said he would drive his tee ball onto the green at the 1st, which was an ambitious claim, considering it was a full 346 yards to the par-4 hole. In fact, Palmer had tried and failed to drive the green in each of the first three rounds. This time, with the added strength a disagreement can lend a person, he managed it. "A long drive is good for the ego," Palmer has said, something any golfer can empathize with. This Herculean drive, and its reward, set him up for a string of four birdies. Each time he drove the ball as if it were his last. Then he cocked his head characteristically to see where it fell, before handing his club to his caddie and charging down the fairway to go again. The excited crowds charged with him. They had little choice. Unlike Nicklaus—a slow, thoughtful player—Palmer didn't like to hang around. And here was part of the reason the public would always prefer Palmer: he was more fun to watch.

Still, it was Nicklaus who led the field after 12 holes. Then the Ohioan bogeyed 13 and lost momentum. In the final stretch it was Palmer versus Hogan, who was going for his fifth Open win, a glorious end to a grand career at the age of forty-seven. The dour Texan misjudged the 17th, however, putting his third shot in the water. When Arnie holed his putt at 18, he had the title, having shot a round of 65—exactly as he had predicted to Bob Drum.

With his victory at the Masters, and now the U.S. Open title, 1960 was arguably the best year Palmer ever had in golf. And it was not over. He would win three more events, including the Canada Cup, taking $80,968 in prize money for the year. He also crossed the Atlantic to compete in the Open Championship at St. Andrews.

"Winnie, honey. Don't unpack," ordered Arnold when he stomped back into Room 218 at the Rusacks Hotel. Behind him was his Scots caddie, James "Tip" Anderson, a twenty-eight-year-old former St. Andrews Junior Champion, who had come upstairs to put the bag away. The men had just played their first practice round on the Old Course in a virtual gale. The wind was whipping in from the North Sea and the bleak links offered no shelter. Palmer shot a very poor 87.

"Arnie, you came here to win the championship," Winnie reminded her husband. "We're not [going home]."

Palmer turned to his caddie, a whippet-thin fellow with a clever face, nicknamed "Tip" after his father, also "Tip," who worked in a billiard saloon tending tables and tipping cues. "Tip, you've seen me play . . ."

"Sir, I can't judge you," replied the caddie, who had advised against a round on such a very windy day. But the American hadn't listened. "I can't judge you under these conditions."

"Well, do you think I could win the Open Championship?"

"Sir, I wouldn't caddie for you if I didn't think you could win."

Palmer looked out the window, which afforded a splendid view of the 18th hole of the Old Course, the Victorian temple in sandstone that is the Royal & Ancient Clubhouse, the long sandy beach, and the broiling gray green sea beyond. "Unpack, darling," he told Winnie.

People have "played at the golf" on the links at St. Andrews since the Middle Ages. It is the home of the game and the birthplace of practically everything to do with the game. The industry of manufacturing

golf equipment more or less started here, for instance, with local crafts-
men making hickory-shaft clubs that went by archaic names such as
Brassie, Mashie, Wooden Niblick, and Long Spoon. In 1848 the first
Open champion, "Old" Tom Morris, established his golf shop overlooking the 18th green of the Old Course, where he sold items such as
leather balls stuffed with feathers, which had numerous disadvantages
including the fact that the stitching rotted when the balls got wet; when
given a thwack, an old ball would sometimes explode on impact. There
are six courses on the links at St. Andrews, but we are concerned with
only the Old Course, upon which the Open Championship is played
every five years or so (in rotation with other links around Britain). It is
unlike any course in the country and is quite different from prime
American courses such as the Augusta National. For the most part, the
best American courses are private inland parks, artificially created in
the fairly recent past and protected from hoi polloi by gates, guards,
and foliage. The Old Course was originally waste land and seems to be
as nature made it. Also, it is a truly public facility, integral to the daily
life of St. Andrews. The 18th is overlooked by a parade of shops. A
public road bisects the 1st and 18th fairways, and anybody is welcome
to take their exercise by walking the shale path that runs beside the
links. No golf is played on Sundays, and locals walk their dogs on
the fairways (an unimaginable custom at Augusta). None of this dis-
tracts from the charm or dignity of the Old Course. Indeed, it enhances
its appeal. There is a sense that the course belongs to the town and the
townspeople are happy to share it with whoever is interested.

The Old Course itself comprises bare, narrow fairways bumped and
hollowed like a lunar landscape and drilled with numerous deep
bunkers, the sides of which are built up with bricklike sods, bunkers
that rejoice in names such as Hell and the Coffins. Adjacent to the sea,
this is a place of big, ozone-heavy air that gusts about in all directions,
forming the gorse into stunted shapes and blowing golf balls off their intended trajectory. "The wind makes the golf links," says Tip Anderson.

"You never play it twice the same, not really." Over the years, the holes, as well as the bunkers, have been given splendid names. The 4th is Ginger Beer, because a ginger beer vendor would pitch his cart here during championships—the first example of on-course refreshments. The 10th is named in honor of Bobby Jones, who won the Open three times, including here at St. Andrews in 1927.

The front 9 twists back on itself, leading the player beside the Eden Estuary and thence to the town, the skyline of which is dominated by its cathedral. Originally, the Old Course was made up of 11 holes, but in 1764 the first 4 holes—which were short—were made into two, making 9 in total, and it became de rigueur to play 9 out and 9 back. Thus golfers throughout the world play 18 holes. At the 17th, the Road Hole, one has to drive over sheds formerly used to store hickory. The trick is to reach the green without putting the ball in the bunker or on the road that runs up to the Rusacks Hotel. Then to the 18th, playing toward the clubhouse, which stands at the head of the course like Buckingham Palace at the top of the Mall. Possibly the most famous building in golf, the R&A clubhouse was designed along neoclassical lines in 1854 and features a large bay window on the ground floor. Once the golfer has crossed the Swilken Bridge, a simple stone bridge spanning the Swilken Burn (a stream, in other words), a massive chandelier in the Big Room of the clubhouse acts like a lantern to guide the golfer home on gloomy days.

The Royal & Ancient Golf Club does not own the Old Course or, surprisingly, any golf course. The club consists essentially of the building and its members; the links are public land administered by the St. Andrews Links Trust and are open to everybody. Yet the course, the R&A, and golf are bound together inextricably by history and custom. The R&A runs the Open Championship and sets the rules for golf throughout the world (except in North America, where the USGA presides, though even here the rules of golf originated with the R&A). It also exerts an influence of tone. Royal by patronage (starting with King William IV in 1834), ancient by its association with the St. Andrews links, and quintessentially British, the R&A is a gentlemen's club of the type immortalized in the stories of P. G. Wodehouse, and it is worth noting that British clubs of this type are subtly different from American clubs. "If people started talking business in most of the traditional clubs in Britain, this one included, [they] wouldn't last long," explains Peter Dawson, a former Cambridge man who has been secretary since 1999. Though the R&A has included notable businessmen among its membership, together with politicians and royalty, many members are, as Dawson puts it quaintly, "perfectly ordinary tradespeople."

Inside the clubhouse, the decor is ornately Victorian, featuring wood paneling, flock wallpaper, and stained glass. In the Big Room, supernumerary members play cards as the hours of their retirement are measured by the chimes of the grandfather clock in the hall. There are floor-to-ceiling display cases filled with such oddities as the Kangaroo Paw, a gift from the Australian Golf Union, stuffed and mounted on silver. The original Claret Jug trophy is displayed in pride of place in the hall, opposite the porter's desk. The winner of the Open is presented with a replica—though a very old one*—and the original remains safely behind glass under the porter's eye. Both trophies are inscribed with the winner's name. Over the years there have been so many winners that tiny names have been scratched into every available part of the silver body of the cup, and now spread to three silver tiers at the base.

Having presided over the game for so long, the R&A had perhaps fallen into a state of complacency by 1960 when Palmer came to compete in the Open. St. Andrews was the home of golf. The R&A laid down the rules of golf and felt no need to define its Open Championship, like its American cousins, with an extra noun. It was not the *British* Open, as some journalists erroneously call it. It was and is *The* Open Championship, and the winner was and is "the champion golfer for the year." So it had been for one hundred years (the 1960 Open was

---

*Winners keep the replica for a year.

the centenary Open). But the prestige of the event had diminished in recent times partly because American golfers were reluctant to make the
journey across the Atlantic to compete. (Having won in 1946, Sam
Snead did not even bother to defend his title.) The fact that Arnold
Palmer had chosen to come to St. Andrews was therefore highly significant, doing much to regenerate golf's oldest championship as one of the
game's major tournaments.

All golfers coming to the Old Course require the advice of a sea-
soned caddie, and Palmer found his perfect partner in Tip Anderson,
though they did not always see eye to eye, as became apparent during
the 1960 championship, with particular regard to what iron Palmer
should play to the green at the tricky 17th, the Road Hole, then a par-
5. In the first round, on Wednesday, July 6 (the tournament then was
wrapped up in three days, finishing with 36 holes on Friday), Palmer
hit a good tee shot, clearing the old wood sheds and landing nicely in
the fairway. When he asked Tip what iron he should play, Tip replied
definitely: "Six-iron, sir."

Palmer took the 6 and hit his ball to the middle of the green, but
three-putted for par. In the second round, on Thursday, he drove his tee
shot to within ten feet of where it landed the previous day. "What club
is it, Tip?"

"Six-iron, sir."

Again, Palmer got it on the green but three-putted for par.

Soon enough it was Friday morning and again at the Road Hole he
drove the ball to where he had before. "What club is it, Tip?"

"It's a 6-iron, sir." Another frustrating three-putt for par.

During the lunch break, before the fourth and final round on Friday
afternoon, there was a cloudburst and the course was flooded so badly
in the ensuing downpour that for the first time the R&A decreed the final would be postponed until Saturday. Overnight, in Room 218 of the
Rusacks, Palmer stared at the deserted course, considering how he
might come from 4 behind to beat the leader, the Australian Kel Nagle.
He wouldn't do it by being cautious at the damn Road Hole.

The weather had improved by Saturday, with a wind that evaporated the floodwater from the links. Palmer played well enough on the back 9 to cut deeply into Nagle's lead, and by the time Arnie came to the 17th he was chasing the title itself. Remarkably, he drove his ball to within feet of where he had in the first three rounds at the Road Hole. But now he wanted a birdie, not another par. "Tip, don't tell me it's a 6-iron," he warned his caddie.

"Yes, it is, sir."

"Give me a 5-iron."

"You'll go in the road."

"Shit, I'll get a 5 from the road, won't I?"

"I don't know, sir. But it's the wrong club." According to Anderson, Palmer took it anyway,* and his ball went too far—as Anderson had feared—landing in the road. However, luckily, Palmer knocked it back up onto the green and holed out for a birdie-4. The tension was now almost unbearable. In the heat of the moment, the irrational thought went through Palmer's mind that had he been using the 5 at the 17th all along he might now be 2 or 3 strokes better off, whereas in truth he would almost certainly have been worse off.

"Tip, I want to speak to you."

"Yes, sir."

"You know you've just lost me the championship."

"Why is that?"

"You've been giving me the wrong club all bloody week." Under his breath, Anderson cursed the exasperating Pennsylvanian son of a . . . "I did nae quite say that, but I was thinking [it]. I gave him the right club every round." Despite Palmer's birdie at 18, which looked like it would force a play-off at least, Nagle kept his nerve and won by a stroke, a great disappointment to the American. Still, to come in second was an achievement, and there would always be next year when the Open was at Royal Birkdale, on Merseyside. And Palmer would engage Anderson

---

*In his memoir, *A Golfer's Life*, Palmer writes that he used a 6-iron.

again. Indeed, they worked together for the next thirty-five years, and they would win.

Back in the United States, on Saturday, July 23, 1960, fresh from 18 holes at Scioto, Jack Nicklaus married Barbara Bash. Following the ceremony and honeymoon, they began married life in a house on Elmwood Avenue in Upper Arlington, where their neighbors included Scioto golfing acquaintance Pandel Savic and his wife, Janice. This was really the start of Jack's close friendship with Savic, a shrewd businessman who would prove not only a valued adviser in years to come but also his best friend.

After his honeymoon, Jack competed in the World Amateur Team Championship, a biannual event between four-man teams of international players. In 1960 it was held at Merion Golf Club in Pennsylvania, and Nicklaus played beautifully, leading the U.S. victory. The press speculated whether he would turn professional, and this became a major issue for him as it had been for Palmer and would be for Woods. With all three there was the dilemma of whether they should abandon their college education to play golf full-time. Also, there was a financial consideration. Of the three, Nicklaus was perhaps least concerned with money because he had always enjoyed the financial support of his father. From the endless lessons with Jack Grout, to helping Jack and Barbara buy their home, Charlie had supported his son all the way. By the early 1960s, he was spending $5,000 a year on Jack's travel expenses alone, so that his son could compete as an amateur at the highest level, but he never complained. "It's the most wonderful money I ever spent," he told a reporter. "I figure it's like living my life all over again. I always wanted to be a champ." When Jack needed a job to make some extra money, one of Charlie's buddies brought him into the insurance game and for a while Jack sold policies out of an office in Columbus. He also earned some sponsorship money from a clothing manufacturer, though this required him to step gingerly around amateur status rules. At the same time, Jack was nominally still studying for a degree at Ohio State.

In the summer of 1961 Jack worked on his golf as never before, putting practice ahead of insurance work and college work. In the run up to the U.S. Amateur at Pebble Beach, he also started to use a yardage system, pacing off holes before a match and compiling a reference booklet that would help him select clubs and make shots in the tournament. Jack's friend Deane Beman, a sharp-witted young amateur, had picked up on Gene Andrews's idea, and it was Beman who told Jack and their friends what a great way this was of getting to know a golf course. "Jack and a couple of players kind of laughed at [my system] a little bit, until Jack started using it, and I think the first time he really put it into play was there at Pebble Beach," says Beman. Situated on a spectacular stretch of California coast south of San Francisco, Pebble Beach Golf Links is probably the most dramatic-looking and aesthetically pleasing golf course in the United States, as remarkable in its way as the Old Course. Nicklaus loved it from the first and was inspired to play at the top of his game in the summer of 1961. He drove the ball with a force that earned him a new nickname: "The Brute." Yet he also putted with finesse. When H. Dudley Wysong Jr. conceded on the 12th hole in the afternoon round of the final, Jack won his second U.S. Amateur title decisively, 8 and 6. Part of the credit is no doubt due to Beman's tip about yardages. But did Nicklaus thank his friend? "I don't remember a direct thank-you for it, no," says Beman, laughing, for one of Nicklaus's faults is that his great confidence has led him to be a know-it-all. "I think he probably thought he would have won it without [me]."

Nicklaus's win at Pebble Beach marked the last time, arguably, that the U.S. Amateur could claim the unalloyed status of a major, in the sense that it was the last time amateurs in the field were of comparable ability with the professionals on tour. The tournament would slip in importance (though Woods later did much to revitalize its status), and the slippage started in 1961, because Nicklaus would not defend the title the following year. In September 1961 he and Barbara had their first child, Jack William Nicklaus II, known as Jackie, and that was an incentive to earn serious money. The evidence was that Jack had the talent to make a good living on tour, and so he turned his mind to how he might launch himself as a professional golfer. He decided he would probably start by signing a management agreement with Mark McCormack, who now represented not only Arnold Palmer but the new Masters champion from South Africa.

The appositely named Gary Player was born the son of a gold miner in Johannesburg in 1935. Only five feet seven inches tall and slightly built, he compensated for his lack of stature by becoming a fitness fanatic. Professional golfers took a lax attitude toward fitness as a rule (and many still do). They tended to eat and drink with impunity and could even be seen smoking as they competed in tournaments (and some still do). Player was different. He made the most of his small body by dieting like a jockey, working out like a prizefighter, pumping weights, and doing aerobic exercise long before such things were fashionable. Though many mocked him, this lifestyle was the future. One of the reasons Woods has outclassed his contemporaries is that he takes fitness as seriously as Gary Player did—as seriously as a true athlete. And the introduction of Player to our story presents an opportunity to address the contention that golf is not a truly athletic sport.

A full-fledged sport—though the word has a broad dictionary meaning—is usually understood to be a pastime that requires a high degree of fitness and involves extraordinary physical exertion and/or physical risk as well as skill. Sport is usually fast and exhausting. The aim is usually to be the quickest, the strongest, to score the most points. In contrast, golf is played at a walking pace. The lowest score wins. And there is a lot of luck involved: a gust of wind or even a bug crawling across a green at an inopportune time can deflect a well-struck ball and dash a player's hopes.

Most ardent golfers would argue against this, of course, not wanting people to think their beloved game is a footling pastime. They talk primarily of the skill involved, adding that golf is deceptively taxing. Gary

Player insists that golf is a supremely athletic pursuit. "It is so athletic, it is unbelievable!" he exploded, when I reminded him there are those who say golf isn't a proper sport, because it isn't athletic relative to, say, sprinting. "Take it from a man who [has] worked on training probably longer than any human that's ever lived"—Player is prone to hyperbole— "I have worked on significant weight lifting and exercise and diet and training more than any human being that ever lived, probably . . . rugby to cricket to athletics to soccer. I played all those sports. I played first team and captained them and won the trophy for best all-rounder at school. . . . So I have done all of that, more than probably anybody that ever lived. And I can tell you that you can take one of the world's greatest athletes, like a Michael Jordan, and let him go play 36 holes today and 36 holes tomorrow and he'll tell you, 'I'm pooped. I can hardly walk.' It's so fierce on your body. People don't understand. If an average man of sixty-six had to hit balls and practice like I do, he'd die. That's when you get the message across. He would die. Either his body would break or he would die. He couldn't do it. It's a fierce, fierce pressure on your body. . . . Now look at this." Player lifted his sweater. "I'm sixty-six years of age," he reminded me. Then he slapped his flat belly with his little hand. "It's like a plank." In case I was in doubt he hit himself again.

Though Player lends himself to mockery, he became a truly great champion of the game, and he has an important part in our story as one of the so-called Big Three golfers of the 1960s and 1970s, along with Palmer and Nicklaus. Player has also shown a lot of character in coming from South Africa to play such a major role in world golf. When he first arrived in the United States in 1957 to play the tour, it was an intimidating experience for a young man of twenty-two from the Transvaal, and a lonely one. He was heartened when his wife, Vivienne, agreed to accompany him, though the tour was not an ideal lifestyle for a wife and young family. "It's a vagabond life. I mean, it's not a life for a woman, living in hotels and motels," says Player, who has traveled more than maybe any professional golfer, partly because he continued to base himself in South Africa. Despite the unsettled nature of this life, Vivienne Player offered the same invaluable support as Barbara Nicklaus and Winnie Palmer gave their spouses. "The three of us had phenomenal wives," says Player. "Never once said, 'Where you going?' Nagging you. When you have that as a golfer you've had it. . . . If a man like Tiger got married, and married a woman that's the wrong woman, it could ruin his career."

The grueling travel and hard work paid off. In 1958 Player won the Kentucky Derby Open and finished second in the U.S. Open. The following year he won the Open Championship at Muirfield, and in 1961 he won the Masters, emerging as a fine adversary for Arnold Palmer (who tied for second at Augusta in 1961). While Player would never be as popular as Arnie with the American public, Mark McCormack saw that the adversarial relationship was good for the game, and he could sell Player all over the world, as an international star of a truly global sport, almost as easily as he could sell Palmer. So, in May 1960, Player became McCormack's second major client.

Sports management was turning out to be a highly successful business for McCormack, and Palmer was making a fortune, too, endorsing everything from Wilson golf equipment to a dry-cleaning franchise. McCormack's logic was that if one opened a regular dry cleaner in a town, nobody would be much interested, but if one opened an Arnold Palmer dry cleaner, people would at least come to look, and that was an edge with which to launch a business. The strategy was surprisingly successful. More than a hundred Arnold Palmer Dry-Cleaning Centers opened in the 1960s, each paying $30,000 for the franchise. More prestigiously, Palmer was the omnipresent television pitchman for Pennzoil motor products, in an ad campaign built around the old Toro tractor his father used at Latrobe. Pennzoil, it seemed, kept it going. The golfer's face also appeared on breakfast cereal cartons, and he endorsed Liggett & Myers cigarettes, which he virtually chain-smoked on the course. (Having encouraged so many to take up the habit, some might consider it rich that in 2001 Palmer made his money on the back end, paid by GlaxoSmithKline to "educate the public about the dangers of smoking.") Player was packaged and marketed with similar thoroughness by McCormack, and almost as much success, becoming known as Mr. Fitness or the Black Knight (partly because of his gimmick of wearing all-black clothing on the golf course). Could McCormack have the same success with Jack Nicklaus?

Despite his brilliance as a golfer and the fact that he was the quintessential Middle American, a conventional young man from Ohio with a charming wife and a child, Nicklaus did not have the five key selling points that made Palmer a world-beater in the commercial sense. In a way, Nicklaus was an even harder sell than Player. On count one—looks—Nicklaus had a problem. As McCormack said, "They called him Fat Jack." He looked even bigger on TV. When Nicklaus opened his mouth, he had an unattractive, high-pitched voice (surprising considering his size), and maybe because he was less confident in company than he appeared to be—there was a shyness to the man deep down—he tended to gabble. He could also be as boastful and humorless as Player, with whom he got along famously. (Arnie, by contrast, was eloquent, modest, and witty.) Then there was the matter of Nicklaus's background. "He was also born to a fairly well-to-do family and had lessons at a private country club from a professional," notes McCormack, "whereas Arnold was the son of a professional and a caddie." As far as McCormack was concerned, this was very important in terms of how the public would relate to the golfers. They would always like Palmer better. However, Jack's sensational ability was such that he was going to be a star of the game whatever his personality, and so McCormack was happy to meet with him at Scioto to discuss his prospects, telling Jack smoothly that if he turned pro he could earn up to $100,000 in his first year from endorsements and appearances. Jack was impressed, as McCormack meant him to be, of course. But Jack did not act immediately and was anxious to keep their discussions secret, as even the suggestion that he was thinking of turning professional could jeopardize his amateur status. Nicklaus was already in a delicate position regarding USGA amateur rules. For instance, the golf equipment company Titleist would send complimentary golf balls to Scioto for Nicklaus—later he endorsed Titleist—but they would be addressed to Jack Grout. "And, of course, we knew when the balls came in that they were for Jack [Nicklaus]," says Dom Lepore. "They wouldn't say his name, because it was [against the rules] to do that . . . but we'd hold 'em until we'd see him."

Finally, Jack made up his mind, and on November 7, 1961, he sat down and composed a letter to Joe Dey, the executive director of the USGA and a good friend. "It is with mixed emotions and considerable thought that I am writing this letter to you of my intention to apply for membership in the Professional Golf Association," he began ponderously. He had mixed feelings in part because if he turned professional he would not be able to defend his U.S. Amateur title. It would have been nice to win three times, something nobody had done. Still, it was about time he started to earn a proper living, and there was another overriding reason to become professional. "The amateur [status] wasn't important to me," explains Nicklaus. "I felt if you were going to be the best, you had to play against the best . . . that's really the reason why I turned pro." So it was that Jack Nicklaus made his professional debut on tour in 1962 and set about dethroning the golfer the media were calling the King.

5

DETHRONEMENT

The 1960s were an exceptionally vibrant time in history and in golf. Upward of six million people were playing the game in the United States at the start of the decade, generating a billion dollars a year, and golf had also been revitalized in its historic home, Great Britain, where Arnold Palmer returned in 1961 to compete in the Open Championship. Again he hired caddie Tip Anderson, who knew the venue, Royal Birkdale, well and proved an invaluable partner. The weather was foul, but Palmer's powerful, low drives cut through the wind and, in the final, he beat Welshman Dai Rees by a stroke, becoming the first American to win the Claret Jug since 1953. It was another triumph for the man who was regenerating the game. "Arnold Palmer came into golf like Muhammad Ali came into boxing," says Chi Chi Rodriguez, recalling the Palmer effect. "Arnold Palmer was the best ambassador that golf ever had."

Palmer's every tournament appearance was charged with excitement and drama. In April 1962 the so-called King of golf played flawlessly during the first three rounds of the Masters and went into the final 2 strokes ahead. Then he faltered, making a series of mistakes, and, after

15 holes, he had fallen 2 behind his friends Gary Player and Dow Finsterwald, one of whom seemed certain to win. The situation became worse still for Arnie when his drive at the par-3 16th fell forty-five feet short of the hole. Then, overhearing a commentator say a birdie was impossible for him now, Palmer was goaded into doing the near impossible. He shot another birdie at 17 and ended the round tied for first place, wonderful entertainment for those watching. In the first three-way play-off in Masters history, Palmer beat Finsterwald by 9 strokes and Player by 3 to take his third green jacket. As if that wasn't enough, he returned to Scotland to defend his Open title at Royal Troon, winning for the second time. For many aficionados of the game, this was one of the greatest victories in the history of the Open Championship, with Palmer's 276 breaking the tournament record by 2 strokes. "I've never seen golf like it in my life. We beat the field out of the park," says Tip Anderson. "Never mind Tiger Woods. . . . Ach, the man!" At home, Arnie also won the Palm Springs (Bob Hope) Desert Classic and the Phoenix Open, beating Jack Nicklaus, who finished second, by a margin of 12 strokes. It seemed that Palmer had the measure of every course and every player on tour, including the young man from Columbus.

Nicklaus had not made much of a showing thus far in his first year as a professional. His debut at the Los Angeles Open in January 1962 resulted in fiftieth place and prize money of precisely $33.33, which wasn't much even in 1962. Still, he did better at the Thunderbird Classic, finishing second for a check of $10,000—riches to Jack and his wife. "We were so excited we could hardly stand it," recalls Barbara Nicklaus. Then Nicklaus met Palmer in the defining tournament of their careers—the U.S. Open at Oakmont Country Club in western Pennsylvania.

Oakmont is only about forty miles from Latrobe, so Palmer's fans turned out in force for the 1962 U.S. Open, swelling the crowd to seventy-two-thousand. "There were maybe a dozen people for Jack," recalls Nicklaus's friend Ward Wettlaufer. "His family. Of course, I was there, and a few other people." With neat choreography, Palmer was

paired with Nicklaus in the first two rounds, an opportunity to compare and contrast their appearance and styles. Nicklaus was an unsmil-
ing blond lump of a man. Still, he was impressively strong, driving the
ball as far as 328 yards. "He outplayed Arnold after about the 5th
hole," remembers Wettlaufer. The more personable Palmer, almost slim
in comparison, though hardly a weakling, didn't have quite as much
strength—but he could be a prodigious driver of the ball as he demonstrated at Cherry Hills two years before—and he was also having difficulty putting on what were very fast greens. Still, it was Nicklaus who
faltered in round one and, at the end of the day, Palmer was a stroke in
front with 71. He moved further ahead on Friday to lead the tournament. By the halfway stage on Saturday, he was tied in first place with
Bobby Nichols. Nicklaus was 2 behind. In the final stretch, however,
Palmer's putting let him down and Nicklaus gained until they held the
lead jointly. In the excitement and the heat of the day, some of Palmer's
fans got carried away in support of their hero and tried to put Nicklaus
off his game, heckling him and waving offensive signs. One read
"Nicklaus Is a Pig." The Nicklaus family was mortified. "I just thought
it was very low-class, very unsportsmanlike," says his sister, Marilyn,
her expression darkening with the memory. "They were just people
who didn't know any better." Charlie Nicklaus was particularly upset.
But his son seemed to be oblivious to the abuse, and he and Palmer finished tied for first place, forcing an 18-hole play-off on Sunday. This
was not the result Arnie had wanted, and he told the press wearily that
he had had enough of "that big, strong dude."

Nicklaus maintains that in the locker room prior to the Sunday play-
off, Palmer put a curious proposition to him: he suggested to Nicklaus
that whatever the result, they combine the prize money and split it fifty-
fifty. That way they would both benefit. Nicklaus says he thought this
was a nice gesture, a helping hand from an established pro to a newcomer. But he declined, saying, "No, Arn, you don't want to do that,
that's not fair to you, let's just go play." Palmer says he has no recollection of this conversation, which has caused much comment over the

years, though he admits he may have suggested it. Purse-splitting in play-offs was commonplace at the time, but it was done privately, without the knowledge of the fans, who had come to see a no-holds-barred competition, and was therefore hardly sporting. In fact, purse-splitting was later outlawed. The incident also seems to indicate that Palmer was not confident of winning, and Nicklaus's rebuttal must have shaken him further. After Palmer had gone outside, Nicklaus lingered in the locker room, refusing to be rushed even though friends told him Arnie was waiting on the tee and had been there for several minutes—swiping at invisible balls, knitting his brow, and chain-smoking. "I don't think he did it on purpose," says Bob Hoag, who was with Nicklaus that day, adding that Nicklaus is rarely on time. Still, this delay can only have taken an extra toll on Palmer's nerves.

When Nicklaus finally stepped outside, he was met with jeers while his opponent's fans cried "Attaboy, Arnie!" It was the older player who bogeyed the 1st, however, while Jack took par. Nicklaus moved further ahead at the 4th and soon Palmer found himself 4 strokes behind, which caused him to mutter to himself about his shortcomings. With a great effort, he rallied and reduced Jack's lead to 1 by the 12th. This was why the public loved him. Under pressure, Palmer played out of his skin. But Nicklaus was resolute. "Most people get flustered when Palmer does this and [they] start bogeying," he said later. He reacted to a classic Palmer charge by playing as if he had all the time in the world, knowing the more excitable man was capable of mistakes. Indeed, Arnie bogeyed 13. Now, Nicklaus was 2 ahead, and he increased the pressure by boldly going for every remaining birdie opportunity. Palmer could not break Nicklaus's lead and, as they teed off at the par-4 18th, Nicklaus was still 2 ahead. An eventful day ended in high drama when Nicklaus drove his ball into the rough, and Palmer, following a more accurate drive, almost managed to pitch in with his third shot to force them to go to another hole. Unfortunately for Arnie, his ball rolled past the cup. The outcome was still unsure when Nicklaus then missed his putt. Palmer could still have continued the game, but he missed again.

After tapping in, Nicklaus tipped his cap to the gallery to acknowledge the grudging applause. In truth, most had wanted the other guy to win. It was a particular dilemma for Mark McCormack, who had recently taken on Nicklaus as his third major client. "I'm sitting there rooting for both of them really," he recalled. "But Arnold I had known longer, and he was my first client, and it's his home state. It was sad to see Arnold not win at Oakmont."

If Palmer was the King, his reign was short and he was dethroned at Oakmont by a pretender ten years his junior, with many good years ahead of him. After the match, Palmer lamented: "I'm sorry to say he'll be around for a long time." For Nicklaus, it was the start of the greatest professional career in the history of golf, and the rewards were immediate. He took home a $15,000 first prize, plus a play-off bonus of $2,500, and his face graced the cover of *Time,* which predicted he would earn $250,000 from prize money and endorsements in 1962, and could be a millionaire by twenty-five. The press compared the numbers wonderingly with money earned by players of previous generations. "When Jack first came out, they used to say, 'Oh, he's making so much money!' And then they would put Sam Snead over here and compare what Sam Snead won to what Jack won," recalls Barbara Nicklaus. "Well, of course, now Jack's in this column and Tiger's in the [big money] column. I mean, the money is probably the biggest change in professional golf."

The last of the four major tournaments of 1962 was originally scheduled to be played at the Wilshire Country Club in Los Angeles. But the PGA of America was forced to find a new venue after California Attorney General Stanley Mosk became aware that the PGA had a clause restricting its membership to white players and decided to confront the association. Charlie Sifford claims he got Mosk interested in the issue as early as 1959. Others say Bill Spiller was responsible. Either way, Mosk took up the case with the view that the Caucasian rule violated California law. He informed the PGA that it could not hold its 1962 tournament in California unless Sifford was invited to compete, arguing that the PGA was denying Sifford—who was a resident of the state—his civil rights. As a sop to Mosk, the PGA had given Sifford a provisional tour card in March 1960, making him a "tentatively" approved tournament player for a limited time. Because he was not a full-fledged member of the association, he was still ineligible to compete in its premier championship, however. In fact, giving Sifford a card in 1960 seems to have been a wholly cynical exercise.

Confronted with Mosk's demands, the PGA relocated the 1962 championship to Aronimink Golf Club in Pennsylvania. As Sifford points out, they went to that much trouble to avoid being forced into having a black man in their tournament. But faced with the prospect of never being able to hold another championship in the most populous state in the union, the PGA decided to delete the Caucasian clause from its rules. This happened finally in November 1961. "As an association, we look back on the Caucasian clause and we were remiss," admits Jim Awtrey, CEO of the PGA of America. "[But] when the Caucasian clause was dropped in the United States it was years before the Civil Rights Act was instituted." While this is true—the civil rights legislation banning discrimination came in 1964 and '65—black golfers say the PGA had other ways of maintaining the racial homogeneity of golf.

"What happened, they pulled down one fence and put up some invisible fences," says Porter Pernell of the UGA. The principal problem was that would-be professionals had to establish substantial savings before they could join the tour, the theory being that golfers should be able to support themselves whether they won or not. This went back to the days when top-level golf had been the preserve of moneyed gentlemen such as Bobby Jones. In 1962 savings of $12,000 were required. The rules affected poor people of all races, of course. It had been a problem for Arnold Palmer when he joined the tour. But a white man had a chance of getting sponsorship (as Palmer did, signing with Wilson). Black golfers usually had less luck in this regard and were thereby effectively still shut out of what we now know as the PGA Tour, much to the anger of activists like Pernell, who also notes that the PGA of America took no account of the achievements of black golfers on the UGA circuit when it came to qualifying for tour events. Because of these restrictions, the UGA was still fighting to get black players into PGA Tour events ten years after the Caucasian rule was struck out. So much for the boast that reform came in advance of civil rights legislation.

So the 1962 PGA Championship was held at Aronimink. Although Palmer was the clear favorite, Gary Player took the title, 3 strokes ahead of Nicklaus, who was tied for third, with Palmer way behind, tied for seventeenth place. Player believes that Palmer's popularity and success were hindering his golf at this stage, paradoxically; he was distracted by the hype that had developed around him. The noisy adulation of his fans at Aronimink was such that it was hard for a fellow to concentrate. "They killed him with kindness," as Player puts it. Arnie was also increasingly distracted by the business deals Mark McCormack was making for him, to the extent that Palmer often seemed to have his mind on something else altogether.

Although Nicklaus did not win at Aronimink, 1962 was a very successful year for the Golden Bear. Aside from the all-important U.S. Open, he won two further tour events as well as the *World Series of Golf*, a TV special. The following year would be equally as rewarding, starting with a win at the Palm Springs Golf Classic. High winds made conditions difficult in the first round of the Masters that year, with Mike Souchak and Bo Wininger leading the field at the end of Thursday. On Friday Nicklaus played a sterling round of 66, putting him 1 behind Souchak, who was still in the lead. On Saturday the course was subjected to a downpour, and while most of the players splashed around complaining about the weather and making mistakes, Nicklaus remained focused and scored 74; considering the conditions, it was enough to propel him into the lead. As is often the case at Augusta, the sun seemed to appear in honor of the final. Nicklaus was playing well under benevolent skies when he heard a roar from the 14th green. Sam Snead, now fifty, was making what would be his last great play for a green jacket and had scored a birdie. At the same time, Player was moving into contention.

When Nicklaus arrived at the 13th, Snead was 2 ahead. But Nicklaus made a birdie to close the gap to a stroke. Snead bogeyed 16 and Player bogeyed his last two holes, giving Nicklaus a chance at the title. When he birdied 16, he was in the lead by 2 strokes, with only Tony Lema to worry about. When Lema finished with a birdie, Nicklaus was back to a 1-stroke lead and needed nothing less than par on 17 and 18. He got the first par and, though his ball flirted with the lip of the cup at the last, he got the second as well. Tossing his cap in the air, he had his first Masters title. Now Nicklaus was on a roll. The 1963 PGA Championship was held at the Dallas Athletic Club in baking 100-degree temperatures. Bruce Crampton led into the final round, with a 3-stroke margin. But with a round of 68, Nicklaus beat him to become the fourth man in history to win the PGA, the U.S. Open, and the Masters. And he was only twenty-three.

Palmer, who tied for fortieth at the Dallas Athletic Club, seemed to be fading almost as fast as Nicklaus was coming up in the game. Maybe Palmer was spreading himself too thin with his myriad business commitments. Maybe his loss of form had something to do with quitting smoking briefly. Maybe the burly young man from Columbus was simply too good. Palmer didn't really know the answer himself, but he had no doubt about the younger man's ability, and it was unnerving the way Nicklaus seemed to think of Palmer as just another tour player to be swept aside on his inevitable progress to glory. This bluff confidence engendered some rancor with Palmer, who had not expected his great career to land in the bunker quite so soon. For his part, Nicklaus was quietly hurt that so many members of the media and the public seemed to judge him on appearances. In this sense, he would always fall short of the better-looking, eloquent, and generally more engaging Palmer. That struck Jack, and his friends and family, as a little unfair, because Nicklaus was a great player and deep down he had fine personal qualities including loyalty, determination, and a basic decency. And Palmer's enduring popularity among galleries seemed to defy logic. In the six months leading up to the 1964 Masters, Palmer played in eleven tournaments without winning once, and was clearly not the man he had been. Yet he was idolized. By the same token, golf fans looked on Nicklaus as an upstart, somebody who was spoiling their fun, and for years to come they were prone to call out unkind comments at tournaments, just as sports reporters were quick to score points in print against him. All of this made for a complex relationship between Palmer and Nicklaus—though they were civil when they met—and the level of feeling among golf fans vis-à-vis their perceived rivalry caused Clifford Roberts to have a code of conduct printed on the pairing sheets at Augusta to remind the patrons how to behave. He didn't want the Masters descending to the level of a boxing match.

With much to prove, Palmer shot 69-68-69 in the first three rounds at Augusta in 1964—to Nicklaus's 71-73-71—and went into the final 5 strokes ahead of the field. Although Nicklaus challenged strongly, driving his ball prodigious distances, and although Palmer three-putted twice, it turned out to be an unexpectedly easy victory for the man from Latrobe. He won by 6 strokes on Easter Sunday, a big enough margin to relax a little on the back 9 and relish the experience of coming up the 18th fairway a winner. It was no mean achievement. He was the first to win the Masters four times, and he did so with a score that showed it was not a fluke. "I really won this one," he told reporters proudly. "This time there was no doubt." (His only regret was finishing 2 strokes off Ben Hogan's record low score of 274.) The media loved it. "Palmer is a hero to all, the darling of an era in which television has put golf into millions of homes," fawned the *New York Times,* showing how pro-Palmer the press was. "He has also captivated the public perhaps as no other athlete since Babe Ruth or Jack Dempsey. He is golf's finest showman." In fact, it was the pinnacle of his career. Palmer would never win at Augusta again. Indeed, at thirty-four, he had claimed his last major title.

It is a remarkable fact that every Masters between 1960 and 1966 was won by Palmer, Player, or Nicklaus, a fantastic achievement for them, and even more gratifying perhaps for Mark McCormack, who managed all three. "Mark McCormack was a genius," says Player. "To sign up Arnold Palmer, Gary Player, and Jack Nicklaus, in that order. The first three clients [and] to build an empire—genius." The money they generated was unprecedented, not only in prizes but even more so in endorsement work, exhibitions, and personal appearances. McCormack thought up so many money-making schemes that he had to create more than two dozen corporations to handle the business. He also developed television vehicles for his players, including *Big Three Golf*, which first aired on NBC in 1964, with the trio competing for a prize of $50,000. With money and fame came influence. McCormack was an increasingly powerful man in golf. So were his clients, particularly Palmer, who won over almost everybody he met, even the arch-traditionalists at the R&A, talking them into changing the qualifying rules for the Open Championship, for instance, so winners of all major events would be invited, thus enfranchising more Americans. This was a sensible idea, but also evidence of his influence at the highest level in the game.

Herein lies an indictment of Palmer, Player, Nicklaus, and McCormack. The agent and the so-called Big Three did not use their fame and influence to campaign publicly for integration and equality in golf, and there was still much injustice in the game, despite the fact the PGA had removed its Caucasian clause. One of the enduring complaints of African American golfers was that no matter how talented they might be, they were never invited to the Masters, which was autonomous of the PGA Tour. The members of the Augusta National alone decided whom they wanted to play in their tournament, creating a set of criteria for qualification that to men like Charlie Sifford seemed rigged to exclude black Americans. There was a loophole, however. Masters champions could nominate a player who had not otherwise qualified. If enough former champions agreed, almost anybody could get in. Knowing this was the case, the UGA and activists such as golf writer Maggie Hathaway approached the leading players, including the

Big Three, asking them to nominate a black golfer for the Masters. With their virtual monopoly of the Masters title at this time, and their close relationship with the club (Arnie in particular was well connected at Augusta, not least because of his friendship with the former president Dwight Eisenhower), the Big Three might have been able to make this happen. At least they could have *tried*. But most of those players who were approached did not even reply to requests for help. "I think we only got one response," says Porter Pernell, who wrote to just about every leading golfer of the day on this issue, including the Big Three, and the reply he received was illuminating (though Pernell feels bound by a confidence not to identify the one player who did respond). "[He] said he would love to invite a nonwhite golfer, but the risk was too great to him personally." Pernell further understood from this letter that there was an unwritten code at Augusta that African Americans were not to be invited "knowing or understanding how Bobby Jones felt about blacks."

Palmer, Nicklaus, and Player were united in having conservative views with regard to the way golf was run, including, to some extent, integration in the game. For instance, Arnold Palmer takes the view that golf clubs can have any kind of membership policies they like. He admits he did virtually nothing publicly for black golfers in his heyday, in terms of speaking up in support of them. By nature, he wanted to be everybody's friend and preferred to resolve such delicate matters in private. People have criticized this lack of engagement, including the late tennis star Arthur Ashe, who said he was saddened that somebody of Palmer's influence did not do more. When questioned on the matter now, Palmer is adept at deflecting the issue. "There's no question they were not admitted to the organizations and so on," he says of black golfers. "But I suppose the fact that it eventually came around to equal for everyone is what we were working for." (Not that Palmer did anything at all, that one can point to, to help the process.)

Gary Player was never as adroit a politician as Palmer and in his salad days he made crass statements with regard to race. In the 1960s, when he was the most famous sportsman in South Africa, he was a vociferous champion of its apartheid system. "I am South African. And I must say now, and clearly, that I am of the South Africa of Verwoerd* and apartheid," he wrote in his 1966 book, *Grand Slam Golf*. In the book, Player also criticized the American civil rights struggle, scoffing: "A good deal of nonsense is talked of, and indeed thought about, 'segregation.'" Comments of this kind made him a target for antiapartheid campaigners, and he was taunted at tournaments as a racist. Player later renounced apartheid. He now names Nelson Mandela as one of his heroes and funds a school for black children in South Africa. "My grandchildren are gonna say to me, 'Grandpa, how did we have these rules in South Africa?' I'm going to say, 'I don't know,'" he says, looking back on South Africa's past. Yet the system existed in part because people like Player paid lip service to it.

Jack Nicklaus, who is color-blind as far as red and green are concerned, appeared to have a problem with black when he was quoted in a Canadian newspaper in 1994 saying blacks were not as prominent in golf as whites because "black golfers have different muscles." He later said he had never knowingly made a racist statement and suggested he might have been misinterpreted. Still, Nicklaus did not help get black players into the Masters in the sixties and he could have done more. So could Palmer and Player.

Again, it is worth remembering the social backdrop to the game at this time, for the Big Three were dominant in an era when civil rights was a burning issue. A few days before the 1965 Masters, for instance, in the neighboring state of Alabama, Martin Luther King Jr. led his famous march from Selma protesting against literacy tests and other qualifications that were used to stop blacks from being able to register to vote in the state. Police teargassed the demonstrators, which caused national revulsion and hastened the passage of the Voting Rights Act.

---

*Hendrik Verwoerd, the prime minister of South Africa from 1958 to 1966 and a champion of apartheid.

But none of these momentous events of the day penetrated the pines of the Augusta National, where the self-regarding world of golf seemed happy to continue as it always had, a bastion of people of one color. Indeed, the members and players enjoyed a delightful tournament in the spring of 1965. The weather was fine and low scores resulted; Nicklaus was particularly commanding. On Saturday he played one of the best rounds in his life, ending 8-under-par. On Sunday he ran away with the tournament, shooting a 69 and bettering Ben Hogan's record by 3 strokes. Bobby Jones was so impressed that he praised Nicklaus with these memorable words: "Jack is playing an entirely different game—a game I'm not familiar with."

Unlike previous decades, the 1960s were lived and recorded in color. Technicolor movies became standard; Kodachrome film gave photos "those nice bright colors," as Paul Simon would sing; and almost every American craved a color TV. This innovation was particularly important for the broadcasters of golf, because the beauties of nature added greatly to the experience of watching the game. Few courses are as luscious as the Augusta National, and it was therefore a significant development when the Masters was broadcast in color for the first time in 1966. "I think the biggest breakthrough aesthetically came with the advent of color cameras," says Frank Chirkinian, doyen of the broadcast. It was a glorious day when he climbed up into the control truck and saw the monitors glowing like rainbows. "I just stood there transfixed and stared and absorbed what I was watching, because this was a dream come true."

If Palmer was the first golf star of television, in its early black-and-white incarnation, Nicklaus—with his straw yellow hair and, as the years passed, increasingly garish clothes—was golf in color. The Golden Bear had been preparing for the 1966 tournament since the start of the year, and outstanding play meant he led the field at the end of the first day. However, his putting let him down on Friday. Although Palmer took the lead briefly in the final round, he faded as Nicklaus picked up his game, and it seemed that Jack was destined to become the first back-to-back Masters winner. During the fourth round, the crowd got behind him as never before, partly because galleries had had time to get used to Nicklaus and because everybody likes a winner. After a fine shot at the 16th, they stood and applauded with particular warmth, moving Charlie Nicklaus to remark to Pandel Savic: "They have finally accepted him." A couple of missed birdie opportunities meant that Nicklaus did not win outright but finished tied for first with Gay Brewer and Tommy Jacobs. In the play-off on Monday Nicklaus proved his supremacy, beating Brewer by 8 strokes and Jacobs by 2 to make golfing history.

Palmer had another chance at glory at the U.S. Open in June, held at the Olympic Club of San Francisco. The title appeared within his grasp on Sunday—the tournament was now being held over four days—and furthermore it seemed as if Palmer might win with a very low score. (Ben Hogan held the record; he had won the U.S. Open in 1948 with only 276 strokes.) Caught up in the idea that he might better Hogan's score, Palmer started taking chances. Before he knew what was happening, he had lost a 7-stroke lead to tie with Billy Casper at 278, 2 strokes more than Hogan. And now he had to go into a play-off, which he lost. Palmer was the architect of his own defeat, and he knew it. He walked from the course hunched over with dejection, smoking heavily again after a failed attempt to quit. Doc Giffin, who came to work for Palmer at this time as an aide, counts this as Palmer's most lamented defeat, saying it has been "an open wound" for years. Meanwhile, Nicklaus kept winning, and he reached one of the early peaks of his career that summer when he won the Open Championship at Muirfield, becoming the fourth player ever to have been the victor in all four modern majors. The others were Ben Hogan, Gene Sarazen, and Gary Player (who had completed his Grand Slam the year before). Palmer was not in this club. Although he had won three of the majors, the PGA Championship had always eluded him, and now it was all but too late.

Perhaps Palmer's last bid for the brass ring, and his last great head-to-head with Nicklaus, came the following year in the U.S. Open at

Baltusrol Golf Club in New Jersey. Nicklaus had not been playing well all season, actually missing the cut at the Masters, and had fallen behind Palmer in the Money List. Palmer had won a couple of prestigious tournaments, including the Los Angeles Open. Palmer played well in the first two rounds of the U.S. Open to take the lead, with Nicklaus just behind him. In the third round they were paired together, and in their game within a game both men seemed to lose sight of the fact that they were competing against a field of players (Palmer scored 71, Nicklaus 72). In the all-important final, Nicklaus took the title with a tournament total of 275, which was a low enough number to beat Hogan's record, the target Palmer had set for himself the year before.

One of the subplots to the U.S. Open at Baltusrol was the emergence of a brilliant newcomer, twenty-seven-year-old Lee Buck Trevino. Born illegitimate in 1939, Trevino would become one of the great personalities of the tour—individualistic, fearless, and hugely talented. Trevino could not have been more different from the country club crowd Nicklaus epitomized. Indeed, he made Palmer look like an aristocrat. Never knowing his father, Trevino was raised in poverty by his gravedigger grandfather, and Lee made his living hustling games and working as a laborer in El Paso, Texas. The name of a former girlfriend, Ann, was tattooed crudely on his right forearm. Though he thought of himself as Mexican American, Trevino did not suffer the same degree of discrimination that African Americans faced in the game. (In later years he had a series of disputes with the Augusta National and he never got along with Clifford Roberts, but that had more to do with a personality clash than the club's not wanting Hispanics in the tournament.) More noteworthy was Trevino's unabashed enjoyment of boozing—even during tournaments. As he says, for years drinking was "a way of life" for him. Because of the humidity in New Jersey during the 1967 U.S. Open, Trevino downed a dozen or more beers each afternoon following his round. Yet he still managed to finish fifth, heralding a great career.

Trevino's drinking during a tournament week was not unique, though most players swore off heavy boozing at a major. There had been several famously bibulous golf champions, notably Walter Hagen, who turned up for tournaments direct from all-night parties. The life of a tournament golfer lent itself to the consumption of alcohol. Players would commonly sit around in the hotel bar during the evenings of a tour stop. "You normally got shit-faced every night," admits Doug Sanders, one of the reprobates of golf, who later reformed his ways and turned to God. Sanders packed a case of miniature bottles in his golf bag for when he wanted to take the party out onto the course the next day, particularly in events like the Bing Crosby celebrity pro-am, which took place at Pebble Beach in January, when the weather was often damp and cold, and many of the celebrity competitors enjoyed a drink, too. Actor George C. Scott sometimes showed up for the Crosby with a bag so heavy his caddie could hardly lift it. "George had about eighteen beers in the bag," recalls Sanders. "A beer a hole." Professional players frequently competed and won with hangovers. Boozing was part of the culture, accepted by most people in the game. Alcohol was their drug of choice, but some players also took pills, such as Librium, to calm themselves during a tournament and thus help them putt. Beta-blockers have also been misused for the same reason. Abuse of narcotics to get high was rare. By and large, pro golfers were drinkers, which went along with those other popular recreations on tour: gambling (always a favorite with players) and womanizing.

Although the idea of golf groupies may seem ridiculous, professional golfers have particular opportunities when it comes to picking up women. "Let me tell you the difference between golfers and other sports figures," Doug Sanders offers, conspiratorially, for this was another pleasure he indulged in. "You are out there practicing. You're putting. And they can see you. You can talk to them. Now, how you going to make contact with someone [on] a football field? . . . You can't do that. But you are walking along and you see someone and you make eye contact, you send your caddie over. He says, '[Doug] would like to know, would you like to have a drink, and do you have a phone number?' 'Oh yes! Tell him to call me.'" Flirting with girls became part of Sanders's image. He would pick flowers on the fairways and look for the prettiest girls in the gallery to give them to, a routine he claims was highly successful, as women literally fought to get into his hotel room.

Sanders's skirt-chasing was not unusual. Many tour players took advantage of the opportunities he describes. Sanders is notable only in that he enjoys boasting about his past—the bad old days when, as he says, the devil had him. But there is a serious point here. Most tour stars in the history of American golf have been married men. Indeed, there is a conservative culture in pro golf whereby players marry and start families young. They also tend to use their family image to attract endorsements. Moreover, the PGA Tour itself has a clean-cut image. There is a Tour Wives Association and a well-attended Tour Bible Study Class that was cofounded by Kermit Zarley, a player who concedes that there is moral dishonesty on tour. "Sure. That hasn't changed, in the sense that there were people like that forty years ago on the tour, and there are some people like that today," he says. "The more you're away from home, the more temptation." The fact that some married players screw around on tour has not been well publicized, however, because of the cozy relationship between players and golf writers, who know it is more than their job is worth to highlight unseemly goings-on. In private, players and sportswriters laugh themselves silly over the shenanigans of the stars of golf. Indeed, the bigger the star, the more opportunity and temptation.

Despite his long and apparently happy marriage to Winnie, Arnold Palmer has had a reputation within golf as having an eye for the ladies. It has hardly ever been alluded to in public. But his friend Bob Rosburg did let something slip in a 1988 interview when he recalled being on the road with Arnie during the early days of their professional career. They sometimes shared a hotel room, and late one night the telephone in the room rang. It was a man asking if Palmer was there. Rosburg looked over at Arnie's bed and saw that he had not come back yet, though it was about 2:00 A.M. "No, he isn't," he told the caller.

"I damn well know he isn't, because he's out with my wife," came the reply. "So when he gets in, tell him I'm going to come down there and kill him."

"Before you do that," said Rosburg, "can I just say that mine is the bed by the window?"

Arnie and Winnie Palmer were dismayed when they read this story in a newspaper. "It did disturb Arnold quite a bit that that came out," says Rosburg. "I shouldn't have said it. . . . It was true, but [when] Winnie saw it, I think it hurt her. . . . You know, the women loved him, and he's the same as the rest of us."

Tour players had a relaxed view of many matters—including purse-splitting, drinking, womanizing, and discrimination—but they took a stand when it came to one subject that was close to all their hearts.

As Palmer and others created a golden age of golf, money flooded into the game. Much of that money was controlled by the PGA of America, to which all tour players had to belong, but which did little for them in return. The fundamental problem was that the PGA was run for the benefit of the bulk of its membership, who were workaday club professionals. The tiny percentage of members who made their living playing tournament golf did not receive the special attention they felt they deserved. Also, tour players had to cope with all manner of restrictive PGA rules. Until 1961 the PGA had its racist membership policy, of course. That had been largely unchallenged by the players. Other restrictions that affected their earnings, including the number of paid exhibition events members could take part in, caused endless complaint. But it was when the PGA began to negotiate rich television contracts without consulting the players that they rebelled.

Aside from the majors, most of the early golf on American television consisted of made-for-TV events such as *Shell's Wonderful World of Golf,* which started in 1961, and the *World Series of Golf,* which began in 1962. The players became very angry when the PGA negotiated contracts for these shows without asking them what they thought. Moreover, the proceeds were put into the general membership fund, which did not benefit them specifically. TV rights to individual tour events were controlled by the relevant sponsors, and they sold them without consultation on an ad hoc basis. Sometimes sponsors got a lot of money and sometimes rights were almost given away in exchange for the exposure. And the proceeds did not go into the purses. Players insisted that sponsors cease selling TV rights without consultation and argued that in the future proceeds should be shared. The sponsors resisted, and the final straw came in 1967 when the sponsors of the Phoenix Open negotiated a TV contract without involving the players. In response, the players said they would not compete in the event again until there were radical changes in the way all tour stops were run. "We said, you're not going to have any players," says Doug Ford, one of the leading malcontents. "You can't run your tournament without players." Ford and others wanted the proceeds from future contracts split—a quarter for the PGA, a quarter going into a retirement fund for players, and the rest going to the sponsor, on the condition that some of that money be put back into the purse. Over the next few months, most tour events agreed to this proposal, and purse money started to rise as a result.

The problem remained that the PGA was fundamentally unsuited to running a professional tour, and so in 1968 Ford and others founded a rival organization, the Association of Professional Golfers (APG), lining up an independent tour and signing most of the top players. Jack Nicklaus was the biggest star behind the APG, giving it his full and public support. Palmer was more wary. "Arnold Palmer never takes a stand on anything," says Ford. "He's very involved in his image with the public and he won't do anything that would mar it in any way."

Palmer took the view that there was a lot wrong with the PGA, but it would be better to change it from within, and he was one of the advocates of a compromise whereby an independent division of the PGA would be created for the tour players. It would have its own schedule, its own boss, and player-directors on the policy board. So it was that in 1968 the Tournament Players Division was created, with Joe Dey, the former head of the USGA, becoming the first commissioner. The APG was duly disbanded and the independent tour forgotten. Still, not everybody was happy. Ford says he and others did not want Dey because of his amateur background. "We needed a professional in there who had the background to negotiate for the TV [deals]." That would come later when the Tournament Players Division evolved into the PGA Tour and Deane Beman succeeded Dey as commissioner.

As Nicklaus's involvement in the 1968 rebellion showed, he had matured into an independent-minded (always less clubbable than Palmer), feisty personality with an interest in the governance of golf. He was also becoming interested in the business side of the game. The first step in Nicklaus's business career, aside from endorsement work McCormack brought to him, was a dream he had to build a golf club in his home state that would be as special as the Augusta National, with a tournament inspired by the Masters. He asked his friend Ivor Young to scout for some land and Young found several suitable plots, including farmland northwest of Columbus, near the town of Dublin. Like that former indigo plantation in Georgia, it had natural undulations and a creek. There was also an old barn that might be of use.

Today, that barn is a maintenance building for Muirfield Village Golf Club, and around it has grown a sprawling real estate development. Named in honor of Muirfield in Scotland, Muirfield Village is much more than a golf course. In fact, there are two courses: the Country Club at Muirfield Village and Muirfield Village Golf Club, home to the annual Memorial Tournament, the final of which is held during the Memorial Day weekend in May. Threaded between the courses are five thousand homes, together with shops and commercial property—a huge subdivision of land that is the city that Jack built. Nicklaus owns a substantial home adjacent to the 2nd fairway of the championship course and, lest anybody forget who built all this, there are reminders, including a life-size bronze statue of the golfer at the entrance to the clubhouse and another on Muirfield Drive. Nearby Interstate 270, which forms a ring around Columbus, the capital of Ohio, is the Jack Nicklaus Freeway. Almost in the dead center is the Jack Nicklaus

Museum, on Jack Nicklaus Drive, next to Ohio State University, where Nicklaus went to college and on whose airstrip he lands his Gulfstream jet. Muirfield is an impressive monument to Nicklaus, his ego, and the Mammon golf can generate. But it almost ruined him.

Back in 1966, it seemed simple. Jack personally bought 195 acres of the farmland Ivor Young had found, and that was all they needed to build a golf course, which was the limit of Nicklaus's ambition at this stage. However, he needed financing to develop the land and to build a clubhouse, and he could not raise the extra capital. This was why it was decided to expand the project into a golf and real estate development, with residential plots that would offset the cost of the course and provide a profit for investors. It was at this point that Nicklaus was reintroduced to Putnam S. Pierman, a childhood friend. Another Scioto Country Club kid, Put, as he is known, had inherited his father's heavy construction business (the family made a fortune building highways, including the Ohio Turnpike) and had money to spend plus contacts in the Ohio business community. Invited to Augusta to renew his acquaintance with Jack, and then to Jack's new residence at Lost Tree Village, a gated community outside Palm Beach, Florida, Pierman became intrigued with the golf course idea and agreed to lend Nicklaus enough money to buy more land. By 1968 the partners had acquired 567 acres. A year later they had more than 1,500 acres. But still the figures didn't work. "If we could have done it with 350 acres, we would have," says Pierman, explaining that part of the problem was that some of the land they wanted belonged to a company that wouldn't sell small parcels. "You had to buy all of their six hundred acres to get the hundred you wanted." Then money had to be found to build roads, bring in the utilities, and do all the other work that would make property lots viable. As they kept enlarging the project, trying to make the numbers balance, the land they were buying became ever more expensive, as sellers realized Nicklaus was behind it all, and Nicklaus and Pierman became overextended. "I don't know how much Jack had in it," says Ivor Young of the money involved, "but way too much." Pierman adds that he wanted to call the project The Anvil, because it almost dragged them both down.

Pierman found himself drawn into other aspects of his friend's financial affairs. "I think Jack is getting screwed," Charlie Nicklaus confided in Pierman, regarding his concerns about his son's relationship with IMG, adding that he thought Mark McCormack's priorities were Palmer first, Player second, and Nicklaus last. "Would you take a look at it?" he asked, so Pierman called in some accountants and conducted an informal audit of Jack's finances, including his relationship with IMG, which not only brokered Nicklaus's contracts but invested his savings and even did his tax returns. When Pierman had his report, he went to meet Nicklaus at the Dallas Open to tell him what kind of financial shape he was in, "and it was for shit. It was terrible. He was not in good financial shape . . . he was just getting drained [by IMG]. . . . He was not merely, as Charlie suspected, getting the third-in-line-type deal from McCormack, but the triple-dip was in play."

By a triple-dip, Pierman meant that IMG took a commission on three earning streams. Dip one was a cut of Nicklaus's prize money. The second dip was a charge for managing his business affairs and negotiating contracts. Pierman considered this legitimate. "Then he got a third dip that had to do with [money] that came from equities or investments made." This Pierman considered dubious—at least the way it was being done. When Pierman explained everything to Nicklaus, who apparently had only a superficial understanding of his own affairs, it soured the golfer against IMG and led to a parting of the ways with the company. McCormack remained unapologetic: "You're taking a percentage of somebody's gross income, so what's the difference if it comes from winnings, endorsements, or investments?"

Nicklaus asked Pierman to meet his buddy Gary Player, to tell him what he had found out. But Pierman implored Nicklaus to keep the information confidential, worried that McCormack would take legal action if they started talking to other IMG clients about their concerns. He says that the most dangerous thing he could do was plant a seed of distrust in tour players' minds. "Because they don't know, anyway. . . . I mean, business is not their background. It's not their bag." As their careers progressed, the so-called Big Three would enjoy giving the impression they were businessmen as well as golfers. But none was highly educated, and most of their forays into business were merely as front men. "I always thought that, of the three, Arnold was the brightest," says Pierman. "He was *this* bright: he was bright enough that he took absolutely no shit of Mark McCormack's, like 'Well, Mark said that, so it must be true.' He wasn't like that. He was much more demanding on Mark [than] Gary or Jack."

In fact, Palmer showed more acumen generally. While Nicklaus was struggling to raise a new Augusta National out of the Ohio mud, Palmer simply acquired a preexisting club and tournament in central Florida. The Bay Hill Club and Lodge, home to a small event called the Florida Citrus Open, was lost in the boondocks outside what was then the unprepossessing city of Orlando. Palmer liked the club partly because it was so secluded, and in 1969 he took out a five-year lease, with McCormack as an investor, and an option to buy. He and McCormack were rewarded a year later when it was announced that Walt Disney World was to be built in Orlando, the first in a series of theme parks that made the city an international tourist destination, dramatically increasing its size and the value of real estate, including the value of Bay Hill. At the same time, the club's tournament—renamed several times, but best known as the Bay Hill Invitational—became a premier event on the tour calendar. Over subsequent years, the most famous golfers in the world drifted south to join Arnie in Florida, establishing colonies in the Orlando suburbs as well as at resorts such as Ponte Vedra Beach, Jupiter Island, and Palm Beach. Greg Norman, Gary Player, and Tiger Woods would all settle in the state. The golfing was good in the winter. It was quicker to fly to Europe from here than it was from the West Coast or the Midwest, and crucially Florida is one of a handful of states that does not have state income tax. For all these reasons, Florida became the golf state, and Palmer led the way as he had in so many other respects.

In contrast, Nicklaus's proposed golf course was in Ohio, where the winters were cold and summers could be insufferably hot. In May, when Jack was planning to have his tournament, rain often swept through the Ohio Valley, making golf almost unplayable. These were problems for the future, however. In the late 1960s, Nicklaus was still trying to get the thing built; at the same time, his father was dying of cancer. Pierman recalls that Jack asked him to visit Charlie at his condominium near Scioto to give him an update on the golf course, which had become such a worry to them all. "I can remember Charlie saying, 'Put, no shit, you really think it'll make it? You really think you're going to be able to pull it off?' And I said, 'Charlie, I *really* do.'"

Charlie Nicklaus died on February 19, 1970. It was a huge blow to Jack, who had adored his father and been supported by him throughout his life, financially at first and always emotionally. However, Nicklaus came into his own after his father's death, taking charge of his life in a way he hadn't before—finally, truly growing up—and playing better and looking fitter than ever. Put Pierman had recently lost thirty-three pounds on the Weight Watcher's diet and, learning from this example, Jack went on the diet, too, getting down to a relatively trim 180 pounds (for a man five feet eleven inches tall). After he lost the weight, he grew his hair longer, as was the fashion, and as a result he started to look good for the first time in his life. He knew it. Sponsors knew it— in the past, when he was modeling clothes, he had to be photographed from the waist up—and television knew it. "The camera hated Jack originally. Jack weighed 250 pounds and he had a Prussian haircut. He was not well liked by the gallery or the cameras and then the metamorphosis took place," says Frank Chirkinian. "All of a sudden, he lost that big belly, and he let his hair grow, and now he's got these lovely blond locks down to his neck, and the camera fell in love him. That was just an amazing turnaround." When Jack rejoined the tour, he found that he had female admirers, some of whom were surprisingly persistent in wanting to get close to him. "All of a sudden they were writing notes and passing them to Angie [Argea] the caddie. I got notes passed to me heading for Jack," laughs Put Pierman. "It [did] wonders for his ego."

It was the new, slim, highly motivated Nicklaus who arrived at St. Andrews for the 1970 Open Championship. The defending champion that year was Tony Jacklin, a working-class boy from Scunthorpe who in 1969 had been the first Briton in eighteen years to win the Open. Like so many top players, he had signed with Mark McCormack, but like Nicklaus he soon became disillusioned with IMG. "All they were interested in was making money out of me," bemoans Jacklin, whose problems started the week of the 1969 Open. "I won it on a Saturday. I sat down and met with Mark McCormack on Sunday and, of course, I was spent. I had given everything I had to give to that week. . . . I said, 'I want to go away now and just digest what's happened, cos my life's changed beyond this moment. It's going to be different.' And he said, 'You can't have any time [off]. You've got to go over to Westchester and play the Westchester Classic.'" Jacklin flew to the United States on Monday only to miss the cut at Westchester, and for three consecutive weeks after that. "What should have been the greatest month of my life was the most miserable month I ever spent." Jacklin was also unhappy with the way IMG handled his money. "Sometimes they invested your money that you'd earned and paid tax on and took 25 percent of that. But none of the investments they ever made for me made any money—*ever*."

At the end of the Thursday round at St. Andrews, Nicklaus was tied with Jacklin in second place behind Lee Trevino, a position they held into the final on Saturday, with Doug Sanders making it a three-way tie for second. Nicklaus, in the group ahead of Trevino and Sanders, finished the tournament 1-over-par. Trevino and Jacklin had dropped out of contention and Sanders found himself in the lead at the last hole. He only needed to make par at 18 to win the championship, and everybody thought he would do it. Sanders didn't make the cleanest job of getting to the double-green, with his second shot leaving the ball thirty feet from the hole. Still, he had two putts to get it down. He should have been able to manage that. However, showing off for the gallery in characteristic style, trying to be a "little bit showbiz," as he puts it, he made a sloppy first putt that stopped short. Even so, he only needed to make this three-footer and he would win the world's oldest golf championship here at the home of golf. As he says, "It would have changed my life." Sanders's personality was his undoing. He swaggered up to the ball. Then something caught his eye and he bent over to pick up what he thought was a piece of dirt. There was nothing there, just a bent blade of grass, and he heard somebody snigger. "I don't know why in the hell they started laughing." When he should have backed away to gather his thoughts, he rushed into the putt and pushed the ball by the hole. Now he was in an 18-hole play-off with Nicklaus on Sunday. Nicklaus commanded from the start. Sanders clawed his way back to within a stroke by the 16th. Both took 4 at the 17th and were level going into the final hole. Sanders had the honor, but his drive was short. Nicklaus slapped his ball through the green to land on the grassy bank behind and finished with a birdie. Here was victory at St. Andrews, after three years without a major title, and he tossed his club in the air in jubilation. It almost hit Sanders coming down.

Upon his return home, Nicklaus and Pierman met with Mark McCormack to tell him that Nicklaus was leaving IMG. To lose the most successful golfer in the world was a considerable blow to McCormack, who felt that it happened because Jack was jealous of his close relationship with Palmer. "Let's face it, Arnold was getting all the press adulation in those days and Jack, starting in sixty-two, was beating Arnold most of the time," he said, identifying what he considered the nub. Nicklaus saw things differently. "I think that when Mark McCormack was younger, I think he made mistakes with me, and I think he [knew] he made mistakes with me," he says, with the directness that is so typical of him and such a contrast to Palmer's emollient manner. "He didn't make me any money to start off with, and I was second fiddle to Arnold and Gary."

It is, of course, far from being the case that IMG did not make Nicklaus *any* money. The company just didn't make Nicklaus enough to finance his ambitions: to build his golf course and live in the style of Arnold Palmer. And he had to blame someone. "He could blame two people," reasoned McCormack. "Himself or me. And it's easier to blame somebody else, usually."

Having fired McCormack, Nicklaus set up a corporation with Put Pierman as his chairman and agent, though the patrician Pierman shuddered at the latter term. "If you had called me an agent, I'd have twisted your goddamn neck off," he says. "Boxers had agents [and] they are all thieves. . . . I [was] a business partner of Jack's." The new company was Golden Bear, Inc., and they established a small office on North Lake Boulevard in Palm Beach, with a skeleton staff and so little start-up money that there was even a question whether they could pay the telephone bill at first. "He really was in [the] shit. I mean, really deep trouble," says Pierman of Nicklaus's financial situation. But there was always money from somewhere for Keeping Up with Arnie. Having proved his dominance on the golf course, Nicklaus felt compelled to compete against Palmer in lifestyle, which was perhaps unwise, for Palmer was a good deal wealthier than Nicklaus, mostly because of more and better endorsement deals. Not only was Palmer rich enough to lease his own golf club in Florida, in 1971 he bought Latrobe Country Club as a gift for his father. Furthermore, he was the first player to have his own airplane, having learned to fly in 1957. As the years passed, Palmer owned ever faster and more expensive aircraft, acquiring a Learjet in 1968. If Arnie had a jet, Nicklaus had to have one, too, and the players rivaled one another to have the best and fastest. Apart from the considerable price of the aircraft, maintaining, fueling, and insuring them was almost ruinous. "Arnold was the only guy in the [jet] business and it cost the shit out of us, cos Jack had to have it," recalls Pierman. At least Arnold was qualified to fly his jet, having to hire only one copilot to meet aviation regulations. Jack had to employ two full-time pilots and inevitably the jet was parked at tour events for days at a time while his pilots stayed in a hotel on expenses. As Pierman puts it, expressively, "Running those fucking jets around the country, pal, they'll eat your lunch."

But Nicklaus was fulfilling his end of the partnership with Pierman, which was winning tournaments. In February 1971 he triumphed in the PGA Championship at the new PGA National Golf Club in Palm Beach Gardens, becoming the first golfer to win all four major titles twice. He went on to win three more tour events in 1971, including the Tournament of Champions, and finished second in the Masters. The U.S. Open was held at Merion Golf Club in Pennsylvania, and Nicklaus looked like a potential winner in each of the four rounds, with Lee Trevino as his main challenger in the final. Trevino, in the group ahead of Nicklaus, finished with 280 on Sunday. Nicklaus could win with a birdie at the last and, knowing this, Trevino went into the locker room to wait. Unable to do anything more than he had done, Trevino closed his eyes and listened to the sound of the crowd through an open window. The people were excited as Nicklaus came to the green, knowing a birdie putt was possible. As Nicklaus bent over the ball they fell silent; then, after a couple of seconds, Trevino heard a collective sigh. He opened his eyes and smiled, knowing he was in a play-off.

A paradoxical character, Trevino is reticent in private life. On the course, he is a garrulous showman whose nonstop patter and antics can unnerve an opponent, even one as formidable as Nicklaus. The next morning, at the 1st tee, with all the tension of the event and the expectation of the people gathered, Trevino pulled a snake out of his golf bag and waggled it before Nicklaus and the crowd. It was a toy, of course, and Nicklaus laughed in a good-natured way, but a crazy prank like that stuck in the mind and had its effect on a fellow's concentration. Lee Trevino beat Jack Nicklaus that day, showing not for the last time that he had the measure of the Golden Bear.

Nineteen seventy-two was another wonderful year for Nicklaus, but again it would have been better without Trevino. In April Jack won his fourth Masters. In the summer he romped home the winner in the U.S.

Open at Pebble Beach with a score of 290, thus equaling Bobby Jones's record of 13 major titles. Now he had a chance at the modern Grand Slam, the dream of every great champion—to win all four majors in the same season. The next leg was the Open Championship at Muirfield in Scotland, a golf course Nicklaus knew and had loved since his first Walker Cup.

Despite suffering with a stiff neck during the first three rounds, he managed to stay within six shots of the leader, Trevino, and five behind Tony Jacklin, and these three made for a vintage final. Nicklaus played brilliantly on the last day and finished with a round of 66. However, either Jacklin or Trevino, who were still on the course, could beat his total of 279 by making par on the last two holes. Trevino's drive at 17 went in a bunker and, though he got out okay, his fourth shot missed the green, landing on a bank behind. Almost as if he knew it was hopeless, Trevino chipped the ball carelessly and, in one of those unexpected moments in golf, it went in the hole to save par. Jacklin bogeyed 17 in surprise. But it was Nicklaus who was most affected by Trevino's luck. "I was just flattened when Trevino chipped the ball in," he says. All Trevino needed now was par at 18, and he did it, beating Nicklaus by a stroke. Jack's friends watched as the normally stoic Midwesterner lost his composure and wept. "It was pretty tough on him," says Ivor Young, who recalls this as being one of the very few times in all the years he had known Nicklaus, man and boy, that the golfer was overcome with emotion. His Grand Slam dream had ended at Muirfield and Nicklaus was not used to failure. Maybe if he'd suffered a few more disappointments early in life, he would have been a more rounded individual.

Ironically, when Jack got back to Ohio he broke ground on that other Muirfield, Muirfield Village, after Put Pierman convinced John Walton Wolfe, one of the richest men in Columbus and the owner of the Ohio Company securities firm, to go into partnership with them. Essentially, the Ohio Company underwrote Muirfield Village in exchange for a third of the stock.

Nicklaus turned thirty-two in 1972 and could not remain the world's greatest golfer forever. Sportswriters cast about for the New Nicklaus. For years, almost any American player who rose to the top was seized upon as a successor to the Golden Bear and, aside from Trevino, few seemed better suited than Tom Weiskopf. "I was the world's best player for one year—1973. No one had a better record," says Weiskopf, a giant of a man at six feet three inches, with a fine swing. "I won five out of eight events that I played in and finished no worse than sixth in the other three. . . . [It] was wonderful. It was exciting. It was easy." For a while, Weiskopf seemed invincible. But he did not have Nicklaus's mental strength—neither his confidence nor his ability to focus. The two men were close, but sometimes Weiskopf caught a look in Jack's eye that told him the Golden Bear doubted he had what it took to endure as a champion. And he was right. "I can honestly say I did not have the motivation or the desire or the determination to become the greatest player that ever lived. Jack Nicklaus did that." To cope with the pressure of life on tour, Weiskopf comforted himself by drinking, not with the bonhomie of Doug Sanders or even Arnold Palmer, who also liked a drink. Weiskopf drank alone, not all the time, but too much and too often, until it was a problem. "That was my escape at night, and it doesn't do your nervous system any good. Nobody is stronger than the bottle." There were times when he competed with a hangover. "I won tournaments with hangovers," he claims, though he won't specify which. The pressure and the booze ate away at Weiskopf quicker than he or anybody else might have thought, and soon the comer of 1973 was nowhere at all.

It was at this time that another Nicklaus friend stepped forward to take a leading role in the game. Deane Beman had known Jack since they were amateurs. He'd taught Jack about yardages and played with him as a professional. Beman enjoyed some success on tour himself, but he was never a household name like his friend. He was, however, a very intelligent and capable fellow. When Joe Dey decided to retire as commissioner of the PGA Tour, he wanted Beman as his replacement. Dey's choice was backed by J. Paul Austin, chairman of the PGA Tour's executive committee, who was also chairman of Coca-Cola and a prominent member of the Augusta National, showing how close-knit the governance of the game was.

When he took over in March 1974, Beman found the tour in poor health. Total prize money for the year was $7.4 million;* there was no senior tour and no second-string tour as there is now. Events were run by volunteers in an uncoordinated way and few tournaments were televised. Dwarfed by football, basketball, and baseball, golf was a minor sport in America, probably no more important than bowling, and the prospects were not auspicious. Networks were wary of investing in golf, not least because it was very expensive to cover. In the mid-1970s, it cost about $40,000 to film and broadcast a football game; by comparison a golf tournament could cost $300,000. Faced with so many problems and with little revenue, Beman initiated a series of changes that over fifteen years or so transformed the tour.

Discovering that board meetings were bogged down with discussion about the grade of greens and so forth, the first thing Beman did was to appoint a full-time golf course superintendent and two agronomists. "So we would not be spending policy time with a lot of discussions that didn't have a lot to do with how to improve the business." He appointed another staff member to compile a standard operation manual on how tournaments should be run. It became clear that tournaments could not operate efficiently without full-time tournament managers, and gradually that began to happen, with the managers liaising closely with the PGA Tour headquarters. As standards improved, Beman turned to the key issue of television and sponsorship. To offset the cost to the networks of covering golf, he had the idea of marrying tournaments with corporate sponsors so that a company name became part of the tournament name. In exchange, the sponsor would agree in advance

---

*In 2003 the PGA Tour was aiming toward a $7 million purse as the standard for *each* event.

to buy 50 percent of advertising time from whatever TV station carried the broadcast. With events packaged in this way, networks' production fees were covered. "Golf turned around from being a risk-to-buy to a guaranteed profit-to-buy."

Beman was making much progress, but one issue he did not address so quickly was the remaining vestiges of racism in the professional game. The PGA Tour still patronized golf clubs that had discriminatory membership policies, and tour members who happened to be black were still not receiving invitations to the Masters. Granted, the Masters was not a PGA Tour event, but to all intents and purposes it was part of the tour calendar. The field at Augusta was made up of players who qualified in a variety of ways, including past winners of major championships, the reigning U.S. Amateur champion, the four best professional players who had not otherwise qualified, and players nominated by a ballot of past Masters champions. Throughout the 1960s, a single win on tour was not enough to earn an invitation, and so, despite winning two full-fledged PGA Tour events—the 1967 Greater Hartford Open and the 1969 Los Angeles Open—Charlie Sifford, for one, was never invited. His only hope was to be voted in by his fellow players. Former champion Art Wall Jr. cast his vote for Sifford in 1969, but others voted for Bob Murphy, and it was Murphy who competed. What irritated Sifford and people such as Porter Pernell at the UGA was that the Augusta National seemed to ignore good black American players in favor of overseas golfers who were arguably less accomplished. The club would say it wanted the tournament to have an international flavor, which is why it was more open to overseas players. After all, African Americans were first and foremost American. Should the club have treated them like foreigners? "If it's necessary [to] get them involved," argues Pernell. "All we wanted was opportunity. That was the old thing of Martin Luther King: we're not asking you to give us anything but opportunity."

Things were changing slowly, however, even in Augusta. Bobby Jones died in 1971, having spent his last years confined to a wheelchair,

and Clifford Roberts was in failing health. Although Roberts had supposedly said that while he was alive blacks would only ever appear at
the Masters as caddies, he was still in charge when the club decided in
1972 that any winner of a PGA Tour event or cosponsored event in the
year preceding the Masters would receive an automatic invitation. As
David Owen points out in *The Making of the Masters,* Roberts must
have known that this change increased the chance of a black golfer
qualifying. Indeed, it was only a matter of time. On the other hand,
Roberts was also aware of concern in Washington, D.C., that a black
man had not broken the color bar at the Masters so long after the rest
of sport had integrated.* By subtly altering its rules, the club was opening the door to the possibility of a black competitor without being
forced into inviting any one individual, such as Sifford, who had become a thorn in its side. And it should be remembered that this qualification rule was changed a quarter of a century after Jackie Robinson
broke the color bar in Major League Baseball. The Augusta National
had not rushed into anything.

Reform was too late for Sifford, who turned fifty in 1972. But another African American reached his peak at the right time. Born in
Texas in 1934, Lee Elder was orphaned at a young age and raised by
relatives. He dropped out of school to work as a caddie at Tenison Park
Golf Club in Dallas, making extra money hustling games in partnership
with the charismatic Alvin C. Thomas, known as Titanic Thompson.
Elder and Thomas bet hapless victims, who didn't know how good they
were, on the outcome of a game, or made money by giving themselves a
bizarre handicap. (Elder would play on his knees, and still win.) Like
Sifford, Elder became a star on the black circuit, winning a string of
UGA National Open titles, and by 1967 he had saved enough to go out
on the PGA Tour. In April 1974 he won his first tour event, the Mon-
santo Open in Pensacola, Florida, and as a result of the recent change in

---

*In 1973 members of the U.S. House of Representatives would petition Roberts about the fact
that no black player had competed in the tournament.

the Masters qualifying system, he received an invitation to compete in the following year's invitational in Augusta. It happened so easily, as if there had never been a race problem at all. Even though Elder missed the cut at Augusta in 1975 (Nicklaus won for the fifth time), his presence in the tournament was a landmark event in the history of American golf. And with storybook symmetry, it happened the year that Tiger Woods—the first player of color to win the Masters—was born.

6

THAT'S INCREDIBLE!

Truth and fiction have become mixed up in the story of Tiger Woods's early life, especially with regard to his father. The ending of Earl Woods's first marriage to Barbara Ann Hart, and the circumstances of how Earl met and married his second wife, Tiger's mother, are particularly murky, and the true story does not reflect well upon Earl.

After joining the army and marrying his first wife, Earl was posted to West Germany and then back to the United States, training as an information officer. He and Ann had three children along the way: Earl Dennison Jr., known as Denny, who was born in 1955; Kevin Dale, born in 1957; and Royce Renee, born in 1958. In July 1961 Earl was posted to Korea; he stayed there for six months before being diverted to Vietnam, where the United States was being drawn into war. When he returned to the States, he volunteered for the 6th Special Forces Group, commonly known as the Green Berets, and was stationed at Fort Bragg, North Carolina, where Earl and Ann celebrated their tenth wedding anniversary. Promoted through the ranks, Earl was then sent back to the Far East. Ann wanted to go with him, but Earl said it was an "unaccompanied tour," so she took the children to San Jose, California, where she had family, and waited for him to return.

On July 8, 1966, Earl traveled to Bangkok, Thailand, where he assumed duties as a special services officer, meaning he was in charge of recreation for U.S. servicemen. One of his calls took him and a junior officer, who happened to be white, to a Bangkok office. The receptionist there was a young woman named Kultida Punswad, known as Tida (pronounced Teeda). Born in 1944 to a family that owned a tin mine, Tida's racial background was almost as complex as Earl's. She was part Thai and part Chinese, with Caucasian ancestors. On meeting the officers, Tida assumed Earl was junior to the white American. When she realized her mistake and apologized, Earl asked her on a date, arranging to meet at nine o'clock. When Tida did not show up that evening, Earl thought she had stood him up. In fact, she had assumed the meeting was for nine the next morning and, when they eventually did meet, she brought a chaperone. Earl has told this engaging story repeatedly as part of the background to Tiger's life. However, Earl neglects to say that he was still married to Ann when he met Tida (a woman twelve years his junior, by the way). And when asked if he told Tida that he was married, with three children waiting for him at home, he snaps, "That's my business." His first wife sees why he is so sensitive. "I think he told her the marriage was over," says Ann, who was waiting for Earl in California, believing their marriage was a happy one. "He had to tell her something to lead her into that."

When Earl returned to the United States in August 1967, he was stationed at Fort Totten in New York. Ann noticed he was quieter and moodier than before. She attributed this behavior to the work he was doing, only later thinking it was the way people typically behave when they are having an affair. Earl was teaching psychological warfare to ROTC students—brainwashing, Ann calls it—and she believes he tried some of the techniques on her. Earl seemed to pick at everything she said and did, a barrage of criticism that made life increasingly miserable. One evening in May 1968, Earl invited a lawyer-friend to the house. When they were all sitting down together, the lawyer produced a document that he read aloud to Earl and Ann, presenting it as a "separation agreement." The friend had put this document together for Earl as a favor because, as Earl later conceded, he did not have the money to hire a regular divorce lawyer. When Ann asked Earl if this was what he really wanted, he replied that it was, and she had little choice but to agree to part. As Ann walked back to their bedroom, very upset, she heard the clink of glasses in the room behind and her husband exclaiming to his friend: "We did it! We did it!" Feeling pressured into agreeing to what Earl wanted, Ann signed the separation papers on May 29, 1968. Earl then took her and their children—ages nine to twelve—to San Jose, where he left them, though he would continue to provide for their upkeep and maintain contact.

In August 1969, Ann went into a hospital in California for a hysterectomy, which was paid for by the army, because she was still a serviceman's wife. She was recuperating when Earl visited to inform her that he had just returned from Mexico where he had used the separation agreement to help him obtain what he called a "Mexican divorce." This had been granted by the Mexican authorities in the border town of Juárez on August 23, without Ann knowing about it, let alone being represented legally. An ex parte (or one-sided) foreign divorce was of dubious value in the United States. Most states tend not to recognize such decrees. Indeed, the U.S. consulate in Juárez had warned Earl in writing when he had the document witnessed that it could not vouch for the "validity [or] acceptability" of the divorce in any part of the United States. In order to have her marriage dissolved to her satisfaction, Ann felt obliged to file a complaint for divorce in the Superior Court of California, which she did in San Jose on August 25, 1969 (citing mental cruelty). Experts in matrimonial law say this was a sensible action on Ann's part as California is one of the states that, by and large, does not recognize ex parte foreign divorces. Rather, such decrees are looked at on a case-by-case basis. If Ann wanted to be confident that her marriage to Earl was dissolved as far as California and most other states were concerned, and certain that her status could not be challenged in the future (if she wanted to remarry, for example), she would be well advised to go through a U.S. court. This she did, and it would be more than two and a half years before the marriage was dissolved by the Superior Court of California.

Despite publishing a memoir, and giving many interviews over the years, Earl has always skated around the details of how and when his first marriage ended and his second marriage began, perhaps because the facts reveal a tangled and unhappy story. Earl married his Thai girlfriend, Tida, in Brooklyn, New York, on or around July 11, 1969. New York marriage records are not publicly available, but in an interview with the author Earl agreed that this date—gleaned from other personal documents—"sounds about right." When it was pointed out to him that this predated his Mexican divorce, he changed his story. "No," he said. "I did not marry [Tida] until after the divorce." When pressed, Earl failed to give me an exact date for his marriage to Tida, excusing himself by saying, "I don't know anniversaries," and Tida declined my requests for an interview. Earl does not dispute the fact that he and Tida married in 1969, however. Because New York is one of the states that did not tend to recognize ex parte foreign divorces at this time, legal experts say this may have been an illegitimate marriage in New York as well as in California where Ann Woods did not *begin* divorce proceedings against Earl until late that summer. The interlocutory judgment was not entered in the Superior Court of California until two and a half years later, on February 28, 1972. As stated in the official paperwork: "the parties are still married and . . . neither party may remarry until a final judgment of dissolution is entered." The final judgment was granted on March 2, 1972, restoring Earl and Ann only at this time to the "status of unmarried persons" in California (and therefore most of the rest of the country). All of this information is public record and Earl was fully aware of the case at the time. He engaged a lawyer to represent him in court, and the lawyer brought Earl's Mexican divorce decree before the court. Yet the case went ahead and Earl did not contest the action. Ann still considered herself to be Mrs. Woods in the meantime. She continued to receive benefits due an army spouse and did not presume to remarry until after the case was finished. Unlike Earl. "He got married and it was bigamous, I guess," says Ann. "Because he was still married to me until 1972." She actually accused Earl of bigamy in a written declaration filed with the Superior Court in April 1995, at which time she was seeking a share in his army pension (which was denied by the court). Ann did not press the point and no legal action resulted—her marriage to Earl had by this stage been dissolved by the California court, of course, and she re-married in 1981—but she believes firmly that, in 1969, Earl remarried improperly, morally speaking and as far as her position was concerned in California (legal experts agree that she has an argument on that score, and that Earl's New York marriage to Tida may have been found to be invalid had it been challenged in court). Earl insists he did every-thing legitimately and is blithely unconcerned that between 1969 and 1972 he was married to Tida Woods in New York while still married to Ann Woods in California. "I don't know anything about California. I didn't live in California," he says, adding: "I do not consider myself a bigamist."

The facts of this strange affair certainly show Earl's previous ac-counts of how he met and married Tida to be misleading, to say the least. In his memoir, *Training a Tiger,* he wrote that when he met Tida, "I had three children from an earlier marriage and was not eager to em-bark on a new relationship. . . ." This makes him seem most consider-ate. Yet when he wrote "earlier marriage," he surely meant he was *already* married (and would continue to be so for years as far as the California case was concerned). Like his tale of being orphaned at thir-teen, and his assertion that he broke the color bar in the Big Seven, the story Earl has disseminated regarding his marriage to Tiger's mother is an improvement on the truth.

In the summer of 1970 Earl returned to Vietnam, where war was dragging on under Richard Nixon's presidency,* and took up duties as assistant to Colonel Vuong Dang Phong, a South Vietnamese officer who was leading his forces in Binh Thuan province against the invading Communists. For twelve months Woods and Phong saw active service throughout the country and were involved in many dangerous situations. Earl was so impressed with his friend's fearless character that he came to call him by the nickname Tiger. "Tiger handled the military, and I was his adviser," he explains. "Whenever there was [enemy] contact or anything like that we jumped in. We went in. Got a helicopter and landed there." Several times, enemy fire pierced the floor of their chopper. On one occasion Earl and Phong were in a ditch, directing air support, when Phong shouted to get down. A sniper had fired two shots at Earl, the first to the right of him, the second to his left, "bracketing" the target before firing the third, deadly bullet. Saved from the sniper, Earl fell asleep in the ditch. When he awoke, Tiger hissed: "Stay still."

"Why?"

"There's a bamboo viper about three inches from your right eye." So Earl had two brushes with death in one day and was saved both times by his comrade. As Earl says, he'd had other friends, but "none that . . . saved my life two or three times and vice versa." Experiences of this kind made for a special bond between the men.

In recognition of his service in Vietnam, Earl was awarded several decorations, including the Army Commendation Medal, the Vietnam Gallantry Cross (with Silver Star), and the Bronze Star. A couple of years later, in March 1974, he completed twenty years of service and retired as a lieutenant colonel. He and Tida then moved to Southern California, where Earl got a job with Arrowhead Products buying components for the Delta rocket satellite launcher (he would later do similar work at

---

*As the conflict continued, the president asked friends and advisers how it might be ended. He even entertained the counsel of Arnold Palmer, of all people. "Why not go for the green?" Arnie asked Nixon, turning the bomb into a metaphorical golf ball.

McDonnell Douglas); they settled in Cypress in Orange County. It was here that Tiger Woods was born, and he was shaped by where he grew up as much as Arnold Palmer had been by western Pennsylvania, or Jack Nicklaus by Ohio, so it is worth knowing something about the place.

Until 1956 Cypress was farmland with a rural population of less than two thousand. Then the strawberry fields and dairy pastures were bulldozed into lots, and a bedroom community of thirty-eight thousand people was created; it became an almost indistinguishable subdivision of the suburban sprawl south of Greater Los Angeles. L.A. was only a short drive away, but there was none of the glamour and excitement of metropolitan life in Cypress. The city and its environs are bland, and that is how residents like it. Orange County is a relatively safe place in which to live, with cheaper property and less traffic congestion than one finds in the metropolis. The area also has its attractions: Disneyland, the original theme park, is here, and there is easy access to beaches and a plethora of golf courses. In fact, Earl chose the house he and Tida bought—a three-bedroom, timber-frame bungalow on a quiet side street—because it was five minutes from the Navy Golf Course, a military facility within Seal Beach U.S. Naval Weapons Station. Earl had taken up golf during his last months in the service and looked forward to many happy hours playing the Navy Course as a veteran.

Though Cypress is now a mixed community, Earl and Tida were the only nonwhites on their street when they moved in, and Earl says this caused them to be the victims of racism. Kids threw windfall limes at the home of the "black"* family and shot at the windows with an air gun. But the Woodses were not frightened away. Their only child, Eldrick Tont Woods, was born at the Memorial Hospital Medical Center in Long Beach at 10:50 P.M. on December 30, 1975. On the birth certificate, Earl gave his occupation grandiosely as "buyer [of] space ship

---

*Earl Woods explains: "My wife is Thai and when she came to the United States I told her, 'Look, forget being Thai, because in the United States there are only two colors: white and nonwhite. Everybody else is lumped in the same boat.' "

products." The name Eldrick was an invention of Tida's, using letters from her and Earl's first names. Tont is a Thai name, also chosen by Tida. "It was her way of identifying and transferring the Thai heritage to her son," explains Earl. Dad provided a nickname. It was a brilliant choice, one of the cleverest things Earl ever did: he chose a highly un-usual moniker that distinguished his son from the herd and would later be a boon to sportswriters and commentators, appealing to their love of puns. His son would be known as Tiger. Tiger Woods, the most famous golfer in the world, forever prowling, until he showed his claws and pounced, causing golf clubs to improve their tiger traps, and so on. . . . Earl named the boy after the friend he had left behind in Vietnam, whom he hoped to meet again one day. Earl had tried to locate Phong without success, but figured his former comrade might find *him* via his son. "[I] thought that some day, somewhere, Phong would see the name of Tiger and Woods together and make the connection." This was a strange idea, assuming as it did that Tiger would become a person of renown throughout the world. It was also sadly misplaced because, un-known to Earl, Phong had died in a Vietnamese concentration camp within a year of Tiger's birth.

At the relatively mature age of forty-three, Earl was starting over as a father, and he was determined to make up for the mistakes of the past. Earl says that he had not spent as much time with his first three children as he knew he should have, because of the peripatetic nature of army life, and his relationship with them suffered because of that. Of course, he had also left his first family when his children were entering their formative years—to run off with a woman ten years younger than their mother—which surely caused more damage. This time, Earl had a reg-ular job, with normal hours, and was therefore able to be a much more conscientious parent. Seizing that opportunity, he doted on Tiger, who he decided was a special child, and went out of his way to introduce his boy to some of the pastimes he enjoyed so that they would have an even stronger bond. For example, Earl loved jazz, so jazz was playing when Tida brought the baby home from the hospital. "I established my personal imprint on his mind, at least about [music]." Apart from the egotism of this remark, it is striking that in talking about Tiger, Earl invariably describes a relationship between father and son, not father, mother, and son. Earl is unapologetic about that, saying he cannot speak from a mother's perspective. However, Earl, a complicated man, also maintains that Tida's role was *more* important than his own, "because her job was to raise Tiger. My job was to make a living. Typical black family. Wife stays home. You go out and get all the hassle. Tiger was taught a lot of things by her that I don't even know about. These are mother-things, and I'm not a mother, so I would not be able to teach him those things, because I don't know. Just like she wouldn't be able to teach him the things of the father, because she doesn't know. We all have our jobs, and we have our roles, and no one is more important than the other. And the idea is that the most important thing is the child." This was great for Tiger, who was always the center of attention. It proved less healthy for the marriage.

Just as Tiger was exposed to jazz at a very early age, he was also introduced to his father's newly discovered passion for golf. Earl had a practice net in his garage, and he beat balls off a scrap of carpet to hone his swing. As he did so, Tiger sat in a high chair to one side, watching him. The baby must have been mesmerized—one might say brainwashed—seeing that club brought back and then swung through the ball again and again. Earl says that when Tiger was ten months old he took him out of the high chair and let him play with a small club and golf balls, which is when a eureka moment apparently occurred. "He picked up a putter, put a ball down, waggled, and hit a ball into the net. First time." Earl almost jumped out of his skin. "I was screaming to my wife, Kultida, 'Honey, get out here! We have a genius on our hands.'" When Tida stepped into the garage, Tiger was apparently getting ready to go again. Earl's instinct that his son was exceptional seemed to be confirmed a week later when Tiger switched from a left-handed grip to a right-handed grip, like his dad's. "That's when I knew I had something special," says Earl, who claims he knew then that his son would be "an international, world-famous golfer." Moreover, Earl believes he had been entrusted by God Himself to raise a child of destiny. It was humbling and exalting. "I looked at it as an opportunity that was given to me, a trust," he says, with almost religious intensity. "And many times I've said, 'Why me? Why me? What did I do?'" It is tempting to mock this kind of passion, and it is natural to question how Earl could possibly have known that a toddler had the potential to be a world-class sports figure. Perhaps the truth is that Earl set out to make such a thing come true, in the manipulative way parents have pushed children to succeed in show business. Earl denies this vehemently, but much of the evidence points this way. One is also reminded of how Earl himself was raised in Kansas, with his father and then Hattie Belle telling him he was special and talented, as if by saying such a thing, it would become true. It hadn't in his case—interesting man though he is, Earl has no outstanding talent—but maybe it would come true for this second-chance son, this kid whom Earl was giving extra attention to in order to make up for his past mistakes.

By the time he was two years old, Tiger was accompanying Earl to the nearby Navy Course, an eccentric-looking golf course ornamented with military memorabilia, including a surface-to-air missile by the putting green and a scale model of the USS *Los Angeles* floating in a pond at the 9th. The child's progress was a source of amazement to all who saw it, including the course superintendent Paul Moreno, who remembers the boy wielding a putter taller than himself. At age three, Tiger supposedly shot 48 on the back 9, apparently confirming that he was something special. However, not all was well between the Woods family and the people who ran the Navy Course.

As Earl sees it, the men who operated the facility were mostly former navy officers who were used to dealing with subordinate African American sailors. "Then I show up at the navy base, and I turn out to be a low-handicap golfer—I eventually got my handicap down to a 1 after three years—and, lo and behold, they couldn't handle that," he says. "I remember in the bar they used to call me Sergeant Brown. That's

OK, I don't mind that. But one night the bartender got pissed off about it and he stopped everybody, and he said, 'I want to introduce you to Lieutenant Colonel Earl Woods, ex–Green Beret, served two tours in Vietnam.' And I outranked them all. So they had a long way to go to accept me, see. They had no history to help them. And that's why I feel sorry for them. And then on top of that along came Tiger and that's like really kicking them in the ass, and they couldn't handle that either. So they tried to prevent Tiger playing on the golf course."

There was in fact a rule forbidding children under the age of ten from playing. Earl was welcome to practice with Tiger on the putting green, and the people who ran the course say they turned a blind eye when the kid played a couple of holes now and again. But there was a limit. "Before the age of ten he was playing 2 or 3 holes," says Moreno. "But he couldn't play the entire 18 holes. . . . There was a regulation for everybody." Since it was a military facility, rules were perhaps more rigidly enforced than at a regular club. One would have thought Earl would understand that. But he took the view that he and Tiger had been slighted, possibly for racial reasons, and so he removed Tiger from the course. "It was never racial," responds Moreno. "As far as I'm concerned, [Tiger] was very well liked. Very nice kid. Very polite. [I] can't say enough about him. . . . Tiger was treated pretty well here [and] this was Earl's doing, removing him from the facility for a short period."

Tida took the boy to see Rudy Duran, a golf professional at Heartwell Golf Park in Long Beach. Duran, an intense young man who had played the PGA Tour, was in his shop when Tida walked in, lifted her son onto the counter, and asked Rudy if he would be his teacher. "Well, I don't teach four-year-olds," replied the professional. But he was willing to watch Tiger demonstrate what he could do. Tiger marched over to the range with alacrity. Then Duran watched in astonishment as Tiger took out a little 2½-wood and smacked three or four perfect little shots—with a tiny bit of draw—seventy yards in the air. "This is unbelievable!" declared Duran, who had never seen such a thing. Next, Duran watched Tiger working with his cut-down 7-iron.

"He had a little bit of a stutter and he used to say, 'I'm going to p-p-pop it up,' and he'd pop [the ball up]. He could change his swing so he could hit the ball high on purpose, and he could hit the ball low, and normal. He could actually hit [on] three different planes [with] his little 7-iron the very first day I saw him, when he was just a shade over four years old." In subsequent years, as Tiger's extraordinary career inspired children to emulate his success, Duran met many four-year-old Tiger wanna-bes. "Most of them can't even hit it at all. Let alone hit it perfect," he says. "At four, he was like a shrunken 5-handicapper."

So Duran started working with the boy. In light of Tiger's age, there was no point using technical words or complex ideas during lessons (although bright, Tiger wasn't as intellectually advanced as his game). Instead, Duran talked to Tiger in terms of the way the ball moved, as in: "Can you make the ball curve like *this*?" Invariably, the prodigy was able to do what was described. Aside from that, Duran devised games such as who could hit the ball the highest or lowest, or make it stop quickest. "All practice sessions basically involved some sort of game." Earl joined in on weekends, picking up tips for his own game and, importantly, learning about the world of golf. "I was the family golf pro and I brought most of the golf information to the Woods family," adds Duran, who was not paid for the work he did with Tiger. He considered it a reward in itself, believing, as did so many people who came into contact with the boy, that he was working with a genius, comparable to a figure such as Einstein or Michelangelo.

Tiger's progress was rapid. "By the time he was five years old, [and] I'd been working with him [for] a year, there was no doubt in my mind that he was going to be a touring pro," says the coach. "And I don't think there was any doubt in Earl's mind." It was not that Tiger was a particularly advanced child physically. In fact, he was small and wore spectacles, which lent him a delicate appearance. His outstanding ability was to hit his best shot the first time, as every pro needs to do. Tiger also had a great capacity for hard work. Like his father, he was self-disciplined and stubborn. As an only child, he also benefited from the undivided love of his parents, and no doubt he wanted to do well to please them. All of these factors, combined with aptitude, made him unusually good at the game.

Tiger came to the attention of the media at a very early age, or, to be more precise, his parents brought him to the attention of the media. It started when he was two. Tida telephoned local TV sportscaster Jim Hill inviting him to watch Tiger play at the Navy Course. The kid was a natural on TV, telling Hill in his tiny voice, with an endearingly childish speech impediment, that he was good at golf because of "pwactice." It was "pwactice" that kept him out of sand twaps.

"How much do you practice?"

"About a whole bunch."

And what was the secret to good golf?

"Keep your head still and fowwow thwoo."

Tiger graduated to syndicated television shows. His first appearance was on the *Mike Douglas Show,* a ninety-minute afternoon chat and variety program filmed in L.A. Hosted by talk show star Mike Douglas, it featured show-business guests and occasional sports figures. On October 6, 1978, Douglas was joined by Bob Hope and James Stewart. The three stepped across to an artificial putting green where Douglas introduced the next guests. "Right now, I'd like you to meet Tiger Woods and his father, Earl Woods." Tiger trotted onto the AstroTurf, toting a little golf bag his mother had made, and then drove a ball into the back of the studio. Douglas suggested a putting contest with Hope. The comedian sidled up to Tiger and asked slyly, "You got any money?" The audience laughed, and laughed again when the boy picked up his ball and moved it closer to the hole.

A couple of years later Tiger appeared on the ABC show *That's Incredible!,* cohosted by former NFL quarterback Fran Tarkenton; it featured ordinary people doing extraordinary things—and, often, extraordinarily stupid stunts, such as the unfortunate fellow who burned himself running through a tunnel of fire. Tiger performed his shtick and

piped up to Tarkenton: "When I get big I'm going to beat Jack Nicklaus and Tom Watson." You had to smile at such a little character.

Tiger gave countless interviews over the next few years, appearing
on major television shows, including the *Today* show and *Good Morning America*. Yet he did not particularly enjoy being interviewed, especially when reporters came down to the range where he was working
with Rudy Duran. Apart from the fact that he was a shy child, interviews interrupted his golf time, which was also his fun time. "So Tiger
never really liked it," says Duran. "Then he actually learned it's part of
the business. [His parents] were training him to be a touring pro and
deal with the media." So he resigned himself to it, enduring reporters'
questions, very much as he does to this day. Still, Duran insists that Earl
and Tida were not putting undue pressure on Tiger. "Golf was not who
he was; it was just something he did, and his parents had an environment where he wasn't measured on the results." Other people who
came into contact with the family at this stage, including Tiger's teachers at elementary school, took a different view.

In the fall of 1981 Tiger was enrolled in kindergarten at Cerritos Elementary, across the street from his home. One of the foundation
stones of the Tiger Woods story, as widely reported, is that on his first
day at school he was tied to a tree by white boys who taunted him with
racial epithets and threw stones at him. Like the stories of Earl's youth,
this incident casts Tiger in the sympathetic position of somebody who
was unfairly treated at the start of his life, thus making his eventual success more special. In fact, like some tales of Earl's early life, this story
of abuse on Tiger's first day of school seems to be a myth. Tiger's
kindergarten teacher, the person in charge that day, was Maureen
Decker. "It's untrue. Absolutely untrue," she states categorically.
"None of it ever happened." Indeed, the first she heard of the story of
Tiger's being tied up and abused was in 1997 when Tiger spoke about
it in a TV interview with Barbara Walters. If a serious incident occurred
that for some reason Decker did not know about, presumably it would

have come to the attention of the school principal. But former principal Donald Hill has no memory of any such incident involving Tiger. "I have never heard of that story [and] something that was that serious, I would question why didn't the father come to me and complain? . . . It certainly didn't come to my office." And it is not a case of simply not remembering. In fact, Hill remembers Tiger very well, because he is a golf fan and, when Tiger was in the first grade, Hill and his son played a match with Tida and Tiger. "And quite honestly he beat me!"

Staff at the elementary school remember Tiger as an unusually intense child whose parents had a conviction that his life would turn out a certain way. "I can remember telling his dad that there was more to life than golf," says Cerritos teacher Linda Behrens. "He was not too happy about it. . . . I told him [that Tiger] has to have other interests, that he needs to have friends his own age, so he would be a well-rounded person." Maureen Decker believes golf got in the way of a normal childhood. "I think he wanted to be involved in more than golf," she says, noting that Tida would take her son to golf practice after school when the other kids were getting together for team games. "So he didn't have the opportunity to have the other sport activities that the other children did. But look where he got, and all he has got!" Furthermore, Decker believes that the often-repeated first-day-at-school story might have been invented to add to the Tiger mythology. Having watched some of Tiger's TV interviews, she suspects he does not actually remember what happened but is telling a story he has learned. "Maybe his dad just wanted more publicity."

Like several other questionable aspects of the Woods story, the truth is less dramatic than reality, and race is involved. The difficulties of his early life notwithstanding, and accepting the fact that race relations is a major problem in American society, Earl seems obsessed with race. And journalists have been happy to regurgitate his lively stories, about himself and about Tiger, without checking the facts. Part of the tone of the first-day-at-school story, for instance, is that Tiger was unusual at

Cerritos because he was a person of color. That was why he was picked on, apparently. Yet there were children of Asian and Hispanic origin in Tiger's class, kids as dark-skinned as he was (he never looked classically African American), and the neighborhood itself was increasingly diverse. So why pick on Tiger? If there were ever any problems (and the staff denies this), maybe it was because he seemed different for other reasons, this geeky kid with glasses, a weird name, and a speech impediment, this boy whose mother took him to golf—of all things—every afternoon.

In preparation for tournaments, Earl began to toughen his son mentally around the age of six. Tiger was given audiotapes with subliminal messages such as "My Will Moves Mountains!" To get the boy used to distractions, Earl would drop the golf bag when Tiger was about to swing. Tiger was forbidden from saying anything when his father was playing tricks like this, though there was a release word he could use if and when Earl became too vexing. Whether any of this helped Tiger is debatable. He certainly became a precociously mature junior golfer, a serious-minded, highly focused kid. But so had Jack Nicklaus, with a lot less nonsense from Jack Grout. Like Nicklaus, Tiger established himself early on as an outstanding competitor in junior golf championships, winning the Optimist International Junior World in the under-ten category when he was only eight. He did so with a remarkable comeback on the final 9. "Winning that first tournament, the way I won it, is still my biggest thrill in golf," he said in 1990, and he would win the title again at ages nine, twelve, and thirteen.

When Tiger was ten, Earl took him back to the Navy Golf Course to play almost every day for the next seven years. "Rain or shine, they were out here just about from daylight until dark," says Paul Moreno, who was happy to see the boy back now that he was old enough. "They were having fun, but also he was very dedicated to his game. [It was] also like work. A little of both: work and fun. You can see it in his face. He enjoys it every time he hits that little white ball." Tiger's game

was formed by the Navy Course, just as Arnold Palmer's was by Latrobe and Nicklaus's by Scioto. The Navy Course was a challenging
long course, affected by ocean breezes that tended to dry the greens in
the afternoon, when it could play 7 or 8 strokes differently than in the
morning. It was a good training ground, and Tiger put in abundant
practice. One day, the finance manager, Walter Olsen, found the boy in
the middle of the 9-hole Cruiser Course after having hit about four
hundred balls in the fairway. "Tiger!" he exclaimed. "You've got to
pick this up."

When Rudy Duran left to run a club in central California, in
the spring of 1986 when Tiger was ten, Earl engaged John Anselmo as
a replacement coach. A native of Los Angeles, Anselmo was a small,
white-haired sexagenarian who had played the tour in the 1940s; he
turned to coaching after being hit in the left eye by a ball, which im-
paired his vision. "[Earl] wanted to know my psychology, or whatever
you want to call it, my method of teaching, which is very simple. You
don't do a lot of things. You just do things natural. And you grow with
that natural sense," says Anselmo, recalling his early dealings with the
family. "You've got to have a *feel*-sense. See, Tiger has tremendous feel.
That's why he can do all the shots he does. If you ask him, 'What do
you do?' He says, 'I don't know, I just feel it.' So he feels what he is going to do, and that's what golf is all about." Anselmo was so impressed
with what he saw that he declined payment, taking the same view as
Duran: to be part of this boy's education was enough.

They worked together at Meadowlark Golf Course at Huntington
Beach, a thirty-minute drive from Tiger's home. As he got to know the
boy, Anselmo discovered that Tiger's golfing hero was Jack Nicklaus.
Hitherto, Tiger had not been much interested in tour golfers of the past,
many of whom must have seemed like old men. For instance, when Duran spoke about Arnold Palmer, it became apparent that Tiger had never
heard of the King. Yet he had a deep interest in the Golden Bear and for
good reason. At an age when most professional golfers are in decline,
Nicklaus was on top of the world again.

At the age of thirty-five, and again at forty, Nicklaus had won the PGA Championship for the fourth and fifth times, respectively (thus equaling Walter Hagen's record of five PGA crowns). In 1977 Nicklaus battled wonderfully against the latest comer, stocky, red-haired Tom Watson of Kansas, for the Open Championship at Turnberry. For many, the final was the best man-to-man finish in the history of the modern majors. "To put it in a nutshell, I beat the best player in the game playing about the best I'd ever played, and that's the pinnacle," says Watson, who established himself as one of the great golfers of modern times by winning eight majors between 1975 and 1983, including a remarkable five Open Championships. "Being from the United States, I value [the U.S. Open] higher than any win, because it's my national open. But winning the British Open is like winning the Open against the world," he says. "It's like the Olympic championship of golf." For a time, Watson seemed to have an exclusive arrangement with the R&A, but in 1978, when the Open returned to St. Andrews, it was Nicklaus who won again, becoming the first player to win all four major titles at least three times. At this stage in his career, there was little doubt that Nicklaus was the best golfer ever. But he wasn't done. As he moved into his forties, Nicklaus showed he still had much to offer, winning the 1980 U.S. Open at Baltusrol (as well as that year's PGA Championship) and fighting to the last at the 1982 U.S. Open at Pebble Beach, against Watson and Bruce Devlin, a match that Watson ultimately won with the help of a wondrous chip-in at the 17th.

Behind the scenes, Nicklaus and Watson were involved in an equally dramatic showdown of a different kind, this time with PGA Tour Commissioner Deane Beman. "They wanted to fire me," says Beman, who had worked strenuously to transform the tour since taking over from Joe Dey in 1974. Unfortunately, many of his innovations did not sit well with his leading players. Among other concerns, players did not approve of the way he had married corporate sponsors with long-established tournaments so that company names—Michelob, Honda, and so

forth—became part of a tournament title. This offended the players' aesthetic sensibilities. More to the point, it cut across personal interest, because sponsors that had previously backed individuals now had the
option of spending their promotional money with the PGA Tour directly. For instance, Coca-Cola dropped Tom Watson to sign a deal with
the tour, which meant that Watson lost income to his own professional
association. "That was our point," he says. "They conflicted with us."

What really upset the likes of Nicklaus and Watson was when Commissioner Beman opened the first Tournament Players Club in Sawgrass
in 1980, near the Florida beach town of Ponte Vedra, where the PGA
Tour had located its headquarters. The TPC at Sawgrass was the first of
a series of courses owned and run by the tour and designed as a kind of
golf stadium: mounds were built for people to stand on and look down
on greens and fairways, because Beman had come to realize rightly that
the public often had difficulty getting a good view at crowded tournaments. Beman also had a problem in that the premier events of the
game—notably the majors—were owned and operated by other organizations (the USGA, PGA of America, and R&A). Beman wanted the
PGA Tour to have its own facility for its own headline events, which he
helped create: the Tournament Players Championship,* first held in
1974 (Nicklaus won), and the Tour Championship, first held in 1987
(Watson was the victor).

The TPC was criticized by players and press for its unusual design.
Moreover, players who had an active interest in building golf courses did
not think the tour should be building and running clubs. They considered
that their business. "Jack Nicklaus, Arnold Palmer, Tom Watson, Ray-
mond Floyd, Hale Irwin, and maybe a dozen other players were all very
specifically opposed to the development of the PGA Tour production
facility, the Tournament Players Club, the licensing and marketing, [and]
they did everything they could to prevent that from happening," says
Beman. He is quick to agree that those players made a significant

---

* Renamed the Players Championship in 1988.

contribution to the growing popularity of golf. "But from a business standpoint of doing the hard, detailed, in-the-trenches innovation and implementation of those things necessary to bring the sport to the level where it is now, they're not responsible for that. As a matter of fact, quite the contrary. Had it been in their power, they would have prevented it."

They tried. In the summer of 1983 fourteen leading players put their names to a letter criticizing Commissioner Beman and his innovations. Essentially they wanted Beman fired. On June 9, 1983, the players had a showdown with the commissioner at Westchester Country Club during its annual tournament.* At the head of the delegation were Arnold Palmer and Jack Nicklaus, who had signed the letter. The names of another twelve players, including Watson, were included as an addendum. In essence, the players accused Beman of exceeding his authority. "In particular, we didn't agree with the Tournament Players Golf Clubs that the tour started to invest in," says Watson. "It was a direct conflict with what many of us were in the business of doing." Beman felt his responsibility was to *all* the members of the tour, not only the stars, and journeyman players were not in the business of building golf clubs. He figured if he made the tour prosperous and successful generally, everybody would benefit. "I felt strongly that if I built a golden goose, [Tom and] Jack and Arnold could get more than their fair share. But they did not see it the same way I did." The conflict was resolved when Beman pointed out that in their haste the players had made errors of fact in their letter. Jack and Arnold were embarrassed by the mistakes and withdrew. Thus Beman was saved and in fact he stayed in his job for another nine years, during which time he continued to develop the tour. However, friendships had been tested to the limit, and from his experience Beman offers this indictment of the tour superstars: "They're not interested in the PGA Tour and golf, they're interested in what's best for *them*. And that's just a fact. It's not a criticism. It's a fact."

---

*A good example of the way tournament names had been changed: the Westchester Classic became the American Express Westchester Classic and by 1983 was awkwardly named the Manufacturers Hanover Westchester Classic. Since 1990 it has been the Buick Classic.

The root of the 1983 dispute was that premier tour players had become more than golfers. Following the example of Arnold Palmer, the
stars of the tour were parlaying success in golf into rich business careers.
They were in the endorsement business and, increasingly, in the golf
course design business, which was a very lucrative business indeed. Jack
Nicklaus was in the vanguard of this movement. His first great project
was Muirfield Village, of course, which had finally been completed. As a
matter of fact, it didn't make him much money, and he didn't retain any
financial stake, other than owning a house there. Muirfield members
bought the club and land from him and his partners at cost a few years
after the development was completed. Indeed, owing to a dip in the real
estate market, Nicklaus, Put Pierman, and the other investors were lucky
to come out even. Still, the image the golfing public received was of a
player-mogul lording over his domain, and the public came to hear a lot
about Nicklaus's Muirfield Village because, starting in 1976, Nicklaus
hosted the annual Memorial Tournament there. Part of its success was
due to the quality of the course, which Nicklaus and his associates had
modeled on the Augusta National. "I liked Augusta's golf course, which
was a fair amount of room off of the tee," he explains. "I thought most
people enjoyed hitting the golf ball off the tee, enjoyed hitting it and
having fun with it, and then you take the difficulty of the golf course in
the second shot."

As he got older, Nicklaus saw himself increasingly as a golf course
architect, a second career that he took very seriously, though, frankly,
anyone can call him- or herself a golf course architect. Player-architects
spend little, if any, time at the drawing board. Typically, Nicklaus has
always employed name "architects" to realize his ideas. One former
employee, Jay Morrish, says: "[Jack] couldn't draw plans." But Nicklaus
and other players knew how to walk the property and talk subjectively
about what they wanted. And once a draftsman had made the plans, a
guy on a bulldozer had shaped the earth, and the turf had been laid—
with the player-designer coming by the site now and again, depending
on how interested he was and how much time he had to spare—there was

a gala opening to attend. This was where the celebrity played a useful role: in public relations, not in the actual design and construction. "The golf course would probably be just as good—or better—if the celebrity never showed up," says Ohio course designer Michael Hurdzan, speaking generally about player-designer courses. The whole industry of golfers designing courses is therefore questionable. But then the notion that golf course design is "architecture" is risible. There are no mandatory exams to take before a person lays out a golf course. (As Hurdzan admits, anybody can do it. All you need is a client.) A failure in golf course architecture poses no threat to life and limb, as the failure of a structure might. Golf courses are just bumpy fields for knocking a ball about. Deciding where the bunkers go and so forth is an amateur business and always has been. The revered Dr. Alister Mackenzie, who worked with Bobby Jones to create the Augusta National and designed other famous courses, was a general practitioner who took up course design as a hobby. This is fine, but few in golf course "architecture" have the modesty to admit the limited nature of their work.

In the summer of 2002 I spent an afternoon following Nicklaus around the holes at Muirfield Village Golf Club as he modified some of his design work. He was supervising the reshaping of the greens in preparation for reseeding before the 2003 Memorial. The grass had been stripped, exposing polymorphous areas of soil. Before the new grass was laid down like a carpet, there was a good deal of discussion about where the bumps should go. Half a dozen men, including a professor of agronomy from Ohio State University, stood around under a blazing sun, nodding earnestly, as Nicklaus inspected each patch of earth at great length, talking rapidly about the undulations he wanted. Nicklaus explained himself with thousands of words, a good bit of poking at the earth, general gesticulation, and, at one stage, a scribble on a piece of paper. Although there was some laughter when he offered to sign this scrawl, the work was undertaken for the most part with a seriousness that extends to all of Nicklaus's design work. In fact, he believes himself to be the only player-designer who works at golf course architecture with diligence and dedication. When I suggested to him that other players claim to pour their souls into their signature courses, including friends of his such as Gary Player, he dismissed that idea. "Gary does promotional stuff and, [OK,] a little bit more. Arnold's basically promotional. The guys that are involved, most of the rest of them, I can't imagine any of them doing much. They don't know enough," he said bluntly (and these are his friends). "Good gracious, it took me six years before I knew enough. And I'm still learning."

There have been times in Nicklaus's career when the high calling of golf course architecture has been reduced to truly childish behavior, especially with regard to the Golden Bear's rivalry with Palmer, which is as fierce in business as it was in tournament golf, maybe more so. (They manage to be friendly when they meet, though, and indeed have collaborated on a course, the King & Bear in St. Augustine, Florida.) For example, Nicklaus used Toro irrigation systems in his courses until Arnie was hired by Toro to advertise its products. One day a picture appeared of Arnie holding a bag of Toro fertilizer. "Soon as Jack saw that, it was over," laughs Jack's erstwhile designer, Jay Morrish. "He never used [Toro] during the rest of my time with him." Another story involves contractor Dave Harman, who built courses for Nicklaus until he also started doing freelance work for Palmer. "Once I kind of became Arnold's guy to build golf courses, I wasn't going to build them for Jack. There's no doubt about that."

As golf became more popular in the 1960s and '70s, there was a boom in golf course design that extended into the 1990s. In the early years of this boom, environmental regulations were not as rigorous as they later became, and this is significant because it has been increasingly argued that golf courses are detrimental to the environment. Until very recently courses have invariably been maintained with noxious pesticides, and some architects say that pesticides are still essential in order to keep courses pristine. The use of pesticides and fertilizers means pollution in the runoff, which worries environmentalists. Jay Morrish derides the most strident of these as CAVE people. "That stands for Citizens Against

Virtually Everything. And there are a lot of those people around," he says. "I would like some environmentalist to point out to me what is wrong with Pebble Beach. What does that hurt? And the sad thing is, if you were trying to do a Pebble Beach today, you'd *never* be allowed to build that golf course. Because it's on the ocean, and the pesticides would be going in the ocean. They wouldn't allow it today. And I find that sort of sad." Others might say thank goodness.

Aside from the problem of pollution, water conservation is also an issue. A golf course in a parched part of the United States, such as Arizona, covering about 110 grassed acres, can soak up half a million gallons of water a day. In the peak period of May through December, this means the use of 120 million gallons, enough to meet the domestic needs of a small town for a year.* And it comes in clean and goes out dirty. Getting that volume of water is such a problem that developers in Arizona have to pay water authorities as far away as Colorado for what they take out of the system. One might argue that this is not a sensible way to marshal natural resources. Others, like Dave Harman, insist that golf courses beautify and preserve the landscape. After heavy construction is finished, the community is left with what amounts to a wildlife sanctuary that will be maintained and protected. "It becomes a wonderful environment. I mean, would you rather have that or a shopping mall?"

Apart from golf course design and prize money on tour, the other main source of income for player-businessmen like Jack Nicklaus was from the exploitation of what the Internal Revenue Service (IRS) terms "name, likeness and image." This means endorsements—lending one's name to advertising campaigns for corporations and putting a logo on clothing and sports equipment. Again, Palmer trailblazed this business. As far as logos were concerned, he had a distinctive multicolored umbrella badge on a plethora of clothing and other items. Nicklaus had a

---

*U.S. Geological Survey figures state that domestic water usage in 1995 was 100.38 gallons of water per day per person.

logo, too, a golden bear. In its early incarnation, the bear was not quite as golden or ursine as it might have been, however. On a trip to Japan with Jay Morrish to build a course, Jack was aghast when the client pointed and asked: "Where you get the shirt with the little yellow pig?"

Income from these ventures is designated by the IRS as personal services income and taxed at a high rate. To alter the tax classification, agents such as Nicklaus's man Put Pierman tried to get their clients involved creatively in the design process. "What you do is you try to get them involved in such things as photo shoots, color consultations, design work [on] a catalog." Income would then be taxed at a lower rate. "In fact, it's horseshit," adds Pierman. "[Those] business functions are to escape the personal services categorization." Unfortunately, by being involved in this way, players were encouraged to think of themselves as businessmen, capable of complicated decisions. Few had the acumen, and this led to costly mistakes.

In the mid-1970s Pierman brought a deal to Nicklaus whereby American Express would take over management of the problematic endorsement work from Golden Bear, Inc., and the revenue from it, in exchange for an allocation of Amex shares. Pierman was working on closing the deal when Nicklaus played a round of golf with some guy who advised him against it. "I said, 'Fuck it, Jack. You'll listen to anybody. You're impossible.'" Pierman, who parted company with Nicklaus in the mid-1970s, believes that had they taken the Amex deal, there would have been so much money it would be hard to spend it all. "It was the dumbest thing we ever did. . . . But that was the start [of] Jack wanting to 'own my own conglomerate.' That did nothing but get his ass in trouble."

After Pierman left Golden Bear, Inc., Nicklaus built up the company until he was employing hundreds of people, many of whom worked in course design. "Give me your money! Show me your money! I'd love to be your employee, Mr. Nicklaus, Mr. Palmer, etc., etc. I'll kiss your ass. I'll nod every time you want me to," ridicules Pierman, who believes Nicklaus could have run his operation with a dozen staff. Golden Bear,

Inc., also diversified into businesses such as oil and insurance that had nothing to do with Nicklaus's core interests. In short, Nicklaus got carried away with himself, as he had with Muirfield Village. Then, in the summer of 1985, Nicklaus's advisers informed him that, as a result of the apparent mismanagement of certain divisions, Golden Bear, Inc., was virtually broke. Jack owed $12 million personally, which he did not have, and he had to go cap-in-hand to the banks to negotiate a repayment plan. It was the biggest worry he had ever had in his professional life, a financial disaster. Yet this fiasco was the backdrop to an extraordinary triumph.

When spring 1986 came around, Nicklaus traveled as usual to Augusta for the Masters. At forty-six, he had not been playing well for over a year. Younger men such as Tom Kite and a number of foreign golfers—notably Spain's Seve Ballesteros, Germany's Bernhard Langer, and the charismatic Greg Norman—were the new stars of the game. Though he had not yet won a major, Norman in particular was feted like a movie idol. In contrast, journalists were writing Nicklaus off, despite his brilliant run of form into the early 1980s, noting that the Golden Bear had not won anything since his own Memorial Tournament in 1984.

A particularly dismissive column in the *Atlanta Journal* made Nicklaus feel he had something to prove in 1986. But the trip to Georgia also had a personal dimension that year. In the past, the Masters had been a male preserve in the Nicklaus family: Charlie Nicklaus and his buddies went south on a stag outing. Jack's mother, Helen, had only been invited once or twice. Now a widow, she told Jack she wanted to go one last time. "She always thought she was going to die," recalls Jack's sister, Marilyn. "She didn't die until 2000. But in 1985 she was thinking she was going to die." The arrangements were duly made, and in April 1986 Jack found himself playing in front of not only Barbara and the kids—together with old friends Hoag, Savic, and Young—but his sister and her family and his mother. To make it a true family affair,

Jack's eldest son, Jackie, was caddying for him. How could he let all those people down?

He played well on the first three days, scoring 74-71-69, but Norman led the field, 4 strokes ahead, with seven players between them. Remarkable competitor though Nicklaus was, even his most loyal friends had got used to the likelihood that at forty-six his glory days were behind him. It was also a hassle getting out of Augusta on Sunday evening. So Hoag, Savic, and Young had got into the habit of leaving early and watching the final on television. Young pulled out Friday night. Hoag went Saturday. Pandel Savic tarried into Sunday, but even he was planning an early exit.

Nicklaus always competed to win, of course, and when he woke up on Sunday morning he calculated that he needed a round of 65 to claim the green jacket—an ambitious thought indeed. After a birdie at the 2nd and a bogey at the 4th, he was virtually out of contention by the time he found himself in trouble on the 8th. With nothing to lose, he played an audacious 3-wood to the green and made par. He then birdied the 9th, 10th, and 11th. Excitement in the crowd grew as he strode into view at Amen Corner. But a deflected putt at the 12th gave him a bogey. Now came the turning point. Nicklaus birdied 13, putting him level with Norman but behind Ballesteros and Kite. (At this juncture, Pandel and Janice Savic left for the airport. Despite the fact that Jack was doing well, surely he wouldn't *win*.) Jack parred 14 and approached the 15th knowing he needed an eagle to have a hope. And he got one, to an enormous cheer. Then he parred the 16th and approached the 17th as Ballesteros hit his second shot at 15 into the pond. Also behind Nicklaus, Norman started making birdies, determined to catch up. (At the airport, Savic met his wife in the bar area after checking the bags. She was watching TV. "I says, 'How's he doing?' She said, 'He's on 17 now and if he knocks this putt in he'll go 9-under.' . . . I said, 'Oh my God!' [But] they're calling the plane now, see, and I couldn't take the bags off.") Nicklaus came to the last hole figuring par would win the tournament. His second shot at 18 stopped about forty feet from the hole. (On the airplane, Savic found a fellow traveler with a portable TV and was leaning over the seat to watch.) The 18th green at Augusta is big and wide, like a stage. Experienced patrons arrive early and arrange their chairs in tiers, as if at the opera, waiting through the long day, fortified with snacks and shielded from the sun with hats and dark glasses, for the climax of the world's greatest golf tournament. Television cameras and press photographers are ranged above on platforms. By midafternoon, as the shadows lengthen, there is an intense atmosphere. As Nicklaus strode onto this stage everybody cheered, a cheer that became a collective roar, and millions more gathered around televisions (including Pandel Savic, on the plane back to Ohio) urged him on, too. This was something special. Even if you didn't much like golf or warm to Jack Nicklaus personally, there was drama here. It was "the most thrilling thing we've ever experienced," says his sister. "I still get goose bumps thinking about it." Gracious! Jack was seventeen years older than Ballesteros (who had fumbled his chance). He'd already won this tournament five times, more than anybody else. The thought that he might do it again was extraordinary. He took his putter, bent over the little white ball, and hit a long putt uphill, left to right, that slowed and stopped six inches from the hole. Then he tapped it in—a round of 65, exactly as he had aimed for. Jackie leaped in the air and then flung his arms around his dad. But Nicklaus knew it wasn't over. He had to wait while the others finished. Kite and Norman were close enough to tie for a play-off. Having made four birdies in a row, Norman looked like he was up to the challenge. All he needed was a par at the last. But the Australian's ego got the better of him. Instead of playing it safe, he tried for another birdie and suffered a bogey, which meant Nicklaus was the winner by a stroke.

"All the majors were very important," says Nicklaus, looking back on his career. "But I think the '86 was pretty special, since nobody ever thought I was going to win, including myself" (and his best friends, who missed it). In fact, it was his last hurrah. Nicklaus would never win another major. He would never win another PGA Tour event; his next victories would be on the senior tour, and in the future he would spend more and more time on golf course design. But he had gone out in the grandest style, the champion of eighteen professional majors, a record nobody would seem man enough to challenge until Tiger Woods came to maturity. In fact, ten-year-old Tiger, at his home in Cypress, was watching Nicklaus's last triumph. It was the first time the Masters had made an impression, and it was one that would stay in his memory. When *Golf Digest* printed a list of Nicklaus's golfing achievements, Tiger clipped it out and fixed it to his bedroom wall. This man Nicklaus would be his model, and these were the records he would try to beat.

7

JUST LIKE JACK

Not long after Jack Nicklaus won his last green jacket at
Augusta, Earl Woods underwent a triple heart bypass. A heavyset heavy
smoker in his midfifties who liked a drink, Earl was a prime candidate
for a coronary unless he changed his ways. He did alter his lifestyle after the operation, but perhaps not in the way his doctors would have
wished—he continued smoking and drinking but retired from his job at
McDonnell Douglas. His health was a factor in this decision, but the
main reason was to spend more time with Tiger, training him to be the
next Nicklaus. Tida had stayed home with Tiger while Earl went out to
work in the early years. Now she would go back to work—in a bank—
and Earl would stay with the boy. (Throughout Tiger's childhood, it
was a point of honor that he was never left with a baby-sitter.) With
Tida's salary and Earl's army pension, they would be able to make ends
meet, though finances would become stretched as Tiger often had to
travel farther afield to compete in tournaments. Although Earl did some
scouting work for IMG, for which he was paid expenses, he never took
another job. Tiger's career was his occupation, his obsession even, just

as Miles Woods had obsessed about Earl's becoming a professional sportsman.

To help achieve the ambition he and Tiger shared, Earl built a support team of experts, what the media would come to term Team Tiger. Earl and Tida had already shown unusual foresight by getting golf coaches for Tiger when he was a little boy. Golf coaching even in the adult game was not commonplace when Tiger was growing up, and it was distinctly unusual for a very young player. (Golf teaching came into its own only after David Leadbetter helped Britain's Nick Faldo reconstruct his game and thereby win six major championships between 1987 and 1996.) Earl also got a psychologist to work with his son—another unusual strategy for the time, especially for a junior. Like Earl himself, all the people enrolled to help Tiger had a military background. Rudy Duran was a former U.S. Air Force man. John Anselmo served in the Marine Corps during World War II. The psychologist was Dr. Jay Brunza, a captain serving in the U.S. Navy Medical Service Corps, who, like Duran and Anselmo, was not paid for his help, though Tiger rewarded him when he eventually turned professional. What Brunza did with Tiger is hard to pin down, but it involved what the psychologist calls "elements of the hypnotic." He shrinks from the term hypnotism, concerned that people might imagine him swinging a watch on a chain (which he did not do). But it seems to have amounted to much the same: teaching Tiger to focus intensely on what he was doing, blocking out what Brunza calls "distracters," thus entering into a trancelike state on the golf course. One can observe this when Tiger is in a tournament. He will pass crowds of people, even his own mother, without apparently realizing they are there.

At the same time, Tiger continued to work with John Anselmo, a straightforward old fellow who did not hold with psychology—"or whatever you call it"—or the voguish coaching methods of David Leadbetter. He was content to sit and watch the boy beat golf balls into the breeze that blew in from Huntington Beach, making the occasional comment but for the most part saying nothing. When they did chat, it was often about the history of the game. Anselmo was a good source of golf lore. Back when he was growing up in L.A., he frequented a golf course on Western Avenue where many prominent African American golfers would congregate. Anselmo played with Bill Spiller and well remembered Spiller's close friend Teddy Rhodes, perhaps the best black player of the 1940s. A thin, elegant man with a gentle manner and a fine game, Rhodes was barred from mainstream tournaments because he was black, as we have seen. After years of battling the PGA, mostly in vain, he died in semiobscurity in 1969. It was a dispiriting story that saddened Anselmo. But Tiger also reminded the coach of Rhodes. As he grew up, the boy became tall and skinny like Rhodes was. He had a similar swing. "And he had the same quietness," adds Anselmo, who told Earl it was as if Rhodes had been reborn. One could only hope that the game would treat Tiger better than it had Rhodes and Spiller (who ended his days working as a caddie at Hillcrest Country Club in L.A.). Yet how open was golf now to people of color? This question was answered dramatically in the summer of 1990.

The 72nd PGA Championship was held in August 1990 at Shoal Creek, a new country club outside Birmingham, Alabama. Designed by Jack Nicklaus and his associates in 1977, Shoal Creek was quickly becoming established as one of the prime courses favored as venues for major championships in the United States. Indeed, it was the second time the PGA Championship had been held at Shoal Creek, the first being in 1984 when Lee Trevino won. The patronage of the PGA was a source of pride and revenue for the owner and club members, all of whom were white—a fact that didn't bother the PGA, evidently. Nor had it been a concern to the United States Golf Association, which held its Amateur Championship there in 1986. "We never asked in the early eighties, which would have been the time we selected Shoal Creek for the U.S. Amateur, 'What is your membership makeup? Do you have African Americans?' " says David B. Fay, executive director of the USGA, adding that the organization was focused on the quality of the golf course. Still, everybody in golf knew Shoal Creek was not inte-grated. "You knew it, but no one ever seemed to speak up about it," as Fay says. Shoal Creek was not unique in this respect, of course. Many notable clubs still practiced discrimination. Some excluded blacks. Some didn't want Jews. Many didn't entertain the outlandish idea of women members. After all, discrimination was part of the tradition of the game.

That tradition was about to be challenged. In the run-up to the 1990 PGA Championship, William Bell, a council member in Birmingham, suggested the city should withdraw public funding for the event, because Shoal Creek excluded African Americans. Mayor Richard Arrington agreed that the club's all-white membership was an embar-rassment. Goodness knows, Birmingham had a bad enough image when it came to race relations. It was here in April 1963 that Martin Luther King Jr. was jailed for leading a civil rights protest. The follow-ing month police dogs were set on protesters gathered at the Sixteenth Street Baptist Church. That September, members of the Ku Klux Klan detonated a bomb in the same church, killing four black school-girls. One would have thought, given the history, that the leading citi-zens of Birmingham would make a special effort to be fair and openhanded in everything to do with race. Not over at the golf club, apparently.

Following the comments of the mayor, a reporter for the *Birming-ham Post-Herald,* Joan M. Mazzolini, went to Shoal Creek to ask its founder, Hall W. Thompson, about membership. A wealthy sixty-seven-year-old businessman, owner of the Thompson Tractor Company and Thompson Realty, and a member of the Augusta National, Thomp-son was a southern gentleman of impeccable manners but outdated views that he foolhardily shared with Ms. Mazzolini. In her article on June 21, 1990, the reporter quoted him as saying, "We have the right to associate or not to associate with whomever we choose. The country club is our home and we pick and choose who we want." He pointed out that Shoal Creek admitted women, Jews, and various ethnic groups.

In fact, they did not discriminate in any area "except the blacks." Asked if club members would feel comfortable bringing *the blacks* in as guests, Thompson replied, "No, that's just not done in Birmingham, Al[abama]." This remark made national news and brought opprobrium on Thompson, Shoal Creek, and the PGA.

As ever in golf, social justice was of little importance to those in the game who, by and large, resented the criticism of outsiders (as they still do). It was money that mattered. Action was taken only when sponsors withdrew from the telecast, and the PGA saw its premier tournament headed for financial disaster. Thompson was pressured into making an apology of sorts and, with only two weeks to go before the players teed off, the PGA insisted Shoal Creek take in a black member—a local businessman named Louis Willie. "My first thought was that the best result was for Shoal Creek to invite a minority to join the club," explains Jim Awtrey, who had become CEO of the PGA of America two years earlier and found himself in the eye of the storm. Some may think that the tokenistic way in which Willie was invited to join the club is as bad as the fact that there had previously been no black members. "The Reverend Joseph Lowery, who I was working with, who was a person of the Southern Christian Leadership Conference,* his statement in that regard was 'Yes, but everything must start with one step,'" says Awtrey in his defense. "So when he was asked if that was tokenism, as a prominent black leader, he said you must start with one step, and that [was] the first step. . . . It started with one and grew from there." The 72nd PGA Championship went ahead. Australian Wayne Grady won. But that was of little consequence compared with the political ramifications of the affair. "Everyone in the game at that moment reflected on the issue of minority participation in the game," says Awtrey. "As a result of that I think there's been some significant change, and discussion and openness, which has led to some positive things in the game of golf."

---

*The SCLC was threatening to picket the tournament.

The most significant result was that the PGA of America announced that henceforth its tournaments would not patronize clubs that discriminated against minorities or women. At the PGA Tour, Commissioner Beman moved swiftly to set a similar policy. A few clubs felt unable to declare their membership open—notably Butler National in Illinois, which had black members but no women, and Cypress Point in California, which did not give a reason why it could not conform—and these venues were no longer used by the tour. Most clubs accepted that nondiscriminatory membership was the way forward, however. Of course, one may ask why the tour hadn't thought of this before 1990. ("We can be criticized for not having taken some action before that. I accept that," admits Beman.) The Masters was independent of golf's governing bodies and could, theoretically, please itself. But even the men in green blazers got the message. At the end of 1990, television executive Ron Townsend was invited to become the first black member of the Augusta National. One out of three hundred, after fifty-seven years.

The United States Golf Association also announced it would no longer patronize clubs that discriminated and, like Jim Awtrey, the leader of the USGA came to think of the Shoal Creek affair as positive. "In the United States we talk about 25 million Americans who play golf. Well, that means that there are about 235 million who *don't* play golf and, for many of those, their feelings about the game of golf are probably somewhat negative," says David B. Fay. "I think that Shoal Creek, and the reaction to Shoal Creek, may have made a statement [that] golf is not an exclusionary game. But, yes, it had been." In the wake of the cause célèbre, the executive committee of the USGA cast around for its first black member, and it approached John Franklin Merchant in the late summer of 1991. A keen amateur from Connecticut who worked as a trial lawyer but had no direct connection to top-flight golf, Merchant was surprised when an acquaintance came to him with the idea that he might serve on the committee. "I didn't know what the hell the USGA executive committee was." He soon found out that it was a highly influential body of grand personages who, without salary, guided the policies of America's premier golf association. They did not invite Merchant to join because he was knowledgeable about golf, of course. They wanted to appear politically correct, as Merchant realized. Once admitted, though, he worked to introduce black Americans to golf and to generate jobs for blacks in the golf industry, leading him to establish the National Minority Golf Foundation and, incidentally, to strike up what would become a significant friendship with Earl Woods.

In the years since 1990, Shoal Creek has not been patronized with another major golf tournament, to the chagrin of Hall Thompson. In a letter to me in 2002, he complained that the city of Birmingham had always been "a target for the liberal media" and blamed media coverage for prejudicing the club's chance of ever hosting a major again. Some might think the club, and Thompson, are due a second chance. But during subsequent telephone conversations with me, Thompson did not show any remorse about his past comments or the way the club had been run in the past. Indeed, his phraseology and views seemed unchanged. During our first conversation he referred to the history of Birmingham and the time the police "got after the Negro marchers with fire hoses and police dogs." For a white man to use the term Negro is, in itself, offensive to many African Americans. Then he talked about the repercussions of the 1990 affair, including the decision of the PGA and other organizations not to work in the future with clubs that discriminated. This is the positive outcome Awtrey and Fay speak of. Yet it seems a cause of regret to Thompson, who says: "What's really sad about it is great [clubs] chose not to make their golf courses available under those circumstances." And what about his own club? Back in 1990 one black man, Louis Willie, was made a member to appease those who were angry about the all-white membership. Awtrey defended the tokenism because, he said, reform had to start somewhere. The numbers would grow. Thompson revealed that in more than a decade African American membership at Shoal Creek has indeed grown— from one member to two, and that is "totally as a result of the 1990 championship." Two black members out of 610 (and this is in Alabama, where African Americans make up almost a third of the population). As Thompson says, not much has changed at Shoal Creek.

Perhaps surprisingly, Thompson has recently been negotiating with the PGA Tour to hold its Players Championship at Shoal Creek, and he has also been talking to the USGA about hosting its Senior Amateur. Although the PGA Tour bid fell through, it might be thought inappropriate that these organizations are even thinking of returning to Shoal Creek as long as the man at the top holds the views he does and expresses himself in the way he does regarding, as he puts it, "the Negro."

A chance meeting at Shoal Creek during the troubled 1990 PGA Championship led to a significant business venture involving Arnold Palmer, at a time in his life when he was beset with almost as many business problems as Jack Nicklaus faced in 1985.

Now sixty, Palmer was no longer a competitive golfer, but he had matured into an elder statesman of the game, who continued to make appearances at major championships and PGA Tour events, as well as events on the Senior Tour. Golf fans loved to see him, and Arnie continued to enjoy signing autographs and posing for photographs. He was perhaps even more endearing than in his youth. His voice had become growly with age—he was more of a bear of a man than the Golden Bear himself—and even the added weight he carried seemed to suit him. Arnie had become a truly avuncular character. So it was that he turned up at the PGA Championship with Winnie, as usual, and because of his position in the game the PGA made arrangements to make sure his stay was especially comfortable. People who owned properties within the Shoal Creek compound were asked if they had room to accommodate VIPs, and the Palmers were given the guest house of residents Joe and Kay Gibbs. Joe was a forty-one-year-old accountant who had made a fortune in cable television and the cellular telephone business. During the championship week, he and his wife struck up a friendship with the Palmers, having dinner with them every evening. When Arnie missed the cut and departed for home, the Gibbses thought that was the end of it. But the Palmers reciprocated politely by inviting them down to their winter home for Thanksgiving. "We want you to come to Isleworth, where we live in Florida," said Arnie. "See where we live and spend a week with us playing golf."

By Isleworth, Palmer was referring to a new golf and real estate development next to his Bay Hill club. Isleworth (pronounced Aisle-worth) is integral to our story not least because it later became the home of Tiger Woods. It was also one of the disasters of Palmer's business career. At the start, it seemed a splendid opportunity. Just up the road from Bay Hill was the town of Windermere, founded by an Englishman in 1889 and named after the picturesque British lake. Nearby was a long-established citrus grove facing a series of natural lakes. Local people had built fishing shacks on the foreshore and some had come to live by the water in regular homes, including Bob Londeree and his family, who had a house on Lake Bessie, a 175-acre landlocked lake. A land planner by trade, Londeree knew the citrus grove on the opposite shore was ripe for redevelopment, and sure enough, in 1983, following a harsh winter that killed many of the fruit trees, the Concord Corporation of Texas bought 1,600 acres of orchard for $27 million and began to redevelop the land into a luxurious gated community with a golf club. The front man was Palmer. Typically, he did not invest his own money in the project. (The bulk of the development money was raised on a mortgage from the Mellon Bank based near Latrobe.) Palmer received his share of the profits by letting the developers use his name, which helped in getting permits and would help sell the lots. Mark McCormack got a piece, too, as his agent. To sweeten the deal, the golf course would be designed and built by Palmer's people: his architect, Ed Seay, and regular subcontractor, Dave Harman. The golfer also planned to live at Isleworth Golf and Country Club, as it was to be called.

Built in opulent style, Isleworth was an ambitious enterprise, rivaling Muirfield Village in size. Sidewalks were paved with pink granite. A nursery was built so that the club could grow plants for its gardens. The clubhouse was a palace finished with Brazilian walnut and stone embedded with fossils. Arnie's office had a leather floor (which he ruined by walking on it in spiked shoes). And no expense was spared on the construction of the golf course. Arnie announced proudly that Isleworth would be potentially "the capstone to my entire career." Rather, it became a millstone.

Unusually for such a project, it was built in one phase, so the developers were spending millions before they recouped money from sales, though Palmer was getting paid up-front for the golf course. There were problems from the outset. As we have seen, a major part of maintaining a modern golf course is irrigation, which uses millions of gallons of water and produces contaminated runoff. A development like Isleworth needs a way of holding and dispersing runoff and storm water. So two water retention ponds were created near the main gatehouse entrances at Isleworth and, under permits obtained in Palmer's name, at times of high water the excess from these ponds would discharge into the Butler chain of lakes. However, residents on Lake Bessie—which was not part of this chain—noticed their lake rising as Isleworth was built. Although the level fluctuated slightly during the year, it was coming up and staying up. The water was also becoming murky. Bob Londeree contacted his neighbor Don Greer, an engineer, and together they checked the Isleworth plans. Contrary to what had been approved by the county, a forty-two-inch diversion pipe was emptying storm water and runoff from Isleworth into landlocked Lake Bessie, which was like a giant bathtub spilling over the top. Londeree and Greer enlisted another neighbor, John Robertson, a trial lawyer, who asked the people at Isleworth if they would turn the water off and install a pump to send the storm water where it should go, into the Butler chain of lakes that naturally drained into the Everglades. This would have cost a relatively modest $300,000. The developers refused. So Londeree, Greer, and Robertson got together with more neighbors, and they filed a lawsuit in April 1987 against Isleworth that named Palmer among the defendants, because his name was on the permits. The case took three years to reach trial, and during that time the rising water flooded the foreshore, killing trees, flooding docks, and drowning Robertson's pet dog. According to some of the lakeside residents, the defendants' representatives warned them darkly that if they lost they would have to sell their homes to pay the legal costs. The plaintiffs were ordinary people, some of them elderly, and they became anxious. Londeree describes the stress as "gut-wrenching." Only one family backed out, however.

As this was going on, the Palmers moved into their new house at Isleworth, in a part of the estate that faced Lake Louise. It was here that they entertained Kay and Joe Gibbs for Thanksgiving 1990. Although the Palmers treated the Gibbses to a delightful weekend, Arnie was going through one of the most difficult years in his life. Apart from the Lake Bessie case, he was being pilloried in the Orlando press for negotiating to sell Bay Hill to a Japanese consortium for $50 million, which would have been a handsome profit on his investment. "It was a PR disaster, as his wife kept trying to tell him," says local journalist and Palmer friend Larry Guest, who covered the story in the *Orlando Sentinel*. Some local people were of the opinion that to sell Bay Hill to the Japanese was unpatriotic, considering that there were veterans who had fought the Japanese in World War II living in and around Bay Hill. In any event, the Japanese did not come up with the money. So Palmer and his partners didn't get the $50 million, and he suffered the bad publicity. Some of those close to the golfer blamed IMG for the way this and other problems were being handled. There was a culture, according to Ed Bignon, an executive on Palmer's team, that Arnold did not need to know everything that was going on in his name.

It was sometimes hard to keep track of what was going on; the golfer had so many and such diverse business interests—including selling cars. Until now, Palmer's stake in the automobile business had proved remarkably and surprisingly successful, with the chain of General Motors dealerships that carried his name—the Arnold Palmer Cadillac Dealership—generating huge revenues. In 1988–89, one of the six dealerships Palmer lent his name to sold an astonishing 74,792 cars.

Nominally, this made Palmer the biggest car dealer in the United States. Hertz alone bought sixty thousand vehicles and paid Palmer an additional $400,000 to appear in its commercials. The car dealerships were generating more money than any venture the golfer had been involved in, and he and his partners estimated they were sitting on a $15 million business. Then Palmer's right-hand man in automobile sales, Jimmy O'Neal, attempted to go one better and turn the dealerships into a public company, the Arnold Palmer Automotive Group. Before this deal could go through, the business got into difficulty, partly as the result of a buyback clause whereby Hertz could return cars it did not need. When Hertz returned thousands in 1990, the business virtually collapsed with debts of $13 million.

Meanwhile, Isleworth was not proving the success Palmer had envisaged. Planned before the stock market crash of 1987, with no expense spared, the lots were offered for sale from $150,000, which seemed expensive during a recession, and almost half remained unsold by 1990. Then there was the Lake Bessie lawsuit. It must have seemed a petty matter in comparison to Palmer's other problems: a pipe where it shouldn't be (arguably), people complaining about a fractional rise in water level. Flooded docks. A drowned dog. There were numerous chances to resolve this irritating dispute, but Palmer's associates failed to seize the opportunity. Or, from the residents' point of view, they thought they could bully their way through it. "They thought they'd beat us down," says Londeree. The case went to trial in April 1990 and Palmer had to suffer the indignity of testifying. Essentially, he said he didn't know anything, but being cross-examined was an uncomfortable experience for a man so concerned with maintaining a positive public image, and the evidence presented made him look bad by association. Apart from the flooding and polluting of Lake Bessie, it was alleged that the two retention ponds at Isleworth were actually sections of the Butler chain of lakes, owned by the state, that had been snipped off without permission. One doubled as a water hazard for the golf course. Also, the main gatehouse encroached on state land. All in all, Palmer and his associates came across as arrogant, rich people who thought they could do whatever they wanted. The trial dragged on for seventeen weeks, the longest civil trial in the history of the county, and when it ended on August 17, 1990, in the week following the PGA Championship at Shoal Creek, the jury found against Palmer and his partners. They were fined $162,000, and the Lake Bessie residents were awarded $300,000 each, plus legal costs—which proved ruinous. When everything was added together, Palmer's side faced a bill of $6.5 million. And when this bill was not paid, sheriff's deputies went into Isleworth and repossessed anything of value, including forty golf carts. Arnie was in Japan at the time and, in his absence, Winnie had to run around to save his trophies.

Without equipment, the club shut and the Mellon Bank foreclosed on Isleworth in April 1991. Arnie had to move out of his new home and back into his condominium at Bay Hill. He would not be making any more money out of Isleworth; indeed, the grand development seemed to mock him. There it was, next door, the very streets named for him— there was a Latrobe Drive, a Deacon Circle (after his father, who had died in 1976), and so on—and he owned none of it. It would be a long time before he was even comfortable going there to visit friends. And his problems were not over.

As if he had not received enough negative publicity, his journalist friend Larry Guest wrote an article in the *Orlando Sentinel* a couple of years later, in March 1994, questioning the golfer's philanthropic work. In recent years, one of Palmer's pet projects had been the endowment of the Arnold Palmer Hospital for Children and Women in Orlando. One of the principal ways he helped the hospital was with charitable gifts from the profits of his Bay Hill Invitational (at this time known as the Nestlé Invitational). In 1994 most PGA Tour events contributed about half a million dollars to local charity. Guest revealed in the *Sentinel* that Palmer's tournament only gave his hospital $60,000 in 1993, and was expected to give just a little more than that in 1994. Yet Palmer and his partners were splitting profits on the tournament estimated at up to

$1.5 million. "When I exposed that, that was a great source of embarrassment to them and they couldn't deny it and a lot of the volunteers for the tournament quit, saying, you know, we're happy to work eighty hours that week to build a hospital, but if it's just to make you and your IMG cronies richer, forget about it," says Guest, who adds that the article ended his friendship with Palmer. "He really got his nose out of joint."

Despite such problems, Arnie was still the highest-earning sports figure in America in 1991, with $12.5 million in income from endorsements and appearance money. And the failures of recent years had not blunted his entrepreneurial ambition. Far from it. He was about to do something he had never done before—invest his own money in an idea hatched by his new Shoal Creek friend Joe Gibbs. With a background in cable television, Gibbs decided there was a market for a twenty-four-hour cable TV golf channel and did some research into the idea during 1991. "I called Arnold at the end of the summer and said, 'Let's talk . . . '" Gibbs told Palmer he wanted to go halves with him as founding partners of what became the Golf Channel, both investing equal amounts of seed money. "He had never put money in a deal. He had always got his piece for his name," says Gibbs. But after some thought, Palmer agreed to be his partner and chairman of the company, and Gibbs went about raising the rest of the $100 million start-up capital. It was not an easy process, and part of the problem was Palmer himself.

Gibbs liked Arnie enormously, for the same reasons most people warm to the golfer. "He's genuine. If you're Arnold Palmer's friend, you're his friend for life [and], when you're around him, he lets you know that. The way he treats you with so much respect, even though you're way down on the totem pole compared to him, he makes you feel like you're his equal. Not that many people have that knack in life. And if you have somebody that makes you feel good when you're around them, you wanna be around them more." But Palmer was a nervous investor. "Arnold was being pulled by a lot of people not to do this over that first year, [because] they thought it was too much exposure for him. . . . He literally called me three times during that year and said he wouldn't do it, and I had to fly to Bay Hill and sit down and say, 'Arnold, [it's] gonna work, you know.' And finally got him back in the boat. Three times he jumped out of the boat, and three times he got back in."

It took Gibbs two years to get the capital he needed. Many potential investors did not perceive him as the right man for the job, because he had no golf background. Also, many could not see why subscribers would want a twenty-four-hour golf channel. But by the spring of 1994, Gibbs had $60 million, and that was enough to start building a studio, hiring staff, and buying rights to tournaments. On January 17, 1995, the Golf Channel first went on air. "Day one you don't have any subscribers. You don't have the advertising dollars, [so] as you little by little grow the revenue base you have to continue to spend this money." Twice, Gibbs didn't have the funds to meet the Friday payroll until the last minute. But the channel drew a healthy number of viewers from the start, and these were the sort of viewers advertisers wanted to reach: a large proportion of high-earners, aged thirty-five to forty-five. As a result, the Golf Channel broke even in its fourth year, unusually quick for such a project. Gibbs and Palmer then sold their interests, each making a considerable profit, though Palmer continued as chairman and, before long, the Golf Channel would be valued at $1.2 billion.* The sweet success of this venture took away the sour taste of some of Palmer's recent failures and showed once again how much money there was to be made in the business of golf.

In the autumn of 1990, a month after the Shoal Creek furor, when Tiger Woods was approaching his fifteenth birthday, he enrolled at Western High School in Anaheim, California, where he would remain until graduation four years later. During this formative time he

---

*Valuation in 2001, when Comcast bought a controlling share.

naturally developed physically and as a personality, and he won his first important national tournaments. Because Tiger traveled so much to compete in events, he missed a lot of school, but he impressed his teachers by always making up the work, even if it meant writing essays on the airplane coming home. This was Tida's doing. As an immigrant who spoke broken English, she had great faith in education. Because of his self-discipline and politeness, Tiger became a favorite with the staff of Western High, especially those interested in golf. He wasn't a celebrity among his peers, however, because few students followed the game. Fellow honors class student Lesley Aldrich recalls her PE teacher advising the girls to keep their eye on Tiger, "because he was going to be very, very rich one day! Of course, we all chuckled." And on those occasions when Tiger's classmates did get a glimpse of his growing fame, Tiger was quick to dampen any excitement—such as the time a kid in science class announced that they'd read something about him in *People* magazine. "He very politely told the whole class that he didn't want to talk about that," says his teacher Corrina Durrego. This was typical of Tiger, who grew into a modest boy as he passed through puberty, distinctly shy in everyday life though extremely aggressive in golf.

Significantly, in July 1991 Tiger won his first U.S. Junior Amateur Championship, at Arnold Palmer's Bay Hill club. Over 2,000 young players tried to qualify for the match play tournament, of which 140 went through to the competition, and Tiger took the title 1-up. At fifteen, he was the youngest player ever to win this important title. Also in 1991, Tiger made the acquaintance of his hero, Jack Nicklaus, at an exhibition at Bel-Air Country Club, during which they performed for the audience and posed for their picture. Considering the awe in which Tiger held Nicklaus, he behaved with remarkable composure during the encounter. "He was always at ease in anybody's company," recalls Don Crosby, his high school golf coach and accounting teacher, who accompanied him to the event. At the end of the year, Tiger won the Orange Bowl Junior International in Miami, and afterward he and Earl spent some time at Bay Hill meeting notable tour players including Greg Norman and Mark O'Meara, to whom Tiger would become close. Essentially, Earl and Tiger were being introduced to the world of IMG and its clients, with O'Meara in particular being put forward as a mentor. "I had a number of meetings with his father when [Tiger] was still an amateur, talking about what-if-this, what-if-that," recalled Mark McCormack, who noted, "you certainly really knew he was going to be someone who was going to be a factor in golf." Now that he was the head of a huge corporation, McCormack did not have the time to work with the Woods family intensively, as he had with Palmer, Player, and Nicklaus. So he appointed one of his best agents to the case, J. Hughes Norton III, who was handling the important Norman account. It was Norton's job to stay on good terms with the family until Tiger wanted to enter the professional game.

McCormack knew that golf badly needed a new superstar. Since the heady days of the Big Three, the American game had lacked a home-grown player with the ability to dominate the tour and capture the imagination of the general public. Tom Watson was masterly between 1975 and '83, but he didn't have the charisma of Jack Nicklaus, let alone Palmer, and, of course, Nicklaus was still on the scene during Watson's best years. Nick Faldo was another great player, but he was an even colder fish than Watson. (When IMG told Faldo they could double his income if he smiled more often, he replied, "But that isn't me.") Norman had abundant star quality, but as far as American fans were concerned he was also foreign, and in truth he never lived up to his promise, managing only two major titles. Where was the next great born-and-bred U.S. player, a champion of the caliber of Palmer and Nicklaus? As years passed and no such golfer emerged, the American public began to drift away from professional golf. As McCormack observed, interest "flattened as tennis was exploding," and IMG was quick to diversify into tennis, signing leading players such as John McEnroe who did enthuse the public. The titans of golf—players such as Palmer, whom the public still wanted to see—moved over to the Senior PGA

Tour,* which Commissioner Beman launched in 1980 to showcase players over fifty. The Senior Tour proved very popular, its appeal boosted when Palmer won the first event he entered, the 1980 Seniors Championship. The PGA Tour by comparison seemed lackluster. So it was with perfect timing that the future superstar of the game appeared in his first PGA Tour event in the spring of 1992.

The Los Angeles Open is one of the oldest and richest events on the American tour, dating back to 1926, and recently renamed the Nissan Los Angles Open after its main sponsor. It has a prime calendar position at the start of the year, when television ratings for golf are high (because viewers in northern climes are kept indoors by the weather). Held at the Riviera Country Club in affluent Pacific Palisades, an easy drive north of Orange County, it was also Tiger's local event. Tournament Director Greg McLaughlin had tried to persuade the tournament committee to invite Tiger for the 1991 L.A. Open, which meant talking about it the year before, when he was fourteen. "He's winning a lot of stuff, and he's in the paper, and he's highly publicized, and what I was looking for was an opportunity [to] create a little bit of interest in the event [by inviting] this local kid that's beating everybody." However, the committee thought Tiger was too young. The next year Tiger took part in a qualifying event and came so close to earning a place that the committee gave him an invitation. So it was that Tiger became the youngest player ever to compete in a tour event, at sixteen years and two months.

Most of the big names were at Riviera, including thirty-two-year-old Fred Couples, who was embarking upon the best year of his career and had the biggest gallery. The second biggest, approximately three thousand people, walked with Tiger on his first day, Thursday, February 27, 1992. Dressed in a striped T-shirt, he looked very young indeed. Yet everything about the boy spoke of star quality: his distinctive look, his unique name, even the tiger headcover his mother had made to

---

*It was renamed the Champions Tour in 2003.

protect his driver. It was as if Tiger Woods was designed for stardom. His youth and personable manner would not mean much if he did not play well, of course. But he had talent in abundance and played with a joyfulness that was apparent from the moment he pulled his club back at the 1st tee. Here was a kid living his dream, and it was exciting to behold. After shooting a 1-over-par 72, reporters clustered around to hear what he had to say about his first round in a tour event and, when Tiger addressed them, he expressed himself with an eloquence that would have been surprising in an adult player. "I would like to stand behind the curtain a little longer," he told the press elegantly. "But I guess this tournament brought me out."

Likable though Tiger was, the fact that he was a person of color was enough to engender hatred in some people. After the first round, an anonymous caller telephoned the tournament chairman, Mark Kuperstock, and left a message railing against a "nigger" being in the event and went on to make what amounted to death threats. Earl was informed, and extra security was put into place for Tiger's second round late on Friday, though Tiger himself was not told the reason until afterward. Thousands followed him again, and happily there was no trouble. Rather, he was applauded at every green. In return, the youngster gave his followers something to watch. When he holed a putt at the 6th, he pumped his fist, and when he putted out at the 9th, he tossed the ball to his fans. Here was a touch of the showmanship of Arnold Palmer, who had always accepted that golfers were in the entertainment business. Jack Nicklaus was less keen on this aspect of the game. "They call it that. And I suppose we are [in the entertainment business]," he concedes. "[But] I've always thought we were athletes in competition, competing against other athletes in competition, which became entertainment for people." Many younger players made almost no concession to the fact that the fans wanted a show. Tiger was a natural in this respect. He was so engaged in what he was doing that he expressed his excitement spontaneously. Also, he had been performing for an audience, in one way or another, since appearing on the *Mike Douglas*

Show at age two. It is no exaggeration to think of Tiger as a child star. Like Shirley Temple or Michael Jackson, he knew at a very early age what people wanted to see.

At the end of the day, reporters clamored to speak to the kid again. But the PGA Tour had not invited him into the media tent. "The tour didn't want to bring him in, because the story isn't about some sixteen-year-old kid that's an amateur. The story is about their players, the 'members of the tour,' " notes McLaughlin. (There was jealousy among the tour players, some of whom reflected upon the fact that one of their own had to miss a spot in the tournament, and thereby a chance to earn a wage that week, so a schoolboy could be paraded before the public.) So Tiger gave an impromptu press conference outside, telling the press that he'd found it hard to concentrate during the round—he'd shot a disappointing 75—because he'd never had a gallery before. It had been a wonderful experience, though. "These were the two best days of my life," he said, adding sagely: "It was a learning experience. I learned I wasn't that good. I learned I have a long way to go. I'm not competitive at this level. I am at the junior level, but not at the pro level. . . . I just have to grow up, that's all."

Until now, Tiger hadn't had a girlfriend. Then he caught the eye of seventeen-year-old Dina Gravell, a senior at Western High when Tiger was a junior. Dina and Tiger could hardly have been more different. She was white and blonde (a cheerleader for the football team), and her family was active in the Lutheran church. Although Tiger was obviously not white, it was hard to find a word to describe his multiethnic look and, as far as religion was concerned, his mother was a Buddhist (Tiger himself would adopt Buddhist customs as he grew older). He wasn't the most handsome boy in school. Growing fast, he was a very skinny six foot one. Instead of the latest clothes, he wore tennis shoes, khaki pants, and golf shirts (there was no uniform at Western). He was not part of the in-crowd, and Dina barely remembered him from Orangeview Junior High, which they had both attended. He was just a quiet kid who played a lot of golf and had a weird name, which he asked teachers not to use in class. As Dina says, "Who would want to be called Eldrick? My goodness!" Around school, Tiger kept company with three friends: Alfredo Arguello, Bryon Bell, and Mike Gout, all sensible, hardworking boys. Dina wasn't sure what Tiger did outside school apart from golf, of course. Even when she saw him with a book, it was invariably a biography of a golfer. Then they started talking, and she noticed how sincere and unpretentious he was. "He didn't try to be popular. He didn't try to stick out. He was just a gentleman. He just kind of minded his own business and did his own thing. I guess that was what attracted me toward him." Over a period of six months or so they became friends, hanging around in a group. Then he invited her to a movie, and so they became sweethearts.

Dina looked forward to meeting Tiger's parents, but she did not find Earl and Tida welcoming when she did visit the family home. They seemed to think she might be a distraction to Tiger and were hard to get to know. Moreover, it was a strange household in her view. It was evident that Tiger's parents lived for their son—"Their whole life was him"—but they didn't seem to be much of a couple. "There was no communication, no togetherness." (Family friend Bill Orr agrees: "It was a divided house. She had her duties and Earl had his.") The house itself was a shrine to Tiger's golfing achievements, with one wall in the lounge smothered with framed magazine covers, photographs, and plaques. Virtually every horizontal surface was taken up with trophies, which house-proud Tida fussed over. At the same time, she allowed Tiger to practice golf shots indoors—pitching balls over a chair in the lounge, despite the fact that it was not a large room. "Golf had priority over *every*thing," as Dina says. But when Tiger was with his girlfriend, he seemed to want to get away from the game. They enjoyed walking around the little park across from his home, talking about everything except golf. "Maybe he didn't want to talk about it, because that was all he ever did was golf, and I was kind of an outlet for him. When we did things together, it was fun. . . . We talked about life and about silly things, and sometimes quite serious things. He was normal with me. . . . He needed that in his life, [because] his life was very stressful and high-pressured." (It is worth pointing out that Tiger could be light-hearted with other people, too. One day at the Navy Course, his father's golfing friend Bob Rogers asked Tiger to watch him putting on the practice green and then tell him what he liked about his stroke and what he didn't like. "So I hit a few putts and he said, 'Well, what I don't like about your stroke is you are cutting the ball,'" recalls Rogers. "'What I like about your stroke is it's your stroke, not mine.'")

Dina got the impression that Earl and Tida would give Tiger whatever he wanted as long as he stayed on the program. Dina assumed that was why they tolerated her; they certainly did not seem to like her. If Tiger wanted to take Dina out to a movie or to McDonald's, he only had to ask for a few dollars. He never worked at a part-time job, and there was no pressure to get one. School and golf were the job. He was up at 5:00 A.M. to put in an hour at the gym before going to the practice range and then school. One thing that perplexed Dina was the amount of time Tiger spent at the range. He went every day and seemed to love hitting balls. In part, Earl and Tida were the impetus for Tiger's interest in golf, and they pushed him to some degree, but it was also true that he took genuine pleasure in the game. Hitting balls was "pure joy," as he puts it. John Anselmo smiled to himself when Dina began to come down to Meadowlark to watch Tiger practice. "Oh, she was a beautiful lady," he remembers. "How can he not get a beauty? Let's face it."

While Tiger was always welcome at Meadowlark, a bad atmosphere had developed at the Navy Course. The origin of the problem was probably the fact that Tiger had not been permitted to play the course when he was under ten, which had caused Earl to withdraw him for a time. But when he came back to use the course regularly—and he would play here throughout his teenage years—there were further incidents. After one of Tiger's early tournament wins, Tida wanted to throw a party for friends at the clubhouse. She made food and brought it over, but even though the clubhouse was vacant, she was told to have the party out-side. Another time a member of the staff confronted Tiger with a sup-posed complaint from one of the residents who lived adjacent to the course. The staff member apparently told Tiger that the resident had said "that little nigger is hitting over in my yard." In the first place, the accusation was absurd. Tiger did not hook balls into back gardens. Even if a resident had accused him of such, there was no reason to relay the complaint so baldly. The same staff member ran after Tiger on an-other occasion, suspecting he hadn't paid for his golf cart, and de-manded to see the receipt (which he did have). In August 1992 the U.S. Junior Amateur was held at Wollaston Golf Club in Massachusetts. Tiger, the defending champion, beat Mark Wilson in the final 1-up to become the only repeat winner of the title. It was a big moment for the sixteen-year-old and the stress showed when he burst into tears at the end. "You can't believe just how much tension there was out there," sighed Tiger. "I'm so glad it's over." When they got home, Earl offered to let the Navy Course display the trophy in the clubhouse. In reply, he says a senior member of the staff asked what the trophy was. "He didn't even know. And Tiger was the national champion." Highly of-fended, Earl and Tiger offered the cup to Big Canyon Country Club, where they also played. "And they were proud. They knew exactly what it was, and they knew how rare it was."

The specter of racism is never far away in the story of Tiger's life. There were racial overtones to those incidents at the Navy Course, at least as far as Earl was concerned. Tiger and Dina sometimes found themselves stared at as a mixed couple. But these were small things compared to the fact that Tiger had to deal with death threats from an early age. The anonymous call to the L.A. Open was the first, but as he competed in an increasing number of high-profile events across the country, it happened in other cities, too. Dina remembers Tiger being afraid before tournaments (he got nervous enough anyway), but he was reluctant to tell her too much in case she became distressed. The im-pressive thing is that the threats did not stop him from competing. As the years went by, Tiger got into a habit of saying nothing publicly about the threats, maybe because he did not want to give the people threatening him the satisfaction of knowing they had upset him. One of the few times he did let something slip was to his U.S. history class at Western High, when teacher Jim Tozzie invited the students to talk on a subject of their choice. Tiger's talk was about Charlie Sifford and the difficulties black golfers had experienced, showing how much he knew about, and empathized with, minority players of the past. "Then he started talking a little bit about himself, and I remember he'd comment to the class about some of the negatives, and death threats he had received, and the class just sat there with their mouths open. They could not believe what they heard," recalls Tozzie. "They were honestly surprised that he was subject to this. Because he was such a nice guy."

In the summer of 1993 Tiger defended his U.S. Junior Amateur title in Portland, Oregon. With two previous wins, he was the favorite, but was not in the best of health, having recently been diagnosed with mononucleosis. In the final round he missed a putt at the 16th to go 2-down. Coming off the green he was angry with himself, and Dr. Jay Brunza, who was caddying for him, cautioned his student to collect his thoughts. He warned Tiger that he could lose the tournament if he was not careful. When Tiger got to the green at 17, he paused and called upon the best inspiration he could think of before playing the shot. "He's always had a great admiration for Jack Nicklaus," says Dr. Brunza. "That's what Tiger aspired to be . . . the very best." Standing over his birdie putt, which would cost him the tournament if he missed it, Tiger told himself out loud, "I'm going to *will* this one in, just like Nicklaus." It did go in. Then he birdied the 18th to finish even with Ryan Armour and won in a sudden-death play-off. With an exultant roar, Tiger became the only three-time winner of the U.S. Junior Amateur, which remains one of the most remarkable accomplishments of his career. Not only had he won three times, but he had done so in succession while undergoing the physical and emotional changes of puberty and while dealing with schoolwork and death threats.

How much of this success was due to the support and guidance of his team—Earl, John Anselmo, and Dr. Brunza—is hard to say. But at no stage in his junior career was Tiger without expert help. When Anselmo was diagnosed with cancer, for instance, and underwent major surgery at the age of seventy-three, Earl quickly found a replacement coach, choosing another former military man. He and Tiger were in Texas for the U.S. Amateur in August 1993 when they met with Claude Harmon Jr., known as Butch. The son of 1948 Masters champion Claude Harmon, Butch is a stocky Vietnam veteran with a disconcertingly cold expression that is caused by a lazy left eye and a nerve disorder in his face. Despite a forbidding appearance, he is in fact a charming, approachable fellow. Harmon played the tour with modest success from 1969 to 1971, before becoming director of golf at Lochinvar Golf Club in Houston. He was one of those coaches who had benefited from David Leadbetter's well-publicized work with Nick Faldo, which raised the status of golf-teaching generally and brought money into the coaching business. Just as Leadbetter got lucky with Faldo, to some extent, Harmon had good fortune with Greg Norman. It was Harmon who told the strong-willed Australian that he had to change his swing; when Norman complied, he won the Open Championship in 1993. What drew Earl Woods to Harmon was this success and a mutual friend—Greg Norman, who was thinking about how he might get Tiger associated with some of his burgeoning business ventures. "My first impressions were, wow, what an unbelievable, raw talent!" says Harmon, recalling his first meeting with Tiger. "It was just his ability to hit the ball so far, [and] his creativity shone. Also, the other side of that, how unpolished he was. He was very one-dimensional in the way he played. He didn't have a variety of shots. But you saw this raw talent and you just said, wow, I'd sure love to have a chance to see if I could get on board with this at a very early time, because I think I could really help him and this could be a very special human being. History has proved that to be true." As in the past, there was little money available for coaching Tiger. In fact, there was none.

Duran and Anselmo had worked pro bono. Harmon said he would work for free, too, until Tiger turned professional. Then he would send the Woodses a bill, "which I did, and it was a very hefty bill."

In his youth, the most significant tournament Tiger competed in was the U.S. Amateur. To win this title was to join the ranks of Jones, Palmer, and Nicklaus, after which the professional tour provided the next challenges. In August 1994 the Amateur was held at the Tournament Players Club at Sawgrass, Florida. It was not an easy week for Tiger, who played erratically, despite help from Butch Harmon and Jay Brunza as caddie. Yet he made it into the final, against Trip Kuehne of Texas, who was three years his senior. Trip and his brother, Hank, and sister, Kelli, were among Tiger's closest friends. All were outstanding golfers, and the first time Earl and Tida permitted Tiger to travel on his own across the country was to a tournament in the Dallas area on the proviso he stayed with the Kuehne family. No ground was given, however, when Trip and Tiger met in the final of the Amateur. And it was Trip who was the superior player in the first round, opening up a 6-stroke lead. Nobody had ever come back from such a position in the history of the tournament to win. Tiger corrected the situation slightly by winning enough holes on the back 9 to finish a less egregious 4 strokes behind. Kuehne believes the turning point was the 16th, where Tiger had a piece of luck. "He hit it over the trees and was trying to go for the green, and there was no way he could hit on the green," he says. "[But] he hit a tree, and it happened to kick out in the middle of the fairway, and [then] he hit a 4-iron about twenty-five or thirty feet and he made that putt for birdie!"

Playing another 18 holes in the afternoon round, Tiger continued to gain on Kuehne. He birdied 16 again, and they drew even. Then they came to the famous 17th green, built on an island in a lake, with the spectators watching from the other side. The pin was cut on the right, dangerously close to the edge, and part of the sport of this hole is watching golf balls rolling off the green and into the water. In the morning Tiger had hit a daring shot that landed on the fringe of the

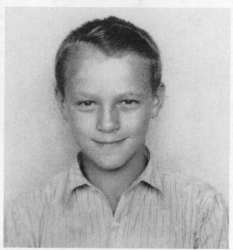

The personal charm of Arnold Palmer is evident even in this 1930s picture of the golfer as a schoolboy. THE ARNOLD PALMER COLLECTION

Arnold Palmer and sister Lois Jean as children with their father, Deacon Palmer.
THE ARNOLD PALMER COLLECTION

Palmer was affected deeply when his college friend Buddy Worsham (standing next to Palmer) was killed in an automobile accident in 1950. Here the friends were celebrating at a junior golf tournament. THE ARNOLD PALMER COLLECTION

Winning the 1954 U.S. Amateur Championship changed Arnold Palmer's life. Here Palmer accepts the congratulations of vanquished rival Robert Sweeny Jr. CORBIS

Arnold and Winnie Palmer, who married in 1954. CORBIS

Upon winning the 1962 Masters at the Augusta National Golf Club in Georgia, Arnold Palmer posed with the club's founder Bobby Jones (seated) and its chairman Clifford Roberts. CORBIS

Like Arnold Palmer, Jack Nicklaus enjoyed a very close relationship with his father. Here young Jack and sister Marilyn are with Charlie Nicklaus at the 1947 Ohio State Fair. MARILYN HUTCHINSON

Jack Nicklaus's sister Marilyn (left) and Jack's wife, Barbara, are seen here in a recent photograph taken outside the comfortable home on Collingswood Road in Upper Arlington, Ohio, where Jack and Marilyn grew up. HOWARD SOUNES

Having won the 1960 U.S. Open, Palmer looked benignly upon up-and-comer Jack Nicklaus, who came in second in the tournament while competing as an amateur. However, Nicklaus would soon end Palmer's reign as the world's number one golfer. ASSOCIATED PRESS

In 1972, Norman Rockwell painted this striking portrait of Arnold Palmer. The picture hangs in Palmer's office in Pennsylvania.

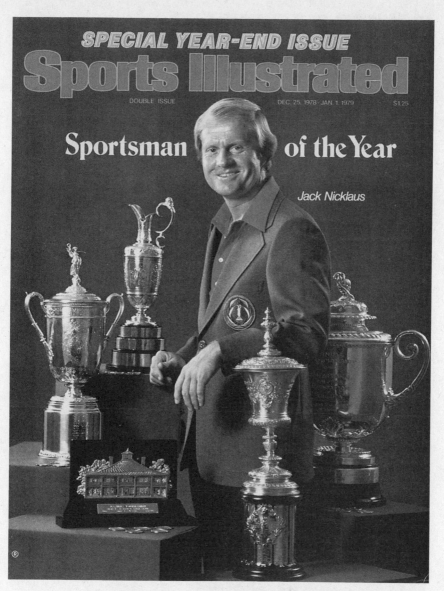

Sports Illustrated

DOUBLE ISSUE   DEC. 25, 1978 - JAN. 1, 1979 $1.25

Sportsman of the Year

Jack Nicklaus

Jack Nicklaus is one of only five golfers in the history of the modern game to have won all four professional major championships. In 1979 Nicklaus posed proudly for the cover of Sports Illustrated *with the four trophies as well as that of the U.S. Amateur.* LANE STEWART/SPORTS ILLUSTRATED

Jack Nicklaus (second from left) with best friends (left to right) Ivor Young, Bob Hoag, and Pandel Savic at Muirfield Village, the golf club Nicklaus built in Ohio. MUIRFIELD VILLAGE GOLF CLUB

Throughout his career Arnold Palmer has been involved in numerous business ventures, including the twenty-four-hour cable-TV Golf Channel, of which he remains chairman. Here he is with Golf Channel founder Joe Gibbs.
DR. HOWDY GILES

Arnold Palmer and Ed Seay, who runs Palmer's lucrative golf course design business, upon disembarking from Palmer's jet airplane. ED SEAY/PALMER COURSE DESIGN COMPANY

Mark H. McCormack founded IMG with Arnold Palmer as his first major client and built the company into the largest sports agency in the world. IMG/DAVID GAMBLE

Arnold Palmer bade farewell to his fans at the 2002 Masters, saying he would not compete again in the tournament. However, he was back the following year. GETTY IMAGES

Arnold Palmer, Tiger Woods, and Jack Nicklaus played a practice round together at the 1996 Masters. Afterward Nicklaus predicted: "You can take all of Arnold's wins in the Masters and my wins in the Masters and add them together, and [Tiger] should win more than both of us." DR. HOWDY GILES

Born in 1932, Tiger Woods's father, Earl, grew up in the racially segregated town of Manhattan, Kansas. An irrepressible character from an early age, he interjected himself cheekily into this photograph of a group of neighborhood boys. HAROLD ROBINSON

Earl Woods's first wife, Barbara Ann. BARBARA ANN GARY

Tiger Woods as a child with his first golf coach, Rudy Duran. RUDY DURAN

By the time Tiger was thirteen, Earl Woods had taken early retirement to devote himself to his son's golfing career. CORBIS

Tiger and his aunt Mae, Earl Woods's only surviving sibling.
MABEL LEE "MAE" MOORE

Tiger was featured in the 1994 Western High yearbook as the boy "Most Likely to Succeed." WESTERN HIGH SCHOOL

Most Likely To Succeed

Tiger is seen practicing his golf swing at Western High School in Anaheim, California, where he was a student from 1990 to 1994. WESTERN HIGH SCHOOL

Tiger's first girlfriend, Dina Gravell, who did not get along with his parents. WESTERN HIGH SCHOOL

Tiger's 1994 school yearbook photograph. WESTERN HIGH SCHOOL

Naturally, Tiger was the star of his high school golf team. In the middle of this group is school coach Don Crosby. Also shown is Bryon Bell (bottom right), one of Tiger's best friends. DON CROSBY

Tiger is seen here at home in Cypress, California, in 1995 with the U.S. Amateur trophy, his former coach John Anselmo (left), and Bill Orr, who customized Tiger's golf clubs. The living room wall is covered with mementos of Tiger's career. BILL ORR

Since becoming a professional golfer Tiger has lived within the high-security Isleworth Golf and Country Club in Florida. This is the palatial clubhouse.
ISLEWORTH REAL ESTATE SERVICES, INC.

"We made it! We made it!" exclaimed Earl Woods as Tiger hugged his father upon winning the 1997 Masters. Associated Press

A grin spread across Tiger Woods's face as defending Masters champion Nick Faldo helped him on with the winner's green blazer, April 1997. Corbis

Tiger won the British Open Championship at the historic home of golf, St. Andrews in Scotland, in July 2000. Here he is holding the Claret Jug trophy, alongside his mother Tida (pointing) and former girlfriend Joanna Jagoda (partially visible, behind Tida). Marc Aspland/The Times

Earl Woods at home in Southern California in a recent photograph.
HOWARD SOUNES

Upon winning his second professional major title in 1999, after a gap of more than two years, Tiger held the PGA Championship trophy to his lips. ASSOCIATED PRESS

Tiger Woods and girlfriend Elin Nordegren in 2002 at the opening ceremony of the Ryder Cup. GETTY IMAGES

Golf has become a huge business. In a promotion for his sponsor Nike, Inc., Tiger Woods's face is painted as a giant mural on a building in Portland, Oregon. ASSOCIATED PRESS

green, but he missed his birdie putt. "We misread it," admits Brunza. That afternoon, Tiger tried the same thing. The ball landed to the right of the flag, stopping three feet or so from the point where it would have toppled into the water. Learning from the lesson of the morning, he made a putt of fourteen feet and thereby won the match, and the tournament, 2-up.

Again, the pressure Tiger had been under was revealed when he dissolved into tears, hiding his face as he wept. In everyday life, Tiger was remarkably composed and rarely showed his feelings—very much like Nicklaus (though quite unlike Palmer). Indeed, Dina thought this aspect of her boyfriend's personality troubling. "I think, probably, the saddest thing is that he has always had to control his emotions, [so] they don't run freely." At times like this, however, the emotional dam burst. It was alarming to watch, though Dr. Brunza insists such a release was normal and healthy, and to some extent Tiger had reason to be overwhelmed. He was the youngest player ever to win the Havemeyer Trophy (breaking a Nicklaus record). He was also the first person of color to win, as Earl was quick to point out. "I said to him, 'Son, you have done something no black person in the United States has ever done.'" By dint of winning, he would be invited to the Masters, the U.S. Open, and the Open Championship. Congratulatory letters arrived from President Bill Clinton and Philip H. Knight, founder of Nike, who was beginning to size up Tiger as somebody who might endorse his products. A great future was beckoning.

Having brought that gold trophy home to Cypress, Tiger confided in Dina about his ambitions. "His goal was . . . to be the best golfer in the world. He wanted it very much. He could taste it. It was funny. He was very confident." To Bill Murvin, his school sports coach, he stated that his aim was to win three U.S. Amateurs. One time teacher Don Crosby overheard Tiger talking with his best school friend, Bryon Bell, about his future. Tiger said that he was going to turn pro and then, when he got old, he was going to play the Senior Tour. His whole life was mapped out in terms of golf, with the support of his parents. Maybe more than just support. "I think his parents pushed him, sometimes when he didn't want to be pushed. . . . I think they controlled him a little too much," says Dina. "From my perspective, he never had a normal teenage life."

One of the last vestiges of normality was going to college. There was a strong emphasis on education in the Woods family, going back to Maude and Hattie Belle Woods in Manhattan, Kansas, and some of the country's leading universities had long been competing to enroll Tiger on a scholarship. The principal contenders were the University of Nevada Las Vegas (UNLV) and Stanford, arguably the most prestigious university on the West Coast, situated south of San Francisco. Annual tuition and fees at Stanford were in the region of $25,000. Alumni included John Steinbeck, and more than a dozen Nobel laureates were on the faculty. In short, this was a world-renowned center of academic excellence, where most pupils had much greater intellectual ability than Tiger. "He was smart. He wasn't *brilliant*," says Don Crosby, who recalls Tiger had a grade point average of about 3.8, making him a B+ student. But Stanford very much wanted Tiger. "Stanford is very interested in winning," explains Wally Goodwin, former golf coach at the university. "Physics is just as important to them as football, and golf is just as important as psychiatry." The incumbent golf team was one of the best ever, winner of the 1994 National Collegiate Athletic Association (NCAA) Championship, and rich in characters. Notah Begay III was a Native American from New Mexico who painted his face for tournaments. Casey Martin excelled at the game despite suffering from Klippel-Trenauny-Weber Syndrome, which withered his right leg (he jokingly referred to himself as a Disabled American). When he was trying to make up his mind which college to attend, Tiger visited Stanford and stayed overnight with another team member, Conrad Ray, a husky Midwesterner who recalls meeting "kind of a goofy kid." That evening, Tiger joined Ray and some of the others at Chili's for dinner, and during the meal team member Brad Lanning fired questions at Tiger about his recent trip to Vegas, where he had visited the campus of UNLV, asking if he gambled, drank, and met girls. "No. I don't gamble because I think it saps your motivation," Tiger replied sanctimoniously. He didn't touch alcohol, either, and said he was happy with his steady girlfriend. The boys were not impressed. As Ray says, "We thought this guy was a robot." Indeed, there was something of the nerd about the young Tiger Woods, this skinny four-eyes whose idea of fun—outside golf—was watching cartoons and playing computer games.

Tiger chose Stanford, enrolling in the fall of 1994 to study economics. Until now, he had been with his parents constantly. The family hadn't so much as moved house during his childhood. Even when he traveled to tournaments, one parent almost invariably accompanied him. To live away from home on his own was therefore a distinct change. It was for this reason that Tiger paid frequent visits to his sister, Royce, now thirty-six and a single mother living in nearby San Jose. Tiger had always got on well with Lala, as he called his sister, and she kindly took in his laundry while he was at college. "Lala, when I get rich and famous I'm going to buy you a house," he would tell her gratefully, which made her laugh, not imagining such a thing would come true. Although Royce was the sibling he saw most often, Tiger's relationships with all three of Earl's older children were reasonably close at this stage in his life, despite the bitterness of his father's divorce from his first wife. Ann was still angry about the way Earl had treated her and their children, arguing that he should have given them the same attention he gave Tiger. But her children were more forgiving of Earl's shortcomings and did their best to get along with Tiger. "They could despise him, because of what he did. But they don't," says Ann of their relationship with Earl. "They know that he hasn't been fair to them. I mean, how do you think you feel when you see your father giving all the attention and money and everything to another sibling, and you're sitting back here watching, and he doesn't do a damn thing for you?"

Because of the extraordinary changes he underwent after he left Stanford, Tiger has come to look back on these college years with special affection. When I asked him at the PGA Championship in 2002 what was the best, and worst, aspect of being Tiger Woods, he replied sharply: "The worst—easy—this," indicating the room filled with media. And though he laughed, one knew that was true. He went on to say that the best memories he had were of his time at Stanford. "I think the toughest part is anonymity. From college to now is certainly a lot different. It's a lot different now than it ever used to be. That's something that I really look back and thoroughly enjoyed—my college experience," he told me. "There was so many different people [at Stanford]. You've got Olympic athletes. There was a kid in my dorm who built his own computer from scratch." Tiger smiled as he remembered. "The kid was, what, sixteen years old. I mean, people are just so bright and special in their own way, and I think that was probably the coolest time of my life."

Some of his former teammates are surprised by Tiger's nostalgic words, remembering as they do a remote person whose monomania for golf set him apart from everyone and made him hard to know. For instance, Coach Goodwin encouraged the golfers to get their academic work done in the morning so that they could practice together on the range in the afternoon. Goodwin wanted them very specifically to practice together in order to foster team spirit, and the boys liked the sociable aspect of hanging out on the range as a team. But Tiger—the star of the team—practiced earlier or later so he could be alone. For him, golf practice was work and he did not want to be distracted by a lot of chatter. As team member Eri Crum remarks, this was "kind of a bummer" for the others who asked themselves, "We're here. Why aren't you here?" Many of the golfers belonged to the Sigma Chi fraternity and encouraged Tiger to join them. Although he showed some initial interest in doing so and attended some parties, he chose not to be initiated. "My feeling was that he was so committed to golf that anything that would get in the way he just wouldn't do," says Crum. "He wasn't willing to join a fraternity if it meant he would have a couple of hours less on the driving range." Tiger also had a different attitude toward studying now that he was at college and his mother was not around to make him do his homework. The young men on the golf team loved the game, of course, and most wanted to turn professional ultimately. But first they wanted to graduate so they had something to fall back on. Tiger seemed to choose the least-taxing classes available in order to have the maximum golf time, and nothing much bothered him as long as he could practice. He wasn't unduly upset when he was mugged on campus. Neither did he allow himself to become distracted by girlfriend trouble.

Although Dina was now living in Las Vegas, she and Tiger still considered themselves a couple and met as often as possible. However, Dina wanted to be able to go on dates if she was asked out by guys she met in Vegas, and suggested to Tiger that they might see other people. He was not pleased to hear this. Tiger had female friends at Stanford, but he wasn't a Casanova, and had a conservative attitude toward life in general. "We got more girls for knowing Tiger Woods than he did for being Tiger Woods," laughs team member Jake Poe, reciting what was an in-joke. An increasingly unsatisfactory relationship limped on until the spring of 1995 when Dina and her parents flew up to the Bay Area to support Tiger in a tournament. Over the weekend, Tiger abruptly ended the relationship by sending some of Dina's belongings back to her hotel with a note accusing her of bragging to people at the tournament about their relationship, and of being interested in him because of his notoriety and possible fortune. Although she did not want to blame his family for the breakup, Dina suspected Earl and Tida had turned Tiger against her. "I guess they were totally afraid of our relationship, because we were so close. Looking back on it now, [they] were probably afraid that I would hinder him." Dina also sees the breakup and the clinical way in which it was done as part of what Tiger had to sacrifice to get to the top. "It's not all peaches and cream, as it seems to be."

A few months later Tiger was at Newport Country Club, Rhode Island, to defend his U.S. Amateur title. In the 36-hole final, Woods competed against Buddy Marucci Jr. A man in his forties, Marucci could not equal the younger player's long drives, but he had a good short game and the match was close, ending at the 35th when Marucci missed a long par-putt and conceded to Tiger, 2-up. Winning the U.S. Amateur back-to-back was another landmark in one of the most remarkable amateur careers in golf history, and a signpost to the future. Earl celebrated by drinking champagne from the Havemeyer Trophy and, thus fortified, made a prediction for the benefit of reporters. "Before he's through," began Earl, once again giving the impression that creating Tiger had been his work alone, "my son will win fourteen major championships." In fact, he was selling Tiger's ambition short. The boy would need to win more than fourteen to beat Jack Nicklaus's record, which is what he aimed at privately and, with this sort of form and single-mindedness, it looked like he could do just about anything he wanted in the game. Arnold Palmer turned pro after winning one U.S. Amateur. Nicklaus waited until he had two. Now that Tiger had matched Jack, his Stanford teammates wondered whether he would even bother returning to college for his sophomore year, or whether he would first try to outdo Nicklaus by winning three Amateurs in a row.

8

GREEN STUFF

Two very different-looking men sat in deep discussion in the Royal Oak restaurant: a college boy and a distinguished man of late middle age with a deep suntan and white hair. The man's hands, when he rested them beside his gleaming plate, were unusually large, and his slightly too loud voice was so distinctive other diners turned to look. It was October 1995 and Tiger had driven up from Stanford to meet Arnold Palmer at the Silverado Resort in the Napa Valley, where the veteran was playing in a Senior PGA Tour event. Tiger wanted some general career advice. "I told him the things my father taught me, that the most important thing is to remain humble, and to protect the game and the future of the game," says Palmer, who had always been happy to help talented new players. It did not seem that long ago that he was advising another Stanford student, Tom Watson. As a matter of fact, he gave Watson some golf equipment, which led to a silly altercation with the National Collegiate Athletic Association over a breach of its rules. Palmer could easily afford the cost of a bag of clubs, though, as he could afford to pick up the check for this dinner with Tiger, which he did at the end of the meal.

Shortly afterward Tiger was playing a practice round with his Stanford teammates at the Northwestern Golf Tournament in Chicago. A reporter who had been following them asked casually, "Hey, did you enjoy having that meal with Arnie?" Coach Wally Goodwin overheard and started to worry, knowing that the NCAA forbade student athletes from accepting what is termed "additional benefits" from outsiders, benefits other athletes did not receive. This rule had been put into place to prevent boosters from influencing college sports—buying athletes, in effect—and even a free meal was against the rules, as was a gift of golf equipment, which was why there had been a problem with Palmer's long-ago present to Tom Watson. When Goodwin elicited the full story from Tiger, he told him he should not have accepted the meal—as he and Palmer surely knew—and that he had to report it. Tiger was promptly ruled ineligible for the Chicago tournament and the matter was referred to the NCAA, which suggested Tiger send Palmer money to cover half the meal. Tiger lost no time in dispatching a check, but still he found himself suspended from college golf for several days while the matter was resolved and this irritated both him and his father. The Woodses had run into such pettifoggery before with the NCAA—when Tiger wrote a Masters diary for a couple of magazines and when he used equipment associated with Greg Norman. Each time the NCAA got upset. But this hassle over a dinner with Palmer was too ridiculous, in their opinion. "It was one of the happenings that made Earl have feelings that the NCAA was 'after Tiger,' because Earl had feelings like that," says Goodwin. Indeed, it was shortly after this incident that Tiger and his father began making plans to leave amateur golf and enter the professional game.

When he spoke with reporters, Tiger insisted that he intended to stay at Stanford until graduation. "I won't turn pro until 1998, after college," he told *Sports Illustrated* in July 1995. However, by February 1996, in private at least, he had essentially decided to join the tour. It was in February that Earl engaged a lawyer to negotiate with prospective sports agents. He chose John Merchant for the job, the Connecticut attorney who became the first black member of the executive committee of the United States Golf Association, from which he had resigned by January 1996. Their friendship started when Merchant was on the USGA's junior golf committee, as he explains: "I made it my business to attend the junior golf championships and that's where I met Tiger's dad and we became very close. And eight months before Tiger turned pro, his father called me and asked if I would, you know, begin to put together all the things that were necessary *in the event* that Tiger decided to turn pro." This was a delicate task because Merchant could not talk to Tiger directly, again because of the rules affecting amateur players. "If I talked to him about any of this stuff, he loses his amateur status." Disgruntled though he was, Tiger wanted to preserve his status long enough to defend his U.S. Amateur title in the summer of 1996, when he hoped to become the first three-time winner.

The business of sports management had grown significantly since Mark McCormack had founded IMG, and there were many reputable agents eager to sign Tiger. Merchant drew up a list of the best half dozen and spoke to them briefly to ascertain their interest. But Earl made his preference clear. "He suggested that I speak to IMG first." Of course, IMG had been courting Tiger for years. There had been meetings with Hughes Norton and McCormack himself. Moreover, Earl had been in a loose business arrangement with the company where he worked as an IMG "talent scout" for a time. He is quick to point out that he did not receive a salary, as such—IMG paid him "expenses"— and he was no longer a scout when it came time for Tiger to choose an agent. Nonetheless, there was a history, and it makes one suspect that Earl had been bought. He refutes this. "Having a job with IMG doesn't mean that I want my son to work for IMG, or for IMG to represent him. And you cannot buy me for [the] money that I got as expenses. You can't buy me like that. I'm too high-principled for that." He says he was disposed toward IMG for another reason. "I wanted someone with international representation, with offices around the world, so they could represent Tiger internationally, because I knew Tiger was going to be an international, world-famous golfer." As he says, he had known this since the boy was ten months old. So there had been plenty of time to formulate a plan. And the plan was: don't waste time talking to others; go with IMG. As a result, Merchant did not meet with any other agents for a "serious discussion," as he says. "All I know is that, when I talked to Earl, he suggested that I speak to IMG first." In theory Tiger knew nothing about this. Not only did Merchant not talk to Tiger directly, he never asked Earl if *he* talked to Tiger about the negotiations. "If I did, I'd commit technically the same violation."

Meanwhile, Tiger entered the last lap of his amateur career and, as he did so, the expectation and drama built with each tournament he competed in. At the Augusta National on the afternoon of Wednesday, April 10, 1996, the prodigy (entered as an amateur) had a practice round with Palmer and Nicklaus—the first time they had all played together. The older men took genuine pleasure in Tiger's talent and after their round Nicklaus made a bold prediction: "You can take all of Arnold's wins in the Masters and my wins in the Masters and add them together and [Tiger] should win more than both of us." Since Jack had the record with six, and Arnold had another four, that was a big number. "Whether he's ready to win the Masters now or not, he'll be your favorite for the next twenty years," added Nicklaus. In the event, Tiger played poorly in 1996, missing the cut. But his future seemed increasingly bright.

Back at Stanford Tiger's growing celebrity was becoming a problem for Coach Goodwin. The telephone in his office rang from morning to night with calls regarding Tiger, who was approaching the point in his life where it seemed almost everybody everywhere knew who he was and wanted a piece of him. There were reporters who would not take no for an answer, girls wanting to date Tiger, every manner of request for Tiger to do this, that, or the other. It was too much for Goodwin to deal with, though none of it seemed to get to Tiger, who had trained himself to block out anything that distracted him, including the attention of media and fans. This concentration was a by-product of the work he had done with Earl and Dr. Brunza, and it was to some extent just how he was. "Focused" is the overused term in golf. The image of a horse with blinkers on also comes to mind. As Goodwin observes, "A cannon could go off in the middle of his golf swing when he was in college and he wouldn't even hear it." A great asset to a team, one might think, but Stanford lost its NCAA Championship title in 1995, coming in second to Oakland. Although Tiger won the individual title, a question is raised regarding whether Tiger is a team player. Goodwin—the type who likes to see the best in everybody—maintains that Tiger was a team player at Stanford. But fellow Cardinals were unsure of his commitment in some respects. At the end of his sophomore year, for instance, they asked Tiger whether he was coming back next year, and he could not give them a straight answer. "After he left we all sort of said, you know, that's probably going to be the end of him," remembers Eri Crum. "He wasn't going to say for sure [if] he was going to turn pro. The truth is, I don't think he knew. Because he wanted to win that third Amateur."

Away from college, during his summer break, Tiger was moving in a world his teammates could only imagine, making star appearances in major tournaments including the U.S. Open at Oakland Hills in Michigan, where he led through 13 holes in the first round, but ended tied for eighty-second. He also flew to Britain for the Open Championship at Royal Lytham and St. Annes. One might wonder how Tiger could afford to flit around the world in this manner, having no obvious source of income. In theory, his parents paid for everything, and they were living beyond their means in order to support him. In 1995 the family's annual expenses exceeded $70,000. Earl's gross earnings, essentially from retirement benefits, totaled $45,000. Tida worked to help make up the difference, but the Woodses were spending more than was coming in. They had a $469-a-month mortgage on their Cypress home— remortgaged to raise funds—plus almost $6,000 of additional debt, mostly on credit cards. This must have been a powerful incentive for Tiger to turn professional and reimburse his parents for all they had done for him.

Yet turning professional was problematic. A player like Tiger, who did not have a PGA Tour card, would only be allowed to compete in seven official tournaments in the United States in his first year, by dint of sponsors' exemptions. And if he waited until after the U.S. Amateur, the season would already be more than halfway finished when he joined the tour. In order to qualify for the 1997 season, he would then have to win one of those seven tournaments, or do well enough generally to finish the year in the top 125 money winners. If he failed to win a tour event or make enough money (about $150,000 would do it), he faced the prospect of having to compete in the PGA Tour Qualifying Tournament for a place on tour next year. This is a desperate affair during which hundreds of would-be tour players (1,153 in 1996) are whittled down by regional events to a field of golfers who compete against one another for a few tour cards (forty-nine were granted in 1996). Tiger did not want to go through that ordeal. Also, if he turned professional in 1996, he would lose his amateur exemption to the 1997 Masters. To get invited back to Augusta, he would have to win a tournament or finish in the top thirty on the Money List. "What people don't understand is I am not exempt anywhere," he said in June 1996, with evident feeling.

At the same time, businessmen were waiting to strike deals with Tiger. At the head of the line was Stanford graduate Philip H. Knight, of Nike, Inc., the corporation Knight built from scratch, starting in 1962, when he sold running shoes from the back of his car. By 1996 Nike (named after the Greek goddess of victory) had a revenue of $6.5 billion. Much of the reason for its phenomenal growth and success lay in clever marketing. Nike products are utilitarian, some would say ugly items: running shoes made with plastic are the mainstay, though Nike would branch out into other types of clothing and sports equipment. To get people to buy, Nike invested heavily in signing the most engaging sports stars of the day to endorsement contracts and presented these stars and the product to the public with slick advertisements and catchphrases, such as "Just do it." For years the main proponent of "Just do it" had been basketball star Michael Jordan. But basketball careers are

fleeting and, as Jordan came toward the end of his, Knight was looking
to invest in a new name. Tiger was the favorite candidate. "Michael was
going to disappear in a short period of time, and they needed a replacement," John Merchant confirms. "I don't think there was anybody [else]
that had the potential." In fact, Woods looked as if he might be an even
better shoe salesman than Jordan. Golf is played all over the world, unlike basketball, and due to his multiethnic look Tiger had greater international appeal than an African American star of what is essentially an
American game. For the same reason, he was also more valuable than a
young white golfer of equivalent ability, had such a person existed. His
mixed ethnicity was not a hindrance, as it would have been in previous
eras. Ironically, it was his ticket. "If I understand Phil Knight and
his people, I don't think a white kid gets the same amount of money,"
says Merchant. "Because you pay the extra money for the novelty, for the
oneness, for the uniqueness of it. And, you know, a white kid, well, hell,
that's what white folks do, they play golf." McCormack agreed, saying
Tiger's multicultural makeup "was a help more than a hindrance."

How much had changed! In the 1950s and '60s, Arnold Palmer was
the ideal salesman for quintessential American products, such as Cadillac and Wheaties. A black Palmer would not have had his face on a
breakfast cereal packet. In the modern era, Woods was a perfect representative for brands that were in almost every American home and, importantly, sold beyond the fifty states of the union. For in the modern
world the most successful companies were global. Herein was a problem, however. Knight built Nike into the money machine it is by sub-
contracting virtually all production to factories in the developing world
where labor is cheap. Knight and his executives worked comfortably in
a smart headquarters in Beaverton, Oregon. The people who actually
glued those shoes together did so for a couple of dollars a day—the
price of a Starbucks coffee—in parts of the Far East where employees
can sometimes be imprisoned for forming unions. Nike is a huge
concern, working with nine hundred factories in fifty-five countries,
a subcontracted workforce of seven hundred thousand people, so its

business practices affect many lives. And though Nike has improved its policies in recent years with regard to foreign workers, its history in countries such as Indonesia, Thailand, and Vietnam has been a cause of concern to organizations such as Oxfam Community Aid Abroad, which established NikeWatch in 1995 to monitor the company. "Nike had led the push to source production in low-wage countries with poor human rights records," says coordinator Tim Connor, explaining why NikeWatch was created. Although wages of a dollar and change per day can be the norm in the Far East, critics say it is not enough to live on comfortably. Certainly, Nike's freewheeling image is at odds with the real lives of the people that make its products. Most alarmingly, there have been allegations of the use of child labor. Nike admits to "past mistakes" in this regard, but has introduced a Code of Conduct that lays down minimum ages for workers—sixteen for clothing, eighteen for shoes—among other things. Nike maintains that it does all it can for the people who make its products. Yet as recently as October 2002 it was claimed that a factory in Thailand that made products for Nike and other companies before it went out of business was asking its workers to put in 110-hour weeks and making amphetamines available to help them work through the night. These sorts of stories have caused Nike to be involved in a seemingly perpetual public relations war. John Merchant foresaw a problem with Tiger's attaching his name to the company, particularly because Tiger's mother is Thai-born. "I want[ed] a letter signed by Philip Knight which says that Nike did not violate any country's labor laws anywhere in the world," reveals Merchant. "I don't want Tiger exposed to [that sort of publicity]." Knight signed the letter, naturally. Nike wasn't breaking laws. The problem was more subtle. As Tim Connor says: "It is distressing that we live in a world where a company like Nike can pay tens of millions of dollars to one golfer, while hundreds of thousands of people, who actually make the company's product, are not paid enough to support their children."

Titleist was another company that made big profits out of banal products—in this case golf clubs, gloves, and balls. To read the advertising literature, one would think the technology that goes into manufacturing a modern golf ball is akin to space exploration. Certainly golf balls are better made than they once were, weighted and dimpled so they travel farther and straighter, and professional players no longer have to carry a metal ring to test that each ball is standard size. Still, they are only little white balls. The fact that companies can charge so much for them—$56 a dozen* for Titleist Pro V1—is another triumph of marketing over common sense. Therein lies the whole story. Like Nike, Titleist could sell such commonplace products in huge numbers at a high price only with the aid of exceptional marketing, which involved getting its brand associated with the best golfers in the world. In theory, the gullible public would follow—which is the model of sports marketing pioneered by McCormack and Palmer. (I use the word *gullible* because there is no logical reason to choose any item over another simply because it has a sportsman's name attached to it.) In fact, Titleist was even more gung-ho for Woods than Nike. "They climbed aboard early and outbid everybody, in effect, before they even allowed anybody to bid," says Merchant, whose mind turned next to sheltering Tiger from tax.

If and when Tiger turned professional, he would be liable for the highest level of state income tax as long as he remained in California (a top rate of 9.3 percent in 1996). Indeed, state and federal taxes would be his single biggest expenditure. But he could avoid state income tax by moving his residence to Florida, one of the few states that does not have state income tax, and, of course, Florida has a good climate for golf. These were two of the reasons that the Sunshine State had become a veritable PGA Tour colony. Tiger began to think about where he wanted to live specifically and canvassed his new friends for advice. His friends were not the same sort of people that most college boys hung out with. "He said, where do I live?" recalled Mark McCormack, who had a home at Isleworth. "[He] didn't want to be a California resident,

---

*The spring 2003 suggested retail price.

[so] we suggested this would be a good place." The fact that Tiger could think of himself as a social equal to McCormack—this much older, powerful, and very wealthy man—showed amazing confidence, which was due in some degree to the way Earl had brought Tiger up, raising him to think he was as good as anybody. It wasn't necessarily egotism, though there was some of that. It was more that Earl was smart enough to know Tiger would mix with rich, powerful people in golf and, if this was going to be his life, he should be at ease with such people. It is also a paradox because, despite his confidence and maturity, Tiger remained basically shy, an almost geeky kid in private. Although now a man of twenty, when he was with friends he could look and talk and behave like a boy of fifteen, wearing his baseball cap backward, delighting in bass-heavy rap music and sugary fast food, and abbreviating words to a juvenile shorthand. High praise was to say something was "kinda neat." Sometimes it was hard to believe this kid might join Muhammad Ali and Pelé as one of the most famous sports figures in the world. It seemed that he had matured schizophrenically. The public Tiger was a man beyond his years. The private Tiger appeared to be stuck in his adolescence.

On July 31, 1996, IMG bought a small house in Isleworth for Tiger for $475,000. There was still no commitment from Tiger, and in public the young golfer persisted in playing dumb with the media. But the fact that IMG bought this house is evidence McCormack's people were confident Woods would turn professional imminently and sign with them when he did. The date of the purchase also undermines Tiger's claim that he intended to return to Stanford and finish his education. As late as August 25—almost a month after the house was bought—he indicated to reporters that he was going back to Stanford in the fall. In truth, he knew he was about to become a college dropout—like Palmer and Nicklaus before him—move out of his dorm, and fly across the country to live in the gated community Arnold Palmer had built.

There was just one more thing to do: win that third U.S. Amateur (though the purchase of the house indicates he would have turned professional that summer whatever happened). In late August, Tiger and his father flew to Portland, Oregon, where the championship was starting a day early so the quarterfinals and semifinals would be played on different days for the benefit of NBC television, which did not usually take such an interest in amateur golf but had realized Tiger was a star attraction. The championship was at Pumpkin Ridge Golf Club, not far from the headquarters of Nike, and Philip Knight attended each day—an austere figure behind dark glasses—his presence adding to speculation that Tiger was about to turn professional. Also in the huge crowd of fifteen thousand were senior staff from IMG. "The fact that all those people were there, it didn't really seem like amateur golf," says Joel Kribel, a teammate of Tiger's from Stanford who found himself playing Tiger in the semifinal. Before the match, Kribel joked that if he won, Tiger would have to stay at Stanford. His friend didn't accept the bet—"he sort of danced around the question"—and won the match 3 and 1. In the 36-hole final, Tiger played nineteen-year-old University of Florida student Steve Scott. After a shaky start, Tiger was behind for much of the match. But he came back, shooting an eagle at the 29th and holing a thirty-five-foot putt at the 35th that broke just as he had hoped, causing him to brandish his right fist in a display of machismo. When they halved the final hole, the match went into a sudden-death play-off and, by winning the 38th, Tiger became the only three-time U.S. Amateur champion.

Tiger had been invited to compete in the forthcoming Greater Milwaukee Open as an amateur. If he wanted to collect prize money, he would have to declare himself a professional before the start of the tournament. On Tuesday, August 27, the press was given a terse statement that Tiger would not be starting college again on September 25. As of that moment, he was a professional golfer. His Stanford teammates heard it on the news, like everybody else. "There were no calls," says Eri Crum. "[No] thanks for the memories and all that. . . . He just moved on."

It was only now that Tiger talked directly with John Merchant about the deals on offer. "The first time Tiger heard anything from me about what was in place was shortly before he signed the documents, when I sat down and explained them to him," says his lawyer. "[I] said to him, 'You don't have to sign these things. You don't have to agree to this. But this is what's there.' " Tiger didn't become overexcited, or even very excited. It was as if he had been expecting as much. "He is a bright young guy, and it wasn't hard to understand what was being said. You know, some of the fine print, obviously, had to be explained to him in some more detail, but the numbers are right there." The numbers were astonishing. When it came to the moment of truth, Titleist offered $3 million over three years for Tiger to use its golf balls, wear its gloves, and carry its bag. (The deal was later boosted to $20 million to include playing with Titleist clubs.) But that was just the appetizer. The main dish was Nike, which offered up a gargantuan $40 million over five years for Tiger to endorse its shoes and clothing. Hughes Norton was elated with the deals, which dwarfed the industry record.* Remaining composed, Tiger signed with Nike and Titleist, together with an agreement with IMG, which would represent him for the next five years at least. "IMG agreed in the contract that I negotiated with them to take less commission than what they told me was standard for them," says Merchant, adding that the agency would receive an enhanced percentage (the exact figures have not been revealed) when Tiger's earnings reached a certain level. "What you wanted was for him not to ever have to worry about paying his bills. You wanted him only to worry about playing golf and getting better and reaching his goals, and so from my point of view the sums of money that were negotiated [were] more than sufficient to allow him to do that," he adds. "He could live where he wanted. He could buy what he wanted. He could go where he wanted. All he had to worry about was working on his golf game and playing tournaments, and winning tournaments, and then winning majors."

On Wednesday, August 28, Tiger appeared before the media in Milwaukee. Everything he wore seemed to have a Nike swoosh on it.

---

*Greg Norman hitherto had the richest golf contract: $2.5 million a year from Reebok.

Sitting to his side in an easy chair was Earl, wearing a Nike cap. Tiger's first words to reporters were: "Hello world." This contrived phrase was part of the copy in Nike's first Tiger Woods campaign, which was launched the following morning with a three-page print advertisement in the *Wall Street Journal*. The ad featured a picture of Tiger as a child hefting a driver, and the first-person-singular copy gave his achievements from age eight. "Hello world. I shot in the 70s when I was 8. I shot in the 60s when I was 12 . . ." Toward the end, it read: "Hello world. There are still courses in the United States that I am not allowed to play because of the color of my skin. Hello world. I've heard I'm not ready for you. Are you ready for me?" The campaign drew immediate criticism from those who saw the issue of race discrimination being co-opted for commercial purposes. James K. Glassman argued in the *Washington Post* that it was untrue that there were clubs closed to Woods. Maybe to some black players. Tiger Woods could play anywhere he wanted. And when Glassman asked Nike to specify which courses Woods was not allowed to play, the company could not give an example. After blurting out "Hello world" at the press conference, Tiger settled down and spoke a little more naturally about how he was fulfilling a lifelong ambition by becoming a professional golfer, something he had thought about since he was a kid watching Jack Nicklaus on TV. Then he turned his mind to the forthcoming tournament. The pressure was on, as he was the first to concede. It was the end of August and Tiger had only a few months to win, or earn a total of $150,000 or so in prize money, and thus avoid the dreaded "qualifying school." It would be nice to win this week and alleviate the pressure. But he was exhausted from the U.S. Amateur and, come Sunday, he could manage no better than a tie for sixtieth place. "Are you ready for me?" already seemed presumptuous.

Next stop was the Bell Canadian Open, where he did slightly better, though a poor final day meant he finished eleventh. At the Quad City Classic in Coal Valley, Illinois, he gave away a 3-stroke lead in the final round to finish tied for fifth. Then he went out and squandered some of his endorsement fortune on blackjack (though he was too young to play legally). Having expressed his disdain for gambling when he first visited Stanford a couple of years earlier, Tiger's views had evidently changed dramatically, and indeed gambling would become a favorite recreation. Perhaps frittering away money that had been so easily obtained put life in perspective. More likely, he had no idea of the value of money. Directly after that was the BC Open in Endicott, New York. When wet weather led to the fourth round being scrapped, Tiger tied for third, picking up $58,000. He was creeping closer to a place in the top 125 earners in the year, but he wasn't *winning*. Tiger then took a couple of days off to see his new house at Isleworth before traveling to Pine Mountain, Georgia, for the Buick Challenge (one of four—now three—tour events sponsored by the car manufacturer because Buick identifies golfers as its market). Tiger arrived at Pine Mountain as scheduled on Tuesday, September 24, to be met by Tournament Director Bob Berry, who says Tiger seemed fine. Early the next morning, however, Hughes Norton informed Berry that Tiger had gone home. He was "exhausted" and wanted to rest before the Las Vegas Invitational. This was a big disappointment for the tournament organizers, naturally, but there was more to it. Part of the reason Tiger had come to Pine Mountain was to receive the Fred Haskins Award, given each year to an outstanding collegiate player. Two hundred invitations had been sent out for a dinner on Thursday evening and now everything would have to be canceled because the honoree couldn't be bothered to show up. Berry was not pleased, though he felt sympathy for a player who had been thrown into the briar patch, as he puts it. "It was overwhelming to a young fella like that." Tour players were more directly critical. Tom Kite said witheringly that he couldn't remember being tired at twenty.

Evidently, the young star was feeling under pressure. In fact, he was miserable. When he was at Stanford, Tiger had been able to live the life of a relatively ordinary person. It was only when he left the campus to appear in tournaments that he was in the spotlight. Now, it was that way all the time. He needed security to get on a golf course, and security to escort him off. Once in his hotel room, he was unable to go out to eat a hamburger or to see a ball game, because fans mobbed him and there was a real fear of cranks who wanted him dead. Nobody wanted to live with death threats, but a different sort of person—a Greg Norman or an Arnold Palmer, say—would have thrived on this circuslike atmosphere. Those players loved attention. Tiger was much more reserved and, like many child stars, he had an ambivalent attitude toward public adulation. He loved performing on the golf course. But part of him wanted to be anonymous. At the very least, he would like to be able to eat outside his room. One night he called Wally Goodwin. "I remember him saying to me this one time, 'Coach, I hate it here. I can't go out for breakfast. I can't go out for lunch. I got to eat up in my motel room. I can't go anywhere. Everybody wants something, and I hate it.' " Friends saw pathos in his position. "I did feel sorry for him," says Joel Kribel. "The life of an ordinary person was pretty much gone." Dina Gravell, who had followed her former boyfriend's career from her home in Las Vegas, felt sympathy for him, too. "You can have all the money in the world, but is it really everything?" asks Dina, who still felt hurt about the way they had broken up. She thought about Tiger often and their paths were about to cross one last time.

Tiger flew into Nevada at the start of October for the Las Vegas Invitational at the Tournament Players Club at Summerlin. He knew Dina was living in town. After he checked into the MGM Grand, he called and left a message, apologizing to Dina for the abrupt way he'd ended their relationship and saying he'd like to see her. When Dina received the message, she called him but was told Tiger was in bed already because he had an early tee time. She might have left it at that, but her friends and family persuaded her to go with them to the tournament as a spectator. There was an opportunity to speak to Tiger. But Dina did not take it. "My family went and spoke to him and saw him," she says, "but I didn't. I just didn't make any effort." Maybe it was because he knew she was there watching that Tiger performed in the final of the 90-hole event like a man with something to prove. He started

4 shots back from the lead, tied with seven others, but finished the five tournament rounds tied with Davis Love III, 27-under-par. When Love missed his par-putt on the 1st hole of a sudden-death play-off, Tiger had his first professional title and a prize of $297,000. Most important, the win meant he would be exempt from qualifying for the tour for the next two years. There would also be an automatic invitation to the Masters. A grin spread across his face as he posed with the trophy and two Vegas showgirls, realizing that he had crossed the Rubicon. "The rest is history," as Dina says, glad she was there to see him win, even though she would not be sharing the success.

Upon turning professional, Tiger talked loftily about using golf and his celebrity to help those less fortunate than himself. For example, in support of the National Minority Golf Foundation, which his lawyer, John Merchant, had founded, he said somewhat fatuously: "What our organization is trying to do is to show kids that there is a new way out of the inner city, out of poverty. There's a great sport called golf." With the establishment of his own charitable foundation within his first year as a tour player, as we shall see, he would be presented to the public increasingly as a munificent philanthropist. While Woods has done some laudable charitable work, the way in which his financial affairs have been managed privately shows, in fact, that he is concerned principally about amassing and protecting as many greenbacks as he can for himself—just like Palmer and Nicklaus before him. Tiger is a product of California's public education system and someone who learned much of his golf on public courses. In the first instance, if he was so concerned about common people, those people he grew up with in Cypress, he might have chosen to continue to reside in his home state and thereby give a proportion of his enormous income back to the community, via the equitable and expeditious method of paying state income tax. Instead, the very first thing Tiger did when he signed his endorsement contracts was to move his residence to the tax haven of

Florida, where he chose to live in a fortress of privilege, and where he returned after that Las Vegas win in the autumn of 1996.

Isleworth had changed considerably since Palmer and his partners lost control of it in 1991, and was now more luxurious than even Arnie could have imagined. This was largely due to British billionaire Joseph Lewis. The Mellon Bank sold Isleworth to one of Lewis's companies, Aviva Land Holdings, in 1993 for $21.65 million. Lewis, who rose from humble beginnings in the East End of London to make a fortune in the restaurant trade and then the money markets, decided to make Isleworth one of his homes. (He also lives in England, the Bahamas, and Argentina, where he is known locally as El Rico—the Rich One.) Because he was going to live at Isleworth, and because he wanted to attract other very wealthy people to reside there, Lewis spared no expense in upgrading the estate. More than one thousand trees were planted each year to beautify the grounds. Property lots were combined to make sites for the construction of enormous mansions. Lewis, who had concerns for his own safety, made sure security was second to none. The estate was enclosed by an eight-foot block wall with the sort of gatehouse entrances one finds at Western embassies in the Middle East. It was virtually impossible to gain admittance without an invitation, and even prospective home buyers had to present bank references before they could look around. When Tiger came through those formidable gates as a resident, he found himself in a pristine park—acres of green fairways rolling down to lakeshores and houses the size of hotels generously spaced along the roads, built in what is known as Mediterranean or Old Florida style (though every house is brand-new and so perfect they look like they've been extruded in plastic, like dollhouses).

Mark McCormack resided in a pink mansion, built from pink coral rock, at the head of a cul-de-sac named McCormack Place. But even McCormack's eighteen-thousand-square-foot palace was not the last word in extravagance at Isleworth. Joe Lewis's home, known as Champions' Gate, was even more extraordinary. Doubly protected within an inner ring of railings and electronic gates, the house is so big that when one is standing in the drive, among the almost casual profusion of Henry Moore sculpture, it is hard to see the boundaries of the place. Inside, one walks through a series of lofty reception rooms, with highly polished and ornate stone floors and wood-paneled walls, most of which are hung with paintings. At first glance, these paintings appear to be in the styles of the greatest modern artists—Joan Miró, Pablo Picasso, and so on—though one assumes they are not originals. If they were, it would be a collection worthy of a museum. But of course they are genuine—unique and important works of twentieth-century art hung in an air-conditioned palace in central Florida, down the road from Walt Disney World, for the edification of one man.

Lewis works at his desk in his huge study, the windows overlooking Lake Bessie. Televisions flicker with data from the financial markets. An assistant glides in from an anteroom with papers and leaves again as the billionaire continues talking on the telephone. An enthusiastic amateur golfer, with a 14-handicap, he has a framed picture of himself with Arnold Palmer on a side table. Above it hangs a Miró. In contrast to such impressive surroundings, Lewis himself is an anonymous-looking man in his midsixties, short, bald, and bespectacled. Yet when he puts down the telephone and walks over to say hello, he has the understated manner of someone who knows that when he mutters, people lean forward to listen. He believes Tiger had limited options when it came to choosing a home. "Tiger can't live anywhere. He would get mobbed." Not at Isleworth, though, where even residents are sent letters reminding them not to ask for autographs and the public has no hope of getting inside to meet the golfer. Apart from the security, the lakes form a natural moat around the development, a moat that is thick with alligators, this being Florida. As Lewis says: "This is as secure an environment [as you can get] without living in a prison." Then he corrected a slip of the tongue: "Or should I say a fortress."

The house Tiger moved into when he came to Isleworth was up near the fortress-clubhouse. A two-bedroom "golf villa" with views over

Lake Louise, it was a mere guest house in comparison to Lewis's mansion but sufficient for Tiger as he established himself in adult life. And, apart from moving into Isleworth, a lot was done in 1996–97 to create an infrastructure for what would be a very busy life. First, a tax-efficient, Florida-registered "S-corporation" was created to receive and distribute his income. It was given the name ETW Corp., the initials standing for Earl and Tiger Woods, who were president and chairman, respectively. Tida was secretary/treasurer. Administration was handled by a team of people initially based at IMG headquarters in Cleveland and later in a small, dedicated office near Isleworth. Aside from agent Hughes Norton, IMG staff who worked with Tiger intensively included a lawyer, John Oney; accountant Chris Hubman; Tara Kreidman, who liaised with sponsors; Kathy Battaglia, who made Tiger's travel arrangements; and Bev Norwood, who fielded press and other inquiries. (The requests IMG received for the golfer exceeded those for any other client.) Outside IMG, Team Tiger also included Butch Harmon and Tiger's caddie, a forty-eight-year-old veteran of the tour named Mike "Fluff" Cowan. Caddies traditionally receive a stipend from their player, out of which they pay their own travel expenses, plus a negotiated percentage of prize money, which is the real reward for the job. Cowan's basic stipend was a generous $1,000 a week, on top of which he received 8 percent of prize money, rising to 9 percent for top-ten places and 10 percent of wins. These bonuses were worth over $69,000 in the first, short season he worked with Tiger.

Team Tiger would grow with the creation of a charitable body, the Tiger Woods Foundation, though this was not announced until January 1997. Earl was heavily involved in setting up this foundation, which would not necessarily be dedicated to golf but would be a philanthropic organization with grander and more nebulous goals. "My father and I established the Tiger Woods Foundation to make a difference in the lives of America's youth," Tiger wrote expansively in one foundation report. "The foundation specifically strives to provide opportunities for children to 'dream big dreams.'" The foundation would do good work, but it also serves Tiger well. Although Florida does not have state income tax, the golfer was liable for federal income tax. But the money he gave to charity was deducted from his gross. He paid tax on the remainder. His income was such that he would always pay a huge amount of tax, so he might as well give some money away as give it to the IRS and, by establishing his own foundation, he could at least influence the way in which his donations were spent. At the same time, having a foundation enhanced his public image and, after it was granted tax-exempt status in February 1997, it did not really cost anything to run, even though there would be a staff of twelve ultimately and a comfortable suite of offices near Cypress. In fact, much of the money that endows the Tiger Woods Foundation does not even come from Tiger Woods. He supplied the $500,000 start-up money and makes other contributions each year, as will be explained, but the bulk of the money is donated by sponsors, corporations, and associates that have reason to keep him happy, including *Golf Digest,* IMG, and Nike.

After Tiger had set up his foundation, made provision for taxes, and paid his assistants and agents directly or via commission, he still had a huge amount of cash that had to be managed and invested. IMG offered a financial management service, though this had not always brought satisfaction, as Tony Jacklin and Jack Nicklaus attest. So John Merchant cast around for an independent manager and invited nine experts to make a presentation in the presence of Earl and Tiger. At the end of the meeting at Isleworth, four financial managers were engaged and, with this business concluded, Merchant felt the essentials were in place for Tiger's future career: he had somewhere to live, a tax-efficient structure for handling his money, and people to service his various requirements. Merchant was pleased with what he had accomplished in a short period of time. It was an unpleasant surprise therefore when Earl took him aside at Isleworth and fired him. Merchant says he never got to the bottom of why. Nor did he ask. After being told, Merchant went back to his room, packed his bag, and called for a taxi to take him to the airport. "Am I happy about it? No, of course not." He left with respect for

Tiger, however. "He was as good a young man as you could ever dream about meeting."

Still, by his actions (and Earl didn't fire people without Tiger's consent), the young golfer showed a ruthlessness that would become more evident as his career progressed. Merchant was not the only member of Team Tiger to be jettisoned at an early stage. Psychologist Dr. Jay Brunza also found himself surplus to requirements. Others would follow.

Earl's life had been increasingly stressful in recent years, as he and Tida risked their financial security to support Tiger's amateur career, and then worked to set him up in his new life as a professional. And Earl was not in good physical condition. In his midsixties, with a history of heart illness, he was overweight and still drank and smoked. It was not altogether surprising therefore when he suffered a heart attack in the early hours of October 25, 1996, during the Tour Championship in Tulsa, Oklahoma. Tida called Tiger's room to tell him the news and Tiger hastened to St. Francis Hospital to be with his father. After staying up all night, a worried and weary Tiger shot 78 the next day, the highest round of his professional career to date. He finished the week tied in twenty-first place. Earl survived, but he would have to undergo a heart bypass in the near future—his second—and the outcome was far from certain. The following months therefore came to have a special intensity as father and son faced the possibility that their time together was nearing its end.

Not long after he was discharged from the hospital, Earl accompanied Tiger to the Fred Haskins Award dinner, making amends for the evening Tiger had missed during the Buick Challenge earlier in the year, and Earl delivered a highly emotional speech to the audience. Almost choking on tears, he eulogized Tiger as his treasure and his joy and suggested that Tiger would change not only golf but *the world*. "He will transcend this game and bring to the world a humanitarianism which has never been known before." Maybe it was medication that made Earl speak in such a grandiloquent fashion. Maybe it was the thought he might die soon. Earl's words were certainly overblown and there was more of the same when, in December, *Sports Illustrated* named Tiger as its Sportsman of the Year. The magazine ran a cover story about the star and his family, and in this article Earl was quoted as saying: "Tiger will do more than any other man in history to change the course of humanity." Earl appeared to have meant this literally. "He's the bridge between the East and the West . . . he is the Chosen One. He'll have the power to impact nations. Not people. *Nations*. The world is just getting a taste of his power." These comments brought ridicule upon Earl at the time and have dogged him since. Earl insists angrily that he did not make the comments attributed to him. It is hard to know what the truth of the matter is, but if he did say such wild things, it would not be wholly out of character, and there were extenuating circumstances.

In addition to the fact that he was facing major surgery, no less than a life-or-death procedure, Earl's marriage was in trouble. When Tiger turned professional, he had given his parents gifts, including an $804,000 house in a gated community at Tustin, part of the sprawl of Orange County, California. Tida duly moved in, but Earl stayed behind in Cypress. Husband and wife still spoke to each other regularly—Tida even came over to cut Earl's hair—but they were no longer together as a couple in the normal sense. Earl tried to make a joke of the situation, saying he didn't feel comfortable living in a big house. Friends and relatives alluded to petty differences between them. Earl's sister, Mae, noted that her brother could no longer stand Tida's Thai cooking. Tida could not abide her husband's cigarette smoke. "She wouldn't let him in the [new] house because he was smoking," chuckles family friend John Anselmo. Of course, these were merely excuses, manifestations of an exhausted marriage. Back when Tiger was an infant, Earl and Tida had made a pact that their son would come first, and they had arranged their lives to give him every opportunity to fulfill what they saw as his destiny. Now that Tiger had gone into the world there was nothing to keep them together. One might say they sacrificed their marriage for Tiger's success, and they seemed to be resigned to that. Both still lived for their son and delighted in his success, much more so than the average proud parents. One gets the impression that Tiger is, and will always be, everything to them.

Tida seemed happy in her new life without Earl; she was content in Tustin, where she surrounded herself with mementos of Tiger's career and was a regular, cheerful presence at tournaments when Tiger was competing. She would appear on the course in expensive, vividly colored outfits (red for finals day) and march steadfastly around the course with the public (not that she spoke to them) as Tiger played—exuding love for, and pride in, her only child. Earl became an almost forlorn figure by comparison. Although he was just as proud of Tiger and was involved in the foundation, inevitably he didn't see as much of his son as he used to. He wasn't well enough to traipse around on tour, and in fact did not enjoy attending most tournaments because he ended up sitting in a hotel room watching Tiger on TV. He figured he might as well be at home if he was going to do that. So he stayed at home. Meanwhile, Tiger was on the road, or he was at Isleworth, and that was on the other side of the country. Earl's older children were based in northern California and in Arizona, but Earl had neglected them for years and their relationship was not close. In fact, as far as the public was concerned, Denny, Kevin, and Royce Woods might as well not exist, for Tiger was presented to the world, via the media, very much as if he were Earl's only child. For his part, Tiger saw less and less of his siblings, though he made good on his promise to Royce and paid for a $450,000 house for her in San Jose.

In his new life, Tiger was surrounded and supported by IMG advisers, a few close friends on tour, notably Mark O'Meara, and a coterie of buddies, most of whom were young men his own age whom he had known for some time. These included his best friend from Western High, Bryon Bell; Notah Begay III and Jerry Chang from Stanford; and the golfing Kuehne siblings of Texas. It was with this crowd that Tiger celebrated his twenty-first birthday in December 1996, in a suite at the MGM hotel in Las Vegas, where Tiger enjoyed playing blackjack. The gambling was something that came with this flash new life, but the desire to associate with old friends from school and college showed the other, quieter side of Tiger—the conservative kid from Orange County who craved normality. That was not easy to achieve when he and his friends left the security of a hotel suite and went into the real world. Trip Kuehne recalls several strange and unsettling experiences with Tiger in the first few months after he turned professional. Down in Tampa, Florida, for the JCPenney Classic, Tiger and the Kuehne siblings went out for dinner at an Outback Steakhouse. During the meal, a man came over and said to the Kuehnes, in front of Tiger: "I can't believe you're having dinner with somebody of that color." This led to the man being thrown out, and it was not the first or last time Trip experienced the naked racism Tiger faced on a regular basis. Part of the trouble was that, when he was relaxing away from golf, Tiger wanted to go to popular chain restaurants where the youthful clientele was less inhibited about approaching him. The public was not always abusive by any means. Most people were delighted to see him, though well-wishers could be a problem, too. One time at a Hooters restaurant so many fans crowded in to see Tiger that a fire marshal had to clear the place. Trip was with Tiger at a hockey game when the people operating the JumboTron display decided to focus the camera on Tiger. When everybody in the arena saw where Tiger was sitting, there was a virtual stampede to get to him. As a result of incidents like this, friends realized that a night out with Tiger had to be planned carefully. "You have to be able to get in touch with the restaurant, or the place you are going, so they can let you in the back," says Trip, "and [you have to] figure out where you are going to sit, [or] it's a mad house." Like a rock star, Tiger found himself sneaked into restaurants through kitchens and sitting at tables in corners with his back to the room for fear somebody might recognize him. It was a weird and unpleasant way to live, but evidence of his popularity.

He was drawing huge galleries on tour. At the Phoenix Open, during Super Bowl weekend, Tiger's presence swelled the crowd to 120,000 on

Saturday—more than the total number of people many tournaments attract all week. Not all were traditional golf fans. This was a rowdy, noisy crowd reminiscent of Arnie's Army. Television ratings were up each time Tiger competed and, when he was in contention, there was a sharp increase. And interest was international, as Earl had prophesied. On February 4, 1997, Tiger and his mother flew to Thailand, where he was paid a $500,000 appearance fee to play in the Asian Honda Classic. His arrival was a national event, broadcast live on television. As the son of a Thai-born woman, Tiger was lionized as a Thai hero, introduced to and honored by the prime minister. And he rewarded his Thai fans by winning the Asian Honda Classic by 10 strokes, showing again that he had what Tom Wolfe termed "the right stuff."

Golf's new superstar returned from the East in time to be near his father as he went into UCLA Medical Center in Los Angeles for his heart bypass. The stakes were high indeed for the sixty-four-year-old, and all his children gathered at his bedside. Even here the siblings were reminded that they were not equal. When a doctor came in to speak to them about their father, he directed his comments to Tiger, as if he were the only child, whereas in fact Tiger was the youngest of four. The others had to point out to the doctor that they were also Earl Woods's children, and they would like to know what was going on. Earl survived the operation, but there were complications a day later when he got the hiccups and told a nurse to bring him iced water to stop it. She replied that he wasn't allowed to have liquids. "So I said, 'Well, get me out of this bed, cos I'm not going to die in this bed.' So I got out, with all these tubes hanging on me . . . and the last thing I remember was drip, drip, drip. . . ." The strain had torn his stitches apart, causing blood to stream from his wound onto the floor, and Earl had to undergo a further emergency procedure, which, as he says, many people did not expect him to survive.

This was the worrying background to Tiger's professional debut at the Masters in the spring of 1997, the key tournament of Tiger's career to date and maybe the most important tournament of his life. Tiger practiced intensively for the event and watched hours upon hours of videotape of past Masters to study how balls broke on the greens. When he arrived in Augusta the weekend before the tournament, he asked to play a practice round with Arnold Palmer. The veteran customarily played with his dentist and close friend Dr. Howdy Giles before the tournament. So they were a threesome. Dr. Giles recalls that Tiger wanted to pick Arnie's brain about the course and, particularly, about dealing with fans, which Palmer did with such grace. In seeking the old man's counsel, Tiger showed wisdom, though in truth he did not choose to emulate the way in which Palmer conducted himself. Whereas Arnie would pause and sign autographs until everybody was satisfied, Tiger signed as he walked, which meant maybe three people got a squiggle on their baseball caps as he passed, the caps being handed back by a relay of assistants to the owners. Of course, he would say that there is no possibility of satisfying everyone—and, truthfully, the way in which golf fans jostle for autographs is less than dignified—but still Tiger treats fans with a coolness that borders on rudeness.

There was another old head to consult in Augusta. Against medical advice, Earl made the journey to Georgia in order to watch his son compete. Earl looked awful. His once-chubby face was hollowed by illness and set in a mask. His complexion was sallow. He was barely able to walk more than a few paces and seemed liable to collapse. Yet he sat out on the range when Tiger was hitting balls and gave his son a last-minute putting lesson that Tiger believed helped greatly. The psychological importance of having his pop there was surely even more significant. Like Nicklaus in the 1986 Masters, Tiger would be performing in front of an aged and beloved parent who seemed on the brink of death.

The sun shone brightly on the first day of the tournament, Thursday, April 10, giving added luster to the green of the grass and the pinks, yellows, and reds of the flowers. As is traditional, the reigning U.S. Amateur champion, Tiger, was paired with the defending Masters champion, Nick Faldo. On the face of it, the tall and powerfully built British star was the bigger name, a man who had won six majors. However, all eyes were on the twenty-one-year-old when the pair teed off. In comparison to Faldo, Woods seemed very young. He hadn't started to shave properly and was youthfully slender. Still, he had an intensity to his manner, in his eyes, that made you think he knew something Faldo did not.

Watching from the clubhouse veranda was Augusta steward Frank Carpenter, soon to retire. "I hope Tiger wins the Masters while I'm still working, so I can prepare the dinner and wine and all," Carpenter said to Earl Woods, referring to the champion's dinner.

"Frank, you may not have to worry," replied Earl. "Tiger is ready right now to win."

He didn't get off to the best start, though. A misjudged tee shot sent his ball into the pines and resulted in a bogey at the 1st. This was followed by three more bogeys, giving him a high score of 40 for the front 9. Nobody who had scored more than 38 on the first 9 of the first round of the Masters had gone on to win. Tiger might have been forgiven if he lost some heart. Instead, he birdied 10, 12, and 13 and made an eagle at 15, finishing the day with a very respectable 70. On an overcast Friday, paired with Paul Azinger, he had just one bogey, at the 3rd. He birdied the 2nd, 5th, and 8th before doing something wonderful at the par-5 13th: his second shot landed twenty feet from the pin, and the putt rolled slowly but surely into the hole for an eagle. With two more birdies at 14 and 15 he finished with 66, leading the field by 3.

Colin Montgomerie was in second place and he and Tiger were paired on Saturday. By his comments and manner leading up to the third-round match—reminding reporters smugly that he had more experience than Tiger in the majors (not that Montgomerie had won any)—the portly thirty-two-year-old Scotsman showed himself to be cocksure. Yet as the two made their way through the green pine canyons on Saturday, Woods outplayed Montgomerie totally, opening an unbridgeable chasm. Driving the ball perfectly, Tiger was emboldened to be daring with his putter. He birdied seven holes and recorded no bogeys. At 18, he pitched his ball to the edge of the green with just the right amount of spin for it to jerk back to within a foot of the flag, as if obeying a command. By this stage, Montgomerie was walking with his head bowed, a dejected figure. His score of 74 would send him tumbling like Humpty-Dumpty down the leader board. Tiger's head was aloft. He was grinning, acknowledging people in the crowd and rolling his bright, brown eyes as if wondering at his own cleverness and good fortune. When all was done, he recorded a score of 65 and had opened up a 9-stroke lead over the field. It was at this point that Nicklaus chose to bestow upon Tiger the biggest accolade he could. Turning the famous compliment Bobby Jones had paid him in 1965, he told reporters: "It's a shame Bob Jones isn't here. He could have saved the superlatives for this young man. Because he's certainly playing a game we're not familiar with."

On Sunday Tiger arrived at the 1st tee dressed in a blood-red shirt and black trousers. He whipped the tiger headcover from his driver and, after a couple of practice swings, brought it around so it came into contact with the ball at 180 miles per hour. Despite some problems on the front 9, he was square at the turn. He did not want anything worse than par through Amen Corner and, in fact, he managed to birdie 11 and 13. He did the same at the 14th. His nearest competitor, Tom Kite, was far behind, as was Italian Costantino Rocca, with whom Tiger was paired. In a sense, it was not meant to be this way. In the daydreams and real dreams Tiger had had of winning the Masters, it always ended in a battle with another player. From the 16th hole, he realized he was competing only against the tournament record. His second shot at the par-4 18th duly landed safely on the green. Coming up the fairway, escorted by state troopers, he later said he was thinking not only of his personal achievement but also about those players of color who had come before him, but had been denied this opportunity: Teddy Rhodes, Charlie Sifford, and the others. "I said a prayer of thanks to those guys." His parents were there to watch, of course. Earl had been sitting beside a CBS monitor all afternoon, inscrutable behind dark glasses, except when a particularly fine shot made him smile. Now he stood to watch his son coming up 18. Having walked the course, Tida was at Earl's side. Among the crowd was Philip Knight. Some business commentators thought Nike had paid too much for Tiger when the company signed him in 1996. Yet Nike sales had doubled since, and now Tiger was playing himself into history. As Knight said, "He's making us look smart." Few black faces can be found among the crowd at Augusta, but one belonged to Lee Elder, who had been the first black golfer to compete in the Masters back in 1975, the year Tiger was born. He had driven up from his home in Florida at the invitation of the club chairman.

When Tiger got to the green he saw his ball was twenty feet from the hole. He bent over the putt, the sleeves of his red sweater rolled up, and hit the ball four feet past and then, on the return, sank it for par. It was a round of 69—a record low of 270 for the tournament—and victory. Tiger swiped the air with his fist and embraced Fluff Cowan. "My first major as a caddie. His first major as a player. . . . It was awesome." Earl put an arm around his estranged wife, and Tida leaned into him gingerly. Tiger walked up, acknowledging fans left and right. Then he made eye contact with his parents, and they all grinned at one another. Earl held his arms open and his son hugged him first, hard, the smile stretched across Tiger's face as they came together. The emotion became overwhelming as he squeezed his father tight and buried his face in his shoulder, screwing his eyes shut. Tida placed her hands on Tiger's right arm, as it came around Earl's back, and rubbed his elbow tenderly.

"We made it! We made it!" exclaimed Earl excitedly. "We made it."

Whatever one thought of Earl, with his embellished stories and sometimes overblown comments, father and son loved each other, and they had come a hell of a long way to stand victorious at the 18th at the Augusta National. Recalling his feelings at that moment, Earl says he was filled with "pride and love and respect for what he [Tiger] had accomplished. I admired him so much, and still do." In the autumn of his days, his fragile health had been part of the reason for Tiger's victory. "Nobody really understands why Tiger won that Masters so early and so fast, except Tiger and I do," says his aunt Mae. "We thought Earl was gonna die." Tiger wanted both his parents to see him win a green jacket. There would be other Masters, but the old man had to see him get one before it was too late. Tiger did it for himself, too, of course. As Nick Faldo helped him on with the club blazer, and Tiger's brown hands slipped into the silky arms of that green garment, it was a fantastic, long-imagined, and thrilling sensation, the dream of a lifetime.

9

FOUR TROPHIES

A Global television audience watched Tiger Woods win the 1997 Masters and that audience delighted in a stylish and charismatic young man—the tournament's youngest winner—bringing an excitement and joie de vivre to golf not seen since Arnold Palmer was in his prime. In truth, Woods was now a bigger star than Arnie had ever been. "For the first time in its history, I think that golf can say that it has perhaps the most recognizable athlete on the planet," observes David B. Fay, executive director of the United States Golf Association. "I mean, when people talk [about] Bob Jones or Harry Vardon or Jack Nicklaus or Arnold Palmer, that would be a joke to say that they were the most popular or most recognized athlete on the planet. . . . But now you have Tiger Woods." It was the way in which he won the Masters that made him such a star. Not only was he the youngest winner, he broke the tournament record and won by a record margin of 12 strokes. This was also the first time a person of African American heritage had won America's whitest golf tournament—a matter of considerable significance in the United States, and in the history of the game. ("I'm so proud," said Lee Elder. "We have a black champion.") And Tiger's win made for compelling television, probably the best TV show that the Augusta National and CBS had ever produced, a show that was beamed around the world and garnered a record audience of forty-four million viewers in the United States.

Among those watching was Bill Clinton, a golf fan like so many presidents before him. He was in the White House resting after knee surgery following an accident at the home of Greg Norman, ironically, when he had tripped on a step. At the conclusion of the tournament, Clinton put a call through to Augusta to congratulate Tiger personally, saying the best shot he saw all week was the shot of Tiger hugging his father. Shortly after this conversation, the White House invited Tiger to New York, where, on Tuesday, April 15, the president was taking part in a celebration at Shea Stadium to mark the fiftieth anniversary of Jackie Robinson becoming the first African American to play Major League Baseball. Robinson's widow would also be attending. But on Monday Tiger was in South Carolina to open a branch of a new restaurant chain, All-Star Cafes, with which he had a deal. Then he had some business meetings before flying to Mexico with friends for a vacation. So he turned down the request, effectively snubbing his president, which generated a good deal of criticism when, to Tiger's chagrin, the White House let it be known that he had turned Clinton down. Woods took the view that if Clinton had wanted him in New York, he should have asked before the Masters. It could be argued that he showed perspicacity in recognizing when a politician was trying to use him. But to turn down the leader of one's country in favor of going on vacation was perhaps arrogant. "In retrospect, Tiger would probably have been better to cancel his vacation," admits one member of his IMG team.

Tiger came home early from Mexico because he was pestered by autograph seekers. Upon his return, he was confronted with the next in what turned into a series of media controversies. On Sunday, April 20, 1997, CNN broadcast videotape of 1979 Masters champion Frank Urban Zoeller (known as Fuzzy, a nickname derived from his initials) talking about Tiger at the Augusta National. A forty-five-year-old veteran of the tour, Fuzzy deported himself like the colorful players of the past. On the course, he was seldom seen without a cigarette—"I drink too! What the hell?"—and he was always good for a joke or a quick comment for reporters. On the final day of the 1997 tournament, as he made his way back to the clubhouse, a CNN crew stopped him and asked what he thought of Tiger. "He's doing quite well," Zoeller replied. "Pretty impressive. That little boy is driving well, and he's putting well. He's doing everything it takes." The "little boy" reference was slightly unfortunate, as "boy" was once a derogatory term for African Americans, but Tiger was so young he almost was a boy. "So, you know what you guys do when he gets in here?" Zoeller asked the CNN people. "You pat him on the back and say congratulations, and enjoy it, and tell him not to serve fried chicken next year. Got it?" Zoeller was referring to the champion's dinner, whereby the reigning Masters champion chooses the menu for the following year's banquet. Fried chicken is, of course, a dish associated with black people. Still, this was not offensive in itself. "Or collard greens," Zoeller blundered on, "or whatever the hell they serve." Was there a sneer in his voice when he referred to "they," as if "they" were different, possibly inferior to white people such as himself? It sounded like that.

Zoeller took a week off after the tournament and had all but forgotten the interview. Journalists were forever asking players for a comment at tournaments, especially the Masters. "Shit, I couldn't remember what the hell [I'd said]." Then on Monday, April 21, he received a call from a friend who told him the tape had been aired as part of the show *Pro Golf Weekly* and said he should get a lawyer because there was going to be trouble. That week Zoeller was entered in the Greater Greensboro Classic. When he arrived in North Carolina, reporters clamored for an explanation of what he had said on TV. Zoeller told them his words were meant in jest. "My comments were not intended to be racially derogatory, and I apologize for the fact that they were misconstrued," he said, which fell short of an admission that he was wrong. He did not, and does not, believe he was wrong, laying the blame for the incident at the door of CNN. "Somebody from Atlanta,* who had no rhyme or reason, just said, 'I'm going to bury somebody and we'll bury him.' " However, he was pilloried and ridiculed for his comments, on television by Jay Leno and David Letterman and also in print. *USA Today* quipped that everybody knew Zoeller was a wit. "In this context, they are half right." On the other hand, some African Americans took Fuzzy's side. "The media got it and blew it out of proportion," says Augusta steward Frank Carpenter.

Reporters wanted Tiger's reaction, but he was busy taping an appearance on *Oprah* in Chicago. Then one of Zoeller's sponsors, Kmart, announced it was not going to renew its contract with him. He pulled out of the Greater Greensboro Classic with another public apology, this time more contrite and tearful in delivery. Still, there was no reaction from Tiger, who seemed to be prolonging Zoeller's misery deliberately. Woods's assistants at IMG say he was just busy. After taping Oprah Winfrey's show, he traveled to Nike headquarters in Oregon for meetings that took up most of Tuesday and Wednesday. Then he wanted to watch a tape of the CNN show before he said anything publicly. Finally, on Thursday, he accepted Zoeller's apology, though he added a humiliating put-down that showed his tough side. "His attempt at humor was out of bounds," he said, "and I was disappointed by it."

Zoeller was probably past his best as a player. But his career never really recovered. "People who didn't even know me were calling me a racist pig," he says sadly. "I'm not racist." The words that were spoken mean very little, in retrospect—an ambiguous remark made by a semi-obscure golfer would never have made news except, of course, that what Zoeller said related to Tiger Woods and, as the newly appointed

*Where CNN is based.

Most Famous Man in Sport, everything that touched upon Woods was a news story in the first few months of 1997.

One of the most interesting stories, perhaps, was the *Oprah* show affair. Tiger had been invited on to the chat show not only because he was in the full flush of his celebrity status but also because of his ethnicity. Having a man of color as the Masters champion was like Jackie Robinson's joining the Brooklyn Dodgers in 1947. Yet, when Winfrey asked Tiger whether being called African American bothered him, he replied that it did. His racial ancestry was more complex than that. "I'm just who I am—whoever you see in front of you," he said. "Growing up, I came up with this name—I'm a Cablinasian." Just as Tida had invented Eldrick, Tiger's real first name, Tiger had put together the words *Caucasian, black,* and *Asian* to make *Cablinasian,* this unwieldy portmanteau term. In fact, he had always said much the same thing when asked about his ethnicity. But because he was now very famous, and because he was talking on *Oprah,* more people took notice and his words precipitated a major debate within the African American "black" community, for the terms are usually taken to be synonymous and, by denying he was African American, Tiger was also seen to be saying he was not black.

Some maintained that all racial descriptions were insidious. The entertainer Eartha Kitt, herself of mixed race, commented simply: "We are all American." Others took the view that Tiger had turned his back on black people. The problem was just a word, but a word loaded with meaning. If black means not white, Tiger was black. But if black was being used as an alternative term for African American, it was an inaccurate description of who Tiger was. With a Thai mother and Chinese ancestry on his father's side of the family he was more Asian American than African American. In an ideal world the unqualified noun would suffice. After all, nobody refers to Jack Nicklaus as German American. Yet American society is still significantly divided by color, though less than it once was. For the most part, people of color are not in the boardrooms or the country clubs, yet they are ubiquitous in service jobs. Statistically black Americans are poorer than white Americans and much more likely to go to jail.* The reasons are complex, but in crude terms black Americans do not have life as good as white Americans and, whether he liked it or not, Tiger was interesting to many people because he was a man of color succeeding in a white-dominated world. Many African Americans were proud, thinking one of their own had come through. So when he told Winfrey he was not black, a lot of people felt insulted, including members of his family. "That hurt me," says his aunt Mae, who considers herself black, as does her brother. "[And] most of my friends are very, very angry about that." Mae asked her nephew to give a fuller explanation of the Cablinasian remark, and he told her in reply that he could not say he was black because that meant denying Tida, who was very proud of being Thai. (In a rare interview granted in 1995, Tida said in her imperfect English: "All the media try to put black in him. Why don't they ask who half of Tiger is from? In United States, one little part of black is all black. . . . To say he is hundred percent black is to deny his heritage. To deny his grandmother and grandfather. To deny me!")

Time and again, Tiger would find himself drawn into intense social issues such as this. He was also the subject of tabloid tittle-tattle. An innately shy young man, he did not much enjoy the attention of the tabloids, and he felt the way he was dragged into serious issues—such as race and, later, sex discrimination—had little to do with him as a golfer. Unlike some of the luminaries of sport in years gone by, notably Muhammad Ali, with whom he had a lot in common in terms of the magnitude and international nature of his fame, Tiger had no desire to be part of social and political debate. Tiger sees himself as a golfer, first and foremost. As we have seen, part of the tradition of the game is avoiding controversy. Golf is a polite, establishment game. Furthermore,

---

*U.S. Department of Justice, Bureau of Justice Statistics, 2001: "an estimated 28% of black males will enter State or Federal prison during their lifetime, compared to 16% of Hispanic males and 4.4% of white males."

Tiger would argue that his background was not enough reason for him to get involved in social and political issues; his ethnicity did not help him strike a golf ball. That was true. But his ethnicity had a lot to do with the fact that corporations wanted him to endorse their products, and he did not complain about the money, and the money kept coming his way. For the same reason Nike and Titleist had signed him in 1996, other companies saw the value in his multiethnic look. In May 1997 IMG negotiated a five-year deal with American Express whereby Tiger would be paid $13 million, and another million was donated to the Tiger Woods Foundation. Soon Rolex would be added to the growing list of his endorsements (though he later switched to promoting TAG Heuer watches).

As long as the public was interested in Tiger, his name was worth a fortune, and he could hardly have been more popular. When it was announced that he would compete in the GTE Byron Nelson Golf Classic in Dallas in the spring of 1997, for instance, a massive three hundred thousand tickets were sold—a number comparable to sales for a very large rock festival. Tiger won that week, and a month later he became the number one player in the world according to the Official World Golf Ranking (a points system devised by Mark McCormack and introduced in 1986). He was the youngest professional to achieve the primary position, and the quickest to get there. He went on to win the Motorola Western Open in July, with CBS again registering a remarkable surge in viewing figures—up 124 percent. Golf was beating tennis in popularity, which was something of a turnaround for the game. When the time came for the new PGA Tour commissioner, Tim Finchem, to renegotiate TV contracts for 1999–2002, the PGA Tour found itself in a strong position because the tour had Tiger and he was drawing millions of new viewers with a demographic that was attractive to advertisers, including as it did a high proportion of the young and ethnic minorities. The latter factor was key. "His ethnic background caused a meteoric growth in our fan base. He brought a whole new group of fans that hadn't really been golf fans," says Henry Hughes, senior vice president of the PGA Tour. "Our ratings are up. Our attendance is up. Our charity is up. When Tiger plays, it's up further." When the PGA Tour completed its negotiations with the networks, the association had contracts worth in excess of $500 million, which was a very substantial increase over previous years. Purse money increased correspondingly. When Tiger turned professional in 1996, total prize money on tour was $68 million. By 2001 it was $175.9 million, meaning average tournament purses tripled to about $3 million. "Tiger's had a huge impact on television, interest in the game, and the purses, so we should all be very thankful to him for that," says tour star and friend Mark Calcavecchia.

Aside from the Masters, Tiger did not shine in the major championships of 1997. At the U.S. Open he finished tied for nineteenth. At the Open Championship at Royal Troon he came to grief on Sunday at the par-3 "Postage Stamp" 8th, triple-bogeying, and ended tied for twenty-fourth. The PGA Championship was another frustrating experience for the young star, who finished tied for twenty-ninth. The cause of this loss of form was that Tiger was undertaking a major overhaul of his game, having detected faults with his swing while watching videotape of himself in the Masters.

"For longevity and to achieve the goals that he wants to achieve—to be the greatest player that's ever played—[he] needed to get more consistent with everything he did," explains Butch Harmon. "He relied a lot on timing in the past. When the timing was fine, he was spectacular. When his timing was off, he wasn't as spectacular." Harmon decided to work through the problems slowly, during which period Tiger did not play as well as he had been. Harmon was impressed that Tiger was prepared to take such radical, corrective action just as his professional career was starting. After all, it would have been easier to continue playing as he was; he probably would have won more often in the short term. As months passed and he failed to win tournaments, commentators began to suggest that he might have been a flash in the pan after all.

It took character to compete knowing people thought that. "It's not like [what] David Leadbetter did with Nick Faldo, when Nick Faldo just kind of quit playing for a year, and they worked on his swing, and then he came back and he was a better player," comments Harmon. "In Tiger's case, he continued to play—'97, '98. You know, he only won one [official] tournament in the United States in '98 and everybody wanted to know what was wrong with him. Well, he actually was doing better. He was just getting used to the changes in his swing."

As a result of his poor form in the season Tiger dropped to fourth place on the Official World Golf Ranking. Still, there were highlights. Earl had recuperated from his heart bypass to the extent that he felt able to partner his son in the AT&T pro-am. There was also a nice moment when Tiger returned to the Augusta National as champion and host of the champion's dinner. Frank Carpenter took special care selecting the wine: a Batard-Montrachet 1995 in honor of the year Tiger first appeared in the Masters, and a Mouton Rothschild 1975 for the year of his birth. The menu was less sophisticated. At Tiger's request it featured his favorite food, which was cheeseburgers. All the living greats gathered for the dinner, including Jack Nicklaus. In fact, the Augusta National members held Nicklaus Day on April 7, which involved unveiling a plaque commemorating the Golden Bear's victories. Then Nicklaus surprised onlookers by making a serious challenge for the title. At fifty-eight, he was in contention almost to the end and finished sixth—the oldest top-ten finisher in the history of the championship—showing once again what a remarkable man he was. By contrast, the considerably younger Tiger tied for eighth. The winner was forty-one-year-old Mark O'Meara, who had improved dramatically as a player during his association with Tiger. "He kind of pushed me a little bit, drove me a little bit," says O'Meara, "and anytime you hang around with somebody as talented as he is, it's going to bring your game up a notch."

Despite an undistinguished season, so much money was coming into the game that Woods made $1.8 million in prize money in 1998, and many times that in endorsements. He was pulling in so much green that older statesmen, such as Nicklaus and Palmer, sometimes grumbled that getting rich quick could curb the killer instinct. "Here is a young man who has the opportunity to break all records. But there is now so much money that it could ruin any desire to keep on winning," warned Nicklaus, who had always had a high-minded, country-club attitude toward golf. Palmer's views were similar, though tempered by the fact that he came from a less privileged background and always had to make a living from golf; in fact, he had done much to make it possible that players like Tiger made millions. Perhaps surprisingly, Palmer, now in his late sixties, remained one of the highest-paid sportsmen in the world, earning approximately $18 million in 1998–99, principally because of endorsements.

In contrast, Jack Nicklaus had stumbled into more problems in his business career. The financial crisis of 1985 seriously depleted Nicklaus's wealth, yet he survived that episode by doing deals with the banks to settle his debts, and he made a characteristically bold bid a decade later to reestablish himself as a golf mogul. In August 1996 Golden Bear Golf, Inc., was launched as a public company on the NASDAQ. In a boom market, where initial public offerings did roaring business, golf companies were prospering. The prime example of how much money there was to be made was Greg Norman's association with Cobra Golf, Inc. The Australian bought a share in the club company for $2 million in 1990 and sold it in 1996 at a profit of $42 million. The Golden Bear flotation raised $37 million, which Nicklaus invested in the business, and the company grew rapidly from there, employing enough people to fill two floors of the North Tower of Golden Bear Plaza, an impressive office development near Nicklaus's home in North Palm Beach. Among the businesses Golden Bear Golf, Inc., was involved in were running a chain of golf centers and golf schools, building golf courses, and licensing Nicklaus's name. Jack appeared to be in good financial shape again. Indeed, with a buoyant stock market and increasing public interest in golf, *Forbes* estimated his personal wealth at $300 million. Then, in the summer of 1998, allegations emerged that executives at the division of

Golden Bear that took care of golf course construction, Paragon Construction International, had misrepresented figures, hiding over $20 million in losses. Paragon President John R. Boyd and Vice President Christopher Curbello were fired, and later sued by securities regulators. (Boyd left the country and was arrested by the FBI in South America in March 2003.) Golden Bear had to issue revised figures for 1997 and as a result the share price collapsed, taking with it much of Nicklaus's notional wealth. Golden Bear Golf, Inc., was subsequently delisted from the stock market and reverted to an inactive private company. Once again Nicklaus had suffered serious business problems, yet his lifestyle was little changed (as Palmer had survived his business problems of 1990–91 almost unscathed). Jack continued to conduct business from Golden Bear Plaza and kept his homes in Florida and Ohio, as well as the private jet. His former partner Putnam Pierman believes Nicklaus has been uncommonly lucky. "His celebrity status has saved his ass. No doubt about it," says Pierman. "Banks don't want to foreclose on people like that."

One of Nicklaus's strengths throughout his career has been his solid marriage. Barbara was his foundation, and he doted on their five children. Tiger was unmarried, of course, which is unusual in a conservative game where players tend to settle down at a young age. In fact, despite his fame and fortune, Tiger had been remarkably restrained, or discreet, when it came to his sex life. In the absence of facts, newspapers linked him with various celebrities. Yet his only serious girlfriend to this point had been Dina Gravell. His next significant girlfriend, Joanna Jagoda, was another girl-next-door type. Born in Poland in 1977 and raised in the San Fernando Valley, north of Los Angeles, she was a political science undergraduate at the University of California at Santa Barbara when she was introduced to Tiger. They soon became a close and public couple, with Joanna walking the course at the Open Championship at Royal Birkdale in July 1998. She spurned attention for herself, however. ("I'm not the superstar here," she says.) And she was impeccably discreet, a quality Tiger valued very highly.

Tiger is obliged to talk to the media at tournaments. But he does not like people in his inner circle talking *about* him. Although the media has grown since the heyday of Palmer and Nicklaus and the media is more intrusive in some respects, meaning Tiger has more to deal with, there is a fundamental difference in his attitude toward the media and in the way he expects his friends to behave. Those friends Tiger keeps close are defensive with outsiders. When asked about Tiger, Joanna will divulge virtually nothing. "I have no comment about him or my personal relationship with him." One of Tiger's closest friends from Western High School to the present day is Bryon Bell, who has kept his position in Tiger's esteem partly because he is so discreet. "I do not do interviews," he wrote in an e-mail to me. "My friendship with Tiger is very personal, and I would like it to remain that way." Others say Tiger will sever contact with anybody who speaks about him in public, revealing a degree of insecurity (after all, why would he worry about friends talking about him?). Even family members have learned to watch what they say. His siblings are very reluctant to comment. "We try to stay as low-key as possible," says his favorite, Royce. Indeed, she and her older brothers seem scared of saying a word out of place in case an already tenuous relationship with Tiger breaks down altogether.

Tida almost never talks about Tiger in public. Earl, on the other hand, was in a unique position. He was doing the talking before Tiger could talk for himself, and Tiger was not going to tell this bullish old soldier to be quiet, though increasingly the impression was that Tiger wished his father was less loquacious. Tiger's best friend on tour, Mark O'Meara, was also in a privileged position, being a public figure in his own right. Questions about Tiger naturally came up at tournaments and he could hardly blank them all. So he devised comments that Tiger could not possibly find fault with, being either lighthearted or eulogizing: insisting, for example, that Tiger was an even better person than he was a golfer (a sugary compliment that other members of the entourage also use). O'Meara had certainly benefited from this relationship. A player who had hitherto been the quintessential journeyman pro, little known to the general public, he won his second major, the Open Championship at Royal Birkdale, just three months after Tiger helped him on with his green blazer at Augusta.

When Hughes Norton became the first of two key members of Team Tiger to be dismissed over the winter of 1998–99, some thought this partly O'Meara's doing. It was understood that Tiger's buddy had never liked Norton. But it was probably more significant that Earl had turned against the agent. "For Hughes, the dollar is almighty. For Tiger, it's not that important," said Earl at the time, in an apparent reference to Norton's ambition to sign Tiger to more contracts (though the assertion that Tiger was not interested in money is nonsense, as will become apparent). Norton was replaced with a younger IMG agent named Mark Steinberg. "It was obviously very important to IMG that Tiger remained a client of the companies, so a few of us were asked to interview and talk with Tiger," explains Steinberg. Apart from his relative youth (he was thirty-one), Steinberg was an unassuming, even drab fellow, much more the type of person Tiger feels comfortable with. His girlfriends Dina and Joanna, Mark O'Meara, and his school and college buddies all were perfectly nice and intelligent but unexciting people. They were conventional, suburban types like Tiger himself. Steiny, as Tiger would call his new agent, with his youthful fondness for contracting names, was representing basketball players at IMG when he came into Tiger's orbit, and Tiger knew Mark through his marriage to another IMG staffer, Tara Kreidman, who worked with Tiger on his endorsements. The golfer started work with Steinberg on a trial basis, later making it permanent. "I think I'm many different roles: his agent, his manager, his friend, his confidant [and] partner," says Steinberg, whose multiple tasks include negotiating contracts, scheduling Tiger's appearances, and traveling with him. Much of the time he seems to be following two paces behind the golfer, chewing gum anxiously and looking like he needs a vacation. "It's a lot of work," he admits. "And you have to be on your toes all the time, and you have to be thinking ahead. [But] representing Tiger is a great job. What makes it, to me, one of the best jobs in the world is the type of person he is. I mean, I've said this before, I think: Tiger is a better person than he is a golfer, and we know how good a golfer he is."

Having changed agents, Tiger turned his attention to perhaps the second most important person on his team, his caddie Mike "Fluff" Cowan, whose association with Tiger had made him into a minor celebrity. Fluff now appeared in television commercials, and at tournaments he was besieged by children wanting autographs. The autograph hunters sometimes got in the way of work. Tiger could empathize with that. He ran a gauntlet of marker pens every time he walked from the locker room to the practice range, shielding his face in case somebody poked him in the eye. Though it can be argued that Tiger should handle the public with more skill and charm, in the style of Arnold Palmer, it is also true that there are few other sports where fans can get so close to the stars. Living with death threats as he does, Tiger is mindful that somebody beyond the ropes could pull a gun on him. In the final round of the Phoenix Open in February 1999, a man who had been heckling Tiger aggressively was wrestled to the ground by security, who discovered he was carrying a gun. (He was arrested and later released.) There was nothing Cowan could do about things like that. But Tiger came to think Fluff was not the best person to have with him when there were problems. Sometimes Cowan seemed too confrontational. He also behaved as if he were Tiger's personal friend, which was not always appropriate. Most experienced caddies are careful to maintain a distance between themselves and their boss. Cowan had always been more informal. Also, Fluff talked to reporters, which Tiger did not like. He was particularly disgruntled when Cowan told *Golf Digest* exactly how much Tiger paid him (see page 193). Ultimately Tiger fired him. "He decided he wanted to move on," says Cowan. "He wasn't pleased with what he was getting out of me and thought he could do better."

Butch Harmon recommended Steve Williams as a replacement—an easygoing New Zealander who never spoke out of turn and did not presume to be friends with his player in a social context, though they have in fact become close. "I've become good friends with Tiger," says Williams, "but you know your boundaries and you don't [abuse the friendship]." Their first tournament, the Bay Hill Invitational, was a poor start. Tiger finished tied for fifty-sixth. But as he got his swing working again, they started to do much better. The breakthrough came on the range at Isleworth in May 1999. Suddenly feeling that he had the right action again, Tiger experimented by hitting different shots with different clubs and everything seemed pure and good. Shortly afterward, he and Williams won the Deutsche Bank–SAP Open in Germany, the start of a streak of wins that included the Memorial Tournament and Motorola Western Open. Like most top-flight caddies, Williams believes caddie and player are a partnership and success is jointly achieved. At the same time, it is not an equal relationship. The caddie is a servant who should know his place and his duties. Part of working with Tiger was dealing with his unusually large, loud, and often noisy galleries, as well as the press. Williams assumed a forceful manner on the course, reminding public and press sharply to be quiet when Tiger was addressing the ball. It helped that Williams was a large and imposing man with a commanding voice. "I try to make his job as easy as I can playing golf. Me, I'm not worried about what people think of what I'm saying. Because, if I can make him at peace and at ease, and enjoy his day, it's better for me." The major tournaments were particularly stressful because, apart from the Masters, a great media caravan was allowed inside the ropes to follow Tiger down the fairways. Sometimes Williams counted up to a hundred people trailing behind them. It was ridiculous.

The last major of the 1999 season, the PGA Championship, was held at Medinah Country Club, near Chicago, with what was considered the strongest field in the championship's history. All but eight of the top one hundred players in the world were entered. The course was very long and rain early in the week meant it presented an even more formidable challenge. Tiger scored an impressive 70-67-68 in the opening three days and went into the final round tied for the lead with Canada's Mike Weir. However, his real challenger was nineteen-year-old Sergio

Garcia of Spain at 2 shots behind. A highly talented youngster with an effervescent personality, Garcia was always entertaining on the golf course and occasionally brilliant. In the final round at Medinah, Tiger scored four birdies in the first 11 holes to build what looked to be an unassailable 5-stroke lead. Then he started to lose his way and, at the same time, Garcia took advantage. The Spaniard made a birdie at 13 to cut Tiger's lead to 3 strokes. When Tiger got to the same hole, he made a double-bogey. At this point, the gallery seemed to decide that it wanted Garcia to win, and Garcia clearly felt the support and believed he could do it, delighting the crowd with his zest. But Tiger was not to be put off. "I knew when I got to 17, I had to play the two best holes of my life," he said later. "Despite everything that had happened, I still had the lead, and I was completely focused on doing whatever I had to do to maintain it." Tiger parred 17 in difficult circumstances, so the title came down to the last hole, a par-4. Casting caution aside, Tiger took out his 3-wood and struck one of the best tee shots of his career. The ball landed in a prime position in the fairway, setting him up for a shot to the green, where he holed out for another par that beat, by a stroke, Garcia's 278. It was Woods's second major title, after a gap of two years and four months that some would call a slump, and it proved he was back; furthermore, it showed that his first major win had not been a fluke. When the champion raised the big silver Wanamaker Trophy to his lips, the cameras caught his blissful reflection in the burnished surface. He appeared to be kissing himself in an ecstasy of self-regard, like Narcissus.

Early the next morning, Tiger flew into Aspen, Colorado, to take part in a charity golf event organized by rock musician Glenn Frey. The golfer was accompanied by his close Stanford friend Jerry Chang and, still elated from the win, they decided to call up another former Stanford teammate, Eri Crum, who lived in Aspen, for a night on the town. Upon leaving Stanford, Crum had tried to break into professional golf the hard way. Having failed PGA Tour qualifying school, he found himself playing the little-watched and poorly rewarded satellite tours in the United States and abroad. Without significant sponsorship and with modest prize money, he had to drive huge distances from event to event and found himself sleeping in cheap motels or even in his car. It was not the glamorous life he had imagined, and to get onto the PGA Tour and do well there he would have to play much better and be much more committed. Realizing he did not have that in him, Crum quit the professional game and took a postgraduate degree, aiming to be a sports chiropractor. Meanwhile, Tiger had become one of the premier sports figures in the world. Crum was not sure what to expect when they met again that evening in Aspen; so much had changed since Stanford and he had never found Tiger easy to get along with anyway, being such a remote figure. "I felt like I got to know him more that night than I'd ever got to know him in college," says Crum. He was not sure whether it was the high of winning the PGA Championship, but Tiger was more open and trusting than Crum remembered. In college, it was as if Tiger was almost too disciplined, "too busy on his road to success to ever really enjoy life." Now that he had proved himself on tour, the anxiety had dissipated and he seemed able to relax and relish the career he had always aspired to. "He never walked around with the smile he [has] now."

Shortly after his win in the PGA Championship, it was announced that Tiger had renegotiated his contract with Nike in exchange for a promise of $90 million over five years. This phenomenal deal followed a falling out with his other main sponsor, Titleist, over a Nike television commercial that showed Tiger practicing a trick shot with his sand wedge: bouncing a golf ball on the head of the club for half a minute and then getting the ball high, pulling the club back, and smiting it baseball-style. The commercial was a hit with the public, but not with Titleist, which paid Tiger to endorse its golf equipment. Titleist considered that the ad gave the impression Tiger was playing with Nike equipment. (Nike had recently started producing its own ball, but at this stage Tiger endorsed only its clothing.) Nike argued it was reasonable to portray Tiger playing golf in its clothing commercials because, after all, golf was what he did. Acushnet, which owns Titleist, filed a lawsuit against Nike, asking for damages and for the offending commercial to be withdrawn, which it was eventually. However, Acushnet did not proceed with the case to court, deciding that the publicity would be harmful to all concerned. Instead, realizing that it no longer had an exclusive agreement with Woods, the company renegotiated its contract with the golf star, paying him considerably less money on a per-event basis only when he used Titleist equipment and golf balls. At the same time Tiger's relationship with Nike became ever stronger. By 2002 not only would the golfer be wearing Nike clothing and hitting a Nike ball, but he would be hitting the ball with Nike clubs, which Steve Williams carried in a Nike bag.

As he evolved into a walking advertisement for Philip Knight's corporation, a Nike man down to the soles of his shoes, Tiger's appearance changed in other ways. He was not fully grown when he first turned professional, a skinny twenty-one-year-old weighing 155 pounds. But a rigorous exercise regimen had built him up to a muscular 180 pounds. He had never looked much like the other professionals anyway, because of his mixed ethnicity, youth, and natural élan. Now he was different by virtue of his physique. Weight training swelled his arms. His chest had expanded like Charles Atlas's. His body fat diminished as he cut back on his adolescent love of junk food, and whenever possible he went on a fast run. By the time the Ryder Cup came around in September 1999, he was starting to look more like a lightweight boxer than a golfer.

From its modest debut in 1927 as the idea of a wealthy British seed merchant, Samuel Ryder, the biannual match-play tournament between teams of professionals from both sides of the Atlantic had grown enormously in popularity largely because of its nationalistic nature. Between 1927 and 1971, the Ryder Cup was the United States versus Britain, with stronger American teams coming to dominate the series. From 1973, Britain joined forces with Ireland to make for better competition. America still won. The tournament began to come into its own when, at the suggestion of Jack Nicklaus, who had a distinguished Ryder Cup career, Britain and Ireland enrolled their colleagues on the Continent to field a European team in 1979. In 1983, led by Tony Jacklin, Europe almost defeated the Americans. In 1985, at the Belfry in England, they reclaimed the Ryder Cup for the first time in twenty-eight years. With Jacklin still in charge, the Europeans won again at Nicklaus's Muirfield Village in 1987, and by 1999 the Ryder Cup was established as an international television event. It was not Tiger's favorite tournament, however. Having competed once before, at Valderrama in Spain in 1997, he did not like the way he had to attend boring social functions as part of representing his country; he found it hard to adjust to being part of a team, and he played poorly—a questionable asset to Team USA, which lost to Europe in Spain.

The 1999 Ryder Cup at the Country Club at Brookline, near Boston, Massachusetts, was another unhappy experience for Woods. In the lead-up to the tournament he and other American players let it be known that they had concerns about the financial side of the event. The PGA of America, which operates the Ryder Cup in conjunction with the PGA European Tour, would gross $63 million in 1999, many times the revenues for any other golf tournament, and a handsome profit of $20 million was to be dispersed among the association's various programs. The players did not have a say in this. Nor were they being paid to compete. This had always been the case, because they were representing their country. But professional golfers were just that; they played for money. David Duval, one of the younger stars of the tour, publicly questioned where all the money went. He did not necessarily want to be paid himself, but suggested some of the profit could go to charity (above and beyond those golf programs the PGA funded). "We ought to be paid," said Woods more directly. "It's the most demanding week of all in the game—the only one where it's mandatory to attend functions, gala dinners, balls, and so on. If you had a choice, fair enough, but we have got to go to those things and, for that alone, we should be paid." The comments by Duval and Woods drew much criticism, and

U.S. team captain Ben Crenshaw said he was disappointed. In a spirit of compromise, the PGA of America came up with a charitable fund of $2.6 million to be divided among the captain and his twelve team members. On behalf of each man, $100,000 would be donated to a university of their choice, and the same again to charity. Most players asked that the first $100,000 go to their alma mater and gave the other $100,000 to their favorite charity or split it among several causes. Phil Mickelson, for instance, gave $100,000 to Arizona State, where he had been a student, and divided his remaining money among ten charities. Tiger requested $100,000 go to Stanford, naturally. But he wanted *all* the rest for his own foundation, which was a circuitous way of giving to charity and showed how he felt about the event and the lack of remuneration.

Many of the fans who came to watch the Ryder Cup at Brookline were unsympathetic to the players and their public complaints about money, considering them rich enough already, and they heckled the American stars freely, especially when the likes of Duval and Woods failed to shine in their early matches. When all was said and done, the Europeans had the lead coming into the third and last day of the 33rd Ryder Cup. But the Americans came out with blood in their eyes for the final, which was either a remarkable victory or a disgrace depending on whose side one was on. European captain Mark James felt that the American players whipped the crowd into such an apogee of patriotism that the atmosphere became hostile to his men. James criticized Tom Lehman in particular for encouraging the crowd to sing "God Bless America" repeatedly at the 1st tee, which was off-putting for Lehman's opponent, Britain's Lee Westwood, who went on to lose the match 3 and 2, which was the start of a streak of wins for the United States in the twelve singles matches that concluded the tournament— each win was worth a point (a half being awarded to both sides when a hole was tied). Colin Montgomerie, who had never enjoyed a happy relationship with American fans, had particular reason to be upset with the rowdy gallery. Shouts of "Monty, you're a fat cunt!" were hardly sporting. Before long Jim Furyk's win over Sergio Garcia had put the United States a point ahead. They needed only another half to reclaim the cup for the first time since 1993. If Justin Leonard could beat José Maria Olazábal or draw, it would be theirs. In its early stages the match between Leonard and Olazábal had been for Europe. But Leonard squared it at 15. At the 17th hole, the American found himself with a challenging forty-five-foot uphill putt, which, surprisingly, went in. Although Olazábal was still to play, and had an easier twenty-five-footer to halve the hole and thereby extend the match, American team members and their supporters ran onto the green and celebrated as if that were the end. This was what Mark James later described in his book *Into the Bear Pit* as "the most disgraceful scenes ever seen at a golfing event." When Olazábal was finally able to play, he missed, to no one's surprise, and America had the Ryder Cup back. It was hardly a glorious victory, though, and Tiger for one was underwhelmed by the whole experience.

Shortly before Christmas 1999 Tiger signed a five-year sponsorship deal with Buick, giving himself a gift worth approximately $25 million, and reflected on a good year in which he had won eight PGA Tour events, including four consecutive tournaments and a major, earning a record $6.6 million in prize money. The new year of 2000 started well, too, when he won another clutch of trophies. Still, it was the majors that really counted and, having finished a disappointing fifth at the Masters, he looked forward to the U.S. Open, which was to be held in the summer of 2000 at Pebble Beach Golf Links, now owned by a consortium that included Arnold Palmer and Clint Eastwood. Tiger considered Pebble Beach the best golf course in America. It would also be the 100th U.S. Open, which made the championship even more special. Despite thick fog on Thursday, June 15, Tiger got off to a brilliant start with a score of 65 that gave him the lead. The second round was carried over to Saturday due to adverse weather, and he finished with 69, despite a bad-tempered incident at the 18th tee when he drove his ball into the ocean and told himself loudly on live television that he was a "fucking prick." Even with his years of psychological training, Tiger can be as foulmouthed and obstreperous as a teenager in a tantrum, and instances like this do not enhance his image. As Mark McCormack noted, part of Palmer's popularity had to do with the way he managed to control his temper in tournaments. Nicklaus, too, had always been classy in this respect. Tiger can be embarrassing to watch, cursing freely and hitting the ground with his clubs in frustration, though some might say this shows he cares. It is at least a display of passion from a man who otherwise glides through public life revealing as little as possible about what he is thinking and feeling, rewarding his fans with a cheesy grin only when he wins. Having scored 71 in the third round, Tiger went into the final 10 strokes ahead of the field and had never looked in better form. His whole game was strong, but his short game in particular was in peak condition.

Sunday was a victory procession. He romped home with a round of 67 to claim that silver cup. The runner-up was Ernie Els, a rangy South African six years Tiger's senior, who would increasingly be the player who came closest to challenging him on tour. In character, they could not be more different. Els is a supremely amiable fellow, totally relaxed with the press and fans, a family man who says he gets up most mornings with a smile on his face and who seems to take whatever happens in golf with a shrug of his shoulders. At the U.S. Open, though, Els finished a very distant second to Woods—15 strokes behind to be precise. "He played at a totally different level, and probably *the* best I've ever seen anybody play," says Els of Woods generously. It was in fact the biggest margin win in the history of the majors, a magnificent performance that astonished all who saw it. Here was something in golfing terms that was more remarkable than the 1997 Masters (though it did not have the symbolism). One had to go all the way back to "Old" Tom Morris at the Open Championship in 1862 to find anything to approach Tiger's achievement at Pebble Beach.* What was more, it felt easy. "I told Stevie [Williams], walking up 18, there comes a point in time when you feel tranquil, when you feel calm; you feel at ease with yourself," Woods said. It was also his third professional major title, at age twenty-four, which meant he was keeping pace with Nicklaus.

After such a commanding display expectations for the next great event of the season, Britain's Open Championship, were high. Golf is about tradition and it was better to win the Open on the Old Course at St. Andrews than anywhere. There were limited opportunities, however, because of the Open roster. Tiger was still an amateur when he first came to St. Andrews for the Open in 1995. He would be nudging thirty when he got his next opportunity, and soon enough he would be past his prime. The Millennium Open, the 129th time the championship had been played, was his best chance to win golf's oldest championship at the historic home of the game. Reminders of the passing of time were everywhere. On Wednesday, July 19, 2000, twenty-two of the living Open champions played a celebratory four holes on the ancient links. One of the champions was Jack Nicklaus, making his farewell appearance in the Open. At sixty, the weary-looking Golden Bear was stout again after years of dieting, only able to walk the course thanks to recent hip replacement surgery. His business problems had clearly taken a toll. He was never going to make the cut, and he knew the real purpose of his visit to St. Andrews was to pause on the Swilken Bridge as he came up to 18 on Friday, to doff his cap and wave farewell for the public and press photographers. Afterward, he refused to absolutely rule out the possibility that he would come back and compete again, however. Like Arnold Palmer, who would make his supposed farewell to the Masters in 2002, Nicklaus found it was very hard to give up the spotlight.

During the week Nicklaus recalled that, when he was an amateur,

---

* In the 1862 Open Championship at Prestwick, Scotland, Tom Morris Sr. won by 13 strokes, which was the previous record margin in a major. But there were only six entrants that year.

Bobby Jones had told him that all great golfers have to win at St. Andrews. Nobody knew that better than Tiger, who was bending to his work under warm summer sunshine. Without any wind to speak of, the Old Course was as vulnerable as it would ever be, and the young American ravaged it, scoring 67 and 66 in the first two rounds. And he did not relent. "Tiger just kept that level of play up the whole week," laments Ernie Els, who started well with 266, but then shot a level-par 72 on Friday, "and that was probably the difference." On Saturday, Tiger shot 67, putting him 6 strokes ahead of the field. His 3-wood to the green at the par-5 14th was, in his own estimation, the only truly perfect shot he made all year. Although he had a poor lie and could not see the green from where he was (he used a TV crane as a guide), he landed his ball precisely on target 260 yards away and went on to score a birdie.

On the final day, he was paired with David Duval. Tiger played cautiously on the front 9, parring each hole except the 4th, which he birdied. Meanwhile, Duval and Els started to close the gap. Then Tiger picked up the pace, scoring birdies at 10, 12, and 14 (his fourth consecutive birdie at this hole). Duval began to lose his way, bogeying holes and landing in the purgatory of the Road Hole bunker, which proved calamitous. (There were 112 bunkers on the course. Tiger's ball had not found one.) When he parred 18, Woods took the title by 8 strokes, a total score of 269, breaking Nick Faldo's Open record. Els was second again, tied with Thomas Björn of Denmark at 277. Duval had slipped to eleventh place. By winning at St. Andrews, Woods became the first golfer since Tom Watson in 1982 to win the U.S. Open and the Open Championship in the same season and only the fifth to have won all four major titles at some point in their career, along with Hogan, Nicklaus, Player, and Sarazen. He did it younger than any of them, beating Nicklaus by two years. So it was that he lifted the Claret Jug, which is smaller than the other major trophies but the richest in history. Here was engraved an extraordinary roll call of names, many of which had near-mythic resonance: "Young" Tom Morris; Harry Vardon (he of the Vardon grip); Hagen and Jones; the triumvirate of Palmer, Player, and Nicklaus was well represented, as were latter-day stars, including Watson, Ballesteros, Norman, and Faldo. The R&A contrives to have the name of the new winner inscribed before the presentation ceremony, and so, as Tiger lifted the cup, he could see another great name added to that illustrious company. And if they kept playing the Open for another 129 years, people would still see that name and date.

The Wanamaker Trophy, awarded to the winner of the PGA Championship, is as ugly as the Claret Jug is elegant. Named after its 1916 donor, New York department store owner Rodman Wanamaker, it is by far the biggest of the major trophies: a twenty-seven-pound silver tub large enough to plant a bush in. Still, if Tiger, the defending champion, could keep possession of this monstrosity in 2000, he would have won three majors in a row. The 82nd PGA Championship was held at Valhalla Golf Club in Kentucky in August. In the first two rounds Tiger's partner was Jack Nicklaus on what amounted to his valedictory tour of the major championships. There is considerable respect and affection between the men, though Tiger is too reserved to gush about how he idolizes Nicklaus and the older man is just as matter-of-fact about Tiger. The mutual appreciation is in the body language, and the looks they exchange remind one of father and son. It was Tiger who led the field after three rounds, but his play was indifferent on the third day and others were closing in. On Sunday, thirty-one-year-old Bob May, who had known Tiger in junior golf, chased him to the finish, playing beyond his form in a truly remarkable final few holes. May was ranked forty-eighth in the world and had never won a PGA Tour event, yet he seemed to be about to defeat the great Tiger Woods. For his part, Woods would not be beaten; he had that same stubbornness Nicklaus had in his prime. The two traded blows to the 18th, playing faultless golf, whereby one mistake would cost one or the other the title, and leaving the rest of the field behind. It was as if the tournament had reverted to the match-play event it had been until 1958. They finished tied at the 18th, having scored 270 (a championship record), and went into a sudden-death play-off. When May missed a birdie-putt at the 3rd, victory was again with Woods. Could he make it four in a row, the fabled Grand Slam?

In the remainder of 2000, Tiger won several tour events and signed a number of new sponsorship deals, including contracts with Wheaties, Asahi beer, and TLC Laser Eye Centers, the latter worth $2 million a year alone. (The laser-surgery deal followed corrective treatment Tiger had had in late 1999.) In the spring of 2001 it would also be announced that Tiger would be paid $22.5 million over five years to represent Disney, which was appropriate considering he had grown up next door to Disneyland and now lived next door to Walt Disney World. His personal life was less healthy than his financial affairs, however. Tiger and Joanna Jagoda were no longer together. Being the partner of a professional golfer had its problems; life on the road was boring and could be demoralizing in the sense that nobody was interested in *you*. The alternative was to wait at home, of course, but that too could be a dispiriting existence. Down in Orlando there was a clique of players' wives and girlfriends—a preponderance of bottle-blondes with drawn-on eyebrows—looking after those big, ugly houses and keeping those big, ugly trophies polished. That was no life for Joanna, a clever woman who aspired to a career as a lawyer. Also, Tiger's father had not encouraged any thoughts of marriage his son might have had. As Earl told *TV Guide* in one of his more provocative statements, "A wife can sometimes be a deterrent to a good game of golf." Asked what happened between her and Tiger, Joanna says simply: "That's personal." She does not want to talk about Tiger or his dad.

It was Arnold Palmer who came up with the idea of the modern Grand Slam, back in 1960 when he was flying to Britain to play in his first Open Championship at St. Andrews, the one where he met Tip Anderson. During the transatlantic flight, he fell to talking with his journalist-friend Bob Drum about Bobby Jones's 1930 Grand Slam and suggested that the idea might be revived with the modern major tournaments: winning all four in one season. Drum and other journalists started to use the term in their articles, and so the notion took root. Palmer did not achieve the Grand Slam, of course. To his regret, he never won the PGA Championship. Nicklaus won all four titles at least three times over, but not in succession. Now Tiger had three in a row, with one more to go, though this notional Grand Slam would be over two seasons.

As a gambling man, Tiger knew the odds were against his winning the Masters in 2001. One of the curiosities of golf is that even the greatest players in their prime do not win consistently. To win, one's game had to be in peak condition, one had to be mentally strong and healthy, and there had to be luck. Then, of course, there were all those other fellows trying to win, too. Woods lost more often than he won. So did Nicklaus. So did everybody. This was true of every event. It was even more true of the majors, where the field of players was stronger, the nervous strain increased, and the conditions more testing and varied. The British links of the Open Championship were very different from the typical Midwestern parklands of the PGA Championship and the narrow fairways and thick rough of the U.S. Open. The Masters had no rough to speak of, but the greens were like glass, with holes cut in exasperating positions. To win each major, one had to play a different game, in a sense. To win any of them at any time was the dream of every professional player. To win any two made a golfer special. More than two and one edged into the company of the greats. For Tiger to have won three in a row was extraordinary. To win four in succession would be unique in the modern game. One had to go all the way back to Jones in 1930 to find a comparison. Of course, Jones won his four major tournaments in the same season, which for many was the only bona fide Grand Slam. Asked about this at a press conference before the 65th Masters, Tiger conceded that the harder Grand Slam was to win everything in one year. "But I think, if you can put all four trophies on your coffee table, I think you can make a pretty good case for that, too."

First, though, he had to win. He began well on Thursday, shooting 70, but not as well as Phil Mickelson, another gambling man who statistically was due a major win. After all, he was ranked number two in the world and had been close several times, earning a handsome living on tour and building a following of fans, but never quite having what it took for ultimate glory, and more often than not finding his path to glory blocked by Woods. Maybe his breakthrough would come this year. He scored 67 in the first round. David Duval, also seeking his first major title, shot 71. The leader was Chris DiMarco, a relative nonentity who had never won on tour, and whose early success—he shot a 7-under-par 65—was evidence of what a lottery tournament golf can be. On Friday, Woods and Duval shot an impressive 66, Mickelson 69. Still DiMarco led the way with 134 for 36 holes. Tiger struggled on Saturday, yet came home with a score of 68, making him the leader, 1 ahead of Mickelson and 2 clear of DiMarco, who would fall further behind in the final. "His goals are different than mine," DiMarco later said of Woods. "I've got kids. I've got other things weighing on my mind. . . . I'm not concerned about winning every tournament." The same was true, to some extent, of Mickelson, who would be paired with Tiger on Sunday. "I love Phil, but he can't hold Tiger's jock strap," says Trip Kuehne, a mutual friend. "Phil's got more money than he can ever spend. If he can go out there and play and be competitive and win three or four tournaments a year, and hopefully put himself in contention in the majors, he's not worried about forever changing the face of golf. He doesn't have that [ability]. . . . Phil isn't going to win twenty-five majors. But Tiger could win twenty-five, thirty majors. Who knows? That's the motivation. They've both got more money than they can ever spend. But one guy can really change the [history] of golf and the other guy can't."

Tiger arrived at the 1st tee on Sunday with a psychological advantage: he had won this before. The men in green jackets were always going to ask him back. Mickelson, on the other hand, was struggling to be more than a chubby footnote in the history of the game. Tiger started badly with a bogey, giving Mickelson a chance, but Mickelson missed his birdie putt and went on to fumble putts at the 4th and 6th. Duval, in the group ahead, was tearing up the golf course with a string of seven birdies, each one applauded with gusto by the crowd. He was level with Woods in the lead at the turn. Mickelson, trailing the leaders, hit a fine, high fade around the corner at the 13th. Tiger decided he needed to match it to maintain his advantage, which he did with a terrific tee shot, which led to a birdie. Although Mickelson scored a birdie here, too, and birdied the 15th, he and Duval then dropped crucial shots and Woods was in the clear coming to the last.

After teeing off at 18, Woods and Mickelson marched up the hill toward the clubhouse, Woods striding ahead. As he scanned the grass for his ball, he was at first dismayed to see a ball in a poor lie. Then he realized it was Mickelson's. His own golf ball was less than eighty yards from the green and the lie was good. His second shot stopped twelve feet from the flag. Players who had finished gathered around to watch him putt out. Earl and Tida were also there, the former as solemn as a judge. All Tiger had to do was make par; a bogey would mean a playoff with Duval. But, in one simple motion, he rolled the ball in the hole for a birdie and raised his right fist, a Grand Slammer. Then he walked to one side, realizing it was over, that he did not have any more shots to play. I'm done, he thought. Done. "It was just a weird feeling because, you know, when you are focused so hard on each and every shot, you kind of forget everything else. When I didn't have any more shots to play, that's when I started to realize what I'd done. I won the tournament, and I started getting a little emotional." He hid his face with his cap but composed himself in time to shake hands with Mickelson, who finished third after Duval. Then Tiger hugged his parents. "You pulled it off," Earl told him. "Now you really are in the history books." And soon after that he received a green jacket, a million dollars and change, and an intricately fashioned model of the Augusta National clubhouse in silver, the fourth trophy in a unique collection.

10

THE MASTERS OF THE WICKED GAME

When Tiger returned home from Augusta on the Monday following the 2001 Masters, it was to a new four-bedroom house at Isleworth that faced the driving range where he spent so much of his time. He turned over his first Isleworth house to Earl, for when he visited. Tiger could have lived in even grander style, of course; his new home cost a relatively modest $2.5 million and could not be described as a mansion. At one stage he bought three lots facing Lake Bessie with a notion of building something bigger. Then he changed his mind and sold the land. As Isleworth owner Joseph Lewis observes, Tiger did not have time to be building houses. Anyway, the new place was nice and roomy—9,253 square feet—with a spa, swimming pool, and boat dock, certainly enough house for a single man who traveled most of the year. Almost the first thing Tiger did after he got in the door and put down his bags was to rearrange his trophies. Already on the mantelpiece in the lounge were the tall, birdlike Claret Jug, the U.S. Open cup, and the Wanamaker Trophy. Next to these he placed the silver replica of the Augusta National clubhouse. Then he stepped back and admired the display. "There was all four major championships right there. And no one else in the world had them but me." It did not represent the classic Grand Slam, as even Earl conceded; that had to be done in one year. It was a Tiger Slam or, as Jack Nicklaus quipped, a Fiscal Slam (for it wouldn't harm Tiger's earnings). Whatever you called it, this was a remarkable achievement, and Tiger was immensely proud. He invited O'Meara and other friends over to see the trophies together and rearranged them several times, like a kid with a prized collection of toys. A photograph was commissioned showing Tiger dressed incongruously like a junior executive in a suit and tie, posing with his cups. He had never looked happier, and he had reason to be pleased with himself. Within five years of turning professional, despite all the hype, he had exceeded expectations. Even friends did not think he would be able to do so much so quickly and "with so much gusto," as his former Stanford teammate Conrad Ray puts it.

Tiger had been well rewarded for his achievements. The life he led at Isleworth was evidence of his wealth. As a result of the interest he had generated in the game, his fellow tour players were also much better off than they had been in the past, despite having achieved considerably less than Tiger for the most part. Even also-ran tour players were living like kings. A case in point was Swedish-born Jesper Parnevik, a distinctive figure on tour in that he dressed stylishly in brightly colored, well-tailored clothing and wore his cap with the brim up, Popeye-style. At thirty-six, Parnevik had not had a stellar career in the United States. He had won a meager five PGA Tour events but no majors. Yet by 2001 he had made $8.3 million in prize money, in addition to which IMG had negotiated sponsorship deals, which allowed the Swede to commission a $6 million mansion on Hobe Sound, a glittering strip of Florida waterway that was also backyard to Greg Norman. The Parnevik residence stood three stories and had twin cupolas, from which flew the Swedish and American flags. The Parnevik household was also enviable because, when Jesper and his wife, Mia, traveled on tour, they brought along their three children and an entourage of eight helpers that included a nanny of uncommon beauty, twenty-one-year-old Elin Nordegren. A fellow Swede who spoke perfect English, Elin had previously worked as a model—she once posed for a series of swimwear photographs—and she was the subject of much attention on tour. Tiger met her in the summer of 2001 at Royal Lytham and St. Annes in the north of England, where the Open Championship was being held, and asked her out, as many had. She did not say yes straightaway, and he had to pursue her with text messages. By chance, Tiger was asked about his love life by reporters when he came into the press tent at Royal Lytham. He said he wasn't ready to settle down yet, adding with characteristic sarcasm that when he was in the marrying mood, "you guys will be the first ones to know."

After the Tiger Slam, Woods seemed out of sorts in the majors. Maybe it was too much to expect him to win everything again. He finished down the leader board at the U.S. Open, the Open Championship, and the PGA Championship in 2001, giving away his titles one by one. Still, it was not a bad year by any means. Aside from the all-important Masters, he won four official PGA Tour events, the Deutsche Bank–SAP Open, and his own tournament, the Williams World Challenge. Founded in 1999, the World Challenge is one of the principal fundraisers for the Tiger Woods Foundation, with Tiger and a small field of leading players competing over 36 holes. The other main fund-raising events for the foundation are Woods's golf clinics and an annual pop concert, called Tiger Jam, sponsored by Coca-Cola. Funds are raised from sponsorship money and ticket sales to these events, and by auctions and exhibition matches held as sideshows. All the events present Tiger as a philanthropist, helping the young and the disadvantaged, as he said he would do when he turned professional, and therefore boosting his public image. However, behind the razzmatazz, Tiger gives little of his time to his foundation—no more than twenty days a year—and relatively little of his own money.

Tiger's friend Greg McLaughlin, former tournament director of the Los Angeles Open who now runs the foundation, declines to say precisely how much Tiger gives in cash to the foundation each year, because he says that no matter what, people will inevitably compare it to his income and find him wanting. All McLaughlin will reveal—"because it's a good sound bite"—is that Tiger donates his winnings from the World Challenge. Taking the fiscal year 2000–2001 as an example, Tiger came second in his own tournament in December 2000, earning $500,000. He may give additional money to the foundation in any given year, but this is the principal cash gift. Half a million seems like a lot. But IRS records show that gross contributions to the foundation in the year ending September 2001 exceeded $11.53 million, meaning Tiger's gift constituted less than 5 percent of the total (and an even more paltry fraction of his gross income, estimated at $53 million in 2001). Most of the foundation's revenue came from the fund-raisers and the corporate sponsors of these events, such as Coca-Cola. And, of course, the World Challenge prize money donated by Tiger did not exactly come out of his pocket. It was put up by the sponsors of the tournament—the Williams power company of Oklahoma (and later Target stores). Still, it is only because Tiger lends his name to the foundation that this money is generated at all. Tiger's foundation gives money to a large number of worthy causes, ranging from inner-city sports initiatives to organizations caring for abused children. Many donations are scraps of money, however, often less than ten grand. In 2000–2001, money paid out to good causes totaled $1.64 million—not such a huge figure considering funds received exceeded $11.53 million. The money paid out was much larger than in previous years, though. TWF distributed only $818,253 in 1999–2000 and $795,423 in 1998–1999. Most surprising is what is left over. Although all charities need to maintain reserves, IRS documents show that in 2000–2001 the Tiger Woods Foundation retained net assets of $16.23 million.

In private, Tiger can be tightfisted with his money, though he has a reckless attitude toward gambling. His public duties as the figurehead of a foundation coincide with an opportunity to throw money away on the tables at Las Vegas each year when he hosts Tiger Jam. In April 2002 Tiger's aunt Mae turned seventy-two, and Tida brought her backstage at the Mandalay Bay Events Center—venue of the Tiger Jam—to greet her nephew, of whom she had always been fond. Mae found Tiger in a private room playing blackjack. When he saw his aunt, he cried out her name and came to embrace her. But Mae was aware of the cardplayers tapping the table in the background, impatient for him to return. "This was serious stuff. . . . Big Money." The Tiger Jams have raised $3 million for charity since 1998. Rumors abound that Tiger has lost millions gambling. He is said to play $10,000 per hand—the amount his foundation donated to Denver Children's Hospital in 2000–2001, which puts his charitable work in perspective.

Before too long, Elin Nordegren was sitting beside Tiger at the green baize tables. "I resisted his courting for a long time," she says. "I was not an easy catch." Elin was similar to Dina and Joanna before her in that she was white, blonde, and from a conventional, middle-class background. Unlike his previous girlfriends, however, she had a touch of the trophy partner about her, being the sort of glamorous girlfriend a man like Tiger might be expected to have holding his paw as he gambled. She also seemed to share his attitude toward money. During one heavy session in Vegas, Tiger put down a $5 tip for the waitress. When Elin reminded him that he had already tipped, he reportedly whipped the money back.

When Tiger returned to Augusta in April 2002 he did so as the defending champion. But it was Arnold Palmer who stole the limelight in the first part of the tournament with his emotional—though not final—farewell. Most people were taken in by the good-bye words and sad, crumpled face of the former King of golf, now a grandfatherly figure in his seventies, white-haired and wistful for the days when his career was as fresh as the smell of cut fairways. The stars who paid him tribute seemed to take him at his word when he said this was his last Masters. Woods commented smoothly that one day he would tell his grandchildren he had played with "the great Arnold Palmer." Not everybody was moved, though. Ken Venturi, retiring from the Masters for real in 2002, after many years as a CBS commentator, remarked:

"I think he waited too long." The other talking point at Augusta in 2002 was that the club had extended the course by 285 yards in an attempt to present a tougher challenge to youngsters such as Woods who could hit the ball farther and farther as a result of better equipment and a higher level of fitness. Nicklaus and Palmer were among those veterans appealing for more action to stop the long hitters outplaying classic golf courses. They wanted a tournament ball, one that did not travel as far as the balls the players got from Nike, Titleist, and other companies (and it is a nonsense that in golf players can essentially bring their own ball to a tournament, a ball designed to suit their game). "The golf ball is kinda ridiculous now, because it is so fast and so forgiving," says Palmer. "It's far too fast. It's far too technical, from an aerodynamic point of view, and the one place that we can keep golf courses like Augusta and Oakmont and Troon and Carnoustie and Birkdale and St. Andrews in the realm of great courses is to slow the golf ball down."

Because of play being suspended on Friday, owing to a storm, Tiger played a total of 26 holes on Saturday, finishing 8-under par for those first holes, and in overall place alongside Retief Goosen, a mild-mannered South African who was the reigning champion of the U.S. Open. Sunday was ravishingly beautiful, a morning when all nature seemed to cry "Fore!" as P. G. Wodehouse wrote, when the fairways "smiled greenly up at the azure sky." The leading pairs were met with applause as they came to the 1st tee: Ernie Els and Sergio Garcia; Vijay Singh of Fiji and Phil Mickelson, who was increasingly desperate for his first major win. The final group was comprised of Goosen and Woods, the latter's red shirt already damp, Tiger having worked up a sweat on the range. He and Goosen were starting at 11-under-par with 205. But players in the groups close behind had a chance of catching up. Woods parred the 1st hole, while Goosen bogeyed, and Tiger birdied 2 and 3. Goosen bogeyed 4, putting him 4 behind, a position he found psychologically crushing. "I knew it was all over for me on the front 9," he said later. "I was just playing for second." Of the leading groups, Els and Garcia were the first to reach Amen Corner. Els seemed a challenger when he made three birdies on the front 9. He played par through the first two holes of Amen Corner, 11 and 12. By the time he reached 13 he was 3 behind Woods, with a chance to catch up on a hole where one hoped for a birdie or an eagle. Despite knowing he must not let the ball go left, where the creek and trees are, Els's tee shot hooked onto the bank. His caddie advised a recovery shot to the fairway. Instead, Els gambled on a shot through the trees, a mistake that sent his ball *in* the creek. He took a drop on the fairway side and reached the fringe, only to see his ball tumble back into the water. Els finally got his ball in the hole for a triple-bogey. After stepping across to the 14th tee, he removed his cap, scrunched his eyes shut, and rubbed the fingers of his left hand gently through his hair and over his face, as if trying to wake up from a bad dream. "I knew that my chances were gone and I had made a terrible mistake."

Mickelson was level par when he reached Amen Corner and had birdie chances at 11 and 12, missing both as he had so often when it came to crunch moments in majors. The second was the killer. "Oh God!" he gasped when his ball slipped past the edge of the hole. At 13, he hit his tee shot into the trees and, despite one more birdie, his chance was also gone. Singh was all square at the 13th tee and needed something special to surpass Woods, but his second shot rolled into the creek. Singh saved par, but bogeyed 14. At 15, a par-5 that afforded the player a chance to make up ground, it all turned to shit. He took 3 to reach the green, and then his ball slithered off the finely cut surface into the pond. He took a drop, went again, and found water again. A quadruple-bogey was the result, reminding one that it was indeed a wicked game. Garcia also failed to live up to expectations, scoring five bogeys during a round of 75. Woods made fewer mistakes than his ill-starred colleagues and stayed ahead with 71. "I've never seen players literally crumble," comments David Leadbetter, who was coaching Ernie Els at the tournament. "It was an amazing thing, because you would have thought that at least one of the players would have come out of the pack to challenge

Tiger." Leadbetter points to what he calls an intimidation factor with Woods. Maybe if it was another player in front, the result would have been different. And so Tiger took the title, 3 ahead of Goosen with a score of 276. Thus his tally of professional major wins reached seven, equaling the lifetime total of Arnold Palmer. In the history of the Masters only Palmer and Nicklaus had won more green jackets.

Amid all the excitement of Palmer's supposed farewell and Tiger's win at Augusta in 2002, many missed a small but significant news story in *USA Today*. On the Thursday of the tournament, Lloyd Ward, CEO of the U.S. Olympic Committee and one of the handful of black members of the Augusta National, was quoted as saying that the club should admit women members, and that he was doing what he could to effect change from within. "I want to talk to members of Augusta and [say] you've got to have a broader membership that includes women." Over the years the men-only nature of the club had received little publicity, overshadowed perhaps by the race issue, and that lack of interest might have continued had the *USA Today* article not come to the attention of Dr. Martha Burk, chair of the National Council of Women's Organizations (NCWO), a feminist pressure group in Washington, D.C. A sixty-one-year-old, twice-married mother of two, Dr. Burk (the title refers to a Ph.D. in psychology) admits to not being learned in golf. "I don't have to be an expert on golf. I'm an expert on sex discrimination, and I know it when I see it." Having decided that the situation at the Augusta National was iniquitous, she wrote to Chairman Hootie Johnson on June 12, 2002, in support of Lloyd Ward, copying the letter to him. Burk's letter read in part:

> *We know that Augusta National and the sponsors of the Masters do not want to be viewed as entities that tolerate discrimination against any group, including women. We urge you to review your policies and practices in this regard, and open your membership to women now, so that this is not an issue when the tournament is staged next year.*

Ward did not thank Dr. Burk for what she considered her moral support and has been silent on the subject since. The problem, perhaps, was that Johnson was infuriated by Burk's missive. On July 8 he returned a curt reply to Dr. Burk, saying that the Augusta National was a private club and he had no intention of talking with her about anything. He then issued a public statement that played into Burk's hands, in that it gave the matter publicity. "Our membership alone decides our membership," he wrote, claiming that Augusta National, Inc., and its tournament are separate entities. "One is a private club. The other is a world-class sports event" (a fine point, as the tournament is run by club members and held on club premises). He expected the NCWO to instigate a media campaign, but declared pugnaciously: "We will not be bullied, threatened or intimidated. . . . There may well come a day when women will be invited to join our membership, but that timetable will be ours and not at the point of a bayonet." So battle lines were drawn, and the battle would perhaps be the most significant for the game since the Shoal Creek affair; maybe more so, because sex discrimination affects not only American golf clubs but the international golf fraternity.

The Royal & Ancient Golf Club of St. Andrews does not have women members either, and this is arguably a more significant matter than the situation at Augusta because the R&A, together with the USGA, governs the game throughout the world, presuming to tell millions of people how to behave on the golf course. "We don't see any reason at all why every golf club has to be the same," says Peter Dawson, secretary of the R&A, defending his membership from the standpoint that the R&A is a private club and can therefore please itself as to its makeup. "We think the game is enriched by diversity." Dawson's counterpart at the USGA is, perhaps surprisingly, one of those who does not see things in quite the same way. "It's not about private clubs. It's about are there entities out there that are more than private clubs, which are indeed golf organizations," says David B. Fay, "and I think that when an entity is a golf organization it cedes some of its rights of freedom of association." Moreover, the R&A is the historic home of golf, the heart of the international game. If golfers cannot be integrated and treated equally at St. Andrews, what hope is there for the game at large?

The Augusta National is in a similar position to the R&A, because of the importance of the Masters and the influence its members have within the wider game. Few of those associated with the club believe it should change, however. Long-standing member Dr. Stephen W. Brown says typically that he doubts there will ever be women members at Augusta, and he does not want any. It goes back to his friend Clifford Roberts, the original dictator-chairman. "When the club was first started, they had a few women as associate members," recalls Dr. Brown. "[Mr. Roberts] didn't think well of that and dropped it off." When I asked veteran player and Masters rules official Dow Finsterwald what he thought about the suggestion that there should be women members of the club, he was highly amused. "Isn't that something? Ha ha ha!"

"Does that make you laugh?"

"Yes."

"Why?"

"Why does a woman have to be [a member]? She can play as a wife."

Martha Burk was in touch with a businesswoman who had contacts within the Augusta National and who asked some of the members discreetly whether they would help to get a woman into the club. When the reply came back that the members would not help, Dr. Burk wrote to the PGA Tour and the sponsors of the Masters—the Cadillac division of General Motors, Citigroup, Coca-Cola, and IBM (those companies that ran commercials during the telecast)—asking that they suspend their links with the tournament until the club reformed its discriminatory membership. Burk also wrote to CBS, asking it to stop broadcasting the Masters. Although CBS, IBM, and the PGA Tour returned robust letters, Burk got the impression that others were worried about their image, particularly Citigroup, which said in its response that it was talking privately with the club about its views (not that it made its views known). Before the year was out, two Augusta National members had resigned because of the controversy, and the chairman of American Express, Kenneth Chenault, one of the few black members, said publicly that he believed women should be admitted. The club that Clifford Roberts and Bobby Jones had built was being challenged as never before.

Apart from employing the rhetoric of oppression to sell shoes for Nike, Tiger Woods avoided politics assiduously; indeed, he cared little for politics. He saw his work as winning golf tournaments and making money, and having won the first major of the year, he had another shot at the classic Grand Slam in midsummer 2002.

The first U.S. Open since the terrorist attacks of September 11, 2001, was held on the Black Course at Long Island's Bethpage State Park. Its proximity to Manhattan aroused feelings of patriotism and defiance—despite all that had happened, one of the year's premier sporting events would be held on schedule. More significantly as far as the history of golf is concerned, Bethpage is a municipally owned course; it was the first time the USGA had brought its premier event to such a place and a gesture toward opening up the game. "To have our national championship finally played on a muni, you know, it was interesting how people even danced around it," says David B. Fay, who has been a liberalizing influence within the golf establishment. "They would call it a 'truly public golf course.' Just call it a muni! That's what it is. That's how people can relate to it."

Tiger led from the start, finishing 3-under-par at the end of Thursday, with Sergio Garcia a stroke behind, another four players at 1-under, and the bosomy form of Phil Mickelson filling out a group at par. Friday was cold and wet, making the course increasingly difficult. Tiger was fortunate to play early in relatively light rain, scoring 68, before deteriorating conditions presented serious problems for those chasing him, notably

Garcia, who, to the exasperation of many watching, had developed a highly irritating habit of gripping and regripping his club repeatedly, like a chronic masturbator, before striking the ball. The New York gallery advised him in forthright ways to get on with it. Garcia responded by giving them the finger and ended the day tied for third, 7 shots adrift of Tiger. When the Spaniard returned on Saturday, his mood and the weather had improved and Garcia played his way back into second place, still behind Woods, who was now at 5-under. The other challenger was Mickelson, a surprisingly popular figure with the public, who celebrated his thirty-second birthday on Sunday and was making his fortieth attempt to win a major. Many in the crowd evidently hoped this would be Mickelson's moment, and he was going into the final with a chance in third place.

On Sunday Tiger played conservatively, maintaining his lead and letting others make mistakes, as he had at the Masters. An electrical storm stopped play just after 6:00 P.M. when he was on the 11th green, 3 clear of Mickelson (Garcia was out of contention). After the storm passed, Mickelson made a birdie at 13 that cut the difference to 2. But Woods matched it when he got to 13, and Mickelson threw away whatever chance he had by bogeying 16 and 17. Even though Tiger bogeyed three of his remaining holes, he putted-out for 72 in the fading light, 3 shots better than Mickelson. At the age of twenty-six, Tiger became the youngest player ever to win eight major professional titles, four years younger than Nicklaus had been when he reached that tally. Accepting his trophy in the gloaming, camera flashes casting his face in stroboscopic light, and Mickelson standing behind, watching and listening with disguised envy, Tiger reminded fans, media, and fellow players that, although he was now set up for what many considered the real Grand Slam, he felt he had already done that trick.

In his heart, however, Woods knew that a rare opportunity lay ahead. Suitably, he was the first player since Nicklaus—against whom he judged himself constantly—to have won the first two majors of the year. And back in the summer of 1972—as America was getting its first glimpse of Watergate and Bill Withers's song "Lean on Me" was a hit on the radio—Nicklaus's next challenge was the Open Championship at Muirfield. Nicklaus went into the event with high expectations, knowing the course and loving it, only to lose to Lee Trevino, which was perhaps the most sorely felt defeat of Nicklaus's career. By coincidence, the 2002 Open would be at Muirfield, too. Would Woods be able to succeed where his hero had failed? It was a tantalizing notion.

The world had changed enormously in thirty years, of course, and in almost every respect. The mellow sound of Bill Withers had been supplanted by Eminem. Nixon was dead. There had been a technological revolution. But in golf, one might be forgiven for thinking that everything was as it had been in 1972, or even in 1744, when the Honourable Company of Edinburgh Golfers was founded. Since 1891 the oldest golf club in the world had been ensconced at Muirfield on the Firth of Forth. The history is incomparable; the course is links golf at its most delightful. But like the R&A and the Augusta National, the Honourable Company is a stubbornly men-only club, and the vexatious issue of sex discrimination—the battle feminists might be forgiven for thinking had been fought and won thirty years earlier, but was apparently news to male golfers—came up again in the days before the 131st Open Championship.

While the vast majority of British golf clubs are mixed, the venerable institutions on the Open roster tend to be men-only, including Muirfield, Royal St. George's, and Royal Troon (venues for the 2002, 2003, and 2004 Open, respectively). Muirfield was open to the public in the sense that one could pay to play a round there as a nonmember. That went for women, too, as long as they were accompanied by a male member (as if women were not to be trusted unsupervised). But women were very definitely not allowed to be members, and this attracted adverse publicity in the summer of 2002. Richard Caborn, Labour government sports minister, criticized the R&A for holding the Open at an all-male club. The distinguished British golfer Vivien Saunders made her displeasure clear, telling BBC Radio 4: "I think it's a shame that the

Royal & Ancient doesn't do something about it, and try and kick golf into the twenty-first century. [It] perhaps hasn't even moved into the twentieth century yet."

The R&A and the Honourable Company were unmoved, however. Indeed, they seem to resent being challenged on this issue. At Muirfield, they hung up the telephone on inquiries about the matter. When I pressed R&A Secretary Peter Dawson on the men-only issue, he became so irritated that he asked to stop the interview. When we resumed a few moments later, he conceded that the R&A had a problem. "I think the club accepts that this is an area requiring further examination, and the club is examining it at the moment. And that is the issue of how the R&A's governance committee should be formulated, and who should sit on it. . . . If we think it's in golf's best interest to be more representative on our governance committees, then that's what we will do." In other words, the R&A sees its committees—most importantly, the Rules of Golf Committee, which is made up of twelve members taken from various golf organizations, including the Ladies Golf Union—as separate from the club itself (as the Augusta National apparently thinks of the Masters as being apart from it, though to the outsider both clubs are indivisible from their committees and tournaments). Even though Dawson says the club might reform its governance committees, he is adamant that there would not be women members of the R&A. "I would be very much against the token woman member of any club," he says. Yet in almost the next breath he voices concern, as the head of golf's governing body, that girls' golf is in serious decline in Britain. Apparently girls don't think of golf as a game for them. When it is suggested that the R&A hardly sets an example to encourage them, Dawson snorts that he doesn't see "any correlation." To others, it is plain as day.

And what about the sponsors of the Open? MasterCard, Nikon, Rolex, and the Royal Bank of Scotland all have a multitude of female customers and staff. Yet none are apparently concerned that all those women are ineligible to be members of the R&A or many of the host venues of the Open simply by nature of their sex. When asked about this, senior executives at these corporations either ignore the question or wriggle out of it, like the director general of Rolex, Patrick Heiniger. "Rolex does not see itself in a leadership stance in this matter," says Heiniger, from the company headquarters in Switzerland. "The management and direction of the sport is we believe rightly the responsibility of the relevant governing bodies."

Tiger was drawn into the sex discrimination issue when a reporter asked him at Muirfield about Dr. Burk and the Augusta National. By his answer, Tiger appeared to think one sort of discrimination less serious than another. "It would be nice to see everyone have an equal chance to participate, if they wanted to, but there is nothing you can do about it," he said, a lamentably weak position when one compares this with his "Hello world. There are still courses in the United States that I am not allowed to play because of the color of my skin" baloney of 1996. In 2002 he reasoned: "If you have a group, an organization, [and] that's the way they want to set it up, it's their prerogative."

Tiger shot 70 and 68 in the first two rounds of the Open, starting Saturday 2 back from the leading pack, which included most notably Ernie Els, who scored 70 and 66. Though Tiger made hard work of the course at times, with displays of bad temper, he was well placed to make his move for the title when he teed off on Saturday afternoon. Half an hour before he struck his first shot, however, the foulest British weather rolled in from the North Sea and a veritable gale developed, a howling wind lashing rain in all directions as the temperature dropped precipitously. Clad in Nike waterproofs, Tiger staggered about the links like a sailor on the deck of a storm-tossed ship. Although he had often said that he enjoyed the challenge of adverse conditions, he was blown completely off course at Muirfield. The superior design of his golf equipment and his much-vaunted long hitting all counted for naught as he knocked his golf balls into the rough and in and out of pot bunkers, carding seven bogeys and two double-bogeys at the 5th and 13th. He thrashed at the ground and cursed. Then, as the hopelessness of his position became apparent, there was a look of surprise on his face and, comically, it seemed that he might cry, as indeed Nicklaus had in 1972. Despite a birdie at 17, he finished with a round of 81, the worst of his professional career to date.

On Sunday the sun was shining benignly. The Firth of Forth was a dreamy blue; the sand dunes winked between grassy hillocks, and birds cheeped cheerfully. Tiger returned early to shoot a fine 65, and then, to his credit, departed the scene without a word of complaint or a disgruntled look. Although he sometimes behaved like a petulant child on the course, Tiger had never been a bad loser. Later in the day, four players—Stuart Appleby, Steve Elkington, Ernie Els, and Thomas Levet—finished 6-under-par and went into a play-off, which Els won, his third major title.

Back in the United States, Martha Burk scored a victory of sorts in her campaign to change the Augusta National's all-male membership. For some time she had been getting the impression that sponsors of the Masters telecast were uncomfortable about the matter and that these companies were talking privately with the club about the possibility of admitting a woman member. This seems to have been correct, for on August 30 Hootie Johnson announced that rather than bow to pressure from outsiders or suffer its sponsors to come under such pressure, the 2003 Masters telecast would have no sponsors. For years, commercial breaks in the CBS telecast and the type of advertising allowed had been restricted by the club so viewers could enjoy long stretches of uninterrupted golf almost to the standard of public television. Still, major sponsors such as Coca-Cola and Cadillac paid an estimated total of $12 million to broadcast a few, specially made advertisements that were in keeping with the tone of the event—muted colors, a throaty voice-over, references to the great champions of the past, tradition, and so forth. The Augusta National was apparently rich enough, and pigheaded enough, to run the tournament without any sponsorship revenue in 2003. Indeed, Johnson later said the club could afford to forgo sponsorship indefinitely. Aside from a handful of dissidents, the members were united in supporting him. In the fall of 2002 close to one hundred stalwart men wearing green blazers gathered at the Augusta National for a closed party. When Johnson entered the room, and before a word was said, they gave him a standing ovation. "He knows the position of our membership because he's our leader!" exclaims Hall W. Thompson, one of those present (and with members like that, who could wonder at the club's attitude?).

The issue of sex discrimination would not go away, though. In October, at the Disney Golf Classic, Tiger Woods was asked for his view once again, and this time he tried to be more of a diplomat. "Hootie is right and Martha is right. That's the problem." Dr. Burk was not impressed by this mealymouthed comment. "Tiger is trying to have it both ways. He's trying to say we are both right," she says. "And we're not both right." Arnold Palmer and Jack Nicklaus were pressed for their views, as prominent figures in the game and moreover as the only two professional players ever to be made members of the Augusta National. Just as they had failed conspicuously to take a position on the race issue in the early days of their careers, they sidestepped sexism. Palmer said only that he regretted the controversy, implying that there were more important things in the world to worry about. Nicklaus wanted to keep his thoughts to himself, arguing that he had no sway over policy at the club. This was just as disingenuous as the claim that Palmer and Nicklaus had had no influence years before, when black players were fighting to get into the Masters. Obviously, if both veterans had bothered to get involved, they could have made a difference— that is, if they thought women should be treated as men's equals, which is highly doubtful.

In April 2003, Dr. Burk would take her campaign to Augusta. Her protest, moved half a mile from the club gates by the sheriff's department, was poorly attended and degenerated into farce as an Elvis Presley impersonator and other publicity seekers horned in on the demonstration. The protest failed to do Burk's cause much good and made no impact on the Masters tournament (in which Woods played indifferently, and which Mike Weir won in a play-off). Certainly, most local people seemed unsympathetic. However, it is in the nature of demonstrations to be undignified at times, and the fact that Burk put on a poor show at Augusta did not mean her point was less valid or that this issue would go away. Indeed, in the long term it is hard to see how the Augusta National and other clubs that take part in running golf at the highest level, notably the R&A, can persist in discriminating against any group of people on a membership basis.

If there was anything Tiger enjoyed less than being quizzed about politics, it was the ordeal of the Ryder Cup, which was held at the Belfry in England in September 2002, having been postponed from the previous year as a result of the terrorist attacks on the United States. Aside from September 11, the other event that cast a shadow was the 1999 tournament at Brookline, when American exuberance so upset the Europeans. This time the European captain, Sam Torrance, and America's Curtis Strange were determined that sportsmanship and good humor would prevail.

Tiger seemed ill at ease during the long and tedious opening ceremony. He would have to sit through a gala dinner later and a display of Irish dancing before he could get to bed, and he still wasn't getting paid, though once again the American team had $2.6 million to donate to charity and, again, Tiger gave the maximum to his foundation. Apart from Tiger, the U.S. team was blessed with numerous star players, including David Duval and Phil Mickelson. Sam Torrance's team seemed threadbare in comparison, featuring the likes of Welshman Phillip Price, ranked 119th in the world. (Tiger apart, the teams had one thing in common, though. All the players were white—almost unthinkable at any other international sporting event, and further evidence of the need for greater diversity in golf.)

Apart from the lack of remuneration in the Ryder Cup and the tiresome social functions, Tiger did not find it easy to change his individualistic approach to practice and exercise to fit in with a team—very much the same problem he had had at Stanford when Coach Goodwin wanted him to practice with the boys. For instance, he turned up at the practice range at the Belfry on the first morning of the tournament on his own and not wearing correct Team USA gear. Then he went to the left side of the range, which he favors because he draws the ball, though he knew the Americans were supposed to work on the right, and started swinging with the opposition.

Woods played his first match paired with Paul Azinger in a four-ball* against Irishman Darren Clarke and Thomas Björn. Tiger wore a long-suffering expression, said little or nothing to his partner, and there were moments of bad temper. "For Christ's sake!" he snarled when a photographer presumed to take his picture at the 1st. Not surprisingly, he and Azinger lost. In the afternoon foursomes, Woods and Mark Calcavecchia lost to Garcia and Lee Westwood, 2 and 1, partly as a result of mistakes by the world number one. Furthermore, the Europeans seemed to be having much more fun—the team spirit was particularly evident with Garcia and Westwood—and that was part of the reason that, at the end of the first day, Europe was a point ahead.

On Saturday Woods managed to get on the winning side when he and Davis Love III beat Björn and Clarke in foursomes, 4 and 3. (Woods and Love won again in the afternoon four-balls.) As Tiger worked his way around the course, Elin Nordegren trotted along inside the ropes, masticating a wad of gum and clapping dutifully when Tiger holed a putt. Nordegren and the other players' partners were part of the show, paraded at the opening ceremony like mascots and sent out onto the course each day in team colors. Yet those impertinent enough to talk to Elin were dismissed imperiously.

"Elin, do you mind if I ask you a question?"

"Yes, I do mind!"

---

*Two teams of two play a full round, using a ball each, and the better score of each team at each hole counts toward the final result. In foursomes, a team of two shares a ball and plays alternate shots.

Golfers who have handled fame most gracefully and successfully have followed a policy of engaging with fans and the media cordially, and that has also been true of their life partners. One only has to think of Arnold Palmer and his late wife or the Nicklauses. Despite the fact that these people are approached constantly when they are in public, they accept it as part of the life they have made and are courteous and charming. Palmer treats strangers as if he wants them to become his personal friends. If this affability comes naturally, it is admirable. If it is contrived, it is cleverly done. Either way (and in Palmer's case, one believes that he is sincere), engaging with spectators and press is surely part of the contract a celebrity makes with the public when he sells himself and the products he is paid to endorse. Woods and his entourage deport themselves differently. Woods talks to the media only when he has to, entering the press tent like a man who must report to a police station. He will sign a few token autographs when walking through public areas, but seems to take no pleasure in the process and avoids eye contact. Watching him breeze past his fans, and even allowing for his special security concerns, one is reminded of the photograph of Richard Nixon shaking hands thoughtlessly with a member of the public as he checked his watch for his next appointment. At golf tournaments, which are, of course, public events held in huge parks where people mingle freely, Tiger, his mother, his girlfriend, and his cronies treat public and press, whom they inevitably brush up against, as if they are interlopers at a private function, giving an impression of arrogance mixed with insecurity. It is not an attractive combination.

The teams went into the singles matches on the last day of the Ryder Cup with 8 points apiece. Torrance put his strongest players out first, hoping any early success would enthuse the home crowd and create momentum. Curtis Strange played into this strategy by sending his best players out last, Tiger last of all. So it was that in the first match Colin Montgomerie, so often a bumptious figure, became something of a European hero by defeating Scott Hoch decisively, 5 and 4. The crowd then lent its enthusiastic support to the next European, Sergio Garcia, as Torrance had hoped they would. Although Garcia would lose his match, Padraig Harrington beat Calcavecchia soundly, Bernhard Langer beat Hal Sutton, and Björn beat Stewart Cink. By the time Tiger came out to play, again not wearing correct team colors, the Europeans were in command with excellent morale, which was boosted when Tiger began to struggle against Jesper Parnevik, even though the Swede's game was in a parlous state. Meanwhile, the world number two, Phil Mickelson, was beaten by Phillip Price, 3 and 2. If Niclas Fasth, a young buck from Sweden, could beat Azinger and gain one more point, then Europe would win. It looked like Fasth's match when he was 1-up and on the green at 18, and Azinger was in a bunker with apparently no chance of holing out. Yet the American pitched the ball out of the sand and straight into the cup—one of the best shots of the tournament. Azinger was overjoyed, scarcely able to believe his luck. Fasth was now under considerable pressure to make a long putt from the fringe. If he missed and halved the match, it would be for others to decide the outcome of the tournament. He took an interminable time and then he did miss. "It's such a wicked game," sighed Nick Faldo, commentating for Sky television.

With Europe needing another half point, the burden of securing victory fell upon Irishman Paul McGinley, who had been trailing Jim Furyk for much of their match but had got himself back to level at 17. It came down to the last hole and a ten-foot putt for McGinley. When he made it, the European players forgot their disapproval of the American antics at Brookline and started capering about on the green. An unimpressed Davis Love III agreed to halve his unfinished match (not that it would have made any difference, unlike the last moments at Brookline). Woods, midway to the 17th hole, appeared to feel upstaged and showed every sign of wanting to complete his round, though again this would not alter the result. At the 18th, Torrance was already swigging from a magnum of champagne, and Curtis Strange was telling British television that the better team had won. When Woods and Parnevik finally got to the 18th green and were actually putting, Torrance was on the edge of the green taking a congratulatory cell phone call from Seve Ballesteros. Considering the fact that the public were forbidden from bringing their phones onto the course, on pain of having them confiscated, this was rich indeed. Then, just as Woods drew his putter back, a cork popped! He went again and missed. Still, he insisted on putting out. Four mallards had waddled up from the lake onto the green and stood there staring at the American, as if even they thought he should quit. When Tiger missed his second putt, he did, and the Europeans sent the ducks flapping for safety as the golfers got on with the important business of showering one another in champagne and jumping in the water.

The traits that make Tiger Woods a so-so Ryder Cup player are, paradoxically, the characteristics that make him the supreme tournament golfer of modern times. For the most part golf is not a team game, and Tiger has no need to be a team player. The life of the tour player suits loners. To dominate in Woods's imperial way also requires tunnel vision. Pejoratively put, a nerdish disposition is helpful (a more lively personality would tire of the practice, asking: "Isn't there more to life than this?"). The life of a tour player—where one is partly judged by one's place on a Money List—also suits a fellow with an avaricious nature. Tiger has that, too. In the run-up to the Ryder Cup, he showed how much money meant to him vis-à-vis sporting glory when he was asked to choose between winning the $1 million first prize in the American Express Championship in Ireland, which he had just done, and a Ryder Cup win. He chose the former, and when asked why, he said he could think of "a million reasons."

It is hard to overemphasize the importance of money in the professional game. Tiger's golfing forebears, Arnold Palmer and Jack Nicklaus, worked at being golf moguls almost as hard as they worked on their swing, as we have seen. No doubt this is the future for Woods, too. Perhaps it is because professional golfers come up through club golf, where they socialize with accountants and lawyers, that they aspire to be businessmen as well as sportsmen. In truth, Palmer and Nicklaus have made almost as many mistakes in business as they have enjoyed successes. Many of the companies and grand projects that bear their name are just that: using a famous name, sometimes with efficacious results, other times not. And at the end of their careers it is interesting to see how they compare financially.

Nicklaus's brilliant career as a player has not been matched in business. He has virtually no financial interest in that great development in Ohio, Muirfield Village. His companies have almost gone under several times. He has worked his way through a surprising number of business associates, two of whom have come to the attention of the FBI. As he has grown older and his business career has not gone as planned, Nicklaus has become increasingly concerned about leaving a legacy that will support his family. "The biggest thing I've got as a legacy for [my children] is my name and my trademarks," he says. However, by the spring of 2002 he no longer had deals to endorse golf balls, gloves, or shoes—bread-and-butter income for most players. At the same time he had more than one hundred staff on his payroll. Knowing that his family could not afford to keep the business going the way it was if something happened to him, Nicklaus cut his staff by two-thirds. Furthermore, three decades after he quit IMG to manage his own affairs, Nicklaus conceded defeat and asked Mark McCormack to represent him again. "I think over the thirty years that I've been gone from Mark McCormack he's learned an awful lot," said Nicklaus, explaining his decision to return to IMG and putting a little spin on it. "He's been very successful. He's had hundreds of people that he handles . . . it's no longer two or three people, and you have to worry about one person getting preference over another. He takes care of all of them, takes care of all of them fairly equally, and I think he's learned that. He learned from my experience, as I've learned from his experience." In the twilight of his career, having made and lost fortunes, associates estimate Nicklaus's wealth at no more than $40 million, which, while a very large amount of money, is not as impressive as the fortunes of the other principal characters in our story.

Born into a blue-collar family during the Depression, Arnold Palmer has been more careful with his money. He maintains a much smaller staff than Nicklaus (and seems better able to keep staff); he has a smaller family; and, aside from his beloved airplane, he lives fairly modestly. At the same time, Palmer owns substantial assets, including homes in California, Florida, and Pennsylvania; he owns Latrobe Country Club outright and has shares in the Bay Hill Club and Lodge and Pebble Beach Golf Links. His golf course design company is highly successful (and once you have paid for a Palmer course, Arnold Palmer Golf Management can run it for you). He is also under contract to promote products and services for twenty companies, ranging from Microsoft to Office Depot. For these reasons, even in old age, he remains one of the highest-paid sports figures in America, earning about $18 million a year. His fortune is therefore estimated in the mid–eight figures, though $100 million might be nearer the mark.

Neither Arnie nor Jack made much prize money in his heyday, relative to what players earn now. On the PGA Tour, Nicklaus won a total of $5.7 million and Palmer $1.8 million. Tiger outstrips them dramatically. In his first seven years as a pro, he earned more than $33 million. *Forbes* estimates he has earned another $200 million or so from sponsorship deals and, as a result, he is judged to be the highest-paid sportsman in the world. Woods has paid millions in commission to IMG, of course, and there is anecdotal evidence that he has lost a lot in Las Vegas. He also likes to play the stock market, another type of gambling. "Anytime you pick up a stock . . . that grows 50 percent, you feel pretty good," he said in 2000. Technology stocks showed that sort of growth, and in the spring of 2000, when the technology bubble burst, Tiger was particularly exposed, because he started investing during the period leading up to the crash. Between the tables and the markets, the young golfer has no doubt lost fortunes by the standards of ordinary people.

Though tightfisted in some respects, Woods has been generous with his parents, giving them cars, homes, and other gifts, including a diamond for Tida that is described as being almost as big as her eye. Still, he lives modestly and most of his daily expenses are taken care of by the companies he has relationships with (provided as he is with cars, clothes, and golf equipment). In 2002 *Fortune* magazine estimated his wealth at $212 million. This may be exaggerated, but he is certainly richer than Nicklaus or Palmer.

As a sidelight, Woods stands to become the richest golf pensioner in the history of the game. Because the PGA Tour is a nontaxed association of self-employed tour golfers rather than an employer of players, it cannot have a pension fund for the players in the normal sense. Instead, each time a player makes the cut on tour a sum of money is set aside in the PGA Tour Pension Program. Because the tour is so prosperous at the moment, the money put aside—what the IRS calls "deferred compensation"—is huge, $27 million for the players in 2001. Contributions for individuals are calculated partly as a percentage of their winnings, so Tiger's deferred compensation is exceptional. Because the PGA Tour is a tax-exempt organization, the beauty of the plan is that this money grows tax free (becoming taxable only when released to players). Since the plan was created in 1983, tour members have been astounded to see how their money has grown, and some have projected funds worth tens of millions.

So who is the most successful man in modern golf, the master of this wicked game—Palmer, Nicklaus, or Woods? Well, they have all been outclassed by the man who took a share of *all* their income.

Having established his sports agency on the success of the Big Three, Mark McCormack expanded IMG in diverse ways, representing tennis players, race car drivers, even fashion models. IMG went on to produce television programs and organize sports events. At the turn of the twenty-first century, it moved into soccer management. Indeed, the company has grown like Topsy, with offices in thirty-three countries, close to three thousand staff, and annual gross revenue of $1.3 billion. And McCormack owned IMG outright. His other assets included several homes, not least of which was the property at Isleworth, a house twice the size of Tiger's. In fact, McCormack was worth far more than Palmer, Nicklaus, and Woods combined. When we met on a wet and windy day in London in October 2002, I asked whether he was a billionaire yet. "I don't know how you compute it," replied McCormack, slightly evasively. "I don't know what IMG is worth." He preferred to reflect on his other achievements. "I do feel that I've made a lot of contributions to golf, in terms of creating new tournaments, in terms of helping existing tournaments grow and flourish, in terms of developing television programming," McCormack said, rattling off his accomplishments. "I've been helpful to the R&A in developing the British Open commercially, and it goes on, you know. So I'm very proud of all that. Creating the World Golf Ranking may be one of the biggest accomplishments of my golf career, and certainly the legacy that I'm going to leave is that, because that was not ever done or thought about until I got involved in it." His sense of pride was evident. But McCormack did not seem to be a particularly contented man, distracted as he was by myriad matters of business, searching about irritably for misplaced papers as he talked, regulating his every hour by a timetable scratched on yellow legal pads that never left his side. He had also grown old, of course, like his friend and contemporary Arnie Palmer. Like Arnie, his hair was now almost white and, though McCormack was not overweight, he had the tired, blotchy skin and watery eyes of old age. And whatever McCormack had done with his life, it was over. Three months after we met, he suffered cardiac arrest and went into a coma. It was while he was lying unconscious in a New York hospital that *Forbes* published its 2003 list of that most exclusive club—the world's billionaires. Among the new entries, McCormack was listed with an even billion. A couple of months later he was dead at the age of seventy-two.

Some would say that golf is not about money at all. It is about playing the game and sportsmanship, and the real achievement of Palmer, Nicklaus and Woods, even McCormack, is that they have made the game more enjoyable and more popular. Tiger is given particular credit, a young man of mixed ethnicity who has apparently brought a whole new

generation to golf, people who would otherwise dismiss the game as boring, silly, and snobby. In fact, not that many more people play golf now
than they did before Tiger came to international attention, a total of
about twenty-five million in the United States. At the grass roots, there is
even evidence that Americans are playing *less* golf. "Tiger has really not
put golfers on the golf course," argues his former coach Rudy Duran,
who owns two courses in California and has seen the number of rounds
played there drop by a third in a decade. "It's still expensive. It's still
perceived as not a comfortable game: it's rules and regulations and kind
of stodgy old men . . . it's still golf." There is a large Hispanic population where Duran is based, and he observes that Tiger creates interest
among minorities, but that does not give kids money to play.

In recognition of this problem, organizations have been established
in recent years to promote golf for minorities in the United States,
including the National Minority Golf Foundation (NMGF) and the
First Tee. Their aim is to get more people of diverse backgrounds playing the game and working in the golf industry, which remains the preserve of white men. Indeed, less than 1 percent of people employed in
the golf industry in America are anything but white men. There are so
few minorities and women that Barbara Douglas, head of the NMGF,
believes she could name them individually. So there is a very long way
to go. And as far as African Americans in tournament golf are concerned, there are fewer black players on tour now than in the 1970s,
when the likes of Lee Elder and Charlie Sifford were active. In fact,
since Tiger Woods and Vijay Singh do not consider themselves black,
there are none.

Tiger's impact is in the number of people *watching* golf; television
ratings have increased by leaps and bounds, bringing more sponsorship
and television-rights money into the professional game, making purses
bigger and players richer. Yet there are problems here, too. During a
time of recession, an easy economy for any major company to make is
to cut back on its sponsorship, and in 2002 eleven PGA Tour events lost
their backers, with three events disappearing. And life was not easy for

those that survived, especially if they were not among those eighteen to twenty tournaments Woods patronizes (out of more than fifty official and unofficial PGA Tour events). "Arguably, right now the major issue in television is the have and have-nots," says Greg McLaughlin of the Tiger Woods Foundation. "If you have Tiger, then life is good. If you don't have Tiger, it's really somewhat of a ratings nightmare."

Even those select tournaments Tiger is almost certain to appear in each season have problems in a shrinking economy. The main sponsor of Nicklaus's Memorial Tournament, insurance company Marsh & McLennan, chose not to renew its contract in 2002, leaving a $1.5 million hole in the budget. At the same time, the Memorial, like other tournaments, was under pressure from the PGA Tour to increase its purse. Although the tour likes to present itself as an organization concerned with the finer aspects of the game and with charitable work, it is at bottom an association of professionals. On their behalf, with the connivance of agents and managers, it squeezes every last dollar it can out of the tournaments. The Memorial, one of the premier tour events, only a step below the majors in prestige, had a purse of $4.1 million in 2002. Yet Commissioner Tim Finchem told Nicklaus's people that that was not enough. "The problem right now [is] the tour is pushing every tournament to move up the purse to a point where you can't run that fast," complains Pandel Savic, general chairman of the Memorial and best friend to Nicklaus. "We're told that we have to move our purse up, by 2005, to a seven-million-dollar purse." The Memorial was big enough to raise it, probably, and they did find a replacement sponsor. But other tournaments in other cities were struggling, and the push for more money engendered bad feeling among tournament organizers. "The veiled threat," says Savic, "[is] that if you don't do it, they'll pick some other city."

Without Tiger, there would not be nearly as much money as there is in the game today. In his first eight years on tour, total prize money more than tripled to $225 million. Having the most famous sports figure in the world as the number one player in golf has been akin to

stumbling upon a reserve of oil—a wonderful bonanza for the game—
and everybody in professional golf should be thankful to him, despite
his shortcomings as a human being. The Woods effect won't last, of
course. In his day, Arnold Palmer was almost as big a name—certainly
in the United States—galvanizing the public in a similar way. But a better, younger player, Jack Nicklaus, took his place soon enough, and
then that player became old and the game fell into the doldrums. Nobody remains on top for long. "No one, not anyone, is the king of
golf," says Palmer. "No one will ever be." If the men who run golf were
shrewd, they would see that the future health of the game lies in diversity, in pulling down all the barriers of the past—all the nonsense that is
excused in the name of tradition—and making golf truly egalitarian; in
persuading establishment clubs to reform with regard to membership;
in making it clear that golf welcomes people of all racial and social
types, and in encouraging the best women professionals, such as Annika Sorenstam, to play alongside men on tour, if they want to do so.
That is surely the way to engage the interest of the general public in the
long term and, by making the game more inclusive, professional golf
would not have to rely on the fortunes of one great star, like Woods,
who will falter and fade. Indeed, the only certainty in Woods's career is
that he, too, will become a has-been.

In the meantime, what binds Palmer, Nicklaus, and Woods together
is that they have been the best in their day. That remains the proudest
boast any of them can make. Nicklaus can add something: he remains
the most successful golfer ever. Even with Tiger snapping at his heels,
Nicklaus has that. So how will he feel if and when Woods surpasses his
tally of major wins? Nicklaus considered this question as he sat on a
golf buggy at Muirfield Village in Ohio at the end of a hot summer day.
The sun had dipped below the trees, casting long shadows over the fairways. Nearby, a group of Jack's friends were taking part in a putting
contest—people he had known since his childhood at Scioto Country
Club, when the world was younger and maybe less complicated—
friends now grown older, too.

It was hard to see the young, power-packed Nicklaus in the sixty-two-year-old man. He seemed almost small; that once-ursine physique was flabby and, at the same time, slightly deflated. His fair skin had been mottled like scar tissue by years of exposure to the elements; the once-thick thatch of yellow hair was dull and thin. His mouth twitched involuntarily, as if betraying inner stress. But he still had spirit and, without a hint of self-pity or regret, he announced that he did not care at all about the prospect of Tiger's breaking his record. Not for a minute. "You do the best you can to make as good a record as you can. You know someday somebody's gonna break it," said the world's greatest golfer, in the voice that was still quick, high-pitched, and emphatic. "And I think it's probably good for the sport to have him break 'em." After all, he and Tiger were so similar in so many ways it would almost be like passing the baton to his own son.

EPILOGUE
CYPRESS IN WINTER

Winter had come to Southern California, a time of year that is barely discernible from the other seasons thereabouts in that there is a chill in the early morning and occasionally there is the excitement of rain. No rain had fallen for weeks in Cypress, however, and on the street where Tiger Woods grew up his former neighbors were obliged to water their yards each evening to keep their lawns and plants alive. When Tiger's father, Earl, was away, they watered his yard as well, at the bungalow on the corner where Earl has lived this past quarter of a century and more. The house was almost indistinguishable from the other tract homes, all built to plan in 1971, except that the two cars parked up against the garage were newer and more expensive than the norm—one of them a sleek, silver-colored Mercedes convertible—and on close inspection the house had been improved in subtle ways without regard for cost. The flimsy front door, for instance, had been replaced by a magnificent portal of carved walnut.

When the heavy door swung open, Earl asked in a gruff but not unfriendly voice: "You afraid of dogs?" Two handsome young Labradors bounded out ahead of him, a brown dog named Hud and a golden Lab named Pepper, brothers, as he explained, trying to calm them. "It's all right, fellas." Eventually, Earl turned and led the way back into an open-plan reception room, where mail was piled high on a ledge to the left: much of it fan mail for Tiger, plus a heap of correspondence from American Express, which has an endorsement relationship with the family (members since 1997, as the advertisements say). Earl shuffled to his leather armchair; a tall, heavy man, bald and bloated, he was wearing spectacles and dressed in gray sweatpants with a Nike swoosh and a gray sweatshirt of different origin with a food stain on the breast. He eased himself down and indicated for his visitor to take the couch to his left, on the side of his hearing aid, explaining that he had just returned from Isleworth, where he had taken charge of Tiger's original golf villa, having overseen its redecoration. "I never considered that place home," he said. "Now, it's got my stamp on it."

Still, Earl was obviously pleased to be back in the house where he raised that remarkable son, dreaming the dreams they fulfilled in such an extraordinary way. In a sense, Earl is custodian of a national monument: the childhood home of one of the most famous sports figures of modern times and, looking around, one was reminded of a museum. Beside Earl was the bronze trophy Tiger won for the 1999 National Car Rental Classic. The wall behind was smothered in golf-related pictures and paintings, including a landscape of the Augusta National. At the end of the room hung a massively enlarged photograph of Earl, Tiger, and Tida, who was now living apart from her husband. Most striking was the large portrait of Tiger's face hanging over the marble-clad fireplace, his smooth, brown features beaming out of a hazy background, eyes wide and teeth gleaming, as though Tiger himself were emerging into the room in the form of a genie. In conversation Earl referred to Tiger fondly as a painting, one "you've sketched out and you've got the canvas partially filled in, but it isn't all filled in yet—that's Tiger. He's still growing." It was right here, between the sofa and fireplace, that Tiger used to pitch golf balls over a chair when he was a kid, and it was here that the kid sat cross-legged watching Jack Nicklaus on TV winning the

Masters. In the garage behind was where the eureka moment occurred in 1976, when Tiger drove his first golf ball into a net, and Earl yelled for Tida to come and see what their genius son was doing. One day, when Earl is gone, this house may have to be jacked-up onto a flatbed truck and rolled over to the World Golf Hall of Fame.

One assumed that the Isleworth house was being made ready for when Earl could not manage on his own anymore and, at seventy-one, he did not look well. Having survived two bouts of heart surgery and prostate cancer (with a hernia the size of a grapefruit, as he says), he continued to smoke heavily and had the sluggish movements of a sickly man. Still, he was mentally alert and, despite the preconception that he would be a difficult, bombastic person, he was a soft-spoken, courteous man of obvious intelligence, moreover a man possessed of wisdom. The wisdom stemmed from his upbringing in Manhattan, Kansas, and the influence of his mother, Maude, who taught him much about life before her untimely death. Not, of course, when Earl was thirteen, as he conceded when I reminded him of the date of his birth and the date of his mother's death. He appeared grateful for the enlightenment and for some other "clarifications" of his biography, exclaiming: "Hell, you taught me some things about my life I never knew about!"

Hattie Belle raised him up after his mother died, and Earl spoke warmly about her influence in his life, recalling one example of her fortitude: the time when he was a boy and the Kansas River flooded, causing havoc in the black district of Manhattan. Water was four feet deep in the little house on Yuma. But Hattie Belle was undaunted. She went into hock to replace the ruined floorboards and, while she was about it, had an extra room put on the house, all to help keep the family together and ensure they had a comfortable and secure base while the younger children completed their education. "She was the one who pulled the family together and maintained the household," says Earl. "She was bound and determined that all of us would go to school . . . and live in the same house. And then, when all of us were graduated and gone, the house would be available for our children to go to school. That was the game plan. You see, the reason is education was of primary importance in our family. It was the cement that held everything together and was the goal of all of us—not baseball, not football, none of that. It was education."

Earl was getting into his storytelling when the doorbell rang. "Oh, sheet!" he cursed, with considerable irritation, for it took him a while to get up and go answer it.

"Hi! How are you?" a door-to-door salesman greeted Earl brightly.

"Yeah, what?" returned Earl grumpily.

"Beautiful car you got there," said the fellow, indicating the Mercedes.

"Thank you," replied Earl more mildly, and then he stood and listened to a long peroration about carpet cleaning, only stopping the man when he suggested coming inside for a demonstration. In dealing with the salesman, Earl showed more courtesy and patience than one might suppose, or most people would muster. "Well, yeah. . . . People do have to make a living," he said when I remarked upon it. "See, that's my mother again. Don't be rude, just because you are imposed upon by others. Everybody has a right. So I'm very understanding about others' feelings and emotions."

Not perhaps when it came to his first family, though. Earl's first wife, Ann, is a fierce critic of Earl Woods, considering him arrogant, selfish, and pompous, a pomposity she believes is a façade to protect his more vulnerable true self from being hurt, as he was as a young man, losing his parents and suffering racism. "She's so insightful," said Earl sarcastically, but with some discomfort. "I don't really think she knows me that well." Some might consider Ann a bitter ex-wife, but most would find fault with the way Earl left his first three children at such a formative stage to take up with a younger woman, and even more hurtful, surely, was the way he wrote so dismissively about his first family in *Training a Tiger*, in which book he referred to that first marriage, those three children, as a "trial run" for fathering and bringing up Tiger. Not surprisingly, Earl is not close to his elder children. He said he didn't believe in that. "I believe in allowing them, and their children, to live lives of their own." Of course, they had grown up without him anyway. "I made mistakes. I went through military service and I wasn't home and, not knowing the difference, I allowed this to continue. In retrospect, I wouldn't have done it that way, because I shortchanged the kids," he admitted. "But I learned, and did a heck of a lot better job raising Tiger than I did the other three, and the reason for that was that I was there all the time with Tiger." Earl went on to say that he did not mean to imply in his book that Denny, Kevin, and Royce were second-best to Tiger. It was more that he was writing from the point of view of being Tiger's father, "from the perspective of I was chosen by God to be this kid's father. Then He has prepared me by giving me [experience] with three previous children, see? That's all that means." He paused and lit a Benson & Hedges to help him think. "There's nothing negative about it from my point of view. I didn't mean anything negative by it. I was merely trying to explain how I felt in preparing myself to be Tiger's father, that I wasn't in control. Somebody else was in control and put me through a series of sea trials to prepare me to be the best parent for Tiger."

But God presumably also meant him to be the father of Denny, Kevin, and Royce.

"Yes, [but] I have never written a book about that."

In writing the book, and calling it *Training a Tiger,* Earl reminded the world that he was behind Tiger's success—something neither Deacon Palmer nor Charlie Nicklaus had felt compelled to do, though they had equal claim to the success of their sons—and an example, surely, of Earl's egocentricity and craving for attention. "I don't consider myself famous," he says. "I'm just Tiger's father [and] I'm not pushy, no. I'm the father, yes, because he had to have a father. Somebody had to be the father and I was chosen."

"By God?"

"Yeah." Here was the melding of religion and ego, which is the essence of the philosophy Earl devised for himself in adult life, and it was this attitude that seemed rampant in the 1996 *Sports Illustrated* article in which Earl was quoted as saying that Tiger had the power to change the world, and appeared to say further he would be more significant than anybody in history, including Buddha and Mahatma Gandhi (though these names were not between quotation marks). The inference was that Tiger Woods was some kind of Messiah. Nothing enrages Earl so much as being reminded of this article, which he claims misrepresented him. "Oh man!" He sighed miserably when the subject came up. He raised himself out of his chair in agitation, as if to end the discussion, before sitting back down again. "Would you say I was a rather stupid, ignorant, unlearned individual?" he asked. "Making a statement like that would be rather stupid, about putting some kind of moniker on your son like that. . . . No way."

The other defining aspect of Earl's personality is his belief that American society is profoundly racist, almost as bad as it ever was. "You have rights now, more [than you did]," he says. "But it's still there. And only those that are very naïve will say that it has gone, and you will not find a black person that will tell you it has gone, because they know. . . . There are more privileges [now], but push-come-shove things are still there. They're still there. You can't legislate against people's minds and their hearts. You can't. You can make all the laws you want—that all people are created equal—but people will want to be superior."

Two levelers, perhaps, are illness and war. Earl's 1997 heart bypass, and the emergency surgery that followed, was almost the end of him, and the inspiration that drove Tiger to win his first Masters. When he woke in postop, Earl says the surgeon told him he should have been dead, adding that he was a "real tough cookie." Earl replied, "Yeah, I been to the place where I met the ultimate competitor, and I thought that it was me." When he talked about Vietnam, it was apparent that this had been the real thing. Earl recalled being under sniper fire and being lifted in and out of battle zones on helicopters with his friend Colonel Vuong Dang Phong, the first Tiger, as bullets whistled about. "Tiger and I were very close. Very close. All he wanted to do was be a schoolteacher," he said. "He wanted to be a schoolteacher, and he wanted to come to the United States and teach kids. He never made it . . ." His voice became husky with emotion, reminding me of Arnold Palmer when he spoke about the prospect of never playing in the Masters again. "Because they starved him to death in their reindoctrination camp."

In our minds we were in Vietnam, when Earl was young and strong and staying alive by dint of his wits, and Tiger's wits, before there was the other Tiger. The years between had flown by as in a dream. Now Phong was dead, and Tiger II had gone into the world, and Earl himself was an old man, barely able to walk a golf course let alone survive on a battlefield. Earl says he has no fear of dying, claiming to have had an after-death experience, which he described as a "wonderful, wonderful feeling." When it is his time, and this house becomes the museum it almost already is, Tiger will be bereft not only of a father but also the main inspiration he has drawn on in life. "I know Tiger's probably trying to accomplish all that he can possibly accomplish while his father is alive," says his friend Trip Kuehne. The question is what will happen when Earl is gone. "[Will] he still have the same fire in his belly?" as Kuehne puts it. Or, with all the money he could ever need, would Tiger retire at the top and let people remember him at his best? Indeed, sometimes one looks at Woods and wonders if his interest in the game is already flagging. His failure to win any of the major championships in 2003, due in part to erratic driving of the ball (leading to his abandoning his Nike driver in favor of a Titleist driver), certainly showed Tiger to be fallible.

Having guided Tiger's career since childhood, Earl had some thoughts as to what will happen in the future. "I think his main rival in the short term, and the long term, is going to be Ernie Els," he said of Tiger's place on the tour. "[Tiger] will play golf until he's tired of it," he added, "and he has achieved all the things that he wants, and somewhere along the line he will marry, and he will have children, and then he will continue with his philanthropic efforts and be like a ambassador without portfolio." In other words, there would be a time when golf was no longer everything, because when all was said and done golf was merely a game. "It always has been a game and always will be a game, that's why he'll be able to walk when he wants to walk. It's a game; it's not life and death. It's a game," said Earl, emphasizing his point. "And I taught him that when he was a little kid. He'd be out there playing and he'd hit a bad shot, and he'd bang the club on the ground and he'd look at me and I'd be laughing, and he'd hit another shot and mess it up, and I would laugh at him some more. Message: it's a game, and quite frankly you're really not that good. And he's never forgotten that."

As the afternoon light faded, and the cool of a winter evening crept in from the west, there was a melancholic atmosphere in the little house in Cypress. Despite all the glory Earl had shared in, despite the money and the prestige of being president of a foundation with invitations to give talks all over the world (Earl would be flying to South Africa shortly to address the South African Golf Association), Earl was alone. After his housekeeper had informed him that his dinner plate was in the oven and that she would return in the morning, there were just the dogs, his interviewer, and the tick of the grandfather clock. Twice the hour tolled loudly, but the telephone never rang. The only caller had been the door-to-door salesman. Asked about his relationship with the absent Tida, Earl said defensively: "That's very personal, [but] I'll tell you this: we're married." He no longer saw so much of Tiger, either, though he insisted he was still "parenting" his youngest, explaining that Tiger came for advice now and again, "then he works it out for himself." In fact, they'd been together just three days earlier, playing golf in Florida. Earl's face brightened as he spoke of being with his boy and the emotional bond between them, which, he said, was as strong as ever.

"A case in point: I was riding in the golf cart, and Tiger had his own cart and he was riding, and I went over to the left rough to hit my ball, and he got out of the cart and he says, 'Hey, Pop! Do you know it was thirteen years ago that we used to have these dog-eat-[dog] fights on the golf course?' I said, 'Yeah. And now look at what has happened to *you*, and look what has happened to me.' And we both started laughing, because his comment to me always was, 'Pop, I'm getting longer and longer, and you're getting shorter and shorter.' And the inevitability of it all was that he was going to beat me, and once he beat me I never got it back. I never beat him, never came close after that. He owned me." Earl smiled slightly at the memory, now that memories were almost all that were left.

TOURNAMENT WINS

Listed below are the wins of Arnold Palmer, Jack Nicklaus, and Tiger Woods in notable golf tournaments in the United States and abroad, including significant amateur events but excluding senior and team events. Majors are in bold.

Arnold Daniel Palmer
BORN SEPTEMBER 10, 1929

1954
U.S. Amateur Championship
  (Country Club of Detroit,
  Michigan)
1955
Canadian Open
1956
Panama Open
Colombia Open
Insurance City Open
Eastern Open
1957
Houston Open
Azalea Open
Rubber City Open
San Diego Open
1958
St. Petersburg Open
Masters
Pepsi Open

1959
Thunderbird Invitational
Oklahoma City Open
West Palm Beach Open
1960
Bob Hope Desert Classic
Texas Open
Baton Rouge Open
Pensacola Open
Masters
U.S. Open (Cherry Hills
  Country Club,
  Colorado)
Insurance City Open
Mobile Open
1961
San Diego Open
Phoenix Open
Baton Rouge Open
Texas Open

Open Championship (Royal
  Birkdale, England)
Western Open
1962
  Bob Hope Desert Classic
  Phoenix Open
  Masters
  Texas Open
  Tournament of Champions
  Colonial National
    Invitational
  Open Championship
    (Royal Troon, Scotland)
  American Golf Classic
1963
  Los Angeles Open
  Phoenix Open
  Pensacola Open
  ·Thunderbird Classic
  Cleveland Open
  Western Open
  Whitemarsh Open
  Australian Wills
    Masters
1964
  Masters
  Oklahoma City Open
  Piccadilly World Match Play
    Championship
1965
  Tournament of Champions
1966
  Los Angeles Open

Tournament of Champions
Australian Open
Houston Champions International
1967
  Los Angeles Open
  Tucson Open
  American Golf Classic
  Thunderbird Classic
  Piccadilly World Match Play
    Championship
  World Cup International
    Trophy
1968
  Bob Hope Desert Classic
  Kemper Open
1969
  Heritage Classic
  Danny Thomas–Diplomat
    Classic
1971
  Bob Hope Desert Classic
  Citrus Open
  Westchester Classic
  Lancome Trophy
1973
  Bob Hope Desert Classic
1975
  Spanish Open
  British PGA
    Championship
1980
  Canadian PGA
    Championship

Jack William Nicklaus
BORN JANUARY 21, 1940

1959
U.S. Amateur Championship
(Broadmoor Golf Club,
Colorado)
1961
U.S. Amateur Championship
(Pebble Beach Golf Links,
California)
1962
U.S. Open (Oakmont Country
Club, Pennsylvania)
World Series of Golf
Seattle World's Fair Pro-Am
Portland Open
1963
Palm Springs Golf Classic
Masters
Tournament of Champions
PGA Championship (Dallas
Athletic Club, Texas)
World Series of Golf
Sahara Invitational
1964
Phoenix Open
Tournament of Champions
Whitemarsh Open
Portland Open
Australian Open
1965
Masters
Memphis Open
Thunderbird Classic
Philadelphia Golf Classic
Portland Open

1966
Masters
Open Championship (Muirfield,
Scotland)
Sahara Invitational
1967
Bing Crosby National
Pro-Am
U.S. Open (Baltusrol Golf Club,
New Jersey)
Western Open
World Series of Golf
Westchester Classic
Sahara Invitational
1968
Western Open
American Golf Classic
Australian Open
1969
Andy Williams–San
Diego Open
Sahara Invitational
Kaiser Invitational
1970
Byron Nelson Golf Classic
World Series of Golf
Open Championship (St.
Andrews, Scotland)
Piccadilly World Match Play
Championship
1971
PGA Championship (PGA
National Golf Club, Florida)
Tournament of Champions

Byron Nelson Golf Classic
Walt Disney World Open
Australian Open
  Championship
Dunlop Invitational
1972
Bing Crosby National Pro-Am
Doral-Eastern Open
Masters
U.S. Open (Pebble Beach Golf
  Links, California)
Westchester Classic
U.S. Match Play
  Championship
Walt Disney World Open
1973
Bing Crosby National
  Pro-Am
Greater New Orleans Open
Tournament of Champions
Atlanta Golf Classic
PGA Championship (Canterbury
  Golf Club, Ohio)
Ohio King's Island Open
Walt Disney World Open
1974
Hawaiian Open
Tournament Players
  Championship
1975
Doral-Eastern Open
Heritage Classic
Masters

PGA Championship (Firestone
  Country Club, Ohio)
World Open
Australian Open Championship
1976
Tournament Players
  Championship
World Series of Golf
Australian Open Championship
1977
Jackie Gleason's Inverrary Classic
MONY Tournament of
  Champions
Memorial Tournament
1978
Jackie Gleason's Inverrary Classic
Tournament Players
  Championship
Open Championship (St.
  Andrews, Scotland)
1VB Philadelphia Classic
Australian Open Championship
1980
U.S. Open (Baltusrol Golf Club,
  New Jersey)
PGA Championship (Oak Hill
  Country Club, New York)
1982
Colonial National Invitational
1984
Memorial Tournament
1986
Masters

Eldrick "Tiger" Woods
BORN DECEMBER 30, 1975

1991
U.S. Junior Amateur
Championship (Bay Hill Club
and Lodge, Florida)

1992
U.S. Junior Amateur
Championship (Wollaston Golf
Club, Massachusetts)

1993
U.S. Junior Amateur
Championship (Waverley
Country Club, Oregon)

1994
U.S. Amateur Championship
(Tournament Players Club at
Sawgrass, Florida)

1995
U.S. Amateur Championship
(Newport Country Club, Rhode
Island)

1996
U.S. Amateur Championship
(Pumpkin Ridge Golf Club,
Oregon)
Las Vegas Invitational
Disney World/Oldsmobile Classic

1997
Mercedes Championships
Asian Honda Classic
Masters
GTE Byron Nelson Golf Classic
Motorola Western Open

1998
Johnnie Walker Classic
BellSouth Classic
PGA Grand Slam

1999
Buick Invitational
Deutsche Bank–SAP Open
Memorial Tournament
Motorola Western Open
PGA Championship (Medinah
Country Club, Illinois)
WGC-NEC Invitational
National Car Rental Classic
Tour Championship
WGC–American Express
Championship
PGA Grand Slam

2000
Mercedes Championship
AT&T Pebble Beach National
Pro-Am
Bay Hill Invitational
Memorial Tournament
U.S. Open (Pebble Beach Golf
Links, California)
Open Championship (St.
Andrews, Scotland)
PGA Championship (Valhalla
Golf Club, Kentucky)
WGC-NEC Invitational
Bell Canadian Open
Johnnie Walker Classic
PGA Grand Slam

2001
  Bay Hill Invitational
  The Players Championship
  Masters
  Deutsche Bank–SAP Open
  Memorial Tournament
  WGC-NEC Invitational
  PGA Grand Slam
  Williams World Challenge
2002
  Bay Hill Invitational
  Masters
  Deutsche Bank–SAP Open

U.S. Open (Bethpage State Park,
  New York)
Buick Open
WGC–American Express
  Championship
2003
  Buick Invitational
  WGC-Accenture Match Play
    Championship
  Bay Hill Invitational
  Western Open
  WGC–American Express
    Championship

SOURCE NOTES

PREFACE

1. MISTER PALMER'S NEIGHBORHOOD

Primary sources for all chapters are the author's interviews and/or correspondence and/or general conversation with those individuals listed in the acknowledgments. In this chapter: Doug Ford, Donald "Doc" Giffin, Dr. Howdy Giles, Eli "Babe" Krinock, Mark McCormack, Dr. Bob Mazero, Jack Nicklaus, Arnold Palmer, Jerry Palmer, Ed Seay, and Dick Tiddy.

8   "Everybody who plays the game of golf": Greg Norman, Golf Channel, April 12, 2002.

8   "[It's] kinda sad": Palmer, author's interview.

8   Palmer changes his mind: 2003 Masters press conference; author's discussion with Giffin.

8   Snead's ball hits spectator: author's notes.

9   Snead dies: *Daily Telegraph,* May 25, 2002.

9   Club's new policy: *USA Today,* April 26, 2002.

9   "That was my life": Palmer, author's interview.

9   Fortune: Palmer's office gives his fortune as "mid–eight figures." Based on research, I estimate it may be as high as $100 million.

9   Tour purses: *PGA Tour Media Guide.*

9   "I suppose, in some ways": Palmer, author's interview.

10   "My goals were to become the greatest player": ibid.

10   "Golf has been labeled a snob sport": ibid.

10   Latrobe Electric Steel: Giffin.

10   Palmer's date of birth: *PGA Tour Media Guide.*

10   Palmer's siblings' births: author's interviews; thanks to Giffin.

10   Bobby Jones's Grand Slam: Wind, *The Story of American Golf.*

11   "It seems as though every record I shot": Nicklaus, author's interview.

11   Background on Clifford Roberts: author's interviews; Augusta National literature (various); Owen, *The Making of the Masters;* and Sampson, *The Masters.*

11   Roberts's suicide: death certificate.

11   "Perfect!": Bobby Jones quoted in Roberts, *The Story of the Augusta National Golf Club.*

12   Jackson Stephens's fortune: *Forbes,* March 17, 2003.

12   Jones and Roberts wanted no blacks inside the club: claimed by Charlie Sifford *(Just Let Me Play),* among others.

12   Membership of Latrobe Country Club: author's interviews; Palmer, *A Golfer's Life.*

13   Link with Fred Rogers: author's interview with Jerry Palmer.

13   Deacon Palmer's community philosophy: author's interview with Mazero.

13   "Few if any automobiles came out this way": Jerry Palmer, author's interview.

14   "We were very poor": ibid.

14   "Hit it hard!": Deacon Palmer quoted in Palmer, *A Golfer's Life.*

14   "I'll knock your ball over the ditch": Palmer, quoted in *Daily Express,* March 10, 1966.

14   "Arnold, pull up your pants": Doris Palmer, quoted in Hauser, *Arnold Palmer.*

15   Interest in football: author's interview with Mazero.

15   Influence of Zaharias: Palmer, *A Golfer's Life.* Zaharias background: Laidlaw, *The Royal & Ancient Golfer's Handbook.*

15   First gallery: Palmer, *A Golfer's Life.*

16   Palmer meets Buddy Worsham: *Arnold Palmer: Golf's Heart and Soul,* Golf Channel, 1998.

16   1953 World Championship: Barkow, *History of the PGA Tour.*

16   Class for the less academically inclined: author's interview with Mazero.

16   "Today he is very outgoing": Tiddy, author's interview.

16   Works as a bricklayer in steel mills: *New York Times*, April 7, 1958.
17   Death of Worsham: author's interviews; Palmer, *A Golfer's Life*; and *Arnold Palmer: Golf's Heart and Soul*, Golf Channel, 1998.
17   U.S. Coast Guard: Palmer, *A Golfer's Life*.
17   Nicklaus first sees Palmer: Nicklaus, *My Story*.
17   1954 U.S. Amateur: *New York Times*, August 29, 1954.
19   "I've never had a better moment": Palmer, quoted in *Daily Mail*, December 20, 1999.

2. AN INVISIBLE MAN

Primary sources: Bill Baker, Dr. Charles Bascom, Sam "Killer" Foy, Barbara Ann Gary (née Hart, formerly Woods), Rosa Hickman, Gene Holiwell, Denzil Kastner, Jerry Keck, Mabel Lee "Mae" Moore (née Woods), Byron Nelson, Charlie Owens, Porter Pernell, Harold Robinson, Patty Schrader (née Keck), Don Slater, Marion D. Socolofsky, Bill Spiller Jr., Ray Wauthier, and Earl Woods. (Thanks also to Kansas State archivist Pat Patton and her colleague Cindy Harris, and Barbara Poresky at the Manhattan, Kansas, Public Library.)

20   "He would have had no chance": Earl Woods, author's interview.
20   Ellison, *Invisible Man*.
20   Supreme Court ruling: Halberstam, *The Fifties*.
21   Robinson background: Boyer, *The Oxford Companion to United States History*.
22   Simkins case: McDaniel, *Uneven Lies*.
22   Caucasian rule: PGA rule book, as displayed at the World Golf Hall of Fame.
23   "I don't remember anything about that": Byron Nelson, author's interview.
23   Background on George Jacobus: Wind, *The Story of American Golf*.
23   "Every caddie wanted to play": Foy, author's interview.
23   Improvised equipment: author's interviews with Charlie Owens and others.
23   Background on Porter Pernell and UGA: author's interviews.
24   "They responded that they couldn't do that": Pernell, author's interview.
24   Rhodes and Spiller: author's interviews with Pernell and Bill Spiller Jr.
25   "I don't think any of them were good enough": Nelson, author's interview.
25   Earl Woods's date of birth: family records and author's interview.
25   Manhattan, Kansas, social history: author's interviews; Kansas State records (special thanks to Pat Patton). Background: Geraldine Walton et al., *A History of Shepherd Chapel, Manhattan, Kansas: 1866–1967*, 1992; *Kansas Kaleidoscope*, vol. 5, no. 3; *Kansas City Collegian*, April 13 and July 19, 1956; and *Manhattan Mercury*, February 17, 1991, and January 12, 2000.
25   Celebration of Emancipation Proclamation in Manhattan on August 4: "Black History of Manhattan," *Flint*, February 21, 1979.
26   African Americans barred from golf in Manhattan: author's interview with Robinson.
26   Freda Woods moved to basement: ibid.
26   "God loves everybody": Hickman, author's interview.
26   Woods family history: author's interviews with Earl Woods and Mae Moore and Manhattan neighbors; Sunset Cemetery records (and headstone inscrip-

tions); newspaper obituaries; and census records. Special thanks to Pat Patton and Cindy Von Elling.

26   Maude Carter Woods graduates from Kansas State: Kansas State records.

27   "old, fussy, cussy man": Moore, author's interview.

27   "and I picked up on it": Earl Woods, author's interview.

27   "Go get it, Tiger": Miles Woods, recalled by Robinson and Earl Woods in interviews with the author.

27   "He had one single obsession": Earl Woods, author's interview.

27   "My mother put her arm around me": Earl Woods, quoted in *Sports Illustrated*, December 23, 1996.

28   "I hate Manhattan, Kansas": Moore, author's interview.

28   In the introduction to *Training a Tiger,* Earl Woods writes, "Mom died when I was thirteen . . ." He also gave his age at the time as thirteen in an interview with *Sports Illustrated* (December 23, 1996) and *Golf Digest* (November 2001).

28   "He has overcome so many obstacles": Tiger Woods in Earl Woods, *Start Something.*

28   "May I ask how old you were" and "I was thirteen": author's interview with Earl Woods, February 2003.

28   Date of death of Maude Woods: gravestone inscription and local newspaper obituary.

28   "OK. That may be a clarification": Earl Woods, author's interview.

29   "If we had to circle anybody": Moore, author's interview.

29   "Hattie was a little dictator": ibid.

29   "See, the whole family" and exchange with Earl Woods: Slater, author's interview.

29   Earl Woods's nickname: author's interviews with Moore, Robinson, Socolofsky, et al.

30   "We were all mixed" and family ancestry: Moore, author's interview.

30   "the prettiest blonde": ibid.

30   "just brown": ibid.

30   "didn't stay on his railroad job": ibid.

30   Earl Woods's high school sports and graduation: *Blue M,* Manhattan High yearbook, 1949.

30   "My American Legion coach": Earl Woods, quoted in *Golf Digest,* November 2001.

31   "I was the first—and only—non-white": ibid.

31   Tiger Woods repeated the baseball team story in his introduction to Earl Woods, *Start Something.*

31   "Do you mean you were the first black" and "First black in the entire conference": author's interview with Earl Woods, February 2003.

31   Robinson background and all quotations: author's interviews. Background on breaking the color bar: *Kansas Industrialist,* September 22, 1949; article by Tim Bascom in *K-Stater,* December 1997; and *Powercat Illustrated,* October 29, 1999.

32   Earl Woods's scholarship claim: author's interview with Earl Woods; *Golf Digest,* November 2001.

32   "He didn't get a scholarship from me": Wauthier, author's interview.

32   "Well, he is correct technically": Earl Woods, author's interview.

33   Holiwell and Earl Woods try out for the team: author's interviews with Holiwell and Wauthier.

33   "Weren't any scholarships": Holiwell, author's interview.

33   Earl Woods on 1951 Kansas State team: 1952 *Royal Purple* yearbook.

33   "I explained all that to him": Wauthier, author's interview.

33   "Because of my race": Earl Woods, quoted in *Golf Digest,* November 2001.

33   "We had black players": Wauthier, author's interview.

34   "Hell, no": Earl Woods, author's interview.

34   "nasty little prejudiced town": Moore, author's interview.

34   "the privations and public humiliations": from an article about Duke Ellington in Cooke, *Fun and Games with Alistair Cooke.* Thanks to Mr. Cooke for referring me to this volume.

34   "The fact that Tiger and Earl had to penetrate this": Moore, author's interview.

34   "kinda complex individual": Gary, author's interview.

34   "I remember him making the remark": ibid.

35   Earl Woods's ROTC training: author's interviews and Earl Woods's military record held at the National Personnel Records Center in St. Louis, Missouri.

35   Earl Woods's first marriage: state of Kansas marriage license.

35   "trial run": Earl Woods, *Training a Tiger.*

3. BLACK AND WHITE

Primary sources: Tommy Bolt, Frank Chirkinian, Doug Ford, Mark McCormack, Arnold Palmer, Chi Chi Rodriguez, Ken Venturi, and Ward Wettlaufer.

36   Platoon leader Earl Woods: Earl Woods's military record held at the National Personnel Records Center in St. Louis, Missouri.

36   "Most people have no idea": Palmer, author's interview.

37   Arnie and Winnie meet: *Arnold Palmer: Golf's Heart and Soul,* Golf Channel, 1998.

37   Wilson Sporting Goods and marriage: ibid.

38   "He's old-fashioned about that": Winnie Palmer, quoted in *Daily Mail,* July 22, 1989.

38   "I was not pleased with the idea": Winnie Palmer, in *Arnold Palmer: Golf's Heart and Soul,* Golf Channel, 1998.

38   "Everybody was different": Rodriguez, author's interview.

39   "In my day": ibid.

39   Background on Tommy Bolt: Bolt, author's interview.

39   "And of course he walked off": Wettlaufer, author's interview.

40   "We had monetary pressures": Bolt, author's interview.

40   Tommy and his wife threw kitchen knives at each other: Palmer, *A Golfer's Life.*

41   Palmers build house; children born: ibid.

41   Background on Charlie Sifford: Sifford, *Just Let Me Play.*

41   1952 Phoenix Open: ibid.

42   "He was one of the greatest players": Rodriguez, author's interview.

42   Sifford wins Long Beach Open: Sifford, *Just Let Me Play*.

42   "Underneath the façade of gentility": ibid.

43   "Charlie Sifford and I played together": Palmer, author's interview.

43   Background on Little Rock Central High: Halberstam, *The Fifties*.

44   Augusta National members critical of President Eisenhower: Clifford Roberts's 1970 Columbia University oral history interview, reported in Owen, *The Making of the Masters*.

44   Sifford's claim that Roberts decreed there would be only white golfers and black caddies at the Masters: Sifford, *Just Let Me Play*.

44   "the most racist and hateful spot on the golf globe": ibid.

44   Roberts and black staff: Owen, *The Making of the Masters*.

44   Story of Claude Tillman and "little black fellow": Roberts, *The Story of the Augusta National Golf Club*.

45   "gift": ibid.

45   "worthless . . . in every respect": Roberts's 1970 Columbia University interview, reported in Sampson, *The Masters*.

45   Derivation of the term Arnie's Army: Palmer's comments at Augusta, April 13, 2002.

46   "They're not real golf fans": Frank Beard, quoted in Hauser, *Arnold Palmer*.

46   1958 Masters: author's interview with Venturi; *New York Times,* April 7, 1958.

47   Bobby Jones's illness: Owen, *The Making of the Masters*.

48   "Why [should I]?": Venturi, author's interview.

48)   "looking down the long green fairways of indifference": Governor Frank Clement, quoted in Halberstam, *The Fifties*.

48   "Eisenhower was interested in golf ": Palmer, author's interview.

49   Palmer achieved 62 tour victories (the larger figure in chapter 1 includes senior and international wins); Snead, 81; Casper, 51; and Nicklaus, 73: *PGA Tour Media Guide*.

49   "He's got a terrible swing": Venturi, author's interview.

49   "Palmer became famous": Bolt, author's interview.

49   Growth of television in America: Boyer, *The Oxford Companion to United States History*.

50   Masters first broadcast: author's interviews; Sampson, *The Masters*.

50   1959 Masters: *New York Times,* April 6, 1959.

50   Background on Frank Chirkinian and "The camera fell in love with Arnold": author's interview with Chirkinian.

50   "The bloody thing's been going around": ibid.

51   "So we watch an awful lot of people": ibid.

51   "I don't know why anyone would go": Ben Hogan, quoted in Hauser, *Arnold Palmer*.

51   "No sport is as much improved": Updike, *Golf Dreams*.

52   "Because the money is really not the primary reason": Chirkinian, author's interview.

52   1958 Masters first prize: *New York Times,* April 7, 1958.

52   In 2001 the first prize for the Masters reached $1,008,000: *PGA Tour Media Guide.*

52   Palmer's endorsements: Palmer, *A Golfer's Life.*

53   "hard nut": Ford, author's interview.

53   Background on McCormack: author's interview with McCormack (thanks also to Penny Thompson at IMG in London) and McCormack, *What They Don't Teach You at Harvard Business School.*

53   Peculiar advantages of golf appealed to McCormack: Shaw, *Nicklaus.*

53   "I had this idea for exhibitions": McCormack, author's interview.

54   "We had all put up": Ford, author's interview.

54   Palmer too nice to be a lawyer: Hauser, *Arnold Palmer.*

54   "Arnold said, 'Look, I'm looking for somebody'": McCormack, author's interview.

55   "He was the first player": Bolt, author's interview.

55   "The Most Powerful Man in Sports," *Sports Illustrated,* May 21, 1990.

55   "I'm flattered that people say": McCormack, author's interview.

55   "One: his appearance": McCormack, author's interview.

56   McCormack–Palmer relationship: author's interviews with McCormack and Palmer.

56   Golf shoes; strategy for selling Palmer; race car drivers: McCormack, *What They Don't Teach You at Harvard Business School.*

56    $60,000 per year: *Sunday Telegraph Magazine,* June 12, 1988.

4. GOLDEN DAWN

Primary sources: James "Tip" Anderson, Deane Beman, Peter Dawson, David B. Fay, Bob Hoag, Marilyn Hutchinson (née Nicklaus), Kaye Kessler, Dom Lepore, Mark McCormack, Jack and Barbara Nicklaus, Robin Obetz, Putnam S. Pierman, Gary Player, Pandel Savic, Ward Wettlaufer, Ivor Young, and Stanley Ziobrowski.

58   "The American Dream was Arnold": McCormack, author's interview.

58   Nicklaus family history: author's interviews with Marilyn Hutchinson; the Jack Nicklaus Museum.

59   "Hardworking . . . hard-driven": Hutchinson, author's interview.

59   Nicklaus's date of birth: birth certificate.

59   "We had everything we needed": Hutchinson, author's interview.

60   "The first TV set I ever saw": Obetz, author's interview.

60   Musical tastes of Jack and his sister: Hutchinson, author's interview.

60   Maid knocked down: Hutchinson to *New York Times,* June 18, 1962.

60   Charlie Nicklaus's injury: Nicklaus, *My Story.*

60   Charlie Nicklaus played the game before: Cooke, *Fun and Games with Alistair Cooke.*

60   Background on Grout: author's interviews; Hornung, *Scioto Country Club.*

60   Grout's conversation with Charlie Nicklaus: Kessler, author's interview.

61   Kessler's conversation with Grout: ibid.

61   "He played about 27 holes every day": Lepore, author's interview.

61   "He [was] remarkably poised": Kessler, author's interview.

62   Older friends: author's interviews with Hoag, Savic, Young et al.

62   1953 U.S. Junior Amateur Championship: author's interviews; Nicklaus, *My Story.*

62   "They said, 'How could you get beat' ": Ziobrowski, author's interview.

63   Derivation of nickname Golden Bear: Jack Nicklaus Museum (thanks to Executive Director Gerald Goodson).

63   "I was just interested in being a golfer": Nicklaus, author's interview.

63   Nicklaus's career plan: author's interview with Obetz.

63   College nicknames: *Time,* June 29, 1962.

64   Nicklaus's first trip to Augusta: author's interview with Obetz.

64   1959 U.S. Amateur: author's interviews; *USGA Media Guide.*

65   "Sissy, I think our son's been born to greatness": Charlie Nicklaus, from author's interview with Hutchinson.

65   1960 Masters: Augusta National literature; *New York Times,* April 11, 1960; Hauser, *Arnold Palmer;* and Nicklaus, *My Story.*

65   "I haven't won it yet": Venturi, quoted in *New York Times,* April 11, 1960.

65   Background on 1960 U.S. Open: *USGA Media Guide.*

65   Oxygen for players: Palmer, *A Golfer's Life.*

65   Background on Ben Hogan and "I'm glad [I] brought . . . this monster": Wind, *The Story of American Golf.*

66   Conversation between Palmer and Drum: recalled by Drum in *Arnold Palmer: Golf's Heart and Soul,* Golf Channel, 1998.

66   "A long drive is good for the ego": Palmer, quoted in Hauser, *Arnold Palmer.*

67   1960 Open Championship at St. Andrews: author's interview with Anderson; Joy, *St. Andrews & the Open Championship.*

67   Palmer's conversation with his wife and Anderson: recalled by Anderson in author's interview.

67   Background on St. Andrews, the R&A, and the Open Championship: author's interviews; visit to the Royal & Ancient Golf Club and the British Golf Museum; and Joy, *St. Andrews & the Open Championship.*

67   "played at the golf ": British Golf Museum.

68   "The wind makes the golf links": Anderson, author's interview.

70   "If people started talking business": Dawson, author's interview.

70   "the champion golfer for the year": Dawson's remarks at the 2001 Open Championship.

71   Palmer's conversation with Anderson regarding club selection: author's interview with Anderson.

72   "I did nae quite say that": ibid.

73   Nicklaus marries: author's interview with the best man, Obetz.

73   Nicklauses as Savics' neighbors: author's interview with Savic.

73      $5,000 a year: Nicklaus, *My Story.*

73   "It's the most wonderful money": Charlie Nicklaus, quoted in *Time,* June 29, 1962.

74   1961 U.S. Amateur: author's interviews.

74   Yardage system: author's interview with Beman.

74   "Jack and a couple of players kind of laughed": Beman, author's interview.

74   "The Brute": Nicklaus, *My Story.*

74   "I don't remember a direct thank-you": Beman, author's interview.

74   U.S. Amateur ceases to be considered a major: author's interview with Fay.

75   Background on Gary Player: author's interview with Player; Player's office; Player, *Grand Slam Golf*; and *PGA Tour Media Guide*.

76   "It is so athletic, it is unbelievable!": Player, author's interview.

76   "It's a vagabond life": ibid.

77   Palmer's endorsements: Palmer, *A Golfer's Life*.

78   Palmer and GlaxoSmithKline—"educate the public about the dangers of smoking": Arnold Palmer Enterprises press release, November 27, 2001.

78   "They called him Fat Jack": McCormack, author's interview.

78   "He was also born to a fairly well-to-do family": ibid.

79   Titleist and "And, of course, we knew when the balls": author's interview with Lepore.

79   "It is with mixed emotions": Nicklaus's November 7, 1961, letter to Dey, at the Jack Nicklaus Museum.

79   "The amateur [status] wasn't important": Nicklaus, author's interview.

5. DETHRONEMENT

Primary sources: James "Tip" Anderson, Jim Awtrey, Deane Beman, Frank Chirkinian, Bruce Devlin, Dow Finsterwald, Doug Ford, Donald "Doc" Giffin, Maggie Hathaway, Bob Hoag, Marilyn Hutchinson (née Nicklaus), Tony Jacklin, Eli "Babe" Krinock, Mark McCormack, Barbara and Jack Nicklaus, Arnold Palmer, Porter Pernell, Putnam S. Pierman, Gary Player, Chi Chi Rodriguez, Bob Rosburg, Doug Sanders, Pandel Savic, Tom Weiskopf, Ward Wettlaufer, Ivor Young, and Kermit Zarley.

80   1960s statistics: *Time*, June 29, 1962.

80   1961 Open Championship: author's interview with Anderson.

80   "Arnold Palmer came into golf": Rodriguez, author's interview.

80   1962 Masters: Palmer, *A Golfer's Life*.

81   1962 Open Championship: author's interview with Anderson.

81   "I've never seen golf like it": ibid.

81   Nicklaus's professional debut: Nicklaus, *My Story*.

81   "We were so excited": Barbara Nicklaus, author's interview.

81   1962 U.S. Open: author's interviews; background from *USGA Media Guide* and *Time*, June 29, 1962.

81   "There were maybe a dozen people": Wettlaufer, author's interview.

82   Length of drives: *Time*, June 29, 1962.

82   "He outplayed Arnold": Wettlaufer, author's interview.

82   "Nicklaus Is a Pig": Hauser, *Arnold Palmer*.

82   "I just thought it was very low-class": Hutchinson, author's interview.

82   "that big, strong dude": Palmer, quoted in Nicklaus, *My Story*.

82   Palmer's suggestion to split the purse: Palmer, *A Golfer's Life*; Nicklaus, *My Story*.

82   "No, Arn": Nicklaus, *My Story*.

83   Nicklaus keeps Palmer waiting: author's interview with Hoag.

83   "I don't think he did it on purpose": ibid.

83   "Attaboy, Arnie!": *Time,* June 29, 1962.
83   "Most people get flustered": Nicklaus, quoted in ibid.
84   "I'm sitting there rooting for both": McCormack, author's interview.
84   "I'm sorry to say": *New York Times,* June 18, 1962.
84   Prize money: *New York Times,* June 18, 1962.
84   "When Jack first came out": Barbara Nicklaus, author's interview.
84   Stanley Mosk and the 1962 PGA Championship: *New York Times,* May
          18, 1961; Sifford, *Just Let Me Play;* author's interview with Bill Spiller Jr.;
          PGA of America Media Guide.
85   The word "tentatively" was typed onto Sifford's card, which expired at the
          end of August 1960 (reproduced in *Just Let Me Play*).
85   "As an association": Awtrey, author's interview.
85   "What happened, they pulled down one fence": Pernell, interviews with author.
85        $12,000 in savings required in 1962: Nicklaus, *My Story.*
86   Ten years later black players still fighting to qualify: UGA correspondence
          thanks to Pernell).
86   "They killed him with kindness": Player, *Grand Slam Golf.*
86   1963 Masters: author's interviews; Augusta National literature; Nicklaus,
          My Story.
87   Background on 1963 PGA Championship: *PGA of America Media Guide.*
87   Palmer stops smoking: Palmer, *A Golfer's Life.*
87   Background on 1964 Masters: *New York Times,* April 13, 1964.
88   "I really won this one": Palmer, quoted in ibid.
88   "Palmer is a hero to all": ibid.
89   "Mark McCormack was a genius": Player, author's interview.
89   McCormack had to create more than two dozen corporations: *Observer,*
          March 31, 1963.
89   *Big Three Golf:* author's interview with Rosburg.
89   Palmer and the R&A: Palmer, *A Golfer's Life.*
89   Did not use their fame and influence to campaign publicly for integration:
          author's interviews with Nicklaus, McCormack, Palmer, Player, and others;
          Sifford, *Just Let Me Play.*
89   Attempts to get African Americans into the Masters: author's interviews
          with Hathaway and Pernell.
90   "I think we only got one response": Pernell, author's interview.
90   "[He] said he would love to invite": ibid.
90   Palmer's views on membership policies: author's interview and Palmer, *A
          Golfer's Life.*
90   Ashe critical of Palmer: Hauser, *Arnold Palmer.*
90   "There's no question they were not admitted": Palmer, author's interview.
91   "I am of the South Africa of Verwoerd": Player, *Grand Slam Golf.*
91   "A good deal of nonsense": ibid.
91   Player taunted at tournaments: *Times* (London), August 18, 1969.
91   Player later renounced apartheid: author's interview with Player.
91   "My grandchildren are gonna say to me": ibid.
91   Nicklaus is color-blind: Nicklaus, *My Story.*

91   "black golfers have different muscles": Nicklaus, quoted by Reuters, August 11, 1994.

91   Selma march: *Encarta Encylopedia* (Microsoft).

92   1965 Masters and Bobby Jones quotation "Jack is playing": Nicklaus, *My Story*.

92   "those nice bright colors": from "Kodachrome," copyright © Paul Simon/BMI, 1973.

92   "I think the biggest breakthrough": Chirkinian, author's interview.

92   Background on 1966 Masters: author's interviews; *Sports Illustrated,* April 18 and 25, 1966.

93   "They have finally accepted him": Charlie Nicklaus, author's interview with Savic.

93   "an open wound": Giffin, quoted in Hauser, *Arnold Palmer.*

93   1967 U.S. Open: Trevino, *They Call Me Super Mex;* Nicklaus, *My Story.*

94   Background on Trevino: Trevino, *They Call Me Super Mex.*

94   "a way of life": ibid.

95   Walter Hagen's drinking: Wind, *The Story of American Golf.*

95   "You normally got shit-faced": Sanders, author's interview.

95   "George had about eighteen beers": ibid.

95   Librium: ibid.

95   Beta-blockers: *Golf* magazine, July 2001.

95   "Let me tell you the difference": Sanders, author's interview.

96   Tour Bible Study Class and "Sure. That hasn't changed": Zarley, author's interview.

96   Rosburg's recollection of being on the road with Arnie: author's interview; *Night & Day,* April 5, 1998 (approached for a reaction in 2003, Palmer declined to comment).

97   "It did disturb Arnold": Rosburg, author's interview.

98   Tour players revolt in 1967–68: author's interviews; Barkow, *History of the PGA Tour.*

98   "We said, you're not going to have any players": Ford, author's interview.

98   "Arnold Palmer never takes a stand": ibid.

98   Palmer's view: Palmer, *A Golfer's Life.*

99   "We needed a professional": Ford, author's interview.

99   Ivor Young finds land: author's interview with Young.

99   Muirfield Village name: Scott Tolley, Nicklaus.

99   Muirfield Village description: author's notes.

100   Background on Pierman: author's interview.

100   "If we could have done it": Pierman, author's interview.

100   Acreage bought: author's interviews (Savic recalls the initial purchase as 195 acres); profile article by Bob Baptist in *Memorial* magazine (undated); thanks to Ivor Young.

100   "I don't know how much": Young, author's interview.

101   "I think Jack is getting screwed": Charlie Nicklaus, recalled by Pierman in author's interview.

101   "and it was for shit": Pierman, ibid.

101   "Then he got a third dip": ibid.
101   "You're taking a percentage": McCormack, author's interview.
102   "Because they don't know, anyway": Pierman, author's interview.
102   Palmer leases Bay Hill: author's interviews; Palmer, *A Golfer's Life.*
102   Florida taxation: IRS.
103   "I can remember Charlie": Pierman, author's interview.   •
103   Charlie Nicklaus dies: author's interviews; Nicklaus, *My Story.*
103   Nicklaus's weight loss: ibid.
103   "The camera hated Jack": Chirkinian, author's interview.
103   "All of a sudden they were writing notes": Pierman, author's interview.
104   Jacklin background and "All they were interested in": Jacklin, author's interview.
104   1970 Open Championship: author's interviews; Joy, *St. Andrews & the Open Championship;* Nicklaus, *My Story.*
105   "little bit showbiz": Sanders, author's interview.
105   Nicklaus leaves IMG: author's interviews with McCormack, Nicklaus, and Pierman.
105   "Let's face it": McCormack, author's interview.
105   "I think that when Mark McCormack was younger": Nicklaus, author's interview.
106   "He could blame two people": McCormack, author's interview.
106   "If you had called me an agent": Pierman, author's interview.
106   Nicklaus and Pierman launch Golden Bear, Inc., on a shoestring: ibid.
106   "He really was in [the] shit": ibid.
106   Palmer buys Latrobe Country Club: author's interview with Jerry Palmer.
106   Palmer's planes: author's interview with Krinock.
106   "Arnold was the only guy": Pierman, author's interview.
107   "Running those fucking jets": ibid.
107   1971 U.S. Open: Trevino, *They Call Me Super Mex.*
107   1972 Open Championship: author's interviews; Nicklaus, *My Story.*
108   "I was just flattened": Nicklaus at Masters press conference, April 9, 2003.
108   "It was pretty tough on him": Young, author's interview.
108   Muirfield deal: author's interview with Pierman.
109   Background on Weiskopf and "I was the world's best player": author's interview with Weiskopf.
110   Beman and the PGA Tour: author's interviews with Beman.
110   Prize money in 1974: ibid.
110   Prize money target in 2003: PGA Tour.
110   Cost of covering events in the 1970s: author's interviews with Beman.
110   "So we would not be spending policy time": ibid.
111   Sifford's record: Sifford, *Just Let Me Play.*
111   Art Wall Jr. votes: Sampson, *The Masters.*
111   "If it's necessary": Pernell, author's interviews.
111   Bobby Jones dies: Owen, *Making of the Masters.*
112   Qualification system and political unrest: ibid.
112   Background on Lee Elder: McDaniel, *Uneven Lies.*

6. THAT'S INCREDIBLE!

Primary sources: John Anselmo, Diane Baer, Linda Behrens, Deane Beman, Maureen Decker, Bruce Devlin, Rudy Duran, Barbara Ann Gary (formerly Woods), Dave Harman, Donald Hill, Bob Hoag, Michael Hurdzan, Marilyn Hutchinson (née Nicklaus), Kelly Manos, Paul Moreno, Jay Morrish, Jack Nicklaus, Walter Olsen, Jane Orbison, Putnam S. Pierman, Joy Rice, Pandel Savic, Tom Watson, Earl Woods, and Ivor Young.

114 Earl Woods's military service: National Personnel Records Center in St. Louis, Missouri.

114 Births of Earl and Ann Woods's three children: family documents.

114 "unaccompanied tour": author's interview with Gary.

115 Background on Kultida Woods: author's interviews with Earl Woods and others. Kultida Woods declined to be interviewed.

115 Woods tells the story of how he met Tida repeatedly: see *Sports Illustrated,* March 27, 1995, e.g.

115 "That's my business": Earl Woods, author's interview.

115 "I think he told her": Gary, author's interview.

116 "separation agreement": copy of same and interview with Gary.

116 Did not have the money to hire a divorce lawyer: Earl Woods's statement in *Gary* [formerly Woods] *vs. Woods* (Superior Court of California, County of Santa Clara, case 226251), October 2, 1995.

116 "We did it!": Earl Woods, quoted in author's interview with Gary.

116 "Mexican divorce": copy of same, filed in the Third Civil Court of the District of Bravos, State of Chihuahua, Republic of Mexico, August 23, 1969.

116 Divorce of dubious value in the United States: experts in matrimonial law, including Professor Herma Hill Kay at the University of California at Berkeley (Boalt Hall School of Law). Also City of New York.

116 U.S. consulate could not vouch for the "validity [or] acceptability": letter from U.S. consul in Juarez, August 25, 1969.

116 Ann files for a California divorce: *Woods vs. Woods* (Superior Court of California, County of Santa Clara, case 226251).

117 Earl Woods has been quoted giving various years for his wedding to Tida, but never a date. For example, in Sampson, *The Masters,* he is quoted as saying he married Tida "in about 1965."

117 on or around July 11, 1969: family documents.

117 "sounds about right": Earl Woods, author's interview, February 2003.

117 "No, I did not": ibid.

117 "I don't know anniversaries": ibid.

117 Legal experts say: Professor Herma Hill Kay.

117 Until late that summer: *Woods vs. Woods* (Superior Court of California, County of Santa Clara, case 226251).

117 "the parties are still married": Interloculory Judgment of Dissolution of Marriage, ibid.

117 "status of unmarried persons": Final Judgment/Dissolution, ibid.

118 He engaged a lawyer: case file, ibid.

118   "He got married": Gary, author's interview.

118   She actually accused Earl of bigamy: letter filed with the Superior Court of California (Santa Clara County), April 13, 1995 (case 226251).

118   She remarried in 1981: case file 226251.

118   Legal experts agree: Professor Herma Hill Kay.

118   "I don't know anything": Earl Woods, author's interview.

118   "I had three children": Woods, *Training a Tiger*.

119   Earl Woods returns to Vietnam: Earl Woods's military file.

119   Nixon and Palmer—"Why not go for the green?": Palmer, *A Golfer's Life*.

119   Background on Colonel Vuong Dang Phong: author's interview with Woods.

119   "Tiger handled the military": Earl Woods, author's interview.

119   Sniper story; Phong saves Earl Woods's life; conversation between them: ibid.

119   "none that . . . saved my life": ibid.

119   Military decorations: Earl Woods's military file.

119   Earl Woods retires and moves to Orange County, California; employment: author's interview with Earl Woods.

120   Background on Cypress and Orange County: author's interviews; local inquiries; *The City of Cypress* (Cypress Chamber of Commerce, 1971).

120   Woodses' home in Cypress: author's visit.

120   Racist attacks: Earl Woods, author's interview.

120   "My wife is Thai": ibid.

120   Birth of Eldrick Tont Woods: birth certificate.

120   "buyer [of] space ship products": ibid.

121   "It was her way": Earl Woods, author's interview.

121   "[I] thought that some day": Earl Woods, quoted in *Mail on Sunday,* April 20, 1997.

121   Phong's death: Earl Woods, author's interview; Associated Press, November 14, 1997.

121   Jazz and Woods—"I established my personal imprint": Earl Woods, *Training a Tiger*.

122   "because her job": Earl Woods, author's interview.

122   "He picked up a putter": Earl Woods, quoted in *Golf Digest,* November 2001.

122   "I was screaming": Earl Woods, quoted in *USA Today Weekend,* July 24–26, 1992.

122   "That's when I knew": Earl Woods, author's interview.

123   "an international, world-famous golfer": ibid.

123   "I looked at it as an opportunity": ibid.

123   Tiger shoots 48 on the back 9: widely reported; see *USA Today Weekend,* July 24–26, 1992, e.g.

123   Moreno's recollection: author's interview with Moreno.

123   "Then I show up": Earl Woods, author's interview.

124   "Before the age of ten": Moreno, author's interview.

124   "It was never racial": ibid.

124   Background on Duran and "Well, I don't teach": Duran, author's interviews.

126   Tida contacted Jim Hill: Strege, *Tiger*.
126   Hill interview: *USA Today Weekend*, July 24–26, 1992.
126   Speech impediment: author's interviews with Duran and others.
126   *Mike Douglas Show* and dialogue: videotape of show. Transmission date: King World Productions.
126   *That's Incredible!:* www.yesterdayland.com; Strege, *Tiger*.
127   "When I get big": Woods, quoted in *Denver Post*, April 9, 2001.
127   "So Tiger never really liked it": Duran, author's interview.
127   Claims that Tiger was bullied on his first day at school have appeared in publications including *Sports Illustrated*, December 23, 1996; Strege, *Tiger;* and Collins, *Tiger Woods*.
127   "It's untrue": Decker, author's interview.
128   "I have never heard of that story": Hill, author's interview.
128   "And quite honestly": ibid.
128   "I can remember": Behrens, author's interview.
128   "I think he wanted": Decker, author's interview.
128   "Maybe his dad": ibid.
129   Audiotapes with subliminal messages: *Sports Illustrated*, March 25, 1995.
129   Distractions and release word: Tiger Woods, *How I Play Golf*.
129   "Winning that first tournament": Woods, quoted in *Los Angeles Times*, August 20, 1990.
129   "Rain or shine": Moreno, author's interview.
130   "Tiger!": Olsen, author's interview.
130   Background on Anselmo and "[Earl] wanted to know": Anselmo, author's interview.
130   Tiger didn't know who Palmer was: Duran, author's interview.
130   Tiger hero-worshiped Nicklaus: author's interview with Anselmo and others.
131   Nicklaus wins PGA Championship in 1975 and 1980: *PGA of America Media Guide*.
131   1977 Open Championship: Watson, author's interview.
131   "To put it in a nutshell": ibid.
131   "Being from the United States": ibid.
131   1982 U.S. Open: author's interviews with Devlin and Watson.
131   1983 rebellion against tour commissioner: author's interviews with Beman and Watson.
131   "They wanted to fire me": Beman, author's interview.
132   "That was our point": Watson, author's interview.
132   "Jack Nicklaus": Beman, author's interview.
133   "But from a business standpoint": ibid.
133   Changing of tournament names: *PGA Tour Media Guide*.
133   "In particular": Watson, author's interview.
133   "I felt strongly": Beman, author's interview.
133   "They're not interested": ibid.
134   Muirfield Village finances: author's interviews with Hoag, Pierman, Savic, and Young.
134   Club and land bought at cost: author's interview with Young.

134   "I liked Augusta's golf course": Nicklaus, author's interview.

134   "[Jack] couldn't draw plans": Morrish, author's interview.

135   "The golf course": Hurdzan, author's interview.

135   . Background on Dr. Alister Mackenzie: Owen, *The Making of the Masters.*

135   Author's afternoon with Nicklaus: Muirfield Village, August 9, 2002.

136   "Gary does promotional stuff": Nicklaus, author's interview.

136   "Soon as Jack saw that": Morrish, author's interview.

136   "Once I kind of became Arnold's guy": Harman, author's interview.

136   "That stands for": Morrish, author's interview.

137   U.S. domestic water consumption: U.S. Geological Survey.

137   "It becomes a wonderful environment": Harman, author's interview.

138   Yellow pig story: author's interview with Morrish.

138   "What you do": Pierman, author's interview.

138   "I said, 'Fuck it, Jack'": ibid.

138   "Give me your money!": ibid.

139   Diversified into oil and insurance: Shaw, *Nicklaus.*

139   Nicklaus's 1985 financial crisis: author's interviews; Nicklaus, *My Story.*

139   1986 Masters: author's interviews.

139   "She always thought": Hutchinson, author's interview.

140   Hoag, Savic, and Young leave early: author's interviews.

140   "I says": Savic, author's interview.

141   "the most thrilling thing": Hutchinson, author's interview.

141   Norman's ego: St. John, *Greg Norman.*

141   "All the majors": Nicklaus, author's interview.

142   Woods watching 1986 Masters: Masters press conference, April 8, 2001.

142   Background on clipping: *New York Times,* August 1, 1991.

7. JUST LIKE JACK

Primary sources: Lesley Aldrich-Linnert, John Anselmo, Jim Awtrey, Notah Begay III, Deane Beman, Ed Bignon, Dr. Jay Brunza, Jimmy Burns, Ron Butterfield, Mickey Conahan, Don Crosby, Eri Crum, Rudy Duran, Corrina Durrego, David B. Fay, Cia Fermelia, Barbara Ann Gary (formerly Woods), Joseph E. Gibbs, Donald "Doc" Giffin, Wally Goodwin, Dina Gravell, Don Greer, Larry Guest, Dave Harman, Claude "Butch" Harmon Jr., Joel Kribel, Mike Kruse, Trip Kuehne, David Leadbetter, Bob Londeree, Mark McCormack, Greg McLaughlin, Casey Martin, John Merchant, Paul Moreno, Doug Munsey, Bill Murvin, Ron Nichols, Jack Nicklaus, Bev Norwood, Walter Olsen, Bill Orr, William G. Osborne, Jake Poe, Conrad Ray, Bob Rogers, Bill Spiller Jr., Hall W. Thompson, Jim Tozzie, Earl Woods, Kevin Woods, Royce Woods, Tiger Woods (at a press conference), and Ed Woodson.

143   Earl Woods's bypass: author's interview with Earl Woods.

143   Tida goes to work in a bank: author's interview with Duran.

143   Tiger never left with a baby-sitter: author's discussion with Norwood.

143   IMG paid Earl's expenses: author's interview with Earl Woods.

144   Leadbetter helps Nick Faldo: Leadbetter, author's interview.

144   Psychologist uncommon for a junior player: author's interview with Duran.

144   Background on Brunza: author's interviews with Brunza.
144   "elements of the hypnotic": ibid.
144   "or whatever you call it": Anselmo, author's interview.
145   Background on Teddy Rhodes: Sinnette, *Forbidden Fairways.*
145   Background on Bill Spiller: author's interview with Bill Spiller Jr.
145   Background on 1990 PGA Championship at Shoal Creek: author's interviews and discussions; *Birmingham Post-Herald,* June 21, 1990; *PGA of America Media Guide;* McDaniel, *Uneven Lies.*
145   "We never asked": Fay, author's interview.
146   "You knew it": ibid.
146   Race history of Birmingham, Alabama: Boyer, *The Oxford Companion to United States History; Observer Magazine,* September 8, 2002.
146   Background on Hall W. Thompson: author's interviews.
146   "We have the right": Thompson, quoted in *Birmingham Post-Herald,* June 21, 1990.
147   "except the blacks": ibid.
147   "No, that's just not done": ibid.
147   Louis Willie: author's interviews; McDaniel, *Uneven Lies.*
147   "My first thought": Awtrey, quoted in Feinstein, *The Majors.*
147   "The Reverend Joseph Lowery": Awtrey, author's interview.
147   "Everyone in the game": ibid.
148   PGA Tour policy change and "We can be criticized": author's interview with Beman.
148   Ron Townsend joins the Augusta National: author's interviews.
148   "In the United States": Fay, author's interview.
148   John Franklin Merchant joins USGA: author's interview with Merchant.
148   "I didn't know": ibid.
149   "a target for the liberal media": Thompson in correspondence with author (July 12, 2002).
149   "got after the Negro marchers": Thompson, conversation with author (August 29, 2002).
149   "What's really sad": ibid.
149   Two black members at Shoal Creek: ibid.
149   "totally as a result": ibid.
150   610 members at Shoal Creek: Thompson's office.
150   Racial makeup of Alabama: 2001 Supplementary Survey, U.S. Census Bureau.
150   Not much has changed at Shoal Creek: Thompson's conversation with author (August 29, 2002).
150   Shoal Creek in talks with PGA Tour and USGA: author's conversations with Thompson and Fay.
150   Chance meeting at Shoal Creek: author's interview with Gibbs.
151   "We want you to come": Palmer, recalled by Gibbs in an interview with author.
151   Isleworth: author's interviews with Bignon, Greer, Harman, Londeree, Osborne, and others; author's visit to Isleworth; and papers in the legal case, *Town of Windermere et al. vs. Isleworth Golf and Country Club et al.,*

Circuit Court of the Ninth Judicial Circuit in and for Orange County, Florida (case C187–2677).

151   Background on Londeree: author's interview with Londeree.

152   Arnie's spiked shoes ruin leather floor: author's interviews at Isleworth.

152   "the capstone to my entire career": Palmer, quoted by UPI, January 15, 1983.

152   Isleworth built in one phase: author's interview with Londeree.

152   Drainage and Isleworth legal battle: author's interviews and documents in case C187–2677. Background: *Orlando Sentinel* (numerous editions); Associated Press, August, 20, 1990; and *Golf World,* March 28, 1991.

152   $300,000 to fix runoff problem: author's interview with Osborne and plaintiffs.

153   "gut-wrenching": Londeree, author's interview.

153   Gibbs visit Isleworth: author's interview with Gibbs.

153   Japanese bid for Bay Hill: author's interview with Bignon. Background: Guest, *Arnie.*

153   "It was a PR disaster": Guest, author's interview.

153   Palmer did not need to know everything: author's interview with Bignon.

154   Palmer Automotive Group: author's interviews; *The Sun* (London), August 3, 1990; Hauser, *Arnold Palmer;* and Guest, *Arnie.*

154   Isleworth lots priced from $150,000: *Orlando Sentinel* (real estate section), January 19, 1986.

154   Isleworth sales: By the end of 1990, 203 out of 370 lots had been sold (*Windermere Sun,* December 13, 1990).

154   "They thought they'd beat": Londeree, author's interview.

154   Retention ponds; gatehouse; seventeen-week trial and outcome: author's interviews; documents in case C187–2677.

155   Winnie Palmer rescues trophies: author's interviews.

155   Arnold Palmer Hospital for Children and Women: author's interview with Guest; Guest article in *Orlando Sentinel,* March 31, 1994.

156   "When I exposed that": Guest, author's interview.

156   Palmer's $12.5 million income: *Sports Illustrated,* May 21, 1990.

156   "I called Arnold": Gibbs, author's interview.

156   "He had never put money": ibid.

156   "He's genuine": ibid.

157   "Day one": ibid.

157   Golf Channel viewers' profile: ibid.

157   Takeover by Comcast and 2001 valuation: ibid; Comcast Corp. Annual Report, 2002.

157   Tiger Woods enrolls at Western High School and opinion of staff: author's interviews with staff members past and present.

158   "because he was going to be very, very rich": Aldrich-Linnert, correspondence with author.

158   "He very politely": Durrego, author's interview.

158   1991 U.S. Junior Amateur Championship: *USGA Media Guide.*

158   Woods meets Nicklaus and "He was always at ease": author's interview with Crosby.

159   "I had a number of meetings": McCormack, author's interview.

159   Faldo story; "But that isn't me": Feinstein, *A Good Walk Spoiled.*

159   "flattened as tennis was exploding": McCormack, author's interview.

159   Senior PGA Tour: author's interview with Beman.

160   1992 Nissan Los Angeles Open: author's interviews. Background: Barkow, *History of the PGA Tour.* Tournament play: *Los Angeles Times,* February 28 and 29, 1992; *Sports Illustrated,* March 9, 1992.

160   "He's winning a lot": McLaughlin, author's interview.

160   Tida Woods made the tiger headcover: Kramer, *Tiger Woods.*

161   "I would like to stand behind the curtain": Woods, quoted in *USA Today Weekend,* July 24, 1992.

161   Death threat; Tiger not told until later: author's interview with McLaughlin.

161   "They call it that": Nicklaus, author's interview.

162   "The tour didn't want to bring him in": McLaughlin, author's interview.

162   "These were the two best days." Woods, quoted in *Los Angles Times,* February 29, 1992.

162   Meets Dina Gravell: author's interview with Gravell. Background: *The* [Daily] *Mirror* (London), July 19 and 21, 1997.

163   "Who would want to be called Eldrick?": Gravell, author's interview.

163   "He didn't try to be popular": ibid.

163   "Their whole life was him": ibid.

163   "It was a divided house": Orr, author's interview.

163   Tiger pitching in the lounge: Woods interview with *Los Angles Times,* August 20, 1990.

163   "Golf had priority": Gravell, author's interview.

163   "Maybe he didn't want to talk": ibid.

164   "So I hit a few putts": Rogers, author's interview.

164   Tiger at the practice range: author's interview with Gravell.

164   "pure joy": Tiger Woods, *How I Play Golf.*

164   "Oh, she was a beautiful lady": Anselmo, author's interview.

164   Rift between Woods and the Navy Course: author's interviews with Earl Woods; Navy Course members Burns and Rogers; and staff Moreno, Nichols, and Olsen.

164   Party; golf cart; resident's stories: author's interview with Rogers.

165   "that little nigger": attributed to a resident who lived near the Navy Course, ibid.

165   1992 U.S. Junior Amateur and "You can't believe": *USA Today,* August 13, 1992.

165   "He didn't even know": Earl Woods, author's interview.

165   Death threats: author's interviews with Gravell and Earl Woods.

166   "Then he started talking": Tozzie, author's interview.

166   1993 U.S. Junior Amateur: Brunza, author's interview. Background: *Sports Illustrated,* August 9, 1993.

166   "He's always had a great admiration": Brunza, author's interview.

166   "I'm going to *will* this one in": Woods, as recalled by Brunza in interview with author.

167   Anselmo's cancer diagnosis: Anselmo, author's interview.

167   Background on Butch Harmon: Harmon, author's interview.

167   Link with Greg Norman: Anselmo, author's interview.

167   "My first impressions": Harmon, author's interview.

168   "which I did": Harmon, quoted in *Golf World,* August 2002.

168   1994 U.S. Amateur: author's interviews with Brunza and Kuehne. Background: *USA Today,* August 29, 1994.

168   Tiger's friendship with Kuehne family: Kuehne, author's interview.

168   "He hit it over the trees": ibid.

169   "We misread it": Brunza, author's interview.

169   "I think, probably, the saddest thing": Gravell, author's interview.

169   Brunza's view of Tiger's emotional outbursts: Brunza, author's interview.

169   "I said to him": Earl Woods, author's interview.

169   Letters from President Clinton and Philip H. Knight of Nike: Strege, *Tiger.*

169   "His goal": Gravell, author's interview.

169   Tiger's prediction to Murvin: Murvin, author's interview.

169   Crosby overheard Tiger: Crosby, author's interview.

170   "I think his parents pushed him": Gravell, author's interview.

170   Stanford background and alumni: author's notes; *Stanford Facts,* 2002.

170   "He was smart": Crosby, author's interview.

170   "Stanford is very interested in winning": Goodwin, author's interview.

170   Notah Begay painted his face: *Stanford Alumni,* June 1995.

170   Casey Martin's medical condition and Disabled American: author's interview with Martin.

170   "kind of a goofy kid": Ray, author's interview.

170   Conversation at Chili's: recalled by Ray.

171   "We thought this guy was a robot": Ray, author's interview.

171   Economics major: *Time,* August 14, 2000.

171   Relationship with siblings: author's interviews with Gary and conversations with Kevin and Royce Woods (both of whom declined full interviews).

171   "Lala, when I get rich": Woods, as recalled by Gary in interview with author.

171   "They could despise him": Gary, author's interview.

172   "The worst": Woods, in reply to author's question at 2002 PGA Championship.

172   "kind of a bummer": Crum, author's interview.

172   "We're here": ibid.

172   "My feeling": ibid.

173   Tiger is mugged: author's interview with Goodwin.

173   "We got more girls": Poe, author's interview.

173   Gravell wanted to date others: *The* [Daily] *Mirror* (London), July 19, 1997.

173   Breakup and "I guess they were totally afraid": Gravell, author's interview.

173   Background on 1995 U.S. Amateur: *USA Today,* August 28, 1995.

174   "Before he's through": Earl Woods, quoted in *Sports Illustrated,* September 4, 1995.

174   Teammates wondered whether Tiger would return to school: author's interviews with Crum and others.

8. GREEN STUFF

Primary sources: John Anselmo, Notah Begay III, Bob Berry, Dr. J. Jay Brunza, Frank Carpenter, Tim Connor, Mike "Fluff" Cowan, Eri Crum, Rudy Duran, Barbara Ann Gary (formerly Woods), Joseph Gibbs, Dr. Howdy Giles, Wally Goodwin, Dina Gravell, Tony Jacklin, Joel Kribel, Trip Kuehne, Joseph Lewis, Mark Mc-Cormack, Greg McLaughlin, Casey Martin, John Merchant, Mabel Lee "Mae" Moore (née Woods), Jack Nicklaus, Bev Norwood, Jake Poe, Conrad Ray, Tom Watson, Earl Woods, Carolyn Wu, and Ineke Zeldenrust.

175   Palmer's dinner with Tiger: author's interviews. Background: *Golf Digest,* November 2001; Strege, *Tiger.*

175   "I told him the things my father taught me": Palmer, quoted in *Night & Day,* April 5, 1998.

175   Palmer advises Watson: Watson, author's interview.

176   "Hey, did you enjoy": reporter's question to Tiger, recalled by Goodwin in interview with author.

176   Masters diary: *Sports Illustrated,* July 17, 1995.

176   Norman's clubs: Edwards, *Tiger Woods.*

176   "It was one of the happenings": Goodwin, author's interview.

176   "I won't turn pro": Woods, quoted in *Sports Illustrated,* July 17, 1995.

176   Earl engaged Merchant: author's interview with Merchant.

177   "I made it my business": ibid.

177   "He suggested that I speak to IMG": ibid.

177   Earl Woods scouts for IMG for "expenses": Earl Woods, author's interview.

177   "Having a job with IMG": ibid.

178   "serious discussion": Merchant, author's interview.

178   "All I know": ibid.

178   1996 Masters: *Sports Illustrated,* April 8, 1996.

178   "You can take all of Arnold's wins." Nicklaus, quoted in *USA Today,* April 11, 1996.

178   Calls to Stanford regarding Tiger: Goodwin, author's interview.

179   "A cannon could go off": ibid.

179   "After he left": Crum, author's interview.

179   Earl Woods's 1995 finances: statement provided by Woods's attorney to Superior Court of California after his first wife challenged the terms of their agreement (case #226251).

179   Cypress home remortgaged: Earl Woods, author's interview.

180   PGA Tour qualifying system: *PGA Tour Media Guide.*

180   "What people don't understand": Woods, quoted in *USA Today,* June 3, 1996.

180   Knight; Nike background: Nikebiz.com.

180   Nike's 1996 revenue: *Stanford Alumni,* January/February 1997.

180   "Just do it": Nike advertisement in *Wall Street Journal,* August 29, 1996.

181   "Michael was going to disappear": Merchant, author's interview.

181   "was a help": McCormack, author's interview.

181   Nike's production issues: author's interviews with Ineke Zeldenrust at Clean Clothes Campaign; Tim Connor at NikeWatch; and Beth Hegde and Carolyn Wu at Nike. Mr. Knight declined to be interviewed.

181   Wages of $1 to $3 a day: NikeWatch, and material supplied by Nike.
181   Subcontracted workforce: Nikebiz.com the inside story.
182   "Nike had led the push": Connor, author's interview.
182   Nike admits to "past mistakes": a response to the question "Does Nike use child labor?" on its Web site, Nikebiz.com the inside story.
182   Nike Code of Conduct: ibid.
182   Amphetamine story; 110-hour weeks (the former Bed & Bath factory, Thailand): NikeWatch. Carolyn Wu at Nike responded: "It would not be accurate to allow the unfortunate Bed & Bath [company] situation to define Nike's presence in Thailand." She could not comment specifically on the amphetamine allegations.
182   "I want[ed] a letter": Merchant, author's interview.
182   "It is distressing": Connor, author's interview.
182   Cost of Titleist Pro V1 golf balls: Titleist press office, March 2003.
183   "They climbed aboard early": Merchant, author's interview.
183   Tiger's decision to move to Florida to avoid California state income tax: author's interviews with McCormack and Merchant.
183   California state income tax: California Franchise Tax Board.
183   Taxes would be his single biggest expenditure: Woods's accountant Chris Hubman, quoted in USA Today, April 16, 1997.
183   "He said, where do I live?": McCormack, author's interview.
184   Woods's conversation and interests: author's interviews and notes.
184   Purchase of house for Tiger by IMG: author's interview with Merchant. Date and amount paid: Orange County Property Appraiser's records.
185   Upon winning his third U.S. Amateur on August 25, 1996, Woods was asked at the U.S. Amateur press conference if his plan was to return to Stanford in the fall and agreed it was.
185   1996 U.S. Amateur: author's interviews. Background: Sports Illustrated, June 10 and September 2, 1996; Guardian, August 27, 1996.
185   "The fact that all those people": Kribel, author's interview.
185   "he sort of danced": ibid.
185   "There were no calls": Crum, author's interview.
185   "The first time Tiger": Merchant, author's interview.
186   Tiger's Nike deal: author's interviews. Background: Augusta Chronicle, August 28, 1996; Milwaukee Journal Sentinel, August 28, 1996; Sports Illustrated, December 23, 1996; Strege, Tiger; and Rosaforte, Raising the Bar.
186   Greg Norman's Reebok deal: Sports Illustrated, December 23, 1996.
186   "IMG agreed in the contract": Merchant, author's interview.
187   "Hello world": Woods, quoted in Wall Street Journal, August 29, 1996.
187   Glassman criticism: Washington Post, September 17, 1996.
187   1996 Greater Milwaukee Open and press conference: Sports Illustrated, September 9, 1996; Times (London), September 3, 1996; and USA Today, August 26 and 27, 1996.
188   Quad City Classic; BC Open: Sports Illustrated, September 30, 1996.
188   Tiger plays blackjack in Illinois: Callahan, In Search of Tiger.
188   Tiger visits Isleworth home for first time: ibid.
188   Buick Challenge; Haskins dinner: Berry, author's interview.

188   "exhausted": ibid.

188   "It was overwhelming": ibid.

188   Tom Kite's reaction: *USA Today,* September 26, 1996.

189   Prisoner in hotels: author's interviews with Goodwin and Kribel.

189   "I remember him": Goodwin, author's interview.

189   "I did feel sorry for him": Kribel, author's interview.

189   "You can have all the money": Gravell, author's interview.

189   Background on Las Vegas Invitational: *Sports Illustrated,* October 14, 1996.

189   "My family went and spoke to him": Gravell, author's interview.

190   "What our organization": Woods, quoted in *People,* September 16, 1996.

190   Tiger Woods played public courses: Duran, author's interview.

191   Sale of Isleworth to Aviva: author's discussion with Lewis and associates.

191   Background on Lewis: author's meeting with Lewis; *Daily Telegraph,* July 15, 2000; *Forbes;* and *Sunday Times* (London) "Rich List," 2001–2.

191   Description of Isleworth: author's tour of the estate and discussions with Lewis and staff, including Marty De Angelo and Lisa Richards. Also: property records.

191   McCormack's property: Orange County Property Appraiser's records; visit to estate; *Daily Express,* June 29, 1989.

191   Lewis's residence: author's visit.

192   "Tiger can't live anywhere": Lewis, author's conversation.

192   Woods's residence: author's notes and Orange County Property Appraiser's records.

193   ETW Corp.: Florida Department of State corporation records; author's interview with Merchant. Additional material: *USA Today,* April 16, 1997.

193   Team Tiger: author's discussions with Norwood.

193   Background on Cowan: author's interview with Cowan. Deal: Cowan's interview with *Golf Digest* (undated).

193   Tiger Woods Foundation (TWF): author's interviews with McLaughlin and Merchant; Internal Revenue Service records; and 2001 TWF annual report (companies that endow TWF).

193   "My father and I established": Woods, quoted in *Tiger Woods Foundation 2001 Year in Review* (annual report of TWF).

194   TWF funding: author's interviews; *Tiger Woods Foundation 2001 Year in Review.*

194   TWF registered as a tax-exempt organization: Internal Revenue Service.

194   Jacklin and Nicklaus unhappy with IMG financial management service: author's interviews.

194   Merchant interviews financial managers and is fired: Merchant, author's interview.

194   "Am I happy about it?": ibid.

195   Brunza let go: Brunza, author's interview.

195   Earl Woods taken ill: author's interviews; *Sports Illustrated,* December 23, 1996; Edwards, *Tiger Woods.*

195   Haskins dinner: Berry, author's interview; *Sports Illustrated,* December 23, 1996.

195   "He will transcend": Earl Woods, quoted in ibid.

196   Earl claims he is misquoted: Earl Woods, author's interview.

196   Earl and Tida separate: author's interviews with Earl Woods and others. Background: Pierce, *Sports Guy*.

196   Tustin house: author's interviews and Orange County (California) property records.

196   Tida gives Earl haircut: Moore, author's interview.

196   Big house/small house joke: Earl Woods, author's interview.

196   Tida's Thai cooking: Moore, author's interview.

196   "She wouldn't let him in": Anselmo, author's interview.

197   Earl's relationship with his older children: author's interviews with Earl Woods, Moore, and Gary.

197   Tiger buys house for Royce: Gary, author's interview, *National Examiner*, August 15, 2000.

197   Twenty-first birthday gathering: Kuehne, author's interview.

198   Incident in Outback Steakhouse; racist remark: ibid.

198   Hooters; hockey game incidents: ibid.

198   "You have to be able": ibid.

198   Phoenix Open attendance: *USA Today*, February 4, 1997.

199   Background on Thailand visit: *Evening Standard*, April 14, 1997; *Independent*, February 4, 1997; *Times* (London), February 6, 1997; and *USA Today*, February 5, 1997.

199   "the right stuff": Tom Wolfe, *The Right Stuff* (London: Jonathan Cape, 1979).

199   Earl's heart bypass: Earl Woods, author's interview.

199   Doctor anecdote: Gary, author's interview.

199   "So I said": Earl Woods, author's interview.

199   Torn stitches: ibid.

199   Many people did not think Earl would live: ibid.

200   Tiger studied videotape of past Masters: Gibbs, who gave Woods access to the Golf Channel library.

200   Woods asked to meet Palmer, to ask for advice: Giles, author's interview.

200   Earl goes to Augusta against doctor's orders; putting lesson: Tiger Woods press conference, U.S. Open, June 18, 2000.

201   Carpenter's exchange with Earl Woods: author's interview with Carpenter.

201   1997 Masters: author's interviews. Background: videotape of tournament and newspaper reports including *USA Today*, April 14 and 15, 1997.

201   Montgomerie's comments: as reported by Strege in *Tiger*.

202   "It's a shame": Nicklaus, quoted in *Guardian*, April 14, 1997.

202   Tiger's daydreams: Masters press conference, April 14, 1997.

202   "I said a prayer": Woods, quoted in *USA Today*, April 14, 1997.

203   Nike sales had doubled: *USA Today*, September 6, 1997.

203   "He's making us look smart": Philip Knight, quoted in *Guardian*, April 14, 1997.

203   "My first major": Cowan, author's interview.

203   "We made it!": Earl Woods, videotape of Masters.

203   "pride and love": Earl Woods, author's interview.

203   "Nobody really understands": Moore, author's interview.

9. FOUR TROPHIES

Primary sources: Jim Awtrey, Bryon Bell, Mark Calcavecchia, Frank Carpenter, Mike "Fluff" Cowan, Eri Crum, Peter Dawson, Kel Devlin, Ernie Els, David B. Fay, Wally Goodwin, Claude "Butch" Harmon Jr., Henry Hughes, Tony Jacklin, Joanna Jagoda, Trip Kuehne, Mabel Lee "Mae" Moore (née Woods), Jack Nicklaus, Mark O'Meara, Arnold Palmer, Putnam S. Pierman, Mark Steinberg, Tom Watson, Steve Williams, Earl Woods, Royce Woods, and Frank "Fuzzy" Zoeller.

205   "For the first time": Fay, author's interview.

205   "I'm so proud": Lee Elder, quoted in *Daily Telegraph*, April 15, 1997.

206   CBS ratings: *USA Today*, April 15, 1997.

206   Clinton's accident: St. John, *Greg Norman*.

206   Clinton's call to Woods: recalled by Woods at Masters press conference, April 13, 1997.

206   Jackie Robinson affair: author's discussions with Norwood. Background: *Guardian*, April 22, 1997, and *Daily Mail*, June 9, 1997.

206   Tiger comes home early from vacation: Callahan, *In Search of Tiger*.

206   Zoeller incident: author's interview with Zoeller; discussions with IMG; *USA Today*, April 22–25, 1997.

207   "I drink too!": Zoeller, author's interview.

207   "He's doing quite well": Zoeller, quoted in CNN transcript, as reported in *USA Today*, April 22, 1997.

207   "Shit, I couldn't remember": Zoeller, author's interview.

207   "My comments were not intended": Zoeller, quoted in *USA Today*, April 22, 1997.

208   "Somebody from Atlanta": Zoeller, author's interview.

208   Ridiculed by Leno and Letterman: *News of the World*, January 11, 1998.

208   "In this context": *USA Today*, April 23, 1997.

208   "The media got it": Carpenter, author's interview.

208   Woods's movements after the Masters: Norwood.

208   "His attempt at humor": Woods, quoted in *USA Today*, April 25, 1997.

208   "People who didn't even know me": Zoeller, author's interview.

209   Woods's comments on *Oprah*—"I'm just who I am": as reported in *Independent*, April 23, 1997.

209   "We are all American": Eartha Kitt, quoted in *Guardian*, April 24, 1997.

210   Income discrepancies between blacks and whites: "Sociological Comparisons Between African-Americans and Whites" by Professor James D. Unnever of Radford University, Virginia (www.runet.edu/~junnever/bw.htm).

210   Crime and imprisonment by race: U.S. Department of Justice, Bureau of Justice Statistics, 2001.

210   "That hurt me": Moore, author's interview.

210   Woods's reason for Cablinasian remark: ibid.

210   "All the media": Tida Woods, quoted in *Sports Illustrated*, March 27, 1995.

211   American Express deal: American Express.com; *USA Today*, May 20, 1997.

211   Rolex deal: *Guardian,* December 23, 1997.

211   TAG Heuer: *Financial Express,* October 8, 2002.

211   GTE Byron Nelson Golf Classic ticket sales: *Sunday Telegraph,* May 18, 1997.

211   Official World Golf Ranking: ETW, *Tiger Woods: How He Did It.*

211   Motorola Western Open; TV ratings: *USA Today,* July 8, 1997.

211   Renegotiating television contracts: PGA Tour and its annual report, 2001–2.

211   "His ethnic background": Hughes, author's interview.

212   Tour purses increase: PGA Tour.

212   "Tiger's had a huge impact": Calcavecchia, author's interview.

212   1997 PGA Tour season: *PGA Tour Media Guide.*

212   "For longevity": Harmon, author's interview.

213   Tiger slips in ranking: *PGA Tour Media Guide.*

213   1998 champion's dinner: author's interview with Carpenter. Background: *Masters Journal,* 2002.

213   Nicklaus's 1998 Masters: Jack Nicklaus Museum, *Jack Nicklaus: Facts and Figures.*

213   Tiger's friendship with O'Meara: author's interview with O'Meara.

213   "He kind of pushed me": ibid.

213   Tiger's 1998 earnings: *PGA Tour Media Guide.*

214   "Here is a young man": Nicklaus, quoted in *Daily Mail,* July 15, 1998.

214   Palmer's views: author's interview; quoted in Feinstein, *A Good Walk Spoiled.*

214   Income and ranking of Palmer and Woods: Forbes.com; also *Daily Mail,* December 20, 1999.

214   Nicklaus's debts in the 1980s: Nicklaus interview with *Columbus Dispatch,* May 24, 1998.

214   Norman's deal with Cobra Golf, Inc.: St. John, *Greg Norman.*

214   Launch of Golden Bear Golf, Inc., on the NASDAQ and subsequent problems: author's interviews; Scott Tolley at Nicklaus; Nicklaus, *My Story;* Golden Bear press release detailing revised losses (June 2, 2002); *The Express,* July 9, 1998; and *Daily Telegraph,* July 29, 1998.

214   Nicklaus's personal wealth estimated at $300 million: reported in *Columbus Dispatch,* May 24, 1998.

215   Paragon executives fired and sued: Associated Press, August 2, 2002.

215   John R. Boyd arrested: *Stuart News,* March 19, 2003.

215   Golden Bear Golf, Inc., delisted: Scott Tolley at Nicklaus.

215   "His celebrity status": Pierman, author's interview.

215   Background on Jagoda: author's discussion with Jagoda.

215   "I'm not the superstar here": ibid.

216   "I do not do interviews": Bell, in e-mail to author.

216   Tiger's tenuous relationship with his siblings: author's interviews with Gary and discussions with Kevin and Royce Woods (both of whom declined full interviews).

216   "We try to stay": Royce Woods, discussion with author.

216   Tida almost never talks: Tida Woods declined to be interviewed.

217   O'Meara may have influenced Tiger's dismissal of Norton: Feinstein, *The Majors*.

217   "For Hughes, the dollar is almighty": Earl Woods, quoted in *Guardian*, October 15, 1998.

217   "It was obviously very important": Steinberg, author's interview.

217   Background on Steinberg: ibid.

217   "I think I'm many different roles": ibid.

218   Tiger shields his face: author's notes.

218   1999 Phoenix Open incident: *Times* (London), February 2, 1999.

218   Cowan fired: author's interview with Cowan. Background: Norwood.

218   "He decided he wanted to move on": Cowan, author's interview.

218   Williams hired: author's interview with Williams. Background: Norwood.

218   Background on Williams and "I've become good friends": Williams, author's interview.

219   "I try to make his job": ibid.

219   Background on 1999 PGA Championship: *PGA of America Media Guide*.

220   "I knew when I got to 17": Woods, quoted in *Sports Illustrated*, August 23, 1999.

220   Tiger's trip to Aspen: Crum, author's interview.

221   "I felt like I got to know him": ibid.

221   Nike commercial: author's interview with Kel Devlin, director of Golf Marketing at Nike; *Dallas Morning News*, August 27, 1999.

222   Background on *Nike vs. Titleist*: *Evening Standard*, July 9, 1999; Forbes.com; *Golf Today* (undated); *Guardian*, August 15, 1999; *Daily Telegraph*, July 9, 1999; and *Times* (London), July 11 and August 25, 1999. Also the June 1, 2000, statement of Wally Uihlein, president and CEO of the Acushnet Company.

222   Exercise and physical change: author's notes; Woods, *How I Play Golf*; *PGA Tour Media Guide*.

222   Background on Ryder Cup: author's interview with Jacklin; Ryder Cup literature.

223   1999 Ryder Cup: author's interviews. Background: *PGA of America Media Guide*; James, *Into the Bear Pit*.

223   Ryder Cup revenue to PGA of America (net and gross figures): Julius Mason at PGA of America.

223   David Duval's concerns: *Guardian*, August 12, 1999.

223   "We ought to be paid": Woods, quoted in *Sunday Times* (London), July 11, 1999.

224   Ben Crenshaw is disappointed: *Guardian*, August 12, 1999.

224   Division of charitable fund: *PGA of America Media Guide 2002*.

225   "Monty, you're a fat cunt"; gallery taunts Montgomerie at 1999 Ryder Cup: James, *Into the Bear Pit*.

225   "the most disgraceful scenes": ibid.

225   Tiger's deal with Buick: *Times* (London), December 17, 1999.

225   Palmer's interest in Pebble Beach: Giffin.

225   Pebble Beach Tiger's favorite course: Woods's comment at Masters press conference, April 8, 2001.

225   2000 U.S. Open: author's interviews. Background: *Times* (London), June 19, 2000; *Daily Express*, June 20, 2000.

226   "fucking prick": Woods, quoted in Eubanks, *At the Turn*.

226   Background on Els, personality, and "He played at a totally different level": author's interview with Els.

227   "I told Stevie": Woods, at U.S. Open press conference, June 18, 2000.

227   Millennium Open: author's interviews with Dawson, Els, and others; *Times* (London), July 24, 2000.

227   Nicklaus's hip replacement: *Augusta Chronicle*, March 15, 1999.

227   Nicklaus on Bobby Jones: as quoted in Laidlaw, ed., *The Royal & Ancient Golfer's Handbook*, 2001 ed.

228   "Tiger just kept that level of play": Els, author's interview.

228   Tiger's perfect shot: Tiger Woods, *How I Play Golf*.

229   2000 PGA Championship: *PGA Tour Media Guide* (including trophy details), *Times* (London), August 15, 21, and 22, 2000.

230   Tiger adds endorsements: *Sunday Telegraph*, April 15, 2001; *Sunday Times* (London), April 15, 2001; Edwards, *Tiger Woods*.

230   Split with Jagoda: author's interviews. Background: *USA Today*, May 30, 2001.

230   "A wife can sometimes be a deterrent": Earl Woods, quoted in *TV Guide*, June 9, 2001.

230   "That's personal": Jagoda, comment to author.

230   Palmer and the Grand Slam: Palmer, *A Golfer's Life*.

231   "But I think": Woods at Masters press conference, April 3, 2001.

232   Background on 2001 Masters: Masters press conferences; *Independent*, April 9, 2001; *New York Times*, April 9, 2001; and *Daily Telegraph*, April 9 and 14, 2001.

232   "His goals are different": DiMarco, quoted in *Newsweek*, June 18, 2001.

232   "I love Phil": Kuehne, author's interview.

233   Tiger sees Mickelson's ball: Masters press conference, April 8, 2001.

233   "It was just a weird feeling": Woods at ibid.

233   "You pulled it off": Earl Woods, quoted in Tiger Woods, *How I Play Golf*.

10. THE MASTERS OF THE WICKED GAME

Primary sources: Deane Beman, Ed Bignon, Dr. Stephen W. Brown, Dr. Martha Burk, Mark Calcavecchia, Don Crosby, Peter Dawson, Barbara Douglas, Rudy Duran, Ernie Els, David B. Fay, Dow Finsterwald, Butch Harmon, David Leadbetter, Joseph Lewis, Bob Londeree, Joe Louis Barrow, Mark H. McCormack, Greg McLaughlin, John Merchant, Jack Nicklaus, Mabel Lee "Mae" Moore (née Woods), Mark O'Meara, Arnold Palmer, Conrad Ray, Pandel Savic, Hall W. Thompson, Ken Venturi, and Earl Woods.

234   Tiger returned home the day after 2001 Masters: Masters press conference, April 8, 2001.

234   Tiger's new home: author's interviews and tour of Isleworth; Orange County (Florida) real estate records.

234   Smaller home for father: Earl Woods, author's interview.

234   Tiger purchased and sold three lots: author's discussions with local resident Londeree.

234   Lewis's observation about Tiger's time: author's discussion with Lewis.

234   "There was all four": Woods, at U.S. Open press conference, June 16, 2002.

235   Earl Woods's view of Grand Slam: *Golf Digest,* November 2001.

235   Nicklaus's quip/Fiscal Slam: *Times* (London), April 10, 2001.

235   Tiger invites O'Meara to see trophies and rearranges them: O'Meara, author's interview.

235   "with so much gusto": Ray, author's interview.

235   Background on Jesper Parnevik: *PGA Tour Media Guide.*

235   Parnevik's house in Florida: author's notes.

235   Parnevik's entourage: author's interview with Calcavecchia.

236   Background on Elin Nordegren: author's conversation with Nordegren; *Sunday Mirror,* September 22, 2002; and *Sydney Morning Herald,* April 14, 2002.

236   "you guys": Woods, at Open Championship press conference, July 17, 2001.

236   Background on Tiger Woods Foundation: author's interview with McLaughlin; *Tiger Woods Foundation 2001 Year in Review;* and tax records. Grants made, programs supported by, and net assets for TWF in the fiscal years ending 1999, 2000, and 2001: IRS forms 990 "Return of Organization Exempt from Income Tax" (Tiger Woods Foundation, Inc.) for the relevant years.

236   Tiger Jam: author's interviews; *Tiger Woods Foundation 2001 Year in Review;* TWF Web site.

236   Tiger gives no more than twenty days of his time to the TWF: author's interview with McLaughlin. ("He probably gives . . . somewhere between fifteen and twenty days a year [to] the foundation.")

237   "because it's a good sound bite": McLaughlin, author's interview.

237   Williams World Challenge prize in 2001: *PGA Tour Media Guide.*

237   Tiger's 2001 income: Forbes.com.

237   Money paid out and kept in reserve: IRS form 990 "Return of Organization Exempt from Income Tax" (see note for page 236, Background on Tiger Woods Foundation).

238   "This was serious stuff ": Moore, author's interview.

238   Tiger's gambling losses: author's interviews; *Daily Telegraph*, March 5, 2003, and November 22, 2002. (It has been claimed improbably that Woods has lost as much as $50 million.)

238   Donation to Denver Children's Hospital: IRS form 990 (see note for page 236, Background on Tiger Woods Foundation).

238   "I resisted his courting": Nordegren, quoted in *Sunday Mirror,* September 22, 2002.

238     $5 tip: *San Diego Union-Tribune,* February 20, 2003.

238   2002 Masters: author's notes.

238   "the great Arnold Palmer": Woods, at Masters press conference, April 11, 2002.

239   "I think he waited too long": Venturi, author's interview.

239   "The golf ball is kinda ridiculous": Palmer, author's interview.

239   "Fore!": Wodehouse, "The Heart of a Goof," in Wodehouse, *The Golf Omnibus*.

239   "I knew it was all over for me": Goosen, quoted in *USA Today,* April 15, 2002.

240   "I knew that my chances": Els, author's interview.

240   "I've never seen players": Leadbetter, author's interview.

241   "I want to talk": Lloyd Ward, quoted in *USA Today,* April 11, 2002.

241   Background on Burk: author's interview with Burk.

241   "I don't have to be an expert": ibid.

241   "We know that Augusta National": Burk's letter to Chairman Hootie Johnson, dated June 12, 2002.

242   Ward didn't reply: author's interview with Burk, approach to Ward.

242   "Our membership alone": Johnson's statement, July 9, 2002.

242   "We don't see any reason": Dawson, author's interview.

242   "It's not about private clubs": Fay, author's interview.

243   "When the club was first started": Brown, author's interview.

243   "Isn't that something?": Finsterwald, author's interview.

243   Burk writes to sponsors: author's interview with Burk.

244   Citigroup reply: letter dated August 22, 2002.

244   Augusta resignations: *USA Today,* December 9, 2002.

244   Kenneth Chenault's statement: American Express.

244   Tiger has no interest in politics: Earl Woods, author's interview.

244   2002 U.S. Open: author's interviews and notes. Background: *New York Times,* June 10, 2001; *USGA Media Guide;* and *Golf Digest,* June 2002.

244   "To have our national championship": Fay, author's interview.

245   Summer of 1972: Mercer, *Chronicle of the 20th Century;* Joel Whitburn, *Billboard Book of Top 40 Hits* (New York: Billboard, 1996).

246   2002 Open Championship; Honourable Company of Edinburgh Golfers: author's notes. Background: *Daily Telegraph,* July 17, 18, 22, 23, and 30, 2002, and *Scotland on Sunday,* July 21, 2002.

246   All but fifty of Britain's golf clubs are mixed: Peter Dawson, secretary of the Royal and Ancient Golf Club of St. Andrews.

246   Richard Caborn criticized R&A: *Sunday Telegraph,* July 14, 2002.

246   "I think it's a shame": Vivien Saunders, speaking on BBC Radio 4, *Woman's Hour,* July 21, 2002.

247   Hung up the telephone: Repeated attempts to speak to the secretary of the Honourable Company ended when the club refused to put the author through and hung up.

247   "I think the club": Dawson, author's interview.

247   "I would be very much against": ibid.

247   "any correlation": ibid.

248   Rolex reaction and Heiniger's response—"Rolex does not see itself": correspondence with author. The author also wrote to MasterCard (no response), Nikon (similar response to Rolex's), and Royal Bank of Scotland (no response).

248   "It would be nice": Woods, at Open Championship press conference, July 16, 2002.

248   "Hello world": *Wall Street Journal,* August 29, 1996.

248   2002 Open Championship: author's notes and interview with Harmon.

248   Woods prefers challenging conditions: numerous comments over the years, including at the Buick Invitational, February 12, 2003.

249   Augusta National drops sponsors for 2003 Masters telecast: author's interview with Burk; Augusta National statement, August 30, 2002.

249   Sponsors paid $12 million: author's interviews. Background: Sampson, *The Masters*.

249   Forgo sponsorship indefinitely: Johnson press conference, April 9, 2003.

250   Closed party and Thompson, "He knows the position": author's conversation with Thompson.

250   "Hootie is right": Woods, quoted by Associated Press, October 17, 2002.

250   "Tiger is trying to have it both ways": Burk, author's interview.

250   Palmer's view on sexism: comments at Augusta, April 9, 2003.

250   Nicklaus's view on sexism: comments at Augusta, April 9, 2003; author's correspondence with Scott Tolley at Nicklaus.

250   2003 Masters protest: *USA Today*, April 14, 2003.

251   Background on 2002 Ryder Cup: author's interviews and notes; Ryder Cup program.

251   Charity money: PGA of America.

251   Woods gave money to his foundation: PGA of America press release, January 23, 2003.

251   Rankings of Price and others as of September 26, 2002.

252   "Elin, do you mind" and "Yes, I do mind!": Nordegren's exchange with the author.

254   "It's such a wicked game": Faldo, on Sky TV, September 29, 2002.

255   "a million reasons": Woods, at the American Express Championship, September 9, 2002.

256   FBI interest in two of Nicklaus's business associates: The FBI investigated and later arrested two former executives of Paragon Construction International, a division of Golden Bear Golf, Inc., following alleged financial misreporting circa 1998 (see chapter 9).

256   "The biggest thing I've got as a legacy": Nicklaus, author's interview.

256   No deals for golf balls, etc., as of April 2002: author's discussion with Tolley at Nicklaus.

256   "I think over the thirty years": ibid.

256   "He's been very successful": ibid.

256   Nicklaus's net wealth: author's interviews and confidential source.

257   Palmer's net wealth: Thomas Hauser used the phrase "mid–eight figures" as an estimate of Palmer's wealth in his 1994 book *Arnold Palmer*, compiled with Palmer's cooperation. In 2002 Palmer's office didn't quarrel with the estimate. Based on research, $100 million seems more realistic.

257   Palmer's endorsements: Giffin (as of 2003).

257   Palmer's/Nicklaus's/Woods's prize money: *PGA Tour Media Guide*.

257   Woods's annual earnings: "100 Top Celebrities," *Forbes*.com.

257   "Anytime you pick up a stock": Woods, quoted in *Time*, August 14, 2000.

258   Diamond Tiger gave to his mother: author's interview with Moore, who described it as being as big as Tida's eye.

258   Woods's wealth: *Fortune,* September 16, 2002.

258   PGA Tour Pension Progam: author's interview with Beman, and *PGA Tour Annual Report to the Membership, 2001–2002.*

258   IMG employees and offices: IMG.

258   IMG's revenue: $1.3 billion in 2002, according to Hoover's Online, www. hoovers.com.

258   Woods's house half the size of McCormack's: Orange County (Florida) property records.

259   "I don't know": McCormack, author's interview.

259   McCormack's cardiac arrest: *Golf World,* February 7, 2003.

259   McCormack in a coma: IMG.

259   *Forbes* billionaires: *Forbes,* March 2003.

259   McCormack dies: *Daily Telegraph,* May 17, 2003.

260   Twenty-five million golfers in the United States: Fay.

260   "Tiger has really not put golfers": Duran, author's interview.

260   "It's still expensive": ibid.

260   Less than 1 percent of people working in golf are minorities: author's interview with Douglas.

260   Eleven tournaments lost their backers in 2002: PGA Tour (Dave Lancer, director of information).

261   "Arguably, right now the major issue": McLaughlin, author's interview.

261   Memorial loses sponsor: Savic, author's interview.

261   PGA Tour purse money: *PGA Tour Annual Report to the Membership, 2001–2002* and *PGA Tour Media Guide* (2003 edition).

261   "The problem right now": Savic, author's interview.

261   "We're told": ibid.

261   "The veiled threat": ibid.

262   "No one, not anyone, is the king of golf": Palmer in *Arnold Palmer: Golf's Heart and Soul,* Golf Channel, 1998.

263   "You do the best you can": Nicklaus, author's interview.

EPILOGUE: CYPRESS IN WINTER

All quotations are from author's interviews with Earl Woods and Trip Kuehne.

BIBLIOGRAPHY

In addition to the works listed below, the author also consulted the media guides of the PGA of America, PGA Tour, and United States Golf Association, which are published annually; The *Royal & Ancient Golfer's Handbook,* edited annually by Renton Laidlaw (London: Macmillan); and numerous booklets relating to tournaments, individuals, and organizations, including *Tiger Woods: How He Did It* (ETW Corp.) and *Jack Nicklaus: Facts & Figures* (a booklet produced in conjunction with the Jack Nicklaus Museum). Newspaper and magazine articles referred to are listed in the Source Notes.

Anselmo, John, with John Andrisani. *A-Game Golf.* New York: Doubleday, 2001.

Barkow, Al. *The History of the PGA Tour.* New York: Doubleday, 1989.

Boyer, Paul S., ed. *The Oxford Companion to United States History.* New York: Oxford, 2001.

Callahan, Tom. *In Search of Tiger.* Edinburgh: Mainstream Publishing, 2003.

Collins, David R. *Tiger Woods: Golfing Champion.* Gretna, La.: Pelican, 1999.

Cooke, Alistair. *Fun and Games with Alistair Cooke.* New York: Arcade, 1994.

Crosby, Don, with James Dale. *Tiger Woods Made Me Look Like a Genius.* Kansas City, Mo.: Andrews McNeel Publishing, 2000.

Duran, Rudy, with Rick Lipsey. *In Every Kid There Lurks a Tiger.* New York: Hyperion, 2002.

Edwards, Nicholas. *Tiger Woods: An American Master.* New York: Scholastic, 2001.

Ellison, Ralph. *Invisible Man.* Harmondsworth, Eng.: Penguin, 1965.

Eubanks, Steve. *At the Turn: How Two Electrifying Years Changed Golf Forever.* New York: Crown, 2001.

Feinstein, John. *A Good Walk Spoiled: Days and Nights on the PGA Tour.* Boston: Little Brown, 1995.

———. *The First Coming/Tiger Woods: Master or Martyr.* New York: Library of Contemporary Thought, 1998.

———. *The Majors: In Pursuit of Golf's Holy Grail.* London: Warner Books, 1999.

Gary, Barbara Woods. *At All Costs.* Salina, Kans.: BWG Publishing, 2000.

Guest, Larry. *Arnie: Inside the Legend.* Nashville: Cumberland House, 1997.

Gutman, Bill. *Tiger Woods: A Biography.* New York: Archway, 1997.

Halberstam, David. *The Fifties.* New York: Fawcett Columbine, 1993.

Hauser, Thomas. *Arnold Palmer: A Personal Journey.* San Francisco: CollinsPublishers, 1994.

Hornung, Paul. *Scioto Country Club: 75 Years of History.* Columbus: Scioto Country Club, 1993.

James, Mark. *Into the Bear Pit*. London: Virgin, 2000.

Joy, David. *St. Andrews & the Open Championship*. St. Andrews: St. Andrews Press, 2000.

Kramer, S. A. *Tiger Woods: Golfing to Greatness*. New York: Random House, 1997.

McCormack, Mark H. *What They Don't Teach You at Harvard Business School*. London: HarperCollins, 1994.

McDaniel, Pete. *Uneven Lies: The Heroic Story of African-Americans in Golf*. Greenwich, Conn.: American Golfer, 2000.

Mercer, Derrik, ed. *Chronicle of the 20th Century*. London: Longman, 1988.

Nicklaus, Jack, with Ken Bowden. *Golf My Way*. New York: Fireside, 1974.

———. *My Story*. New York: Fireside/Simon & Schuster, 1997.

Owen, David. *The Making of the Masters: Clifford Roberts, Augusta National, and Golf's Most Prestigious Tournament*. New York: Simon & Schuster, 1999.

———. *The Chosen One: Tiger Woods and the Dilemma of Greatness*. New York: Simon & Schuster, 2001.

Palmer, Arnold. *Arnold Palmer's Golf Book*. London: Hodder & Stoughton, 1961.

Palmer, Arnold, with James Dodson. *A Golfer's Life*. London: Arrow, 2000.

Pierce, Charles P. *Sports Guy*. New York: Da Capo Press, 2001.

Player, Gary. *Grand Slam Golf*. London: Cassell, 1966.

———. *The Golfer's Guide to the Meaning of Life*. Emmaus, Pa.: Rodale, 2001.

Roberts, Clifford. *The Story of the Augusta National Golf Club*. New York: Doubleday, 1976.

Rosaforte, Tim. *Raising the Bar: The Championship Years of Tiger Woods*. New York: Thomas Dunne/St. Martin's, 2000.

St. John, Lauren. *Greg Norman: The Biography*. London: Corgi, 1998.

Sampson, Curt. *The Masters: Golf, Money and Power in Augusta, Georgia*. New York: Villard, 1998.

Saunders, Vivien. *The Golf Handbook*. New York: Crown, 1997.

Shaw, Mark. *Nicklaus*. Dallas: Taylor, 1997.

Sifford, Charlie, with James Gullo. *Just Let Me Play*. Latham, N.Y.: British American Publishing, 1992.

Sinnette, Dr. Calvin H. *Forbidden Fairways: African Americans and the Game of Golf*. Chelsea, Mich.: Sleeping Bear Press, 1998.

Staff of *Sports Illustrated*. *Tiger Woods: The Making of a Champion*. New York: Simon & Schuster, 1996.

Stout, Glenn, ed. *Chasing Tiger: The Tiger Woods Reader*. New York: Da Capo Press, 2002.

Strege, John. *Tiger: A Biography of Tiger Woods*. London: Piatkus, 1998.

Trevino, Lee, with Sam Blair. *They Call Me Super Mex*. New York: Random House, 1982.

Updike, John. *Golf Dreams*. Harmondsworth, Eng.: Penguin, 1998.

Walton, Geraldine, et al. *A History of Shepherd Chapel, Manhattan, Kansas: 1866–1967*. Manhattan, Kans.: privately printed, 1992.

Wind, Herbert Warren. *The Story of American Golf*. Rev. ed. New York: Simon & Schuster, 1956.

Wodehouse, P. G. *The Golf Omnibus*. London: Hutchinson, 1973.

Woods, Earl, with Pete McDaniel. *Training a Tiger*. London: Hodder & Stoughton, 1997.

Woods, Earl, and the Tiger Woods Foundation, with Shari Lesser Wenk. *Start Something*. New York: Simon & Schuster, 2000.

Woods, Tiger, with the editors of *Golf Digest*. *How I Play Golf*. London: Little Brown, 2001.

INDEX